A Country Between

The Upper Ohio Valley and Its

Peoples, 1724–1774

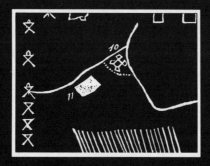

Michael N. McConnell

University of Nebraska Press   Lincoln & London

Maps are adapted from "Indian Villages—Ohio,
Pennsylvania, New York, 1760–1794," in *Atlas of Early
American History*, vol. 2, *The Revolutionary Era, 1760–1790*,
ed. Lester J. Cappon et al. (Princeton: Princeton University
Press, 1976). Used by permission.
Manufactured in the United States of America
⊛ The paper in this book meets the minimum requirements of
American National Standard for Information Sciences—
Permanence of Paper for Printed Library Materials, ANSI
Z39.48-1984.
First Bison Books printing: 1997
Most recent printing indicated by the last digit below:
10   9   8   7   6   5   4   3   2   1
Library of Congress Cataloging-in-Publication Data
McConnell, Michael N. (Michael Norman)
A country between : the upper Ohio Valley and its peoples,
1724–1774 / Michael N. McConnell.
p.   cm.
Includes bibliographical references (p.   ) and index.
ISBN 0-8032-3142-3 (cl: alk. paper)
ISBN 0-8032-8238-9 (pa: alk. paper)
1. Ohio River Valley—History—To 1795. I. Title.
F517.M14   1992
977.1'01—dc20   91-42867
                                                    CIP

For Alice and Michael

contents

illustrations and maps

acknowledgments

This book could not have been completed without the generous cooperation and encouragement of numerous institutions and individuals. A fel-
lowship at the D'Arcy McNickle Center for the History of the American
Indian, the Newberry Library, provided the perfect opportunity to lay the
groundwork in a stimulating intellectual environment. Since then, support
from the National Endowment for the Humanities and a research grant
from the University of Alabama at Birmingham have enabled me to bring
the project to fruition. Along the way the Library of Congress, the American
Philosophical Society, the Historical Society of Pennsylvania, the William
Penn Memorial Museum, the American Antiquarian Society, the National
Archives of Canada, the Rochester Museum and Science Center, the William L. Clements Library, the Virginia Historical Society, the John Carter
Brown Library, and the Milton S. Eisenhower Library of The Johns Hopkins
University provided access to collections and made research all the more
enjoyable and profitable.

Aside from such generous institutional assistance, I have also been the
beneficiary of the wit, wisdom, and guidance of friends and colleagues. In
Jim Ronda and Jim Axtell I have had teachers without peer, and much of
whatever good is contained in the pages that follow has come from their
example and encouragement.

I first met Jim Merrell in 1981 at the Newberry, and since then he has
proved to be the ideal critic: quick to point out errors of fact and weaknesses
of argument, but with good humor and welcome encouragement. Earlier I

was introduced to Dick Haan, and over the past several years he has listened to lengthy discourses on the Ohio Country and has sharpened my insight into events there while generously sharing his own profound knowledge of the eighteenth-century Iroquois and the colonial frontier. Neal Salisbury also read the entire manuscript and offered valuable advice on both interpretation and organization.

Closer to home, Tinker Dunbar, Debbie Givens, and Katharine Stark cheerfully provided much-needed technical assistance—sometimes in response to last-minute and cryptic requests—and I thank them for keeping me in touch with the interlibrary loan system and on friendly terms with word processors. To Dan Lesnick I owe special thanks for his unfailing support and for gently reminding me that this is, after all, only a book.

Finally, to my family I owe special thanks: to my parents, Joan and Fred McConnell, for their steady support and generosity, and to Alice and Michael, who have lived with this project for what must have seemed an eternity and throughout have given patience, understanding, and love.

A Country Between

introduction

In the middle decades of the eighteenth century a new period of conflict and uncertainty began for Indians living beyond the limits of colonial settlement. From the Green Mountains of Vermont to the foothills of the Carolinas and Georgia, by the 1740s native societies found themselves confronting once more the threats that came with European imperial warfare, after the relative calm that had prevailed since the end of Queen Anne's War a generation earlier. Moreover, in the aftermath of the Seven Years' War many Indian societies would find themselves under relentless pressure from British American settlements pushing westward, unimpeded now that the French had been driven from Canada. And by 1775, fratricidal conflict within the British Empire threatened to engulf nearby Indians as well.[1]

Among the leading actors in this drama were the Iroquois, Delawares, Shawnees, and other natives known collectively to the British as the "Ohio Indians." As the name implies, they occupied the upper Ohio Valley, their settlements stretching from the Allegheny River westward to the Muskingum and Scioto valleys. This ill-defined region was itself of central importance in the events that unfolded beginning in the mid-1740s. Identified by Lawrence Henry Gipson as a "zone of international friction," the Ohio Country provided the spark that ignited the last of the Anglo-French wars for empire, and the situation there defined British frontier policies and intercolonial affairs long beyond the surrender of New France. It was a particularly volatile land, punctuated by wars and less organized forms of violence, a place where reputations could be made, as happened to George

Washington and General John Forbes, or ruined—a fate that befell General Edward Braddock.[2]

Yet the upper Ohio Valley was more than a zone of imperial friction. It was also a cultural frontier, a region whose history was shaped not so much by the convergence of rivers, trails, or royal claims as by the Indians who lived there. Indeed, the very existence of the Ohio Indians made the region important to European contestants economically, militarily, and politically. When French or British, Pennsylvanians or Virginians attempted to stake a claim in the Ohio Country, they had to face the Ohio Indians. Finding themselves, as the Ohio Seneca headman Tanaghrisson cogently observed, living in "a country between" competing imperial and colonial interests, the Indians were not merely observers of the events that unfolded in their land. Because of their locale, but even more because of their determination to retain their sovereignty in the face of grasping outsiders, Tanaghrisson and his neighbors played a central role in a contest that was multicultural as well as international.

Given the large gaps in both the historical and the archaeological records, modern histories of seventeenth-century America often label the upper Ohio Valley "poorly known." But much the same could be said of the Ohio Indians in the better-documented eighteenth century. The marginal place Ohio Indians have been accorded in their own history is a function of perspective. Since Francis Parkman, scholars interested in the era of the "French and Indian War" have tended to shove Indians to the margins of frontier history; reading history backward, they have often assumed that, because they ultimately lost the contest for control of the middle west, the natives were always bound to lose and so could be readily summarized or dismissed. Moreover, there has been a persistent tendency within the field of colonial history to separate "Indian" history from "colonial" history, though these were often intimately intertwined.[3]

If their place in colonial frontier history has been clouded by a Eurocentric bias, the Ohio Indians have also lived in the shadow cast by the Iroquois Confederacy. Few American Indian societies in early America have attracted so much attention from their contemporaries or from later generations of scholars. Thanks to Francis Jennings, the myth of the "imperial Iroquois" has largely been demolished; nevertheless, our picture of the northern colonial frontier is still shaped in great measure by the history and diplomacy of the Six Nations and the inclination to assign other Indian societies—including the Ohio Indians—a subordinate status as dependent on the Iroquois Confederacy. This continuing tendency to view the western frontier exclusively from an eastern perspective, as defined by the Six Nations and their Covenant Chain alliances with the British, tells us little about peoples who may have seen themselves as outside such networks. A better understanding of their actions might clarify our ideas about the frontier.[4]

This book offers a different perspective on the history of the Ohio Indians between 1724 and 1774. By approaching events from the vantage point of the Ohio Country, I have tried to reflect the view of Indian participants. Fundamentally, I am concerned with the ways Ohio Indians confronted the challenges of living between competing colonies and empires from their initial settlement of the Ohio Country through Dunmore's War. After that time political revolution within the British colonies fundamentally altered the shape of intercultural relations in the west.[5]

A closer look at the history of the Ohio Indians reveals several important features of these societies and the world they inhabited. Throughout their struggle to maintain cultural and political sovereignty, the Ohio Indians were flexible in their dealings with outsiders, developing a range of creative strategies from armed resistance to accommodation in response to ever-shifting threats and opportunities. Indeed, the resettlement of the Ohio Country by Delawares, Iroquois, and Shawnees was itself a creative response to the pressures of colonial settlement and imperial conflict. Moreover, in confronting challenges from outside, the Indians in the Ohio Country developed a strong attachment to the new homeland, while for the Delawares and Shawnees, collective identity went a significant step further as once autonomous or long-separated bands cooperated more closely, approaching our modern definition of "tribe" or "nation."

The Ohio Indians' success in tackling the problems of warfare, invasion, and colonial expansion was increased by the fluid nature of the cultural frontier in the middle west. Only in the wake of the Seven Years' War did "Indian" and "settler" harden into cultural, eventually racial, monolithic terms. More characteristically, interests and needs dictated alliances and hostilities on the frontier. Thus Ohio Indians could exploit the British army's security needs, the friction between traders and soldiers, and the competition between colonies and empires, fashioning a local version of the "play-off system" most commonly identified with the Six Nations. At the same time, however, Indian towns were often the scene of factional disputes, while ethnic and historical jealousies made regional cooperation between native societies difficult and provided opportunities for outsiders to divide and rule. In one of the best-known events of the area, the 1763–64 war associated with the Ottawa Indian Pontiac, the Ohio Indians' actions reveal how far local and regional concerns, not an abstract pan-Indianism, determined the level and extent of their participation.[6]

Ohio Indian history also reveals how little outsiders, particularly the British imperial government and its Six Nations allies, were able to impose their will on the frontier and native societies. Though the Ohio Country was repeatedly occupied by foreign armies between 1753 and 1772, it does not follow that the Ohio Indians themselves were a conquered people. The French were more interested in enlisting native allies than in subordinating Indian societies, while the British, their official rhetoric notwithstanding, maintained at best a tenuous hold, as was forcefully revealed when in 1763 Ohio Indians and their western allies nearly swept the British army from the region. Thereafter a fragile, symbiotic relationship existed as imperialists conceded their inability to transform de jure control over the Ohio Country into de facto authority over Ohio Indians.

In much the same way, the limits of the Six Nations' influence in Indian America, and the gulf between the reality of the Iroquois Confederacy's power and British rhetoric concerning its role on the frontier, are clearly revealed in the Ohio Country. The Ohio Country was never a central concern for the Confederacy as a whole. Rather, those peoples whose interests lay in the west, notably the Senecas, tended to take a commanding role there. Yet Senecas, like Delawares and Shawnees, defined their interests locally, not in relation to the Six Nations and the Confederacy's political ties to British and French colonies. Moreover, as the Ohio Country became the seat of imperial and intercolonial conflict, the Six Nations were correspondingly more reluctant to be drawn into a volatile and violent country. On the one occasion when the Six Nations did engage directly in negotiations over the Ohio Country, it was to bolster their own prestige with their British allies while shedding any responsibility for a dangerous region. By ceding lands east of the Ohio River in the Fort Stanwix Treaty of 1768, however, the Confederacy further alienated Ohio Indians and helped set the stage for intense border conflict that finally exploded in Dunmore's War in 1774.[7]

Finally, the study of Ohio Indians shows how the history of the Ohio Country grew from the interplay of peoples and interests—Indian, British, and French, economic, political, and cultural. That lesson reminds us once more that colonial history, especially on the cultural frontier, was the product of many participants, Indians as well as Europeans.

one

Native Pioneers

 In the spring of 1724 Delaware Indians were busy establishing a new town west of the Appalachian Mountains. Appropriately, they called the site overlooking the steep valley of the Allegheny River Kittanning—"at the great stream." Having recently left their old towns in the Susquehanna Valley, these natives of eastern Pennsylvania now lived in what was for most a new land. The newness of this region—later generations would call it the Appalachian Plateau—was largely physical. Unlike the lowlands of the Delaware Valley or the rolling countryside east of the Susquehanna that the natives knew so well, the Delawares' new town sat in the midst of rugged terrain cut by numerous rivers and secondary streams. Even entering the Allegheny Valley was difficult; the Appalachians, whose recurrent ridges and valleys led colonial settlers to dub them the "Endless Mountains," were pierced in only two places: by the West Branch of the Susquehanna River and by the Juniata River. And even these streams led only to the base of the escarpment that defined the Allegheny Plateau.[1]

The plateau itself was drained by four river systems that ran through it from north to south. The Allegheny River, whose headwaters nearly met those of the Susquehanna, cut through the eastern portion of the region and would serve as the major highway for natives and Europeans entering the area from Iroquoia and the lower Great Lakes. Access to the lakes was aided by the Chautauqua and French Creek tributaries, which originated in the watershed between the plateau and the Lake Erie Plain. The plain, narrow at first but widening significantly at its western end near the Detroit River,

Map 1 The Ohio Valley and the trans-Appalachian West.

marked the northern limit of the plateau and provided a covenient east-west axis for travel and communication. To the south of the Lake Erie Plain, the plateau was bisected by the Beaver River system and, farther west, by the Muskingum. Beyond the Muskingum, the plateau gradually gave way to the plains of central Ohio, called the Scioto Plains for the river that drained them. These rivers—the Beaver, Muskingum, and Scioto—all emp-tied into the Ohio River, itself the product of the Allegheny and Mononga-hela rivers. The Monongahela and its tributaries, the Cheat and Youghio-gheny rivers, rose in the tangled uplands of present West Virginia. These river systems to a large extent define the physical bounds of the Allegheny Plateau—the "Ohio Country" of early American history. Yet the rivers posed no particular obstacles to human activity within the region; communication throughout the Ohio Country was aided by portages, trails, and the Lake Erie Plain. At the same time, the region's natural history was marked by uniformity rather than by sharp contrasts or discontinuities in climate or physiography.

Place-names given to features within the upper Ohio Valley by French and British colonials—Great Meadows, Laurel Mountain, Chestnut Ridge,

Map 2 Indian societies, about 1720.

Le Boeuf (Buffalo) Creek—all suggest the diversity of resources. Some idea of the rich animal and plant resources the Delawares found as they entered the Allegheny Valley can be gained from the accounts of Anglo-Americans who traversed the region in the middle decades of the eighteenth century. Their reports all speak of a wide variety of game, of the kaleidoscope of forests, fields, marshes, and river valleys, and of the variable quality of the land itself. Cartographer Lewis Evans, basing his narrative on others' eye-witness accounts, insisted that the soils in parts of the Ohio Country were "none of the best; consisting in general of low dry ridges," but he hastened to mention the "very rich low meadow ground." He may well have been alluding to the unglaciated southeastern portion of the plateau, where thin, poor soils supported "great extents of poor pitch pines" as well as "spots of fine white pines.[2]

Others were impressed not only by the varied quality of the land but also by the abundance of game. Passing through the Muskingum Valley in 1751, Christopher Gist found little timber but good meadows and "fine runs for mills." He and his companions also ate well; at one point Gist killed a "fine fat deer," and he remarked that his party "had great plenty of provisions." Gist also found the natural salt licks in the Muskingum area convenient places to hunt. Eastward, in the Youghiogheny Valley, he found elk, bear, deer, turkeys, and even a "panther," as well as good bottomland, though he commented on the "broken country" sometimes filled with laurel thickets that he passed through on his return to Virginia.[3]

Pennsylvanian James Smith probably saw more of the Ohio Country than most travelers during his three years' captivity among the region's Indians. He too commented on the many local variations in topography and ground cover as well as on the availability of game. The valley of Loyal Hanna Creek Smith found to be "exceeding rocky laurel thickets," in contrast to the black and white oak forests, rich bottomlands, and buffalo, elk, and turkeys of the upper Monongahela Valley. In between lay the Beaver River with its gently rolling hills, much covered with brush but also holding stands of black oak, hickory, chestnut, and walnut.[4]

Major Robert Rogers, traveling to Fort Pitt from Detroit during the winter of 1760–61, confirmed Smith's description: Rogers and his men found chestnut and oak east of the Muskingum. The major found the Lake Erie Plain south of Sandusky to be "level land, and a good country. No pine-trees of any sort," but with plenty of oak, black and white walnut, chestnut, and locust. Near one Indian town on the Muskingum, Rogers's hungry troops had no difficulty finding game. Such, then, was the country settled by the Delawares and other natives early in the eighteenth century.[5]

The Delawares entered this bountiful new land unopposed. Only the abandoned "towns and fortresses" referred to by Lewis Evans remained as testimony to an earlier Ohio Indian world. For generations people known to Europeans as Eries, as well as others known to modern archaeologists as the Monongahela, Allegheny Iroquois, and Mahoning cultures, had lived on the plateau as farmers and traders. By the sixteenth century these natives were linked through the trade in exotic materials—especially marginella shell—to a vast exchange network that encompassed the Susquehannocks to the east and the distant Neutrals of southern Ontario. This same network brought the Ohio natives exotica of another kind—glass beads, brass, and iron—as Europeans entered the native northeast. Yet competition for access to these goods, the spiritual power they were thought to convey, and the furs that paid for them transformed the Allegheny Plateau into a battleground, then a no-man's-land, as the New York Iroquois scattered their neighbors and competitors in a series of "beaver" wars. The warfare set in motion migrations of people who would later be known as Shawnees and swept the Ohio region of its other inhabitants: in 1680—more than a generation before Kittanning appeared—the last Erie refugees surrendered to the Senecas.[6]

Thus the Delawares who entered the Allegheny Plateau in 1724 did so not as invaders but as pioneering newcomers who inaugurated a new phase in a rich and turbulent regional history. And though Monongahelans or Eries and Delawares would not have met face to face on the plateau, the migrants shared many broad cultural traits with the region's former inhabitants. Moreover, the Delawares' arrival in the Allegheny Valley was the result of many of the same changes and conflicts that had cleared the upper Ohio Valley of its first native peoples.

Like the early plateau dwellers, the Delawares were horticulturalists who lived in autonomous villages and seasonally exploited the rich ecosystems of the lower Delaware Valley. And also like the early Ohio Indians, the eastern natives had a long, rich history and a culture well adapted to the region they lived in. Unlike the Ohio natives, however, the Delawares and their eastern neighbors met the Europeans, whose appearance in the northeast accelerated some tendencies within native societies and set in motion new, largely unpredictable, changes. Indeed, the new town of Kittanning was itself a direct product of encounters between Delawares and a variety of Europeans.[7]

The Delawares' introduction to the European world came in the form of Dutch and Swedish traders and small numbers of settlers who vied for

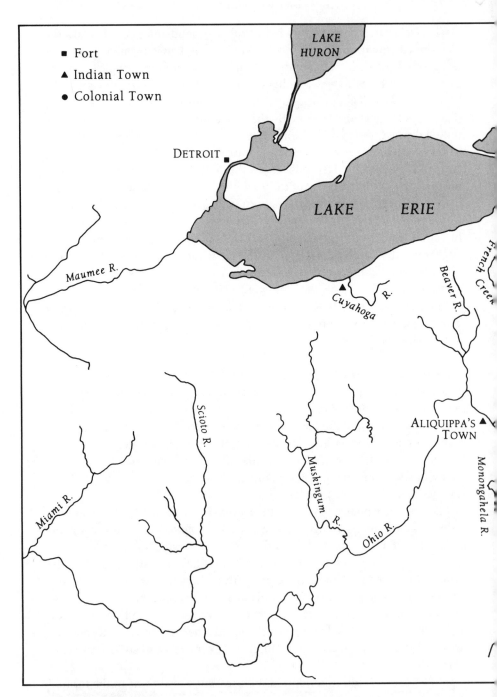

Map 3 Indian migrations to the Ohio Country, 1724–1745.

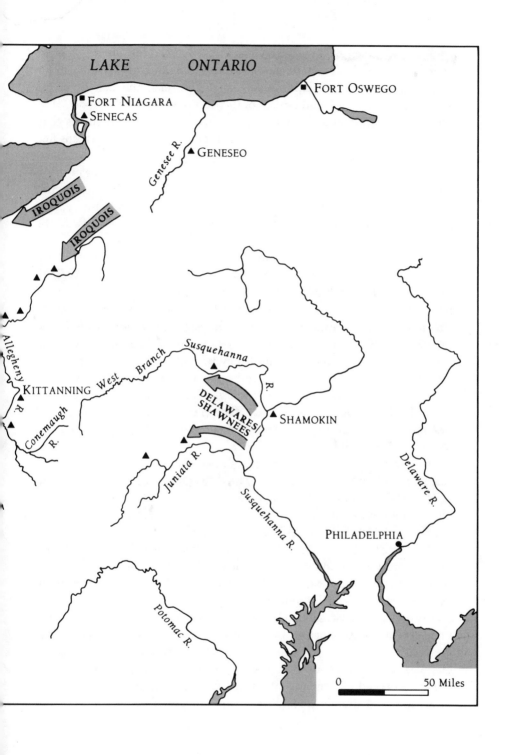

control of the rich fur trade in the lower Delaware (to the Dutch, "South") Valley. These early encounters ran the gamut from mutually satisfying trade to periodic violence to land sales, but all informed the natives of the strengths, weaknesses, and desires of their uninvited new neighbors. Hostilities were minimal and directed more toward Dutch settlements than toward traders. Of far greater significance for the natives was the intensified interethnic conflict that arose as interior groups (Mohawks, Susquehannocks, and others) attempted to gain both direct access to European stores and more reliable sources of the pelts that soon became the medium of exchange. By the mid-1650s the Delawares were caught up in the cycle of warfare that culminated in the destruction of native societies west of the Appalachians.[8]

As disruptive as the Dutch traders and intersocietal warfare may have been, the Delawares' greatest challenge came with the arrival of William Penn in 1682. Though two generations of more casual contact with Europeans enabled the Delawares to learn much about the newcomers, nothing had prepared them for the magnitude of the English invasion that followed the creation of the colony of Pennsylvania in 1681. Within forty years of Penn's arrival, the lower Delaware Valley was all but cleared of its native inhabitants; Shackamaxon had become Philadelphia, and the Delawares found themselves relegated to the margins of yet another English new world. And whereas skins and pelts had been the truck with the Dutch and Swedes, land now became the principal commodity of exchange between natives and colonists.

The new world that Penn's settlers fashioned had its parallel on the other side of the colony's cultural frontier. The natives' material lives continued to change as more and more foreign goods became available. Not only had older communities and territories been abandoned, but by the 1720s the structure of Delaware society itself had changed. The natives met the English advance by a gradual movement westward, as villages traded land for European goods and for the distance such sales created between newcomers and remaining native territory. Native bands from both sides of the Delaware River gradually joined in this western remove, as did the ethnically distinct Munsees living beyond the Delaware Water Gap. At the same time, previously autonomous Delaware villages began to consolidate. What eventually emerged in the east were several composite Delaware groups; one was known to Pennsylvanians simply as the "Schuylkill Indians"—a group composed of remnants of several villages from the lower Delaware, Schuylkill, and Brandywine valleys. This process of social consolidation continued as these natives and those living east of the Delaware River—the "Jerseys"—moved west beyond the Allegheny Mountains.[9]

As villages coalesced, new leaders emerged, men who served principally as brokers between native communities and oncoming colonists. Known as "kings" to Englishmen who misinterpreted both their origin and their influence, such men reflected a tendency among the Delawares for neighboring bands to cooperate through the symbolic leadership of the man most influential locally. Under pressures from Penn's colonists, however, this process was reinforced as villages banded together in collective action, and it found favor among provincial leaders predisposed to deal with one Indian voice rather than many. Among the new group known as the Schuylkill Indians, this leadership role was held for more than a generation by Allumapees, also known as Sassoonan.[10]

Allumapees, like other Delaware "kings," quickly became a major participant in the sale of native lands in the Schuylkill valley to Penn and to proprietary agents. Precisely how individual bands' territorial claims were alienated through Allumapees is unclear, but his central role is undeniable. In 1718 he was the first among equals in Schuylkill society; his name on treaties was followed by those of men who represented specific bands or villages. By 1731, however, the process of consolidation among the Indians had reached a point where Allumapees was referred to as "Chief of the Schuylkill Indians and Indian *owner*" of lands to be transferred. Transfers typically were witnessed now by only a few others, including at least one member of Allumapees's own lineage. Allumapees's influence at home certainly rested on his ability to work with and satisfy the needs of his colonial neighbors. As they so often did, colonists purchased influence within Delaware councils by simply providing "kings" like Allumapees with material goods and political support that both enhanced the headman's prestige and enabled him to maintain a core of followers based on traditional notions of reciprocity, in this instance expressed in Allumapees's redistribution of European goods in exchange for political support.[11]

One measure of the Pennsylvanians' success in dealing with Allumapees was how rapidly the Schuylkill villagers' homelands were given up to colonists. By 1709 some of the Delawares, including their king, were living among recently settled Shawnees at Paxtang on the Susquehanna River; a decade later most of the Schuylkill Indians were settled in the vicinity of Shamokin (Sunbury, Pennsylvania), a multiethnic town at the confluence of the West Branch and main stream of the Susquehanna.[12]

From the vicinity of Shamokin the Delawares had ready access to the upper Ohio Valley by way of the West Branch. Although Kittanning was not founded until 1724, there is every reason to believe that Delawares began to penetrate the Allegheny front much earlier; French accounts speak of Minisinks (Munsees) near Lake Michigan in the 1680s. And others followed seasonally during the first two decades of the eighteenth century.[13]

Anglo-Americans assigned a purely economic motive to the Delaware migrations. James Logan reported in 1731 that "the most of our Delaware Indians [were] about the year 1724 unhappily drawn off to the branches of Ohio for the conveniency of game." His explanation has some basis in fact, as others subsequently learned from natives who complained about the scarcity of game owing to the barren ground in the Juniata Valley south of Shamokin. Yet the scarcity of game, and with it the limited supply of meat and hides for trade, was only an indication of another, equally pressing problem: continuing colonial encroachment on the Delaware land base. In the mid-1720s the natives were already concerned that soon, because of aggressive purchases by men like Logan, aided by pliant "kings" like Allumapees, their children would be "vagabonds." It was undoubtedly to avoid this fate that other natives packed up and moved west, turning their backs on an increasingly crowded, alien world and heading toward a new country whose expanse and geographic security they already knew.[14]

The Schuylkill Indians were soon joined in their westward trek by the Shawnees. The Shawnees, under a variety of names including Savannahs and Chaouanons, had surfaced as far afield as the upper Mississippi Valley and the Carolina Piedmont since their dispersion by the Iroquois in the 1670s. In the west, Shawnee bands had made contact with the French at Starved Rock and other places, and they eventually entered Pennsylvania in 1692 led by French traders, such as Martin Chartier, who were seeking better opportunities among the recently settled English on the Delaware. The Minisinks also met and hosted other Shawnee villagers.[15]

Though their settlements in Pennsylvania (Pequa, Chillisquaque) carried the names of the Shawnees' principal social divisions, the people living in them were still scattered in separate groups, often living among the Delawares or Conestogas. Not only were they still dispersed, but their time in eastern Pennsylvania was no less stormy than their previous experiences had been. Evidence suggests that animosity between Shawnees and Iroquois continued, even as the former moved closer to the Confederacy's homeland. The Shawnees' continued bellicose relations with the Iroquois were matched by conflicts arising from their proximity to colonial settlements and to other natives. Shawnee warriors returning from raids against

southern Piedmont enemies in 1728 provoked hostilities with border settlers; this same group was also blamed for the deaths of two Conestogas.[16]

Such conflicts may have led some Shawnees to rethink their choice of
new homes and to look westward once again. Moreover, the migration of
Delaware villagers seems to have left their Shawnee guests little choice but
to follow, hoping, as one Shawnee later put it, that the Delawares would not
"drink away" the Ohio Country as they had their lands in the east. Finally,
angered by their failure to support a scheme to halt British expansion, the
Iroquois evicted those Shawnees living on lands in the Susquehanna Valley
that were claimed by the Confederacy. Yet the forces that pushed the
Shawnees out of Pennsylvania were offset by positive attractions. Those
Shawnees who turned west in the mid-1720s were really returning home,
taking the first steps in a journey that, over the next fifty years, would see
the Shawnee people reunited in their old Ohio Valley homeland for the first
time in a century. This westward trek was made still easier not only by
strong ties to the Ohio Valley and knowledge of its land and resources, but
also by continued contact with French traders and, through them, with the
colonial government at Quebec.[17]

The Shawnees and Delawares were not alone in seeking new homes and
continued autonomy in the Ohio Country. Although some of the same
forces that pushed the Delawares and Shawnees west were at work here as
well, the Iroquois migrations, which began in earnest in the 1740s, were
rooted in the special circumstances confronting those people and in their
relations with their neighbors.

For most of the seventeenth century the Senecas and other members of
the Iroquois Confederacy had been locked in a series of wars with the
Canadian French and their native trading partners in the Great Lakes
region. The earliest of these conflicts—"beaver wars"—erupted from intersocietal dynamics that predated the arrival of Europeans. Widening competition for control of the trade in European goods added new motives to
traditional patterns of warfare. The Eries and Monongahelans were among
the victims of this struggle, which reached a climax during the last two
decades of the century. By then the Five Nations found themselves on the
defensive. In 1687 a Canadian-Indian army led by the governor Jacques-
René de Brisay, marquis de Denonville, invaded Seneca territory and sacked
the principal towns. For the next thirteen years the Senecas and the rest of
the Confederacy suffered serious losses in their war with New France, and
they were eventually driven to redefine their strategies in confronting an
increasingly dangerous colonial world. In separate treaties at Montreal and
Albany in 1701, Five Nations leaders abandoned their aggressive efforts to

control the flow of pelts from the west. Instead they opted for neutrality between New France and rival British colonies, a position that permitted them to profit from the Great Lakes trade, to maintain the needed Covenant Chain alliance with New York, and to rebuild societies ravaged by years of warfare and torn by factional disputes.[18]

Having made peace in the north, after 1701 the Iroquois turned their attention southward, releasing social tension and replacing wartime losses through raids against long-standing foes in the southern Piedmont, especially the Catawbas and Cherokees, raids that took a far less serious toll than had the earlier conflicts. This southern orientation was reinforced by the growth of Pennsylvania, which held out new opportunities for trade and alliance. Thus warfare to the south and diplomacy with Philadelphia drew the Iroquois more and more toward the Ohio Country and the Susquehanna Valley.[19]

The decades after 1680 also saw growing emigration from Iroquoia. The Canadian mission towns claimed some who tried to escape the conflict between converts and traditionalists. Others resettled in the Susquehanna Valley, eventually becoming members of multiethnic towns at Wyoming, Shamokin, and Conestoga. By far the largest number, however, moved into the upper Ohio Valley. These people were for the most part Senecas, whose towns moved gradually westward toward the upper Genesee Valley and the Allegheny watershed as the threat of renewed French attacks subsided after 1701.[20]

Raids against the Catawbas led some Iroquois to settle permanently on the Allegheny Plateau. Warriors commonly traversed the region in the 1720s and may have helped found Aliquippa's Town as some men, having collected information on the countryside, chose to move into the Ohio Country. Jonah Davenport and James Le Tort made a point of referring to the town as "a great resort" of the Six Nations, a comment that might also reflect the settlement's role in provisioning outbound and returning raiders.[21]

Of greater importance, however, was the continuing rivalry between New France and New York for control of the Great Lakes fur trade. After 1715 the focus of this competition was the Niagara portage, lying within Seneca territory. The Senecas nearest Niagara Falls granted the French permission to build a trading post, a move that clearly benefited Indians near the portage road. The decision also added to the problems facing the Six Nations as they strove to preserve their sovereignty in the face of continued colonial expansion. Louis-Thomas Chabert de Joncaire's post at Niagara (Youngstown, New York), founded in 1720, renewed Anglo-French competition for control of the Lake Ontario–Niagara transportation corridor, and

Senecas and Onondagas found themselves competing with rival colonies for control of their own land. The Six Nations lost the diplomatic contest that ensued, and in 1727 New York's Fort Oswego joined the French Fort Niagara as a colonial enclave in what had once been exclusively Iroquois lands.[22]

The impact of this struggle went beyond strategic or diplomatic considerations. As early as 1717 Senecas heard rumors of an Anglo-French plan to attack the Six Nations, rumors that helped produce the Confederacy's call for a pan-Indian war against all the colonies. At the same time, a lack of consensus on how to respond to French and British pressure for access to the Niagara River and Lake Ontario exacerbated existing factionalism and magnified tensions within Six Nations towns. New York's Indian commissioners were informed in 1716 that the Senecas "are divided into two parties," ostensibly because of an increase in numbers, though the seriousness of the division was emphasized by the notice that "for the future when any presents are given they *must* be divided into six shares instead of five" (for each of the five nations then recognized by the government). And Senecas themselves spoke of "a jealousy and disturbance" in their country that grew from the departure of "two principal sachems, their wives and families" for Canada, as well as the appearance of the French flag in the sachems' towns.[23]

Factionalism was nothing new to Iroquois society, though the underlying causes and the level of intensity clearly changed with mounting pressure from colonial societies; likewise, the ever-present suspicion of French and British activities had become a part of living between two competing empires. What was new in the wake of the Niagara-Oswego episode was the sudden proximity of the western Iroquois towns to trading posts, with their liquor and their propensity for generating violence and spreading disease. Of the two posts, Oswego clearly produced more problems and Iroquois anxiety. Unlike their French rivals, who understood the diplomatic aspects of trade and were under tighter constraints from both church and state, the Oswego traders operated a freewheeling marketplace where profit far outweighed any other consideration.[24]

A litany of grievances from Senecas and their neighbors began even before Oswego was fairly established, as New York peddlers flocked to the site. Liquor, now a staple among British traders, topped the list of native complaints. One of the more disgusting practices revealed by the Senecas was the traders' habit of "cheat[ing] them very much in the sale of rum instead of which they sell them their own water, which in a day or two stinks and is noisome."[25]

By the time Oswego was founded, liquor was commonplace in Iroquois villages. No longer strange drinks that burned the lips and addled the brain, rum and brandy had become part of native experience, their use dictated by local values and needs. The intoxicating effect of liquor hastened the dream states through which men could commune with the spirits that guided life on earth, lessening the need for the arduous vision quests common in earlier times. Drinking also became a form of group recreation and provided an emotional "time out," especially for people who had to face the interpersonal conflicts of everyday life while adhering to the ideal of "autonomous responsibility": the stoicism admired in Iroquois society. Drinking provided an opportunity to vent frustration, fear, and anger at others without having to bear responsibility for acts ranging from theft to homicide, since blame was placed on the alcohol, not the individual.[26]

Yet drunken behavior when normal inhibitions were set aside led to violence that left men and women maimed or dead. Moreover, heavy drinking left villagers, especially headmen, unable to conduct normal affairs. Meetings with colonists were delayed, often for several days, while sachems and their followers overcame the aftereffects of rum or eau-de-vie; Senecas in particular warned their provincial neighbors that the uncontrolled flow of rum into their towns not only harmed people but "unfits them for any kind of business." Such statements and complaints came from village elders who were faced with the complicated task of controlling a substance that was at once a proven danger and very popular. The persistence of such complaints, in the Confederacy towns and elsewhere, testified to a singular lack of success.[27]

The appearance of New York's trading post produced other dangers as well. Both Oswego and its rival at Niagara stood as tangible proof of continuing European expansion at the Confederacy's expense and added to the feeling of being "hemmed in" that was increasingly spoken of by Senecas and others. The posts not only brought manufactured goods and liquor closer to native towns but also introduced diseases, especially smallpox. In 1716 and again in 1733, reports of smallpox reached British officials. The earlier outbreak may have been the result of Six Nations raids into the southeast; in 1733 the sickness was spread through contact with traders and infected native middlemen. The French discovered that the disease had spread through the Great Lakes region as well. The New Yorkers spoke of a "great mortality" among the Six Nations, whose headmen feared that the disease "would have almost destroyed them." To make matters worse, in 1741 the Seneca towns faced a food shortage severe enough for Frenchmen to report that "they are dying of hunger in the Sononatouan [Seneca] territory," while the British in New York felt they must order "a considerable quantity" of corn to help alleviate the famine. The Six Nations Iroquois, especially the Senecas, thus had compelling reasons to leave their homeland altogether.[28]

Like the Delawares, the Senecas and others from the Six Nations were pulled into the Ohio Country. The same abundant land and game that attracted Delawares and Shawnees must have been particularly welcomed by Iroquois, who were short of both by the early 1740s. Equally influential were the new French emporiums on the south shore of Lake Erie. Through adoptive kin such as the Joncaires, the Senecas had maintained close ties with the Canadians since the end of the seventeenth century. These bonds, and the better treatment they received at French posts, led the western Senecas to permit the building of Fort Niagara and would have made other posts at Cuyahoga (near Cleveland, Ohio) and Sandusky equally attractive. Moreover, the Iroquois and French were capable of developing other symbiotic relationships. At Niagara, for example, local Senecas served as porters for the French, "from whom they earn[ed] money" that offered an additional avenue toward the desired manufactured goods. The French derived benefits as well; the small village near Joncaire's post at the foot of the portage raised corn, beans, and other produce and provided game for the nearby traders.[29]

Although some Senecas remained at the Falls, others moved farther south into the Ohio Country. Though French traders were clearly one lure, it is equally possible that for some among the pioneers the Senecas' arrival was a resettlement of ancestral territory. Erie and Monongahelan captives (nominally Senecas, Cayugas, or Onondagas, but never fully assimilated by their captors) may have formed the vanguard of the removals to the south. Many of those taken as children or young adults in the 1680s and still alive thirty or forty years later would have harbored not only memories of home but also intimate knowledge of the region that eased their emigration or that of their children.[30]

The Iroquois migration followed two principal routes: one led directly overland from the Genesee Valley to the headwaters of the Allegheny River, below which the Seneca towns of Conewango (Warren, Pennsylvania) and Buckaloons (Irvineton, Pennsylvania) appeared by the 1740s; the other route led southwestward along the Lake Erie Plain toward Cuyahoga and Sandusky. In both cases the Iroquois were moving into lands that, by their standards, they could legitimately claim as a result of the Erie war. Like the migration of the Delawares and Shawnees farther east, the Iroquois movement into the Ohio Country continued for decades, waxing and waning with changing conditions in Iroquoia and according to relations with European colonies. Yet the number of emigrants by 1750 must have been substantial. In that year Governor James Hamilton of Pennsylvania plaintively observed that the Iroquois in the Ohio Country and westward were "become more numerous there than in the countrys they left."[31]

The Delawares, Senecas, and Shawnees thus found themselves settling on the Allegheny Plateau for a variety of reasons: abundant resources, distance from menacing colonial or Indian neighbors, and strong historical ties to the region made it attractive to migrating natives; loss of lands—by sale or fraud—and the friction generated by increased contact between natives and colonists made the upper Ohio Valley a convenient haven. For whatever specific reasons, however, the towns that appeared in the Allegheny Valley after 1724 were the product of a deliberate strategy as native pioneers attempted to preserve their cultural and political integrity. Although sometimes referred to by the British as "straggling" or "wandering" Indians, the migrants were not a hodgepodge of refugees but were kin-based societies whose subsequent histories included the successful re-creation of familiar ways in a new country.[32]

At the same time, these new towns marked the first tentative steps toward two altogether new developments. As increasing numbers of Delawares and Shawnees moved west in the decades following 1720, there began the process that eventually led to the formation of new societies as independent bands or long-scattered kin groups were reunited in the Ohio Country. And while these and other ethnic groups were strengthening their own particular identities, there began to emerge a growing collective identity with the upper Ohio Valley, at once rooted in the localized dynamics of Indian societies, the natives' locale, and the challenges they ultimately faced from ambitious outsiders.

two

The Indians at "Allegeney"

The arrival of the Delawares, Shawnees, and Senecas inaugurated the resettling of the upper Ohio Valley, which continued for two decades after 1724 as the original pioneers and settlers were joined by others from as far away as Wisconsin and the French mission towns of the St. Lawrence Valley. New towns founded by different ethnic groups ensured that Ohio Country history would be marked by cultural diversity as well as by competition and conflict.

Yet those natives who settled on the Allegheny Plateau brought with them persistent social systems, cultural values, and ethnic identities that quickly took root in the region. Moreover, while the Indians' material world continued to change because of growing reliance on European goods, alien materials were embedded in patterns of native values and practices. Taken together, what emerges from the native pioneering of the Ohio Country is a portrait of continuity and order in the midst of the apparent disruption caused by migrations during a period of rapid material change. Far from being refugees, the natives who settled west of the Alleghenies represented viable societies able to confront the many challenges of fashioning a familiar landscape in a new land. That process, coupled with time, distance, and localism, also produced a growing regional identity, one shared by all inhabitants of the Ohio Country regardless of ethnic affiliation—an identity linked to an emerging "Ohio Indian" world.

The Pennsylvania traders venturing across the mountains in the wake of migrating Indians offer the earliest among the few glimpses of the new cultural landscape taking shape on the Allegheny Plateau. In autumn 1731

Jonah Davenport and James Le Tort provided detailed information to provincial authorities concerning the locations, numbers, and ethnic identities of the Indians living in what the traders called "Allegeney." Davenport's and Le Tort's depositions identified ten towns in the Ohio Country: four Delaware and five Shawnee, plus one small Iroquois hamlet. All of the Delaware towns and two Shawnee towns are identified by name; three unnamed Shawnee towns were probably the "French Town," Peter Chartier's town, and Kiskiminetas, identified in 1737 by trader George Miranda. With the exception of the Iroquois settlement—Aliquippa's Town—all were east of the Allegheny River near Kittanning.[1]

These towns held some 217 families in 1731, with Kittanning and the Shawnees' Sewikaley's Town accounting for fifty each; Aliquippa's Town held only "4 settled families" but was considered "a great resort of those [Iroquois] people." All together, the Ohio towns contained perhaps as many as 1,336 people, and half appear to have been adult males. Such a large number of men indicates the pioneering nature of these towns; advance elements from older parent communities would lay the foundations for new settlements, and such work and the security it required would have initially demanded more men than whole families.[2]

Though they are remarkably detailed, the reports of Davenport, Le Tort, and Miranda offer only a momentary glimpse of an ongoing process of migration and resettlement. Throughout the next two decades the builders of these first Ohio Country towns were joined by numbers of kinfolk. Shawnees were joined before 1731 by groups from the Assiwikales that came to the plateau from the upper Potomac Valley, having earlier moved there from South Carolina, where they were known as "Savannahs." Such migrations continued, culminating in the establishment of Logg's Town in 1744 by a group led by the eastern Shawnee "king" Kakowatchiky. By then elements of Chillocothes, Pequas, and Assiwikales had all settled in the upper Ohio Valley, marking the first time in nearly a century that elements of most of the five Shawnee divisions were living together.[3]

The Shawnees' Delaware neighbors also continued to move west, joined eventually by Delawares and Munsees from northeastern Pennsylvania. As early as 1728 traders reported that "all the Indians were removed from Shamokin"—all save their king, Allumapees, and his nephew Opekasset. Some may have departed early for winter hunting sites, but others would have continued west to join kinfolk under the guidance of Captain Hill, Shannopin, and others, in a slow but steady shift of Delaware people from the Susquehanna to the Ohio Valley.[4]

Few reliable population estimates exist, and those that do are difficult to compare. Nevertheless, the steady influx of natives from a variety of directions, coupled with an increasing birthrate, led to at least modest increases. The Delawares living in the Allegheny Valley in 1730 included 296 adult males; twenty years later one Virginian reported 500 fighting men. The greatest concentration of peoples before 1750 was in the Cuyahoga Valley, where French traders had attracted as many as 2,400 natives (mostly Iroquois) by 1743. Five years later, after considerable resettlement owing to warfare in the region, some 347 Iroquois were living in the upper Ohio Valley, and though all Six Nations were represented, nearly half were Senecas. Less is known about the Shawnees or the Iroquois living far up the Allegheny Valley, but by the mid-1740s Aliquippa's modest village had been joined by Seneca and mixed Iroquois towns at Conawango (Warren, Pennsylvania), Buckaloons (Irvineton, Pennsylvania), and Kuskuski (New Castle, Pennsylvania) on the Beaver River.[5]

One measure of the growing number of people in the Ohio Country is the distribution of towns. In 1730 most, if not all, Indian settlements were concentrated along the middle Allegheny Valley; lands to the west were exploited largely as hunting reserves. A decade and a half later, however, the land west of the Allegheny held numerous villages, large and small. The change reflected the increased need for settlement ground at a time when substantial numbers of Shawnees and Iroquois were joining the Delawares in establishing new homes on the plateau.[6]

Migrations followed patterns rooted in the customs of the local communities that shaped the lives of Senecas, Delawares, and Shawnees. The natives' movement westward itself would have been the result of countless discussions as the villagers weighed the pros and cons of migration and arrived at a consensus on the issue. In some instances long-standing factional divisions within villages led dissatisfied minorities to vote with their feet and seek new homes elsewhere, thus preserving the harmony so highly valued within native societies. In some cases respected clan headmen, such as the Delawares' Shannopin and "Captain" Hill, could influence decisions through their own prestige or through their kin groups. Moreover, among the matrilineal Unamis and Iroquois, the paramount importance of women—as heads of lineages, with the responsibility for selecting clan spokesmen, and as providers of food and clothing—would have led to their involvement at every stage in the process. For example, the Seneca matron Aliquippa appears to have led her family to the Allegheny Valley. Thus those who came to the Ohio Country arrived as the result of purposeful decisions and careful planning, even though the natives faced mounting pressure from colonial societies.[7]

Decisions to leave may have been predicated in part on knowledge of the Ohio Valley obtained by earlier reconnaissance. For the Shawnees, firsthand knowledge of the region, its resources, and its important stream and trail systems extended back to the late seventeenth century. Once a decision to remove had been made, the group would face new challenges, primarily siting the new town and ensuring that a reliable source of food would be available when the families arrived. The new Ohio Valley towns were normally close to major streams, far enough from the floodplains to avoid springtime inundations but near enough to take advantage of river transport. Town location would also have been determined by the availability of firewood and fresh water and by proximity to game trails, reliable sources of fish, and an ever-increasing number of colonial traders. Natives met the more immediate need for food and building materials by sending out advance parties in the autumn to winter on the site, clear fields for spring planting, and collect wood and bark for dwellings; the temporary shelters at these camps could later be used for fuel.[8]

Few descriptions of Ohio valley towns survive for the years before 1760. Davenport and Le Tort went no further than to indicate the number of families and adult men in each village, and later observers were either uninterested in native townscapes or content to take brief note in passing. Thus in 1749 Captain Pierre-Joseph Céloron de Blainville reported that Conewango "consists of twelve or thirteen cabins," while farther down the Allegheny he found at Kittanning twenty-two dwellings, figures that at least suggest the variable size of the Allegheny Valley towns. A better sense of Ohio Indian townscapes comes from descriptions by missionaries and other travelers of the native towns that provided many of the Ohio settlers. Moravian Bishop Gottlieb Spangenberg found Shamokin in 1749 divided into three hamlets, occupied by Delawares, Senecas, and Tutelos. Six years earlier the naturalist John Bartram passed through Iroquoia on his way to Oswego. At Onondaga he found a town "about 2 or 3 miles long, yet the scattered cabins . . . are not above forty in number, . . . but all stand single, and rarely above 4 or 5 near one another." He was also struck by the "strange mixture of cabins, interspersed with great patches of High grass, Bushes and shrubs, some of pease, corn and squash." The "cabins" Bartram found included at least one traditional longhouse that also served as a council house. In contrast was Ganatisgoa, a Tuscarora town David Zeisberger visited in 1750. The missionary found a much more orderly settlement consisting of "almost thirty houses, large and regularly built, with a crude street through the middle of the town."[9]

Towns thus varied greatly, from small hamlets like Aliquippa's Town to large, multiethnic trading towns like Shamokin or, in the Ohio Country, Logg's Town (Ambridge, Pennsylvania). Furthermore, European terms such as "town" or "castle" imply a regular, nucleated pattern and often hide more than they reveal. For example, Zeisberger described Onondaga not as one straggling settlement but as "5 small towns" that also included "single, scattered huts." What Zeisberger observed was a pattern common throughout the northeast as the destructive wars of the previous century gave way to more settled, predictable patterns of interethnic and intercultural relations. The fortified towns that dominated the Monongahelan and Iroquoian landscapes in 1650 had given way to the open, sometimes ramshackle, settlements visited by colonists a century later. In the process, kin groups within the towns tended to settle apart, nearer their fields and away from town centers and village council houses. The result was the five towns at Onondaga, actually clusters of related lineages whose dwellings, like those of neighboring Seneca towns, were "ornamented with red paintings of deer, turtles, bears, etc.," the totemic signs of the clans the lineages belonged to. This atomization was also found in the increasing prevalence of single-family dwellings: Bartram thought the Onondagas' "cabins" would hold at most two families, while traditional longhouses continued to serve principally as council houses.[10]

One existing town plan from the Ohio Country demonstrates how far the region's new settlements reflected these tendencies. Drawn to aid a Pennsylvania force that destroyed the town in autumn 1756, the plan of Kittanning reveals seven clusters of dwellings—most identified with prominent war leaders or headmen—arranged in an arc on terraces overlooking the Allegheny River. Below the town, near the river, were the maize fields, while smaller streams bordering the town were a ready source of drinking water; the entire town, numbering some three hundred to four hundred people, was about 1,100 feet from end to end.[11]

The Kittanning townscape reveals more than just the distribution of people or the placement of fields. Near the center of town stood a "Long House" wherein the "frolicks and War Dances are Held." A ceremonial center, the house would have held annual harvest ceremonies and doubled as a council house. The town was under the leadership of three men: Shingas, Pisquetomen, and Tamaqua, whose maternal uncle, Allumapees, had earlier been the "king" of the Schuylkill Delawares. The presence of these men among the western Delawares, since at least the time of Al-

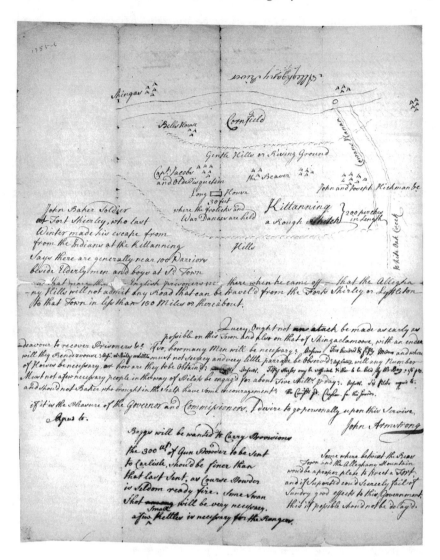

1. Kittanning, about 1755, from John Armstrong, "Scheme of an Expedition to Kittanning." (Courtesy of the American Philosophical Society)

lumapees's death in 1747, suggests a strong continuity in leadership and social order as the Delawares moved west. One of the leading Delawares in the Allegheny Valley in 1730 was "Captain" Hill, further identified as "a Allumappy"—another member of the principal lineage of the Schuylkill Indians.[12]

This same continuity extended to the Shawnees. Shawnee towns in the Ohio Country took their names from the social divisions of which they were a part. Thus, for example, Sewickely's Town was settled by Assiwikales. At the same time, "kings" appeared among the western Shawnees: Missemedi-queety, known to Pennsylvanians as "Big Hominy," and Nucheconner were both important men, with Nucheconner referred to in 1738 as "Chief of the Shawanese at Allegeney."[13]

The traders who committed Indian messages to paper or the provincial clerks who kept minutes of the councils with visitors from the Ohio were careful to record the names of native headmen. This record reveals, in the first place, that Indians in the Ohio Country were represented by a number of spokesmen and village elders; ten such Delawares are known from this period, as are nearly as many Shawnees. Most often several men would affix their marks to a letter or speech. Depending on the skill of the colonial scribe, the lists of names—in some cases several variants for one individual—might seem to imply a cacophony of voices and a number of competing centers of power within western villages. Yet the very nature of native societies, with their emphasis on kinship and localism, meant that all elements of Delaware or Shawnee society had a right to be heard. A closer look at Delawares who participated in diplomatic exchanges, for example, suggests that on issues involving trade and relations with the colony a consensus existed among the principal villages, strong enough to perhaps carry smaller settlements as well. In 1732 a message to Lieutenant Governor Francis Gordon was signed by seven village leaders, including "Merhe-goakehuk" ("Great Hill" or Captain Hill) of Kittanning, Shawanoppan (Shannopin), and Allemykoppy. Two of these men, Captain Hill and Shan-nopin, represented the Delawares at a meeting with Pennsylvanians in 1740 as well. The frequency of their appearance in the records implies that both men enjoyed high esteem among their people. Moreover, cooperation reflected an alliance of interest between these two influential leaders that may have lasted until their deaths near the end of the 1740s and that presaged broader cooperation among the Delawares in the following decades. Captain Hill's status may have been enhanced by his kinship ties to Allumapees; Ohio traders, at least, assumed he enjoyed a position comparable to that of the Delaware "king" at Shamokin.[14]

Information on Shawnee leaders reflects a similar emphasis on collective agreement by men representing autonomous villages. The western Shawnees appear to have gone one step further toward formalizing leadership— and relations with outsiders—by selecting Opessah's son Loyparcowah as titular leader of the headmen meeting in assembly. However, Loyparcowah's

2. A representative example of the Delawares at the time of their migration to the Ohio Country: Tishcohan (1735), by Gustavus Heselius. (Courtesy of the Historical Society of Pennsylvania)

"deputy king," Nucheconner, quickly rose to become the principal representative for the western Shawnees in their dealings with the British. In this way Nucheconner's role paralleled that of Kakowatchiky, the acknowledged "king" of the Shawnees at Pechoquealin and Wyoming. Each man seems to have acknowledged the legitimacy of the other; indeed, Nucheconner, while not deprecating his own standing in the west, was quick to recognize

Kakowatchiky as "the chief man" and deferred to him on at least one occasion. Yet Nucheconner's influence, like that of his Delaware counterparts, rested largely on consensus hammered out in councils composed of representatives from at least most of the Shawnee towns west of the Alleghenies.[15]

Such a picture must remain tentative; the paucity of references and detail makes a close examination of political structure all but impossible. Furthermore, those men who actively engaged in the give-and-take of the council tended to enjoy greater notoriety beyond the Ohio Country than did others. Nucheconner appears frequently in the records. Yet though Peter Chartier is mentioned in his capacity as trader, messenger, and "our Friend," little is known of the role played by others from his town whose names are absent on letters going east. Likewise, whereas men from Kittanning and nearby towns figure prominently in Delaware-Pennsylvania affairs, nothing can be said about those natives who occupied the lower French Creek Valley in the 1740s. At best such negative evidence suggests ethnic or political divisions that might have precluded closer cooperation; the subsequent alignment of Peter Chartier's band with the French—a move not followed by other Shawnees—implies such divisions. The scant references to native leaders, then, leave much obscured. However, the consensus that emerged among Ohio Indian towns casts light on another important dimension of the Indian world that took shape in the Ohio Country.[16]

The orderly towns they lived in and the rapidity and apparent ease with which the newcomers were able to establish relations with outsiders suggests that these people were not "wandering" aimlessly about, seeking sanctuary wherever it might appear. Indeed, the natives' migration westward was not unlike that of seventeenth-century English men and women whose own world was beset with uncertainties that pushed people already on the move to seek their fortunes and security beyond the sea. Thus the natives' arrival on the Allegheny Plateau was the product of planning and was carried out by peoples who, though undeniably under stress from outside encroachment and factions from within, were nonetheless viable, cohesive societies. Moreover, the persistence of ethnic identities and the emerging ethnic boundaries within the Ohio Country suggest that the clans and bands that entered the region were able to maintain—even to strengthen—their particular identities. The lines dividing Shawnees, Delawares, and Senecas were less clear in the 1730s, when most settlements occupied a narrow stretch of the Allegheny Valley. That boundaries existed, however, was made clear in the early 1750s, by which time settlements had expanded beyond the Allegheny into central Ohio, where ethnic territories became more readily identifiable both to natives and to foreign visitors. These ethnic boundaries were neither immutable nor impenetrable. Rather, like the larger cultural frontiers that distinguished native from colonial societies, the more discrete ethnic boundaries *between* Indian societies were often fluid. Trading centers or towns situated on or near ecological or ethnic frontiers were most often characterized by their multiethnic composition. Yet even in such places Iroquois, Wyandots, Ottawas, Delawares, and others tended to form their own clusters of dwellings and continued to adhere to their own leaders, who met in town councils with their ethnic neighbors.[17]

To be sure, there were people in the Ohio Country who were "refugees," notably the Mesquakies (Foxes) who settled among the Seneca and Delaware towns. Over time, their small numbers allowed them to be absorbed by their neighbors and protectors. But the Mesquakies and the small groups of Mahicans who settled the region were the exception rather than the rule. The newcomers to the Ohio Valley experienced nothing like the complex mixing and merging of remnant peoples, shattered by warfare, slave raiding, and disease, that produced the Conestogas, Schaghticokes, and Catawbas—new societies that were more than the sum of their constituent parts. Even among the Shawnees—most peripatetic of all the peoples who eventually called the Ohio Country home—ethnic identity persisted. Peter Chartier's band of Shawnees left the Ohio Valley in 1745 to live among the Upper Creeks; the bonds between these two peoples were rooted in their histories and made fast by intermarriage. Yet many of Chartier's people eventually rejoined other Shawnees in the Scioto Valley. What amalgamation did take place among the Indians on the plateau was largely within ethnic groups rather than across ethnic boundaries.[18]

Although ethnic identities persisted on the plateau, the broad descriptive categories—Shawnee, Delaware, Iroquois—cannot be equated with "tribes" in any political sense. Kittanning, Windaughalah's Town, and Aliquippa's Town were largely autonomous, reflecting traditions of localism rooted in kinship networks that pervaded native societies. Big Hominy, Captain Hill, and Nucheconner were "kings" only insofar as they spoke for and symbolized coalitions of interests that embraced several villages within their societies. These interests—and the factionalism that frequently divided villages and ethnic groups—characteristically developed around specific issues or questions and often represented responses to outside pressures or opportunities. The centrifugal forces within Indian societies were still compelling, however, as the Shawnee "king" Opessah discovered. He abdicated his position, frustrated because "the People differed with him," their difference apparently expressed by "the Young men who lived under no government."[19]

Opessah's difficulties reveal several important points about the nature of native societies. His inability to lead grew from deep and insurmountable divisions within Shawnee society between warriors and their elders. Headmen's interest in social harmony and peaceful relations with neighbors was sometimes at odds with the warriors' desire to earn status through raids or to maintain respect by exacting revenge for insults and poor treatment by outsiders. Shawnee society had long since institutionalized this dichotomy, having headmen—and headwomen—representing both interests. Yet Delaware and Iroquois societies also comprised groups defined by generation or gender, all based on the inherent autonomy of individuals. Individual autonomy, and the need to balance competing—sometimes conflicting—needs within village communities necessarily limited the coercive power of leaders. Opessah could not control ungovernable warriors; neither could he compel obedience in a society that arrived at decisions through the give-and-take of council discussions, where harmony and consensus were more valued than argument and dictatorial pronouncements. In stateless societies, leaders did not so much govern in a European sense as worked to persuade, reason, arbitrate, and maintain social harmony.[20]

Alliances, whether between or within villages, rested on kinship networks and, increasingly after the arrival of Europeans, on the economic influence of native leaders and those who aspired to power. These men stood as brokers between their own people and colonists. Such alliances were inherently unstable, because of the localized nature of Indian societies and because of the shifting sands of intersocietal relations. Over time, however, as the Ohio Indians faced a constant barrage of demands, threats, changes, and opportunities resulting from colonial expansion, coalitions between native groups became more commonplace. Heretofore autonomous villages found advantages to cooperating under the guidance of new "kings" who, as skilled diplomats or as culture brokers, became the leaders of new ethnic alliances from which grew the later Delaware and Shawnee "tribes."[21]

Kinship ties, localism, and the traditions that defined them were also expressed in how the natives in the Ohio Country made their living. In the face-to-face societies of Delaware or Iroquois towns, sharing took precedence over private property and was enforced by a strong ideal of reciprocity. Exchanges of gifts created social bonds between individuals and villages, helped console the relatives of the deceased, and preserved social harmony by emphasizing giving over receiving while also ensuring broad availability of needed or desired goods, whether food in time of poor harvests or trade goods such as iron knives and woolen cloth. Indeed, so important was reciprocity that those who ignored their obligations faced sanctions that placed them beyond the social pale; in some cases persistent stinginess or other evidence of social deviance could result in accusations of witchcraft and summary execution. Headmen bore special responsibility in this regard; they were expected to collect food and redistribute it to those in need, to entertain visitors, and to conduct diplomacy with neighboring societies: in short, to represent in their persons and actions the openhandedness so valued in native societies.[22] Nevertheless, the basis of any town's economy was the local kinship network, a group ranging in size and complexity from nuclear families to the extended matrilineages of the Delawares and Iroquois. Among all the Ohio Indians, labor within kin groups was divided based on gender, yet not strictly segregated. Men cleared new fields for planting, but the care of the fields and the harvest were primarily the responsibility of women and young children. Among the horticultural peoples of the northeast, this division of labor was felt in other ways; men were often away from the villages for extended periods, hunting, raiding enemies, or conducting trade and diplomacy. Women, responsible for crops and lodges, remained more closely tied to the town itself. This pattern contributed to the increased status of women among the Iroquois and may have been equally important in the development of a matrilineal kin system among the Delawares. The arrival of European colonists reinforced this pattern, as men intensified their hunting for the marketplace and as native societies found themselves drawn ever deeper into colonial rivalries and wars.[23]

Though the sexes held different primary responsibilities, the activities and roles of men and women often overlapped. Among the Iroquois, clan matrons played a central role in selecting the men who would represent their longhouses in village and confederacy councils. Women also accompanied hunting and raiding expeditions and, as the heads of kin groups, could encourage retaliatory raids against enemies by demanding that dead relatives be avenged or that captives be taken to replace the dead. In this and other matters concerning village life, however, women seldom appeared before the male council; they chose their own spokesmen, instructing them on how best to present their case, much as their husbands and fathers did in preparing council spokesmen for encounters with neighboring societies. Here, as in other aspects of native life, reciprocity and cooperation remained the ideals that shaped the behavior of men and women, adults and children.[24]

The experiences of a British captive reflect both the cooperation that pervaded relationships within native societies and the seasonal rhythm of

Ohio Indian life. James Smith began his life among the Ohio Indians in 1755 by accompanying his adoptive Caughnawaga family on the annual fall hunt into the territory between the Muskingum and Sandusky rivers. From a log cabin the women and children mended clothing, cleaned deer hides, and prepared food for hunters whose exhausting work was made more taxing by freezing weather that crusted the snow so that it crunched underfoot, frightening their prey. The rising of maple sap in February brought an abrupt change in the work routine as men and women worked together tapping trees, carrying sap, and reducing the liquid to sugar, much of which was stored for future use. By mid-March the extended family was on its way back to Sandusky, where the dispersed wintering parties reunited at village sites that were quickly made ready for planting by women and young children. At this point the burden of subsistence shifted from men to women; while the fields were being prepared, men enjoyed a respite from their most trying season in gambling and in the more serious business of village government. These were also the lean weeks for the villagers: the winter's supply of meat was nearly gone, and the maize crops and wild plants had yet to ripen. The situation was exacerbated in this instance, since so many men spent the spring and summer campaigning with the French against the British frontiers. By August, however, the first harvest was ready, once more a time for cooperative labor and harvest ceremonies that bound the community together. By mid-autumn, Smith and his adoptive kin were preparing for another winter's hunt.[25]

In pursuing this seasonal round, exploiting a variety of resources, the Ohio Indians used a network of trails that also reflected how far the newcomers had transformed the local environment into a meaningful landscape. Doubtless still visible though centuries old, the paths that tied together the corners of the Monongahelan world had been refashioned and extended by 1748 into a complex of trails that bore names like Venango, Catawba, and Shamokin and that gave access to the towns, traders, and enemies peculiar to the newly arrived societies. These paths followed well-drained uplands, spanned watersheds, and included "sleeping places"—cliff overhangs or hollow logs—and examples of native engineering that missionary David Zeisberger knew only as "Indian bridges," which crossed smaller streams or ravines.[26]

Townscapes, work routines, and social systems all reflected normative patterns that had developed over generations and, while never unchanging, represented stabilizing, conservative, aspects of native life. Yet the arrival of natives in the Ohio Country and the rapid appearance after 1720 of new cultural landscapes there bespeaks both change and adaptation. Trail networks were the most visible signs of that adaptation, whose inner processes are now lost. Nevertheless, change and persistence were two complementary sides of Indian life, on the Allegheny Plateau as elsewhere; the capacity to adapt while preserving the essentials of one's cultural identity lay at the heart of any native's strategy in the face of new challenges either generated from within society or imposed from without.

The Indians' continued ability both to meet changes and to preserve their own societies can be measured in their dealings with colonial traders. For over two decades after the founding of Kittanning, these peddlers were the only resident Europeans in the Ohio Country. The trade in deerskins and other commodities was over a century old by the time Kittanning was settled, and during that time what began as a casual encounter was transformed into an economic, political, and social nexus that bound together specific groups of natives and colonists even as it created conditions that drove Indians and their Euramerican neighbors apart.

The western Delawares recalled their people's first face-to-face encounter with Europeans over a century and a half earlier when Henry Hudson, piloting a ship in Dutch service, arrived in their country. What followed was a scene enacted countless times as strangers met. The Delawares met Hudson's men with all the ritual behavior and ceremonial exchange of gifts that befitted any honored guests. The ship's crew responded by passing out what were to them trifling goods—ax heads, beads, and cloth—to people eager to give up their rich bounty of animal skins. Language proved no barrier as the Delawares sampled liquor and examined ironware for the first time.[27]

Hidden beneath the surface of this encounter lay some fundamental principles about what has became known simply as the "fur trade." While representatives of two vastly different societies exchanged things, they also conveyed information and meaning across a cultural divide; as one recent student of the trade has so aptly pointed out, both parties were engaged in an important form of communication, one based on objects and the behavior surrounding their exchange. The Delawares were immediately taken with the iron and glass from another world, but they accepted these goods in ways defined by *their* needs and norms. Thus later visitors found these same Delawares wearing ax heads around their necks—in imitation of the shell or copper pendants and gorgets so common throughout the northeast. It took some discussion to inform the natives of the "proper" use of iron tools. Further, the Delawares obtained these goods through a ritualized set of behaviors that reflected the reciprocal nature of native encounters and the persistent linking of exchange with peaceful intent and friendship. As the Delawares later told missionary John Heckewelder, their people were "hailed from the vessel in a language they [did] not understand," though they were able to answer "according to the custom of their country."[28]

Hudson's men, and those who followed them, also acted according to their own customs. As representatives of commercial companies or settlement colonies, their principal concern was profit as they consciously and unconsciously extended the North American trade nexus to embrace peoples unaccustomed to the ethics of a capitalized, consumer-oriented marketplace. Thus each party interpreted trade according to its own culture-bound assumptions of protocol, need, and value. Yet such exchanges could take place only in an atmosphere free of hostility. The trade promoted cooperation if not insight and understanding among participants. Thus European traders adjusted to the rituals of pretrade gift giving and the metaphorically rich language of the council house in dealing with their native customers, accommodation that found its way into the diplomatic dialogue between colonial governments and Indians who insisted on maintaining their sovereignty to the last detail. The natives, for their part, became discriminating customers, demanding the highest quality at the best prices while learning to turn a competitive marketplace to their advantage.[29]

Another, equally telling, aspect of intercultural exchange is revealed in western New York, where a series of Seneca village sites spans nearly 140 years, from 1550 to 1687. Over time, the variety and quantity of European goods on the sites increased, while there was a corresponding disappearance of native ceramic and stone objects. By 1687 traditional Seneca pottery had all but disappeared, supplanted by brass kettles; likewise, bone and shell beads were in the distinct minority beside their Venetian glass counterparts. Here too, as among the Delawares, foreign goods were absorbed in Seneca ways. Kettles initially disappeared to become brass arrowheads and pendants or became part of the grave offerings that accompanied Seneca dead to the next life. Broken ironware was reworked into scrapers, adzes, or drills. Adaptation, as well as adoption, was the rule.[30]

Yet here and elsewhere the growing preponderance of European goods indicates the increase—often rapid—of native dependence on foreign technology. The Senecas and their neighbors could *purchase* iron and cloth, but they were never in a position to produce such materials. This technological dependence, which eventually carried political significance as well, was not so much forced as voluntary. Conscious decisions guided natives as they selected from the array of goods before them. And their choices were predicated on a realistic recognition that iron was more durable than stone, muskets were more devastating that bows and arrows, and cloth was more easily sewn and decorated than pelts or deer hides. Early natives, no less than modern consumers, saw bargains in laborsaving devices and previously unknown creature comforts.[31]

Though clothes and Venetian beads did not necessarily make the man, and enhanced rather than altered ritual aspects of native life, tools, weapons, and housewares did bring greater efficiency. Firearms, ubiquitous by the 1720s, provided Indian hunters with the means to stop even the largest game and, in a world where virtually all one's neighbors were similarly armed, were a necessary item of defense as well. Brass and iron kettles cooked more quickly and thoroughly, held larger portions, and were more easily carried from village to camp than clay vessels. Yet here too native concepts of utility and efficiency placed limits on how and when such powerful or laborsaving items were used. Although muskets, for example, were found to be very good under some conditions, they were ill suited at other times. Hunters found their trade guns useful in daylight, once they had modified them for use in the woods by shortening and darkening the barrels. But as light faded, darkness made sighting difficult, even against large game; firearms were put aside and hunters relied on their still appreciable skills with the bow to bring down their quarry.[32]

In the same way, Indian women knew the practical value as well as the limitations of their imported housewares. In February and March, at annual sugaring camps, women and children used their iron and brass trade kettles as caldrons for reducing great quantities of sap to sugar, for which the large, sturdy vessels were well suited. Yet these kettles did not find their way to the maple stands. There European technology was no match for the light, easily made bark vessels hung on the trees as sap collectors. This critical and practical application of imported wares extended to their initial purchase as well. Merchants and traders everywhere learned that natives quickly developed a fine eye for quality as they scanned the array of merchandise before them. An exasperated Philip Livingston, a member of one of the great merchant families of New York, found his traders "fantasticall and difficult" to please in their demands for merchandise. Yet the peddlers were only reflecting the needs and interests of an equally "difficult" clientele.[33]

Trade with Europeans brought other changes as well. Regular contact with traders increased the natives' chances of contracting diseases against which they had no acquired immunity. Smallpox, like ironware or beads, often raced ahead of traders themselves, carried along centuries-old native trade networks, and it devastated whole populations. The demographic disaster that often accompanied early encounters between natives and

Europeans upset regional power systems at the same time that increasing competition for the skins and pelts most in demand at the traders' marts contributed to a marked increase in intersocietal warfare. Finally, by the end of the seventeenth century widespread Indian participation in the trade began to erase some distinctions between societies, since all shared a fundamentally similar material culture and technological dependence on foreign colonies. By the early eighteenth century this "pan-Indian trade culture" was firmly in place throughout the Great Lakes region and Ohio Country. This largely material way of life by no means weakened or destroyed ethnic distinctions or differences, but it did give all natives in the west at least one common element when confronting colonial neighbors or intruders. Moreover, the trade culture that bound diverse native societies in a consumer network whose center lay across the Atlantic was paralleled by a similar phenomenon as British colonists underwent "anglicization" through the adoption of, among other things, a wide array of Old World material goods.[34] Thus, by the mid-1720s the traders' store of blankets, bullets, hardware, and housewares had become necessities for Indian consumers rather than objects of curiosity or ritual significance. And the trade itself had become formalized. Experience on both sides of the cultural frontier had taught traders and natives alike how to behave when the two met. One outgrowth of the trade and the lessons learned from hard experience was a shared interest, albeit limited by political and cultural considerations, between traders and their customers, both of whom wished to profit from their partnership with as little outside interference or internal turmoil as possible. These patterns, common from Hudson's Bay to the Carolina Piedmont, were replicated in the Ohio Valley after 1724.

The trade in the Ohio Country was largely an extension of the system that grew up east of the Susquehanna River. The depletion of the deer whose hides were the basic commodity of trade led to a westward movement both of Delaware and Shawnee hunters and of their Pennsylvania trading partners. By the end of the 1720s, references began to appear in provincial records to James Le Tort and others who were known to be trading in the "remoter parts in or near" the colony.[35]

These peddlers—Le Tort, Martin Chartier, Peter Bezaillon, and Edmund Cartlidge, and others—were all seasoned veterans of a trade that had originated among the Delawares and Susquehannock-Conestogas and, after 1698, embraced the Shawnees as well. Le Tort, Chartier, and Bezaillon were all expatriate Canadians who had led their Shawnee customers and kinfolk into relations with Pennsylvania. The success of these traders rested largely on their association with Pennsylvania's provincial secretary, land agent, and merchant James Logan. Through his control, before 1720, of virtually all aspects of provincial finance and management, Logan was able to place Indian affairs in his own hands and monopolize the trade. Using his economic and diplomatic influence for larger purposes, Logan acquired large estates through his agents, usually at the expense of local Indians and the goodwill between colony and natives. In the process, he exacerbated conditions that led his Delaware and Shawnee customers to quit their towns and take refuge in the Ohio Country. Yet growing native dependence and the already dominant role of Logan's traders made it easy for "Shamokin" traders to become "Allegeney" traders as they followed their customers west across the mountains. One of the earliest traders venturing into the Ohio Country was James Le Tort. He and those who followed pioneered their own routes to the Ohio, principal of which was the Frankstown Path, which followed the Juniata Valley. A more direct route for traders living near the towns of the middle Susquehanna Valley, the Frankstown Path nevertheless required travelers to cross several of the Allegheny ridges before reaching the headwaters of streams leading to the Ohio.[36]

The Frankstown Path led Logan's traders to what they called simply "Allegeney": the region encompassed by the middle Allegheny River and its Kiskiminetas River tributary. Here, in the 1720s and 1730s, were the principal Delaware and Shawnee towns. As the focal point of the Ohio trade in its early years, these towns became seasonal trading centers and multiethnic communities. "Allegeny," or Kittanning, is a case in point. Its principal residents were Delawares, and it was their headmen who corresponded with Pennsylvania's government on problems arising from trade. Yet the town and its immediate environs also embraced groups of Shawnees and Iroquois, each with their own leaders. Collectively, the headmen and leading matrons of the resident groups worked to maintain the order and social harmony that made trade possible.[37]

Trading towns like Kittanning were western counterparts of the Susquehanna River towns at Conestoga, Paxtang, and Shamokin, and they quickly became political centers was well as marts of trade. On the plateau, several such towns appeared as the native population continued to grow. Logg's Town, below the Forks of the Ohio, the lower Shawnee town at the mouth of the Scioto River, and a cluster of villages and summer trading camps on the lower Cuyahoga River were the most prominent. Brief European descriptions of these towns also reflect the growing ethnic complexity of the region; the French found mission Iroquois from near Montreal,

Nippissings, Albenakis, Mississaugas, Loups (Delawares), Shawnees, and former Six Nations Iroquois living at Logg's Town in 1749.[38]

When they arrived at Kittanning or Chartier's Town, Pennsylvania traders entered a world unlike the one familiar to them east of the Susquehanna River. There the proximity of settlements, suppliers, and government provided the peddlers with some security. Moreover, by the mid-1720s the traders—and their fellow colonists—were a growing majority set against much smaller numbers of natives whose own power and influence steadily diminished. On the plateau, however, the situation was reversed. Though the number of traders grew rapidly in the 1730s and 1740s, they remained a distinct minority among their Indian customers. The seasonal nature of the trade further guaranteed that the traders would have a limited impact in the west. Logan's men and their packhorse trains typically appeared in the Ohio Country during the summer and autumn, collecting the previous winter's store of hides and pelts, settling debts, and making the necessary advances to trusted hunters. Only later would a few men—notably gunsmiths and blacksmiths, whose skills were especially desired by Ohio Indians—remain at their posts or in native towns year round. Thus the Pennsylvanians, unlike their Canadian rivals, maintained a much more tenuous personal presence among their Indian customers, though ties remained between natives and traders, forged through a generation of contact in the east.[39]

These seasonal peddlers were met at the trading places by native customers who had already adopted a good deal from the traders' roving general stores. Men like the Pole Anthony Sadowsky or like Edmund Cartlidge would have found Delaware or Shawnee men decked out in ruffled shirts and leggings "done off with ribbons and beads," while their wives and children warmed themselves in stroud blankets and calico shirts. At least a few of the Ohio Indians would have cut figures similar to that of the Seneca-Canadian interpreter Andrew Montour, who was described by one fascinated missionary as wearing a "brown broadcloth coat, a scarlet damaskin lappel waistcoat, breeches, . . . shoes, stockings, and a hat." Native and European styles often merged in such cases, as when Montour sported a painted face and pierced ears hung "with pendants of brass and other wires." Village ceremonies on the Allegheny may also have been accompanied, as were those at Onondaga, by European instruments such as violins and flutes in addition to native drums and rattles. And longhouses and other dwellings would have boasted an assortment of wares ranging from kettles, skinning knives, looking glasses, and thread to kegs of gunpowder, bags of gunflints, and long, thin bars of lead, while the fires that warmed the inhabitants and illuminated councils would have been ignited with strike-a-lights and tin-derboxes.[40]

The Indians on the plateau had embraced other elements of European culture as well. Food, including tea, found its way into native towns. And conversations were now peppered with profanities borrowed—if only dimly understood—from hard-swearing traders. Indeed, a later observer remarked that "these words seems to be intermixed with all their discourse" and became functional parts of the trade jargon that emerged in the region.[41]

The extent to which Indians in the Ohio Valley had adopted elements of a foreign culture may be striking, but their experiences made it clear that European material culture was also adapted and that native acculturation carried with it the *assimilation* of foreign objects into familiar patterns of use and value. Andrew Montour may have had a "Countenance . . . decidedly European" and worn clothes to match, but he was no less a Seneca for that. Indeed, his usefulness to British colonists lay precisely in that he was fully wedded to his mother's society. Although the violins and flutes would have added to the rhythmic accompaniment at village gatherings, they hardly altered the meanings behind the social, religious, and curative rituals, all of which long predated and transcended the colonial world that supplied such exotica.

Though the trade reinforced native dependence on colonial producers and merchants, it placed traders in a dependent position vis-à-vis their native customers and paved the way for an interdependence that reflected the mutability of cultural frontiers. Traders lived at the end of a long line of credit and debt that ultimately tied them and their inventories to a much greater Atlantic economy. Though men like Edmund Cartlidge and Jonah Davenport likewise extended credit to native suppliers against the following year's catch, thus replicating the patron-client networks that bound traders to the likes of Edward Shippen and James Logan, the traders were never able to enforce debt payment upon their customers as Logan or Shippen could upon their factors. Unfortunates like Aaron Moore were dunned by credi-tors, had their assets seized, or like the forever debt-ridden George Croghan, were forced to stay in the west, beyond reach of the law. A trader's ability to stay out of jail and remain in good standing with his suppliers often rested, therefore, on the willing cooperation of Indian hunters whose own debts were the sum total of the trader's assets. This became a particularly acute issue as competition increased: new traders, often former employees of their competitors, used liquor to separate native hunters from their deer hides, impoverishing both the Indians and the trader who expected to balance his own accounts with the purloined hides. And coercing Indians into honoring debts had less than the desired effect. The natives could, and did, simply enter into business with someone else. In more extreme cases, conflicts over credit turned violent. When trader John Maddox refused additional credit to Delawares, his would-be customers exercised their own "moral economy" and "fell upon him, beat and wounded him sorely" and threatened to do worse before Maddox's companions surrendered goods valued at £100.[42]

Incidents like these were not common on the plateau, and they stand in contrast to other evidence of cooperation. Traders applied their own short-hand with respect to their customers' names, often replacing tongue-twisting Algonkian or Iroquoian appellations with names reflecting physical characteristics, behavior, ethnic identity, or age. Thus "the Pock-marked Fellow," "the Man Trapper," "the Madman," "the Big Woman," and "the Old King," appear in traders' records, along with "Betty" and "Blind Jemmy." Occasionally such references reveal more than just an outsider's sense of humor or the peculiar. Other Indians were known as "Teaffe's landlord" or simply as "Frank Stevens's son," suggesting how even seasonal business transactions led to more personal ties that allowed natives and traders to meet, swap information, forge new business alliances, and cooperate on matters of shared concern.[43]

Though trade did not destroy the fiber of Ohio Indian societies, it did introduce problems that placed additional strain on native communities. This was particularly true with respect to the proliferation of traders in the region and a parallel rise in the volume of liquor that came into the Ohio Country. From the handful of men who appeared on the plateau in the 1720s, the number of traders steadily grew, while at the same time the colonial origins of these men changed as New Yorkers, Virginians, and Marylanders eventually entered the arena. For the older, established hands, newcomers were by definition a problem; they represented unwelcome competition, they sometimes refused to follow local customs, and their often rapacious manner added another dangerous ingredient to an already volatile mixture of peoples and interests. Logan's men were particularly aggressive in driving out those they considered interlopers, men like the "Severall new Traders," formerly servants of Cartlidge, Davenport, and Henry Baly (Bailey) who were now selling rum on their own account and "debauching" local Indians who bought liquor with their deer hides rather than settling their debts with their trading partners.[44]

Although the flood of traders into the Ohio Country raised the competitive stakes for colonial participants, it had more serious repercussions for natives. By 1740 at least, the traders and border settlers had joined Delaware and Shawnee hunters in killing so many deer that the natives began to fear for their livelihood and complained to provincial officials. But it was the inability of anyone—in particular, colonial authorities—to regulate the behavior of men so far removed from the colony that presented the biggest problem.[45]

Dead game was one thing, dead traders and Indians were quite another. The Ohio trade was occasionally marred by death and injury. John Maddox's confrontation with angry natives was only one example of the conflicts that sometimes punctuated meetings between Ohio Indians and traders. Maddox and his companions escaped with minor injuries to bodies and inventory; others were not so fortunate. Three men—John Armstrong, Woodward Arnold, and James Smith—all traveling to the Allegheny region, were killed by several Delawares led by one Mussemeelin. Once again debts and traders' efforts to collect what they considered their due were at issue. Having suffered the indignity of seeing his property seized by the three men, and failing to obtain any sort of accommodation, Mussemeelin with his companions stalked and summarily killed the traders.[46]

At other times death and injury were accidental. In such cases traders often fell victim to ignorance, doubtless tied to their temporary residence among Indian customers. John Hart died of a gunshot wound in autumn 1730 while hunting with a party of Delawares. His presence had not been welcomed, since he and his companion did not understand the natives' method of hunting by creating fire rings around their prey, and the Delawares were clearly concerned about the trader's ineptitude. At the same time yet another trader, David Robeson, was accidentally shot in the leg when a drinking session with several other traders and Indians got out of hand. Traders were not the only ones who fell victim to the violence that accompanied the trade, however. As late as 1744 provincial officials in Philadelphia were told of Indians "killed at different Times at Ohio."[47] Such incidents placed heavy burdens on Ohio Indian villagers and their headmen. To the natives, acts of violence and homicide, if not properly excused or compensated, led to retaliation as the bereaved kin of the victim assuaged their grief by striking at those responsible, or at anyone else who happened to be within reach. The absence of any effective colonial efforts to regulate traders made the problem much worse. Moreover, village headmen, lacking the coercive authority found in British society, could neither prevent transgressions nor summarily apprehend and punish wrongdoers. Provincial authorities, never fully comprehending that fact, exacerbated the problem by demanding that Indians suspected of attacking or killing traders be sent to the settlements for trial in colonial courts. Colonists also began to insist that continued trade and peace rested on the natives' compliance. In these circumstances native leaders were hard pressed to control intercultural relations that by their very nature bred conflict, while avoiding direct confrontation with provincial leaders; their options were limited. In the case of victims like Hart and Robeson, Delaware headmen, through trader intermediaries, went to great lengths to explain the circumstances and to convince Pennsylvania's governor that the incidents were accidental. At the same time, other Indians used their own restraint as an object lesson to colonials who were too quick to demand retribution. Iroquois attending the signing of the 1744 Lancaster Treaty listened patiently as Pennsylvanians demanded that natives suspected of murdering traders be brought to the bar. The Six Nations speaker then quickly reminded the governor that, though three Indians had recently been killed in the west, "we never mentioned any of them to you, imagining it might have been occasioned by some unfortunate Quarrel, and being unwilling to create a disturbance." Finally, the Delawares and Iroquois admonished provincial authorities to restrict the flow of rum into the west, a point on which both natives and colonists could agree.[48]

Yet agreement on the dangers of liquor in the trade did not produce meaningful solutions. Governors could sign legislation making the sale of rum to Indians an offense, but they had no way of reaching beyond the Susquehanna River to enforce these ordinances. In addition, even had colonial governments found ways to stop the traffic, the flood would not have ended altogether, since rum was a popular refreshment at colonial-Indian councils and at least small quantities could find their way west as part of traders' private stores. But the issue was seldom one of total prohibition; rather, it concerned controlled access. With memories of Oswego and the freewheeling trade along Pennsylvania's border fresh in their minds, and with liquor now a functional part of native societies, Indians on the Allegheny Plateau were determined to strike a balance between total abstinence and violent, self-destructive excess. The challenge produced no easy solutions, but it did promote closer cooperation between Ohio natives and some of their colonial trading partners. Such cooperation was rooted in a convergence of interests as well as in the long-standing alliances between particular native towns and the traders who served them. Logan's men were eager to rid themselves of competitors; they and their Indian customers quickly distinguished "good" traders from "bad"—the latter being recognized by their overwhelming reliance on rum as an article of trade as well as by their unlicensed status. Logan's traders were losing profits to such men and made common cause with native villagers, especially the Shawnees, in petitioning their governor for permission to destroy illicit rum stores; the appearance of Shawnee names on the letter could not but impress the authorities with the seriousness of the matter. The natives' specific endorsement of "good" traders by name was a not inconsiderable bonus.[49]

The Shawnees and others who added their names to such petitions did so not as pawns of colonial traders but for reasons of their own. Lacking any coercive power over fellow villagers, who placed a high premium on personal autonomy, yet faced with potential and actual problems arising from the presence of rum among them, Ohio village leaders made common cause across the cultural divide in an effort to stem the flow of liquor. These efforts were also made by people whose geographic position itself added to the problem. The Iroquois' war road to the Carolinas was also a convenient path for native liquor peddlers such as the Mohawks who appeared in the Ohio Valley with several kegs of rum. And the Shawnees, at least, carried the initiative further than their trader allies. In early March 1738 the Shawnees sent to Pennsylvania an "Indian Resolution Respecting Rum"—what amounted to a temperance pledge—and followed it with another message that the French and Iroquois, as well as the Delawares and Shawnees east of the Susquehanna River, had been instructed "not to bring any Rum here to our Townes, for we want non and that we would stave itt."[50] The trade in rum and other spirits continued, here as elsewhere, despite the best efforts of the natives. Yet these efforts helped produce developments that went beyond the immediate issue of social order. The 1738 "resolution," for example, was underwritten by a majority of the men from the three Shawnee towns whose residents were enumerated a year earlier. In addition, and topping the list, were the names of the three most prominent western Shawnees: Laypareawah (Opessah's son), Nucheconner, referred to here as "deputy king," and Coyeacolinne, the "chief council." In this instance the pressing need to curb the rum trade led to cooperation between autonomous villages and, perhaps, enhanced prestige for men like Nucheconner, who actively pursued the liquor issue and built the consensus that emerged in 1738. This "resolution" did not create a "tribe" where none had existed before, but the liquor question did provide a catalyst that led to increased, if only temporary, cooperation. Furthermore, the problems of trade the Shawnees addressed were peculiar to their—and their neighbors'—circumstances in the upper Ohio Valley. The Shawnees sent their petition to those groups, Indian and colonial, either resident in the region or active there, and this may represent one of the earliest expressions of a distinctly Ohio Valley perspective on the part of its new inhabitants.[51]

Further, during the 1730s the natives took the first steps toward forging relations with other groups to the west. The issue was once again trade, as the Ohio Indians served their own and their traders' interests by acting as pitchmen as well as by providing deerskins. The same Shawnees who were determined to stop the flow of rum into their towns also told Pennsylvanians that they were going "to the Ottawas to inform them of the good news we have from our Brothers [the Pennsylvanians] and to encourage them to come this way to trade." Such activities would later prove important well beyond the immediate economic benefits they could provide.[52]

Between 1724 and the mid-1740s, the Allegheny Plateau was once again occupied by Indian peoples. During that time, migrating villagers from Pennsylvania had established a number of towns along the middle Allegheny River and took the first steps toward transferring their identities and interests from former homelands to a new territory. Their activities were part of a process that began in a small way at Kittanning and with the first Shawnee settlements but soon spread westward into the Beaver, Muskingum, and Scioto valleys and the Lake Erie Plain by 1744 as numbers multiplied with a steady stream of newcomers. The success of this resettlement can be measured in the creation of a complex pattern of village communities that exhibited both cultural continuity and adaptation—communities embedded in a cultural landscape that reflected more and more the settlement patterns and activities of the region's new inhabitants. The westward movements that led to Kittanning or to Aliquippa's Town were deliberate efforts to avoid the excesses of an enlarged colonial world and thus to preserve the social fabric that held Delawares, Shawnees, or Iroquois together.

The success of the immigrants can be measured in another way. During their first two formative decades west of the mountains, the Indians lived in a world of their own making, free from the persistent interference from colonists that had marked their experiences in the east. Yet the new Ohio Indians neither could nor wished to isolate themselves completely from the colonial world outside their own. Traders quickly appeared in the Ohio Valley, reestablishing contacts with long-standing customers, and the two groups in partnership developed a new commercial nexus in the valley—one based on continued native dependence upon European material culture but also controlled by the Indians who dominated the region and the trade. At the same time the trade, and especially its by now familiar problems of disorder and alcohol, demanded that heretofore autonomous villages on the plateau band together to seek solutions while using the trade to forge new links in a commercial chain with Indians living to the west. Their success in this venture, their growing numbers, and the happenstance of their geographic position, however, all but guaranteed that the Ohio Indians and their countryside would become ever more important to outsiders. By the late 1740s, the plateau's inhabitants were finding themselves pulled once more into the treacherous complexity of interethnic and intercultural relations while their own ties to the Ohio Country continued to mature.

three

Allegheny Crossroads

 The Indian settlers in the Allegheny Valley carried into their new homeland a web of trade that bound them to both French and British colonial societies. Nevertheless, the new towns in the west were never mere outlying hamlets of eastern societies, shaped and defined by the same forces and interests that dominated the older centers of Delaware, Shawnee, and Iroquois peoples. Resettlement beyond the Alleghenies encouraged the development of a new, distinctly regional identity that, over time, loosened the bonds between migrants and their kinfolk in the east. Time and distance encouraged this process, but they were strongly reinforced by the inherently localized nature of Indian societies. The widening gulf was also the result of widely differing experiences; the dialogue between Ohio Valley natives and Pennsylvanians over trade and the Indians' raids against southern foes are two examples.

At the same time, however, the movement of Indians into the upper Ohio Valley quickly captured the attention of colonial officers in both Quebec and Philadelphia who sought to gain strategic and political advantages by drawing the newcomers into either the French or the British imperial orbit. In either case, by the 1730s the growing European interest in the Ohio Country presented Indians living there with a challenge at once familiar and new. Delawares and Shawnees had moved west to avoid the pressures of colonial expansion and were predictably reluctant to entangle themselves once more with grasping provincials who now enlisted Six Nations Iroquois assistance in a tentative effort to extend British influence into the west. The appearance of both Canadians and Pennsylvanians in the region, however, raised the specter of intercolonial conflict for control of the land and its people. Although the battle lines were by no means clearly drawn before the mid-1740s, during the previous two decades native pioneers demonstrated both their independence and the emerging regional focus, characteristics that would shape their response to intruders for decades to come.

Within the Ohio Country the natives accommodated themselves to their new homeland. Though the neighboring Hurons, living at Detroit, initially expressed concern for the security of their own hunting territory south of Lake Erie, they and the Miamis joined in inviting the Shawnees to "light their fire" on the Ohio—to settle permanently in the west. For the Shawnees, as for their Delaware and Iroquois neighbors, relations with peoples to the west were expressed in the same kinship terms common within native societies. Indeed, amicable relations with outsiders were characteristically defined as extensions of the kin groups that bound individuals, villages, and societies together; traders or missionaries, for example, might be adopted—literally or fictively—as "cousins," "nephews," or "brothers." In the same fashion, kinship ordered relations between societies living in the Ohio Country. Thus, out of deference to their claim to be the "original people," the Delawares were referred to as "grandfathers," while Shawnees, Miamis, and Hurons met each other as "brothers." The meaning of such terms nevertheless varied with time and circumstance, and words might not easily reflect the realities of a given relationship. Thus, although the Six Nations referred to their Shawnee neighbors as "brothers," the enmity and lingering distrust between the two peoples was well known to natives and colonists alike. Likewise, the Iroquois might refer to the Delawares as "cousins" and be called "uncles," but such terms often masked more complex, as well as less deferential, connections. At best, the use of kinship terms suggests levels of association—closeness—based on historical ties, shifting power, or a group's perceived role in the larger scheme of interethnic relations. And like other aspects of diplomatic protocol, the forms remained though the substance of relationships continued to change.[1]

Kinship terminology tended to define amicable interactions with peoples nearby; traditional enemies and those who lived far away were less likely to be embraced by kinship terms. In the case of the Ohio Indians, enemies lived primarily to the south, in the rugged foothills of the southern Appalachians; the French used the generic term "Têtes-Plates"—Flatheads—to identify a number of societies: Catawbas, Cherokees, and Chickasaws that were at war with Ohio natives and Indians living in the Great Lakes basin.

Distant enemies served a variety of social needs. Participating in raids was a principal route to full manhood for young men. In the case of some young Shawnees, for instance, an argument over "who was the best man" was settled when they all "resolved to make a Tryal by going to war" against the Catawbas. Such trials helped young men acquire status, influence, and good marriages. Yet unlike the destructive trade- and epidemic-induced wars of the seventeenth century that had dramatically altered the cultural landscape of the northeast, the north-south raiding of the eighteenth century was of much lower intensity and represented a pattern of controlled violence whose ultimate goals did not include the kind of destruction visited upon the Monongahelans or the Eries.[2]

The endemic warfare between Iroquois, Shawnees, and Delawares and their Piedmont foes was rooted in hostility whose origins had been obscured or lost by the 1730s. That is not to say, however, that the participants had few good or valid reasons for continuing conflicts that were occasionally punctuated by truces but never fully ended before the mid-1700s. Iroquois raids against the southern nations began to increase after 1700 and represented a shifting focus for warriors as the Five Nations sought to free themselves from the destructive wars against Great Lakes Indians and their French allies. As Iroquois warriors moved south through the Susquehanna Valley, local Indians joined them, drawn into the cycle of raid and retaliation as were two young Conestogas who were killed returning from a foray into the Carolinas.[3]

But by the 1720s the Six Nations were already moving their principal war road west to the Allegheny Valley. In 1718 the French identified the "River Ohio, or the Beautiful River [la Belle Rivière]," as "the route which the Iroquois take" against their southern enemies. By the 1730s, the "Catawba Path" ran through the Allegheny Valley toward the Cheat River to the south. The use of the Ohio Valley as a military corridor increased during the century, especially after Virginia and Pennsylvania sought to protect their own exposed border settlements from northern warriors who often pilfered from settlers on the long journey back home, by negotiating a westward relocation of Iroquois war roads.[4]

The arrival of Delawares and Shawnees in the Ohio Valley added yet another dimension to the north-south raiding. Between the Ohio towns and the Catawba and Cherokee settlements lay Kentucky, and efforts by rival natives to control this large and abundant game reserve provided further impetus for raids and an additional reason for keeping enemies at a distance. The importance of Kentucky did not diminish over time; in 1754 Governor Robert Dinwiddie of Virginia hoped to encourage Catawbas and

Cherokees to join his colony's militia by telling the natives that the campaign would secure *their* hunting grounds on the Ohio River against French encroachment.[5]

Though the intermittent raiding along the Appalachian corridor served important social functions, attack and counterattack nevertheless punished both sides. Catawbas often found themselves besieged by attackers who made travel far from home dangerous, especially for a small nation. The Piedmont landscape was dotted with "heaps of Stone" marking the spots where Saponis and others had been killed, while Ohio Indian raiding parties, equipped with specially wrought prisoner ties, watched the paths between southern towns. Yet the southern Indians could return a full measure of what they received. A party of Shawnees settled in a seemingly inaccessible corner of the Alleghenies on the headwaters of the Potomac River paid dearly for being on the wrong side of the mountains, losing nine men to southern raiders. Catawba raids became so serious by 1740 that two western Delaware headmen, Captain Hill and Shannopin, asked Pennsylvanians to intercede on their behalf. By the 1750s a generation of warfare across the Ohio had taught local Indians respect for their enemies; to many Ohio Indians "Catawba all one Devil Catawba" and their devilish foes were a preoccupation for years.[6]

During the later 1720s the few towns in the upper Ohio Valley drew the attention of French traders who appeared in the region at the behest of the colonial government at Quebec. The French were no strangers to the Indians, especially the Shawnees, who had forged strong ties to Canadian traders during their seventeenth-century diaspora throughout the middle west. Iroquois villagers in the Allegheny Valley likewise knew the French well, as trading partners, missionaries, and adversaries during the long wars of the previous century. Trade, diplomacy, and conversion meant that Frenchmen too had found their way into native kinship networks.

Though Frenchmen knew many of the Indians who lived there, French knowledge of the Ohio Country itself remained limited well into the eighteenth century. Since La Salle's time, the Canadians had known of the upper Ohio River—la Belle Rivière—yet they seem not to have accumulated much firsthand information before the 1720s. Reports on the territories west of Montreal contained little concrete information on the upper Ohio Valley. In 1736 the French were able to report only that the Shawnees were then living "toward Carolina"; they made no reference at all to the Shawnees' numerous Delaware neighbors. And as late as 1749 father Pierre Bonnecamps, accompanying Céloron's expedition, could refer to "this Beautiful River—so little known to the French," even though a decade earlier Charles le Moyne, baron de Longueuil, had passed down the Allegheny and Ohio with Canadian troops on their way to attack the Chickasaws. The reasons for this ignorance are not hard to identify. A half-century of warfare against the Five Nations denied the French direct access to the region. At the same time, the lucrative trade among the natives of the Great Lakes and the need to preserve that commerce from New York and Iroquois competition diverted attention from what was considered a marginal area.[7]

Interest began to build, and the Ohio Country moved closer to the center of French attention during the long Anglo-French peace between 1713 and 1744. Dynastic changes and the fear of political instability in both countries led to foreign policies that sought accommodation rather than conflict. These developments were mirrored in the colonies, where Canadians and Anglo-Americans sought to pursue their own interests in the west free of the conflict that had previously threatened both societies. In Canada, the challenge was to rebuild the network of trade-based alliances with Great Lakes nations that had been jeopardized at the end of the last century by a royal policy of fiscal retrenchment in the west. Moreover, the French hoped that native alliances, coupled with adroit diplomacy with the Six Nations, would negate British influence and secure the colony's vulnerable border-lands. Such a plan was complicated by the creation of new settlements in Louisiana that, if linked to Canada, could provide a year-round port and another source of food for the northern colony while raising an additional barrier to British expansion from Virginia and the Carolinas.[8]

By taking advantage of localism and divisions within the Iroquois Confederacy, the architect of French Canadian strategy, Governor-General Philippe de Rigaud de Vaudreuil, was able to take control of the vital Niagara portage in 1720 in an effort to separate the Iroquois and New York from fur-trading Indians in the west. Vaudreuil's success was checked when New York secured a base at the mouth of the Oswego River in 1726, bringing British goods and influence closer to the heartland of New France than ever before. Consequently, French officials were once again confronted with the challenge of British traders and their plentiful merchandise as Vaudreuil and his successors attempted to hold on to France's inland empire. Correspondence from the western posts, and between Quebec and Paris, became a litany of complaints about Ottawas, Miamis, and Hurons who bypassed Detroit in favor of Oswego, drawn by the "cheapness of the Goods . . . and the Brandy which is abundantly distributed to them." At the same time, the prospect of contraband trade between Canadians seeking quality woolens and Anglo-Americans wanting additional prime pelts once again surfaced, not only in the Champlain Valley, where it was a chronic problem, but in the west as well.[9]

Their attempts to protect their western trade and alliances and further undercut British influence in the west led the French into the Ohio Country. As early as 1718, a Canadian officer had pointed out the importance of the Ohio River, observing that "whoever would wish to reach the Mississippi easily" had only to control "this Beautiful river [the Ohio]." Moreover, the country held such abundance of game that troops—or settlers—could not be threatened with starvation. And in the developing scheme of imperial politics, a firm line of communication between Canada and Louisiana would also serve as a barrier to British expansion. But what made the Ohio Country even more attractive, and led to the first sustained French interest in the region, was the presence of Delaware and, especially, Shawnee villagers who were then pioneering the region. A native exodus westward had all the makings of a convenient buffer zone in the continuing European game of global politics. The Canadians hoped to exploit the resettlement of the upper Ohio through the medium of trade and ties to specific groups of natives in the area. Governor Charles de la Boische, marquis de Beauharnois, expressed satisfaction that his superiors' latest effort to check the brandy trade had ended in 1729, since "liquor is the sole allurement that could attract or preserve [the Indians] to us." The governor may have exaggerated the centrality of liquor in relations with his Indian neighbors, but the French came to the Ohio Valley prepared to offer a variety of goods to local natives. The goal was not profit, however. The deer and buffalo hides that found their way out of the Ohio Country held no attraction for Canadians, whose trade had long been based on beaver pelts and other furs. French trade in the Ohio Valley, as elsewhere in North America, was a strategic tool, a means to the greater end of exclusive control over the middle west and the Mississippi Valley.[10]

In their effort to transform the Ohio Country into a buffer and a secure route to the Mississippi Valley, the French turned first to the Shawnees. Recognizing that at least some were "well attached to the French," Canadians sought to exploit the natives' dissatisfaction with their treatment at the hands of Pennsylvanians and the Iroquois. By 1728 Beauharnois was already laying plans to draw the Shawnees closer to Lake Erie and French-allied Indians west of the Miami River. The following year the governor held a meeting with "three chiefs of the Chawanons." The number of headmen corresponds to the number of Shawnee towns near the Allegheny River and suggests that Beauharnois and his agents had succeeded in establishing cordial relations with all the principal Shawnee bands in the west.[11]

The Shawnees cautiously welcomed Canadian visitors. Beauharnois's optimistic appraisal of Shawnee-French relations overlooked the fact that no immediate changes took place in Shawnee village locations or in their relations with either French or British colonists. The Shawnees did, however, host Canadian agents, among them the shadowy Toussaint le Cavelier and Philippe-Thomas Joncaire, who seems to have remained among the Shawnees through the mid-1730s. Information on the Shawnees and their Canadian guests is spotty at best, though Joncaire's reports in particular suggest the limits of both Shawnee cooperation and French influence in the Ohio Country at the time.[12]

The self-congratulatory tone of Beauharnois's earliest report on his Ohio Valley initiative stands in contrast to those offered by his agents between 1729 and the early 1740s. Some headway was made when Joncaire and others secured Huron and Miami acceptance of Shawnee settlements near their territories. Moreover, growing numbers of Shawnees did resettle at the mouth of the Scioto River by 1735, but they were by no means out of range of British traders, and they were not settling northwest of the Ohio River as Beauharnois had planned.[13]

The Shawnees, though, continued to pursue their own interests. By 1734 Beauharnois was forced to order Joncaire to "watch their actions" and work harder to maintain the cooperative spirit the Shawnees had "felt in *previous years*." Finally, in 1742 Beauharnois had to admit that his plan had, at least for the moment, failed: the Shawnees had not moved to la Prairie des Mascoutens as they were encouraged to do, and the governor was convinced "they had been tampered with by the English."[14]

From the Shawnees' perspective there was no compelling reason to make a new remove west of the Allegheny River. Trade relations with Pennsylvanians were certainly an issue. The Canadians made no effort to check the activities of Pennsylvania traders until the late 1740s; both sides adopted a policy of live and let live. At the same time, the localized nature of Shawnee society and continued ties to kinfolk living in the east provided countervailing forces to any French effort to rally the natives and resettle them en masse farther west. Moreover, the limited success the Canadians enjoyed among the Shawnees also appears tied to kinship. In 1740 Beauharnois conducted negotiations with a Shawnee band led by Peter Chartier, son of Canadian trader Martin Chartier. The younger Chartier appeared "very well disposed" toward his Canadian countrymen, something that helps account for his group's subsequent attacks on Pennsylvania traders during King George's War. Yet, though his partisanship would have pleased French officials, Chartier's decision to take his people to the upper Creeks did not accord with plans for their resettlement in the Illinois Country or at Detroit. And Chartier's group was the only one to respond at all favorably to the French. Those Shawnees who removed down the Ohio toward the Scioto River had good reasons for doing so wholly unrelated to French influence: they had attacked and killed Six Nations ambassadors to their towns. Thus the Shawnees had little inclination—and less reason—to pursue goals set by outsiders during their early years in the Ohio Country.[15]

Both the Shawnees and their Delaware neighbors pursued their own interests by entering into closer relations with Pennsylvania. The historical links between Ohio Indians and the colony had been forged after 1680 as William Penn attempted to build Indian relations in his proprietary grant based on law, fairness, and mutual respect. So well did he succeed that the Iroquois rendering of his name: "Onas" (pen, or quill) became the natives' official title for all succeeding Pennsylvania governors, and memories of the original Onas lingered even as those who followed him corrupted and eventually destroyed the relationships that Penn had carefully cultivated.[16]

Moreover, the Delawares' and Shawnees' departure from Pennsylvania did not sever communication with the colony. Indeed, through the late 1720s and 1730s correspondence between native headmen and provincial leaders continued; by 1728 James Logan was relying on western Delawares for information on the activities of more distant Indians. Meanwhile, exchanges between the Ohio Country and Philadelphia were punctuated by Indian complaints about trade and by growing provincial interest in drawing the natives back to their old towns.

In early December 1731, Governor Patrick Gordon sent separate letters to the Delawares and the Shawnees, but in both cases the message was the same. The natives learned that the governor was "much griev'd that so many of my Brethren are removed to so great a distance," and he worried lest they "fall into the hands of Strangers." Gordon admonished the natives to maintain the exchange of information that was "One Link in the Chain made between you and us." What the governor sought was the Indians' return to towns east of the Susquehanna River, and he extended invitations to that effect by way of Logan's trader, Edmund Cartlidge.[17]

Gordon's motives lay buried in the cryptic reference to the "hands of Strangers." For well over a decade Pennsylvania's leaders had looked to their ill-defined western frontier with a mixture of anticipation and concern. The Allegheny region's resources were fast becoming a significant element in the colony's burgeoning economy. At the same time, the geopolitics of the west made French intrusion into the Ohio Country likely if not inevitable. As early as 1720, Pennsylvanians had expressed concern about the "Extravagent Growth of the ffrench Settlements upon the Back" of their own and neighboring colonies. Not only could the Canadians appropriate territory and trade, but their tireless traders and Jesuits would "debauch" the Indians—with potentially devastating results. It was therefore no coincidence that Gordon's letters to the Ohio Indians followed traders' reports on the activities of Cavelier and Joncaire. Initially, Pennsylvania traders found little in the presence of these French agents that seemed threatening. By 1732, however, the traders conceded that circumstances might change, especially when rumors circulated that the French were about to take up a post in the upper Ohio Valley with "a Fort of Loggs," whose purpose was yet unclear. At the same time, the government in Philadelphia had enjoyed no success in efforts to stem the flow of rum into the west or stop the excesses of their own people in the region. Admitting that traders were both "numerous and under no sort of Security to act honestly" and that they were far from "the eye of all Magistracy," officials could do little more than issue new regulations and admonish Indians to deal only with "honest" peddlers. Yet as abuses continued, the fear increased that disgruntled natives would embrace the French. The solution seemed obvious: by drawing the Indians back east, the Ohio Country could be maintained as a seasonal—and British-controlled—hunting preserve, traders would be more closely regulated, and the French would be robbed of potential allies.[18]

Gordon was not content to rely entirely on messages of invitation and reminders of Onas's lasting friendship. When the western Delawares and Shawnees refused to commit themselves, the governor and the recently arrived proprietor, Thomas Penn, turned to the Six Nations for assistance. The arrival of Confederacy sachems at Philadelphia in August 1732 introduced yet another element into the mixture of peoples and interests that were drawn to the Ohio Country.

The Six Nations' appearance at this juncture represented the latest, and perhaps most ominous, link in a complex intercultural alliance system known as the Covenant Chain. The term reflected the metaphor-rich language of its principal native participants, the Six Nations. In reality the Chain was, in the words of Francis Jennings, "a multiparty alliance" that embraced, on the one hand, the Confederacy and a growing list of client and allied nations and, on the other hand, the governments of British colonies from Massachusetts to Virginia. Forged in the conflicts that dominated the northeast in the late seventeenth century, tempered through numerous treaties and councils, the Covenant Chain continued to link, with varying degrees of firmness, Iroquois and Anglo-Americans in a relationship of mutual convenience. New York's royal governor, Sir Edmund Andros, first entered into alliance with the colony's Mohawk neighbors in 1677 and, through them, with the other confederated Iroquois. In return the Five—later Six—Nations enjoyed a preeminent role in New York Indian affairs. Over the next half-century, warfare and continued Anglo-American expansion altered the relationship: a devastating conflict with New France forced the Confederacy to accept peace on French terms and, in the process, to redefine the Iroquois' relationship with New York from one of military alliance to economic and diplomatic partnership. At the same time, Iroquois leaders, eager to extract their people from overdependence on what had proved to be an unreliable ally, extended diplomatic and trade relations to other colonies; in so doing, they added new links to the Covenant Chain.[19]

Of great interest to the upper Iroquois towns was the appearance of the new colony of Pennsylvania. Penn's province not only lay next to the Susquehanna Valley, it also demonstrated an eagerness to trade and thus offered a convenient alternative source of goods and political support to those within Iroquoia who opposed too close a connection to New York. Meanwhile, the Chain gradually began to serve as a mechanism for Anglo-American expansion at the expense of other Indians, as well as a tool with which the Iroquois fashioned a place for themselves in the colonial northeast.[20]

While the Covenant Chain became a useful device for promoting peace across the cultural divide and protecting the exposed frontiers of northern Anglo-America, it also helped create and sustain a particular image of the Iroquois Confederacy in the minds of British Americans. Since the mid-seventeenth century, the Six Nations had earned a reputation as invincible fighters as well as skilled diplomats. This growing mystique of Iroquois power took a beating during the catastrophic warfare of the 1680s and 1690s. Yet through creative diplomacy the Confederacy survived. In the decades that followed, Anglo-Americans, especially New York's Cadwallader Colden, refashioned the older lore of Iroquois victories and invincibility into a chronicle of conquest. The notion of wide-ranging Iroquois "conquests" of other native societies served British interests well. Since the British claimed the Confederacy both as Covenant Chain partners and, after 1713, as subject peoples, any Iroquois conquests—real or imagined—naturally became the province of the British Crown. By the middle of the eighteenth century the mystique of Iroquois unity and power had taken on a life of its own, often blinding provincial leaders to the realities of Iroquois influence in the Indian world.

In no small measure, this British view of the Confederacy was consciously reinforced by the Iroquois. In reality, however, the Confederacy was often divided within itself. Yet the ability to project an image of unity and purpose became, during the eighteenth century, the cornerstone of the Six Nations' survivial strategy in an increasingly hostile colonial world. Taking advantage of British Americans' limited knowledge of internal Iroquois affairs and their colonial neighbors' own persistent image of what they thought the Confederacy to be, Six Nations leaders, among them Canasetego and Shikellamy, actively reinforced the Iroquois mystique. It was a strategy that other Iroquois, no longer living in the Mohawk Valley towns, would use as well.[21]

The Chain's imperial dimension, its inherent mutability, and the Six Nations mystique were all elements in Pennsylvania's effort to forge its own links with the Confederacy. As early as 1722 both Pennsylvania and Virginia negotiated with Six Nations leaders over access to the Susquehanna and Shenandoah valleys; areas the colonies wished to expand into but that were of strategic importance to the Iroquois. In the process of negotiating new western boundaries with the Six Nations, both colonies gave formal recognition to the Covenant Chain. At the same time, the definition of the Chain began a subtle, but vital, transformation as the Six Nations and Pennsylvania gradually formalized relations.[22]

Interest in lands along the upper Susquehanna and Delaware rivers pitted the colony against Indian neighbors who for over a generation had enjoyed cordial relations with the proprietor and his settlers. Profits, however, soon outweighed intercultural cooperation, and when Delawares and Shawnees continued to resist rapacious land agents, James Logan and the Penns strove to create a formal alliance with the Six Nations. The object was to use Iroquois coercive power to overawe intransigent Indians within the colony. In a larger sense, the eventual Six Nations–Pennsylvania alliance transformed the Covenant Chain into a blatant tool for provincial expansion. In fact, what was fashioned at Philadelphia after 1732 was not merely a new link in an old chain of friendship but in many ways a new Covenant Chain, embracing the upper Six Nations and Pennsylvania and based on assumptions quite distinct from the Andros-Mohawk alliance of the previous century. In the process, eastern Delawares and Shawnees were trapped in an Iroquois-Pennsylvania vise and found their status redefined; they were now viewed as "dependents" of both the Six Nations and the colony and were expected to live wherever those two powerful partners dictated. Those who could joined the exodus to the Ohio Country, and it was there that the Covenant Chain met its most persistent opposition.[23]

Though Indians within the colony ultimately fell victim to the Covenant Chain, they were not the only concern of the 1732 treaty council at Philadelphia. During this meeting the tentative nature of provincial-Iroquois relations was given substance as the colony became the latest link in the Chain. Provincial officials quickly set the tone of their newfound alliance by insisting that the Confederacy recall the Delawares and Shawnees living in the west. Moreover, the proprietor and his governor, not the Six Nations, first cast the western Delawares and Shawnees in the role of Iroquois "dependents," declaring that the westerners were "under their [Six Nations'] protection." Such logic rested on the persistent notion that the Ohio Indians were merely splinter groups from the Susquehanna Valley towns, which were also understood to be under Iroquois dominion.[24]

The Pennsylvanians' assumptions concerning their power and influence notwithstanding, the Six Nations headmen at Philadelphia were slow to acknowledge any special claims to the Ohio Country or any authority over Indians living there. Iroquois backwardness only emphasized that it was not the Confederacy but the colony that sought to extend its influence into the west. Subsequent actions indicate that the Senecas assumed an influential place among Iroquois living in the west, one rooted in their symbolic role as the western door of the Confederacy longhouse. Senecas' interest in the Ohio Country also originated in their raids through the region in the seventeenth century and with the Erie and Monongahelan captives whose children were now considered Iroquois. Use of the region as a hunting preserve and war road and as a new land for settlement would have provided additional grounds for special ties between the Ohio Valley and the Senecas and, to a lesser degree, Cayugas and Onondagas as well.[25]

Yet the 1732 Philadelphia council revealed that the Six Nations' interest and influence in the Ohio Country was still limited and ill defined. Thomas Penn learned that the Senecas had ordered Cavelier out of the region but nonetheless admitted that they knew "nothing certainly of what passed between [Cavelier] and the Shawnees at Ohio." Even more to the point, when pressed by Thomas Penn to recall their Delaware and Shawnee "dependents," the Seneca headman Hetaguantagechy replied for all those assembled that it would be better for the colony to "joyn with them in calling back the Shawanese." Hetaguantagechy further shifted responsibility to the colony by suggesting that the task would be much easier if Penn first recalled his traders. What the Senecas may have privately understood, even if colonial leaders had yet to learn it, was that Six Nations–British influence beyond the mountains had limits.[26]

Those limits were revealed even before the Pennsylvania–Six Nations chain was confirmed at Philadelphia. The Delaware headmen Allemykoppy and Shannopin sent a decidedly noncommital reply to Governor Gordon's invitation that they return to their former homes within the colony. The Shawnees deferred a reply until 1738, when they also declined Gordon's invitation. Reading beyond the governor's solicitous words, the Shawnee headmen insisted that "The Tract of Land You have Reserved for us does nott sute us at Present" and hoped Gordon would not "take itt amiss" that they declined his generous offer. Dramatic proof of the Shawnees' determination to follow their own interests came much sooner, though. In 1732, before the Philadelphia congress, Seneca headmen had appeared in the Allegheny Valley and urged the Shawnees to return east. Their efforts were unavailing, and their meddling was not appreciated. Members of one Shawnee band, "pressed so closely that they took a great dislike to him," later killed Sagohandechty, "a great Man of the Senecas." The incident might easily explain Iroquois reluctance to press the Ohio Indians too far.[27]

The Delawares' response to colonial and Six Nations meddling was no less determined. While they spoke of the "Chain of friendship" that bound them to the Pennsylvanians, Delaware headmen offered no deference to the Covenant Chain and waited until 1740 before finally traveling to Philadelphia in response to Gordon's original invitation. Even then Shannopin, Allemykoppy, Captain Hill, and others came of their own volition, with their own agenda, and only for a brief meeting with their eastern kinfolk and provincial leaders. The Six Nations were nowhere in sight, and their influence may have been further diminished in Delaware eyes by the natives' insistence, expressed by Allumapees years before, that the Delawares and Iroquois "have their own land . . . and each of them are to manage their own affairs." Moreover, the western Delawares were less inclined to accept the provincial-dominated political order of the eastern towns. Soon after the 1732 Philadelphia congress Allumapees, then living at Shamokin, was asked to recall those of his people living in the west. The "king" had no success. His role as principal spokesman had been assumed in the west by others. These western Delaware headmen decided when to accept the governor's invitation to council, waiting nine years to do so. And while Thomas Penn claimed that Allumapees had "called on . . . and brought" the westerners to Philadelphia in 1740, westerners like Allemykoppy and Shannopin demonstrated little deference toward their onetime king. Meanwhile, western Delaware numbers grew by continuing migrations in the face of Penn–Six Nations success in reforging the Chain into an instrument of coercion and dispossession. By 1744 Allumapees's own nephews, Shingas, Pisquetomen, and Tamaqua, had joined the westward movement.[28]

The Indians who occupied the Ohio Country brought with them to their new homes a complex web of relationships that tied them to eastern kinfolk and to native enemies and allies, as well as to colonial societies. These relations precluded isolation in the upper Ohio Valley. The geography of their new homeland also ensured continued links between Shawnees, Delawares, Iroquois, and outsiders. Migration to the upper Ohio placed the newcomers astride an important military highway as well as in a region readily accessible to traders and government agents from both Canada and the British seaboard.

Movement westward did not culturally transform Delawares or Shawnees, but distance became itself an additional barrier to the political and cultural imperialism that was becoming ever more common in the east and typified by the Pennsylvanian-Iroquois redefinition of the Covenant Chain. The Ohio Valley Indians consciously used this distance as a buffer against the pressures and entanglements that had reduced their eastern kinfolk to the status of marginal, dependent peoples in their own land.

The process that transformed migrating native societies into "Ohio Indians"—attachment to new homelands, distance from older settlements, the passing of generations, and a determination to maintain sovereignty, coupled with new challenges arising from a new location—was only in its first stages in the 1720s and 1730s. That process would accelerate, however, as colonial interest in the Ohio Country increased.

four

Warriors from "Ohio"

Throughout the spring and summer of 1747 Pennsylvania's leaders received messages from the Iroquois living in the upper Ohio Valley and along the south shore of Lake Erie. The Pennsylvanians learned that the Indians had taken up arms against local French garrisons and traders and had also forged an alliance with neighboring societies. Moreover, the western Indians were actively seeking provincial support: in mid-May they underscored a request for arms and ammunition by sending a French scalp to Philadelphia.[1]

The messages and scalp, as well as information supplied by traders, generated considerable debate within the provincial government. Though Britain was indeed at war with France, and though any Indian victories could prove advantageous, Pennsylvanians were not involved in the fighting, and colony officials were unsure how to respond to the Ohio Indians. Then, before a tentative decision to supply the natives could be fully implemented, there appeared in Philadelphia, on November 13, a delegation of headmen from the west. Calling themselves "Warriors, living at Ohio," the natives, all Iroquois, announced the formation of an alliance in the Ohio Country and the lighting of a new council fire at Logg's Town. Through their spokesman, an Oneida named Scarouady, they also called on the colony to "put more Fire under your Kettle"—to take a more active part in a joint Indian-British war against the French.[2]

The Ohio Iroquois' initiative of November 1747 ushered in an important new chapter in the history of the Indians living in the Ohio Country. During the previous decades the natives had had only occasional contacts with colonial societies. Within a decade after 1747 the Ohio Indians found themselves confronting French and British military forces in what became a multicultural—as well as intercolonial—struggle for control of the Ohio Country. For the region's native societies, this conflict became only the latest phase of a much longer struggle to preserve autonomy in a colonial world.

At the same time, bonds between towns and societies within the Ohio Country were made stronger by colonial expansion and aggression. In the 1720s and 1730s the Delawares and Shawnees played a central role in shaping relations with colonial societies. By the late 1740s, however, recently arrived Iroquois had taken the lead and were at the center of the growing Anglo-French dispute over the Ohio Country. In the meantime a strong attachment to the region continued to shape the responses of all Ohio Indian societies to intercolonial competition and intrusion.

The war that did so much to alter the Ohio Indians' world erupted in part from the volatility of the region as native migrations continued into the early 1740s. In 1744 Kakowatchiky, the eastern Shawnee "king," abandoned his town at Wyoming and joined his kinfolk at Logg's Town, adding to the already populous Shawnee towns in the Ohio Country. Earlier, increasing numbers of Iroquois had begun to settle new villages along the lower Cuyahoga River. This migration continued through the mid-1740s; in 1743 the French at nearby Detroit estimated that nearly six hundred Iroquois, mostly Senecas and Onondagas, were settled on the Cuyahoga. The sudden arrival of so many Iroquois so close to Detroit gave Canadian officials cause for concern that was only slightly diminished by news that the Indians "earnestly asked . . . for some Frenchmen to supply their wants."[3]

French concerns over the new Iroquois towns south of Lake Erie increased when troubles arose with the Hurons living at Detroit. In 1738 a number of Hurons led by Orontony (Nicolas), one of the principal headmen at Detroit, decided to leave the French post, eventually resettling at Sandusky. Their immediate reasons for doing so rested on growing friction with their Ottawa and Potawatomi neighbors at the fort. Having taken a disproportionate amount of abuse from Cherokee and Catawba raiders, Orontony's people made a separate peace with the "Flatheads." In so doing, however, Orontony earned the distrust of his neighbors. The decision to make peace with the southern Indians also intensified a deeper ethnic division within a western Huron community composed of remnant Petuns, Hurons, and Neutral Indians. The Huron headman Orontony emerged as spokesman for a splinter group that left Detroit, becoming the "Wyandots."[4]

The enmity that existed between Orontony's people and their Indian neighbors at Detroit did not initially include the French. Yet the latter saw the Hurons' departure as a threat to the native alliance painstakingly nurtured over the past four decades, one that provided an important buffer against British expansion. Orontony's departure to the east, toward the Ohio Valley, and his proximity to newly arrived Iroquois intensified French concerns. Officers at Detroit who tried to stem the defection may well have earned Orontony's wrath by exploiting long-standing differences between younger warriors and headmen over the wisdom of peace with the southern Indians. In the meantime Orontony and a majority of his followers consistently refused to return to Detroit, appearing "Indifferent and averse" to French appeals that they return to their old towns. By then, however, Orontony may already have made contact with Pennsylvania traders based at Logg's Town, Cuyahoga, and Kuskuski. Trade with the Pennsylvanians made the Wyandots less dependent on Detroit while providing Orontony with potential allies, though the Pennsylvanians did not hesitate to turn an Indian-French conflict to their own advantage.[5]

Orontony's defection led to more than trading advantages for Wyandots and profit-hungry traders. The Wyandots' resettlement and the simultaneous arrival of Iroquois at Cuyahoga drew two rival colonial trading systems closer than they had ever been. Though they could not hope to disperse the growing Cuyahoga River towns, the French did attempt to profit from them and at the same time undersell British competitors and thereby reduce their influence. The recent lifting of trade restrictions—especially the ban on brandy sales—was applauded at the western posts as a move that would give Canadian traders a valuable competitive edge. But the leasing of posts and a corresponding jump in prices for native customers further eroded French influence in the west. As early as 1740, Indians at Detroit threatened to take their trade elsewhere, and by 1742 colonial officials had to report that more and more natives were being "corrupted" by British traders who, suffering under no government restraints and amply supplied with a wide array of goods, easily outbid Canadians, a task made easier as disaffected Senecas, Wyandots, and others abandoned their former trading partners.[6]

The coexistence that had earlier prevailed between Canadians and Pennsylvanians thus came to an abrupt end as French officials planned to rid their hinterlands of British interlopers. At the same time the Ohio Country, heretofore only on the periphery of the colonial-imperial stage, rapidly became a center of attention. For the Canadians, the region's strategic value was now made abundantly clear as Pennsylvanians came perilously close to

.25"

3. Maskettes from the Wyandotte Town Site, Lawrence County, Pennsylvania, occupied between 1748 and 1751 by Wyandots and Senecas. (Courtesy of the State Museum of Pennsylvania, Pennsylvania Historical and Museum Commission)

severing the communication between Canada and Louisiana. And in the absence of significant numbers of troops, local commanders made every effort to rally native allies to "act against the English settled on the Beautiful River" and to "plunder and kill" British traders at Cuyahoga, thus restoring the buffer between Anglo-Americans and the vital Great Lakes basin. Canadian efforts in 1744 to redress the balance of power in the Ohio Country were given added impetus by the recent outbreak of war between France and Great Britain, which marked the end of the long peace of Walpole and Fleury and the beginning of a new round of worldwide conflict. By the following summer, imperial war threatened to consume the lower Great Lakes region and engulf the area's native inhabitants.[7]

Though officials at Quebec thought they could rely on native allies to drive out or destroy troublesome British traders, events soon proved otherwise. Parties of Ottawas and others sent from Detroit in 1745 toward the Sandusky and Cuyahoga trading posts returned without firing a shot; Governor-General Beauharnois chose to overlook the implications by blaming failure on "Hurons" (Wyandots) among the Detroit warriors. Yet Canadian leaders were clearly disturbed by the lack of native cooperation. Concern turned to alarm when fresh reports from the west told of wholesale native defections and the staggering decline of French influence west of

Niagara that seemed to presage the collapse of the entire inland empire. By late summer 1746 the governor was compelled to acknowledge sporadic attacks on Canadian traders and growing hostility among Indians living beyond Detroit.[8]

The following year proved decisive as simmering resentment and occasional conflict exploded in a wave of Indian attacks on isolated posts and traders. Officers at Michilimackinac spoke of the "confusion that prevails among all the Nations of that post." Such reports included a litany of attacks and losses: three traders killed by Ottawas at Saginaw, two canoeloads of supplies ambushed on Lake Huron and eight men killed, another Canadian killed by Saulteurs (Ojibwas). The attacks spread west to the heretofore secure Illinois Country, and by early October Detroit was, its commander admitted, under siege.[9]

In the midst of the crisis, the only encouraging news came from the Allegheny Valley, where early in 1745 Peter Chartier led his Shawnee village in raids against Pennsylvania traders, plundered eight of them, then took his followers out of the Ohio Valley and toward the Creek towns south of the Tennessee River. Beauharnois was clearly delighted to have good news to report and identified Chartier's actions as the long hoped for movement of the Shawnees closer to the French posts. News of these events reaching Philadelphia did include a reference to Chartier's having "accepted a Military Commission under the French King" and may indeed reflect a small success for the Canadians' twenty-year diplomatic mission to the Shawnees. Yet Chartier's motives appear more complex than merely a desire to stand by his father's people. It appears that Chartier's followers had taken advantage of French support and current hostilities to strike back at two old foes: Pennsylvania and the Six Nations, each in its own way instrumental in driving the Shawnees into the Ohio Country. Nevertheless, whatever hope Canadians had that Chartier would join them was dashed when he and his people demonstrated their independence by moving not to the French forts in the Great Lakes region but to the Creek towns, where kinship ties assured them welcome.[10]

Surveying the shambles of their inland empire, French officials located the cause of their woes in a plot, led by Wyandots and supported by the British, to wreck their trading network and alliances—a conspiracy that had enlisted an unspecified number of Iroquois from Cuyahoga. In addition, Beauharnois and his officers quickly pointed out that they suffered under a severe handicap as Britain's wartime blockade reduced the flow of trade goods to a trickle, complicating the already sensitive relations with natives angered by high-priced, low-quality goods.

As early as 1745 Beauharnois reported that message belts from British traders had been passing "underground" (unofficially) through western Indian towns. Within two years "strange Indians" from Fond du Lac boldly appeared in Illinois villages and, on behalf of the "Iroquois," "Hurons," and British, called those people to war against the French. At the heart of this conspiracy, in the minds of French leaders in the colony, stood Orontony, who in mid-1747 led his warriors on raids that killed five Canadian traders. Orontony's action was intended to signal a general native rising against the French, a plan that failed only when news of it leaked to the garrison at Detroit. At the same time, shortages of necessary supplies meant that local military officers could not hope to match their British enemies in the reciprocal and protocol-laden forms of diplomacy that could strengthen native alliances.[11]

New France indeed suffered from the British navy's blockade, and the disappearance of trade goods clearly contributed to the events of 1747. Yet the Indians who participated in the fighting after 1745 were not materialistic men, nor were they easily led or driven to follow paths marked by others. Natives living in the middle west harbored no illusions about their growing dependence on European technology; the Miamis, for example, asked that the French not deprive them of "their indispensable supplies." Yet what caused resentment was not only the absence of goods, which could be obtained from the ubiquitous British peddlers, but the equal scarcity of reciprocity and fairness on the part of Canadian traders. High prices coupled with shortages did not sit well with people who valued generosity and placed a premium on the reciprocal nature of a relationship defined by Indians in terms of real or fictive kinship rather than by distant political or market forces. The failure of the Canadian traders to behave in an acceptable fashion—including, perhaps, their growing concern about Indian debts—could only lead to trouble.[12]

Though strained relations with the French touched the lives of many Indians, problems were especially acute for the "young men," the warrior-hunters whose social responsibilities included providing for and protecting their families and towns. Price gouging, shortages, and debts all affected these men more than others. At the same time, the highly personal nature of native warfare meant that local French commanders were hard pressed to restrain neighboring warriors who chose to launch raids—for revenge, economic gain, or as a matter of honor—on traders and garrisons. Although village leaders may have understood the folly of such attacks, they too had difficulty restraining their young men. Yet not all men in the Great Lakes towns chose to fight or wished to choose sides at all; as the level of conflict intensified, factions arose within villages from Sandusky to the Illinois Country as natives debated the proper strategy in the face of spreading conflict.[13]

Whatever their particular motives, warriors throughout the region were now in arms. And on the far less secure but no less vital eastern marches of France's inland empire, natives from the Ohio Country joined in the attack. Pennsylvania's official interpreter, Conrad Weiser, learned that one hundred western Delawares were planning to join nearly as many Iroquois at Sandusky in the autumn of 1747. Reports from New France early the following year confirmed the participation of Ohio Indians in raids near Detroit and identified Wyandots, Senecas, Mahicans, and Onondagas among the attackers. More important, the raids were also a manifestation of a growing alliance, anchored in the Ohio Country, that bound members of several societies together and helped shape the region's history for the next eight eventful years.[14]

The Ohio Indians' alliance took shape away from colonial observers, and consequently details concerning its origins are scant. It does seem clear, however, that what initially brought Iroquois, Wyandots, Shawnees, Delawares, and Piankashaws together was a shared hostility toward the French, fueled by British traders. By the time the Ohio Indians arrived in Philadelphia late in 1747, the alliance was already a fact, though its dimensions were still not firmly set. Though its ultimate origins are obscure, the natives' aggressive solicitation of British support offers some insight into the formative stages of the alliance, while the Indians' central role in shaping regional events after 1747 permits the subsequent history of the alliance to be traced in some detail.

On April 20, 1747, Indians living at "Aleggainey" dictated a message to George Croghan for delivery to Pennsylvania's leaders. In it the natives, identified as "Mingow" (Ohio Valley Iroquois) and "Shauenons," spoke of the "Inomy [Miami] Nation in our tratey with them" and were in effect attempting to sponsor a similar alliance between the colony and the Miamis at the latter's request. To promote such a meeting, the Ohio Indians sent along a gift of deerskins and beaver pelts as a means of "clearing the path" between the Miamis and Pennsylvania.[15]

Less than a month later, Pennsylvanians received yet another message from the west, again through Croghan. Sent from the Indians "on the Borders of Lake Ery," this message drew far more immediate attention because it included a French scalp, taken from one of the hapless traders attacked near Sandusky. Included in the message was the news that, having taken up arms at the request of New York and Pennsylvania, the westerners now expected the colonies to provide them with much-needed gunpowder and lead. Heading the list of those natives who sent the message was the Seneca headman Conagaresa.[16]

These messages reveal several things about affairs within the Ohio Indians' world. Though Orontony's Wyandots seem to have triggered hostilities south of Lake Erie, leadership quickly passed to local Iroquois. Orontony gradually lost control over many of his own followers; by fall 1748 many of the Sandusky Wyandots had made peace with the French at Detroit, while Orontony and a smaller group moved first to the Beaver Valley and then into the upper Muskingum Valley. Meanwhile the large Iroquois settlements at Cuyahoga took the lead in the anti-French movement. Farther east, in the Allegheny Valley, Iroquois influence emerged owing to the insistence of a Piankashaw faction led by La Demoiselle (Old Briton) that local Iroquois intercede on their behalf with Pennyslvanians. The Piankashaws' request was an acknowledgment that the Six Nations, and by extension Iroquois living in the west, enjoyed a special relationship with the colony, one that would allow the Piankashaws to be heard in Philadelphia.[17]

The Iroquois were willing to assist the Piankashaws both because of their own hostility toward the French and because of the encouragement they received from the Pennsylvania traders in the west. Quickly recognizing an opportunity to expand their own influence and profits, these men, with Croghan in the lead, urged Richard Peters and others in Pennsylvania's government to take full advantage of the "fair Opertunity" offered by the Ohio Iroquois to "have all the French Cutt off in them parts." At the same time, Croghan apparently misrepresented the actual state of affairs to his Iroquois customers, who later told Pennsylvania's Indian agent that they had attacked the French at the request of the colony's government, a request that originated not in Philadelphia but at Croghan's trading station on the Cuyahoga River. It would not be the last time that private interests in the Ohio Country, native or colonial, would be cloaked in the mantle of public policy.[18]

Finally, the information coming out of the west makes clear the presence of two distinct Iroquois centers of activity. One was on the Cuyahoga River where natives, by late spring 1747, were already actively involved in fighting. Another group of Iroquois who had not yet taken up arms lived in the Ohio Valley. Of the two groups, the one on the Ohio was the older, whereas the Cuyahoga Iroquois had arrived gradually in the years just before the outbreak of fighting. The messages from each group were sent in the names of several men, though three—Conagaresa at Cuyahoga and Orscanyadee

(Scarouady) and Tanareeco (Tanaghrisson) in the Allegheny Valley—would subsequently play leading roles in Ohio Indian affairs.

The precise relation between the Cuyahoga and Ohio groups at the time of their correspondence with Pennsylvanians is unclear. Each represented elements of all the Six Nations; each stood at the center of a number of native communities that embraced Wyandots, Shawnees, and Delawares. Moreover, they shared hostility toward the French that may have reflected the migrants' origins among anti-French factions within Iroquoia. Nevertheless, the Ohio Valley Iroquois continued to be more aggressive in pursuing an alliance with the British and quickly rose to a commanding position in regional affairs for nearly a decade after 1747. Their diplomatic skill, numbers, and perhaps special claims in the region linked to adoption of remnant Eries and Monongahelans gave these Iroquois a paramount role in the Ohio Country. Yet events at Logg's Town in 1748 suggest some competition between Cuyahoga Iroquois and Wyandots and their Ohio Iroquois neighbors. As a group, the Cuyahoga Iroquois appear to have held together only until the end of hostilities in 1748; most subsequently left the Cuyahoga Valley and resettled with Orontony's people at Kuskuski and perhaps farther up the Allegheny River at Venango, Shenango, and Buckaloons. Colonial reports are of little help in this regard, though Pennsylvania authorities initially treated the two Iroquois groups as distinct and shaped their responses to each accordingly. By the end of the 1740s, however, any earlier distinctions between Cuyahoga and Ohio Iroquois blurred under generic terms such as "Mingos," "Ohio Indians," or the even less precise "Six Nations."[19]

The diplomatic offensive undertaken by the Cuyahoga and Ohio Iroquois caught Pennsylvania officials unprepared, though the provincials were quick to grasp the implications contained in the "fair Opertunity" Croghan spoke of. Richard Peters, provincial secretary, reflected the colony's lack of knowledge about western Indians when, in response to the Cuyahoga message and scalp, he instructed Conrad Weiser to learn from the Six Nations all he could regarding the Indians living near Lake Erie. Meanwhile, warnings from Croghan about the immediacy of the Indians' need for some sign of friendship, as well as the possibility that delay would wreck any chance to further weaken French influence, led Peters to request £400 for presents to be sent, in Croghan's care, to Cuyahoga. The decision was made easier by news from Weiser that the Indians near Lake Erie, believed to be "allies" of the Six Nations, were of considerable numbers and aggressively anti-French. Further, James Logan, the colony's elder statesman in such matters, pointed out that the recent collapse of a scheme to invade

Canada through the Champlain Valley, coupled with the persistent and troublesome failure of the Six Nations to abandon official neutrality in its relations with rival colonies, meant that any opening to natives in the west might be not only advantageous from a commercial or strategic point of view, but vital if pressure on the French was to be maintained.[20] To this point, in mid-October 1747, Pennsylvania's interests lay with the Cuyahoga Iroquois, who were already at war with the French and whose dramatic message that spring did not fail to gain the colonists' attention. Yet the presents voted by the assembly had been sent no farther than Harris's Ferry on the Susquehanna River when the Ohio Iroquois seized the initiative and, in the process, held out for provincials even greater possibilities in the west.

The appearance of the Ohio Iroquois at Philadelphia was not entirely unexpected, though the nature of their business was as yet unclear. In the shadowy comings and goings of messengers and agents, native and provincial, during the spring and summer of 1747, Logan learned of an impending visit and warned the assembly that since "Some Indians are expected to arrive . . . during your recess," money for their entertainment ought to be voted in advance. Furthermore, Logan urged that a more substantial portion of the present for the westerners be reserved for the Ohio Iroquois, since, as he had discovered, they were "our much nearer neighbors" and could presumably be more conveniently dealt with. Nevertheless, no one knew precisely what to expect when, on November 13, colonial representatives met Scarouady and his party.[21]

As the party bringing business to the council, the Indians acted on well-understood protocol and spoke first, identifying themselves as "Warriors, living at Ohio" who spoke for themselves and the "rest of the Warriors of the Six Nations." Though they used Covenant Chain metaphors—they came to, among other things, "brighten the chain" and identified themselves as "of the Six Nations, who are your antient Friends"—subsequent statements here and later actions indicate that Scarouady's delegation acted not for the Six Nations proper, but rather for those Iroquois and their allies living in the Ohio Country. Fully aware of the diplomatic and political realities of their world, the Ohio natives may well have used such statements to add to their own legitimacy before the Pennsylvanians. The Iroquois also came with a specific agenda that offers additional glimpses into the Ohio Indian world at a particularly crucial juncture.[22]

The Ohio Iroquois had recently entered the war as British partners, and their trip to Philadelphia, like the scalp from Cuyahoga, was a means of soliciting material assistance, since in the natives' view they had entered the war only after "repeated applications of our Brethren the English"—

Croghan and his fellow traders. However, these natives again went beyond mere requests for powder and shot; the Iroquois took up arms believing the French were aggressors in a conflict that threatened both the tranquility and the security of the Ohio Country. From their own perspective, the Iroquois were attempting to maintain the status quo, siding with one belligerent as much to maintain the balance of power as to obtain needed supplies.[23]

Scarouady made it clear that this had been the warriors' decision. He expressed their frustration with the Six Nations council at Onondaga, which, when asked for help, steadfastly refused to abandon its official neutrality in the face of renewed intercolonial war. Rebuffed at Onondaga, the Ohio Iroquois determined to "lay their old People aside" and to look after their own affairs by exchanging their own inadequate arsenals—"little Sticks and Hickeries"—for "better Weapons, such as will knock the French down." Buried beneath this metaphor-laden discourse was a deeper message: the Ohio Iroquois were fully prepared to turn away from their elders in Iroquoia in favor of direct relations with the colonies at a time when the interests of Ohio Iroquois and their parent communities in New York began to diverge. To that end the Iroquois urged their would-be colonial allies to let their own war kettle boil as high as the Indians' and enter the battle themselves.[24]

Although they asked for material support from the colony, the Ohio Iroquois had other things in mind as well. During a lull in the council proceedings, Conrad Weiser learned that the Iroquois had decided to "kindle a Fire at their Town, and had invited all the Indians to a considerable distance round about them to come to their Fire" the following year. The creation of a separate and distinct Ohio Iroquois council was a bold step for men who identified themselves as warriors rather than sachems. A firm Ohio Iroquois–Pennyslvania alliance would further this ambitious plan by drawing the colonists directly into regional affairs while considerably enhancing the prestige of the Iroquois who promoted such a scheme.[25]

The Ohio Iroquois' dramatic appearance, Weiser's information, and knowledge that Scarouady's delegation represented a formidable body of Indians, "not less than Five hundred Men" by best estimate, prompted colonial officials to reevaluate their plans for treating with western Indians. The council marked a convergence of interests that Peters, Weiser, and others could not ignore. Natives needing assistance against the French to redress the local balance of power, while attempting to strengthen their alliance by inviting colonial participation, also gave Pennsylvanians a singular opportunity to extend their own commercial and political influence far into the Canadians' inland empire, a prospect too tempting to resist. Armed with discretionary funds voted by the Quaker-dominated Assembly, president Anthony Palmer and others at the council quickly reversed their earlier plans; they decided to give the bulk of the present already on its way to John Harris's to the Ohio Iroquois, "and half as much" to the Cuyahoga Indians. Tentative plans were also made for Weiser, as an official representative of the colony, to travel the following year to the Ohio to give further encouragement to the natives and to gather more information on what were to be Pennsylvania's newest native allies. All of this must have pleased Scarouady and those who remained on the Ohio anxiously awaiting his return; the first links had been forged in a new chain of friendship, one designed by *Ohio* Iroquois.[26]

It took little time for the Iroquois-Pennsylvania alliance to mature. Before Conrad Weiser could begin his trek to the Ohio Country, the provincial council, on June 23, 1748, received word that Iroquois and Shawnees from Logg's Town were "coming down to present the Chiefs of the Twightwees, a nation lately come over from the French."[27]

The Twightwees in this instance were the Piankashaws led by La Demoiselle. In 1747 La Demoiselle had broken with the French, and since then he had actively sought an alliance with the British as well as with his Ohio Country neighbors. He abandoned his town on the Maumee River for a new site, Pickawillany, on the headwaters of the Miami River. His removal added considerably to French anxiety, and La Demosielle soon became a special object of French attention as he was alternately threatened and cajoled to return to the Maumee. Nevertheless, the headman consistently led his people closer to the new Ohio Iroquois–Pennsylvania alliance while urging others of the Miami Confederacy to do the same. It was at this time that La Demoiselle began to be known also as Old Briton, a name he may have adopted when he abandoned the French in favor of an alliance the British.[28]

Since Pennsylvanians had previously known little of La Demoiselle's people, the council between the Iroquois and Shawnees at Lancaster provided a useful education for provincial authorities, one that further encouraged them to cement alliances with the western Indians. President Palmer could barely conceal his excitement when reporting to the assembly that the "Twightwees, a considerable Nation of Indians . . . hitherto in the French Interest" had changed sides, a fact made more encouraging since it appeared that Old Briton's people, and presumably all the Miamis, would "considerably" increase the colony's western trade.[29]

At the same time, the Piankashaws' application to enter the Ohio Iroquois–Pennsylvania alliance sheds additional light on interethnic affairs in the west. The Shawnees had accompanied the Piankashaw delegates Assapause (the "young Piankashaw king") and Musheguanockque ("the Turtle"), because, as the Piankashaws explained, the Shawnees lived nearest to them. The emerging alliance thus carried with it a native-based protocol: Piankashaws applied to Shawnees, who spoke to the Iroquois; the Iroquois, as the senior partners on the Indian side and a people who were "heard" in colonial councils, then would "take [the Piankashaws'] Hands, and let them, together with ours, be lock'd close" to those of the Pennsylvanians. Protocol took a different turn, however, when two cultural traditions met for the first time. Whereas the British had adopted from the Iroquois the use of wampum in council, the Piankashaws used calumets, the "peace pipe" of popular lore and something the Pennsylvanians evidently knew nothing about. Observers described in great detail "a Calumet Pipe with a long stem curiously wrought, & wrapp'd round with Wampum of several Colours & fill'd with Tobacco," which all the parties passed and smoked "according to custom." In the ever-changing world of intercultural affairs, another element had been added, one with which the colonists would soon become familiar.[30]

The passing of the calumet at Lancaster concluded one more phase in the development of an Ohio Indian–centered alliance. Yet another potential problem was overcome when, during the council, the Shawnees attempted to make amends for Peter Chartier's attack on provincial traders. Once again the Ohio Iroquois acted as intermediaries for Shawnees representing Nucheconner, Kakowatchiky, and those "who are left at Ohio"—specifically, those Shawnees who had since abandoned Chartier and returned to their old homes. The Shawnees' appearance at Lancaster, and the fear that colonists bent on vengeance would not distinguish friendly from hostile natives, demanded that the "chain of friendship" be mended before there was talk of any alliances; therefore, composing relations with the colony was as important to the Iroquois as to the Shawnees. Scarouady, responding to the Pennsylvanians' demand, orally rebuked the Shawnees for having "abandoned" the colony, yet the colonial officials also spoke approvingly of those Shawnees who had resisted Chartier's blandishments. The whole matter was thus composed in a manner that further showed the superior role of the western Iroquois in the evolving native-British partnership.[31]

Even before the Logg's Town encounter between the Iroquois and Weiser later that year, the Indians' overtures had raised other serious questions of policy for the colony. Conrad Weiser, when asked by the Cuyahoga messengers to deliver their French scalp to the governor, refused even to consider such a thing, since, as he later explained to James Logan, "my commission for the transaction of Indian affairs did not extend to Ohio . . .

but reached on[ly] to the Six Nations." Weiser's explanation struck to the heart of the problem; since the 1720s the principal axis of Pennsylvania's Indian affairs had run north to Onondaga. That axis was symbolically supported by Weiser and an Oneida, Shikellamy, who resided at Shamokin. Shikellamy served not only as the representative of Confederacy interests within the colony, but also as a diplomatic adviser and a conduit of information regarding the several Confederacy "props"—Tutelos, Conoys, and Conestogas living in the colony, as well as the eastern Delawares and Shawnees. Shikellamy and Weiser both had a great deal at stake—prestige, power, and influence—in maintaining an exclusive Pennsylvania–Six Nations alliance. Shikellamy lost little time in recognizing the threat posed by Ohio Iroquois actions and moved quickly to dampen provincial enthusiasm for a western alliance. Accordingly, he told Weiser that one of the members of the 1747 delegation had assured him the Ohio Iroquois were "entirely devoted" to the Six Nations and would take their cue from Onondaga. The purpose behind Shikellamy's report becomes clear when he insisted that, since the Ohio Iroquois were "devoted" to the Confederacy, Weiser's planned "Journey to Ohio would avail nothing." Weiser concurred and initially refused to make the trip to Logg's Town. For lack of anyone better qualified for the task, Weiser was prevailed upon to undertake the mission, but the agent continued to fret and express his disapproval of a new rapprochement with the Ohio Iroquois, insisting that it would anger and alienate the Six Nations and throw the entire frontier into confusion.[32]

Others rose to meet Weiser's arguments and press for the Ohio alliance, foremost among them George Croghan, who, like Weiser, had much at stake in any political decisions on the matter. By late 1750 the lines were clearly drawn. Proprietor Thomas Penn learned that "there is a difference of Judgement between Mr. Croghan and Mr. Weiser," the "two persons who are supposed to understand Indian affairs the best," over how to exploit the opportunities presented by the Ohio Iroquois while avoiding a rupture with the Six Nations. Although he held the Ohio Indians in low esteem—calling them the "scum of the earth"—Richard Peters nevertheless encouraged continued relations with them. Ironically, Weiser himself provided the rationale for Peters's—and the government's—pragmatism. Peters was effusive in recounting Weiser's information about the Ohio Country, especially "the exceedingly good land" to be had there.[33]

Within a month of the Lancaster meeting, Wesier was on his way west bearing official assurances of continued friendship from the colony as well as a substantially larger, and symbolically more significant, present worth £1,000. Virginia belatedly contributed £200 as its great men began to show great interest in the trans-Appalachian region. Weiser made the westward trek by following the Frankstown Path to the Allegheny Valley and the Ohio Iroquois' new council fire at Logg's Town. By meeting native headmen there, Weiser was able both to signify the colony's recognition of the alliance and to enhance Iroquois prestige. A brief side trip to a Delaware town on the Beaver River enabled Weiser to have the necessary council wampum prepared; he then proceeded to Logg's Town, arriving on August 27.[34]

The Indians at Logg's Town seem to have been as eager for the meeting as Weiser's superiors. Weiser reported that when he first entered the town "Great Joy appear'd in their Countenances," and that the assembled headmen immediately came to "shake Hands" with the emissary. Emerging from the crowd was Weiser's host, Tanaghrisson, subsequently known to the British as the "half king." A Seneca though his mother was a Catawba, Tanaghrisson came to embody the growing autonomy and rising influence of the Iroquois living in the Ohio Country. His name first came to the attention of Pennsylvanians when it appeared on the 1747 message from the Ohio Iroquois. From that moment until the Logg's Town meeting, Tanaghrisson remained in the shadows, active diplomacy being conducted by the Oneida Scarouady, who subsequently served as Tanaghrisson's partner in all important negotiations with British colonists. Tanaghrisson's origins, like those of the people he represented, thus remain obscure. His subsequent lofty historical role as a Six Nations "regent" or "viceroy" in the Ohio Country was the product of later generations of scholars. Tanaghrisson's actual influence may have rested largely on his leadership of one of the Iroquois villages in the Ohio Country, as later reported by the French, and on a network of kin and personal allies that ran through the Iroquois towns in the west. Whatever the extent of his influence before Weiser's arrival, Tanaghrisson's authority was clearly enhanced by British generosity as he became the colonists' "half king"—their preeminent ally in the Ohio Country.[35]

At some point during the preceding year, Tanaghrisson seems to have cast himself as the individual best suited to promote local Iroquois interests. Yet even as Weiser approached the Ohio Country in August 1748, Tanaghrisson's position appeared anything but secure. Shortly after Weiser's arrival at Logg's Town a message arrived from the Iroquois and part or all of Orontony's Wyandots from Kuskuski, who, in Weiser's words, "desire of me that the ensuring Council might be held at their town." The challenge from Kuskuski was clear enough: whoever hosted the meeting could well use the event to gain the upper hand in the struggle between former Cuyahoga Iroquois and those from the Ohio for influence in regional affairs. The reaction from Tanaghrisson and his followers was equally clear and swift. Calling Weiser aside, they reminded him that "the Indians at Coscosky were no more Chiefs than themselves" and further insisted that everyone had originally agreed to meet at Logg's Town, since Kuskuski was short of food. "Now that their Corn is ripe," Tanaghrisson complained, "they want to remove the Council." Weiser, closely following the letter of native protocol, rejected the bid, and the council continued as planned. The subsequent British recognition of the Logg's Town council fire—Tanaghrisson's fire— and the transfer of £1,200 worth of gifts to the Indians through the Seneca headman, enhanced Tanaghrisson's prestige and power while for the moment silencing his rivals. Weiser's decision to meet at Logg's Town and work with Tanaghrisson carried other benefits as well. As a self-confessed "new beginner" at council business, Tanaghrisson needed and welcomed signs of colonial support, which included personal gifts for his and Scarouady's "council bags," gifts whose redistribution strengthened Tanaghrisson's influence at home.[36]

By the time the presents were exchanged on September 17, both Tanaghrisson and Weiser could judge the council a success on all counts. Weiser was able to learn the state of affairs in the Ohio Country in some detail. He received a tally of warriors living in and about Logg's Town— some 789 men, mostly Iroquois, Delawares, and Shawnees. Among the Iroquois the Senecas were the most numerous, and the total number of Ohio Country warriors suggests a population of between 3,000 and 4,000 people, exclusive of the numerous Piankashaws and other members of the Miami Confederacy. The emissary also learned that the Ohio Indians were expecting Canadian retaliation and were also fearful of raids by their southern Indian enemies. Thus the natives had compelling reasons for seeking a British alliance.[37]

For their part, Tanaghrisson and his followers managed to hold their own against rivals near at hand while enjoying a considerable political and diplomatic coup. Their earlier efforts to draw the Piankashaws into a regional alliance were confirmed by Weiser, who also asked that the Wyandots be formally admitted to the Iroquois-British alliance, which by virtue of the presents exchanged embraced Virginia as well. By the end of the Logg's Town council, the Iroquois stood at the center of that alliance, supporting a chain of friendship forged at their council fire and stretching from the council house at Pickawillany to the government house in Philadelphia. Nothing better symbolized their standing than the distribution of the treaty present: the Senecas received one (presumably the largest) of the five portions; all the remaining Iroquois shared one portion; and one portion each went to the Shawnees, the Delawares, and the small groups of Wyandots, Mississaugas, and Mahicans. For a "new beginner," Tanaghrisson could be well pleased with the outcome of his initial diplomatic venture as well as with his newfound role as the colonists' ally.[38]

The significance of the Ohio warriors' actions was not lost on the Six Nations. The independence displayed by the Ohio Indians at Philadelphia and Logg's Town and encouraged by provincial leaders clearly upset some within the Confederacy, as Weiser soon learned. While at Onondaga in 1750 to offer condolances on the death of the Onondaga council speaker and Pennsylvania ally Canasetego, Weiser raised the subject of western lands and the prospect of Iroquois negotiations with the governor of Virginia. Explaining that Governor Dinwiddie could not meet them at Albany, Weiser suggested that presents intended for the Confederacy be given instead to the Ohio Iroquois, since, as he believed, "the Ohio Indians were one and the same with the Six Nations and of their own blood." The Onondagas' reply was quick and to the point: the Ohio Indians "were but hunters and no counsellors or chief men, and they had no right to receive presents that was due to the Six Nations." Though the westerners might expect to receive a share, the "must receive [it] from the Six Nations' chief under whom they belong," a statement the Onondagas repeated "over and over."[39]

The Onondagas' exchange with Weiser reflected the anxiety that emerged within the Confederacy as shifting power relations in the Ohio Country threatened their own standing with the British. Any cracks in the Six Nations' carefully cultivated facade of unity and power threatened not only the prestige of the Iroquois in British circles but the security of a people living an increasingly perilous existence between competing European empires. Yet the Six Nations' relationship with the "mere hunters" in the Ohio Country remained ambivalent, something colonials like Richard Peters could sense if not comprehend. Though they were emphatic in their claims to sovereignty in Ohio Country, the Six Nations had remained distant from regional affairs since the beginning of King George's War. Maintaining its declared official neutrality in the face of renewed intercolonial hostilities, the Confederacy as a whole resisted efforts by Canadian Philippe-Thomas Chabert de Joncaire on the one side and New York's William Johnson on the other to draw them into the conflict. Neutrality, though it frustrated the Ohio Iroquois as well as New Yorkers and Canadians, did preserve harmony within a Confederacy divided over the war, allowing constituent members to pursue their own interests without risking internecine conflict. Mohawk warriors, for example, lent support to their British neighbors as they had done in the past.[40]

By remaining neutral, many among the Six Nations may have hoped to spare the Ohio Country as well as their own settlements from the ravages of war. In response to French calls for them to take up arms against New York, Onondagas reminded Quebec officials of the 1701 treaties and urged the Europeans to take their war elsewhere and "leave our hunting grounds undisturbed." Moreover, intercolonial warfare raised once more the possibility of hostilities between the Six Nations and kinfolk now living on French mission reserves at Caughnawaga and Oka, who were active French allies.[41]

The divisions within the Confederacy that sustained official neutrality continued after the war, cutting across ethnic and kinship lines. The tensions evident to outsiders like Weiser or Joncaire were not unique to the 1740s. Rather, they arose from an ongoing debate since the beginning of the century over how best to survive in the disputed ground between rival empires. Factions expressed themselves on the surface as "pro-British" or "pro-French" or "neutral," but they represented differing strategies based on one overriding Iroquois imperative: cultural survival. These factions vied for influence within village and Confederacy councils, and never more so than during and after the first major intercolonial conflict in a generation.[42]

By 1747 Joncaire found the Senecas "all divided," with his own adoptive kin and friends among them "separated from the other villages." Such divisions surfaced among the eastern Iroquois as well, and nowhere was this tendency more evident by the end of the war than at the Confederacy's center, Onondaga. Onondaga sachems blamed a rise in French influence among their people on the British, who characteristically ignored their Iroquois neighbors as soon as the fighting stopped. The depth of bitterness between competing points of view was revealed to Conrad Weiser when he arrived in 1750. Weiser learned, for instance, that not all Onondagas welcomed Canasetego's close association with Pennsylvania, which resulted in the transferral of much of the Confederacy's southern buffer to colonial jurisdiction. In symbolic contempt, one of Canasetego's rivals, Tahashronchdioony, ordered that the dead man's treaty wampum from Pennsylvania be buried with him in order, he said, "to make Canassatogo a Thief after his Death" as many believed he had been in life.[43]

Canasetego's death added to factionalism within Iroquois towns, further reducing British prospects for Confederacy cooperation in distant places like the Ohio Country. Moreover, Pennsylvanians feared that their opponents were gaining the upper hand in the political debate within Iroquoia. Weiser made a point of noting that Onondaga "was thick with French praying Indians," and he learned that "the Onondagers, Cayugers, and

Senecas were turned Frenchmen, and that some of the Oneiders inclined that Way." What Weiser and other colonists perceived was a growing paralysis that prevented the Six Nations from taking the decisive action expected of them by their Covenant Chain partners in a region where, in theory, they and their colonial allies shared important interests.[44]

Internal dissension and genuine reluctance to become embroiled in European conflicts only partly explain the widening gap between Six Nations claims in the Ohio Country and the actions of supposedly dependent peoples living there. Although colonial officials were seldom able to understand the complexities of native societies, Pennsylvania's governor, James Hamilton, may have come closest to explaining what was in fact happening in the west. Discussing his colony's decision to support the Ohio Iroquois, Hamilton observed that "by suffering their young Indians to go and settle" in the Ohio Country, the Six Nations helped promote a "new interest" that challenged the Confederacy's claims to hegemony over the region.[45]

As Hamilton saw things, the migrations that continued into the 1740s had led to a considerable shift in population from Iroquoia to the Ohio Country. Distance came to be measured in more than just miles, however. By midcentury the Ohio Iroquois, as well as their non-Iroquois neighbors, were looking upon the Ohio Country as home, despite Six Nations' and colonists' persistent reference to them as "hunters" or "stragglers." Since Iroquois loyalties had always been tied to kinship networks and local communities, it was natural that the Ohio Iroquois would gradually develop a strong attachment to their new homes as well as a greater preoccupation with events in the west that had an immediate effect on their lives. At the same time, the natives' interest in affairs within Iroquoia would wane, particularly since the Confederacy was being pulled in a number of directions: toward Canada, the Susquehanna Valley, and Albany. The Ohio Iroquois' localism was enhanced by the support given them by the Pennsylvanians. As early as 1750 Conagaresa could boldly assert that "We are now become a stronger Body" than only two years earlier and, as such, "desire to be taken notice of."[46]

Finally, the Ohio Country, like other parts of the Iroquois hinterland, held the attention not of the whole Confederacy, but only of those who had an immediate interest in the region—in this instance the Senecas. This was itself rooted in the localistic tendencies found within the Confederacy, which precluded the "Six Nations" involvement in the west that colonists anticipated. Moreover, the Ohio Iroquois themselves exhibited a certain ambivalence toward their Six Nations kinfolk. Although many among them persisted in identifying themselves as "of the Six Nations," the attachment of others within this group was weaker. The term "Mingo" applied to the Ohio Iroquois by the British implied a mix of people, ostensibly Iroquois but also including Mesquakies, Mahicans, and the descendants of captives taken in earlier wars.[47]

Thus, although a cultural affinity remained between the Ohio Iroquois and their kinfolk in New York, geographical and political interests drove a wedge between them. Yet the Ohio Iroquois were not the only ones hammering that wedge ever deeper. The "new interest" Hamilton identified may well have been a reaction to Six Nations' inertia, a sense of being abandoned and set adrift by elders in Iroquoia. As Scarouady's party explained to Pennsylvanians in 1747, the Six Nations had ignored their request for help against the French, leaving the westerners to face the enemy alone, a situation that made colonial aid even more necessary. Six years later the Confederacy again remained aloof in the presence of a much more serious threat to the Ohio Iroquois. Meanwhile, the physical distance that helped pull Tanaghrisson's people away from Iroquoia seems to have had the same effect on the Six Nations. Confederacy headmen in 1753 referred Ohio Iroquois' calls for advice and help to the colonies, arguing that "they are a great way from us" and that Pennyslvania was better suited to supply "*our* young Men at Ohio."[48]

The Ohio Iroquois were also upset upon learning, apparently for the first time, of the 1744 Lancaster Treaty whereby the Six Nations, led by Canasetego, agreed to cede land between the Susquehanna River and the Allegheny Mountains. The Ohio Seneca headman Conagaresa protested because, though the Six Nations continued to sell land, they "give us no account of the value," in the process violating the reciprocal nature of relations within Iroquois society. Although he did not question the Confederacy's claim to the land, Conagaresa insisted that *all* Iroquois be included in the deal. He went on to ask, on behalf of "the *Ohio Council*," that Pennyslvania's governor intercede for them and "recommend it to the Six Nations that when any lands shall be sold, we may have part of the value." Conagaresa's request made sense to the Ohio Iroquois; they used the territory in question, land that also served as an important buffer between their towns and colonial settlements.[49]

Conagaresa's statements reveal much more, however. In speaking specifically of the "Ohio Council," he was drawing an important distinction between what he, Tanaghrisson, and others outside Iroquoia defined as two coequal bodies, each taking care of affairs within its particular sphere, though still bound together by a shared cultural tradition as well as the larger issue of how to deal with colonial expansion. It was this notion of circles within circles that so worried the Onondagas in 1750, but they could do little about it other than invoke their exclusive sovereignty over the Ohio Country, playing once again upon the colonists' mystique of Iroquois power.[50]

By the early 1750s, however, that mystique had begun to fade. British colonists with interests of their own to advance in the west were as vexed by the Six Nations' inaction as were the Ohio Iroquois. Richard Peters lamented the failure of his own efforts to learn the exact relation between the western Iroquois and the Confederacy: Canasetego, one of the colony's best sources of information on such matters, died before he could provide an answer. Meanwhile, as the flag continued to follow trade into the still uncharted thickets of Ohio Indian affairs, Pennsylvanians and Virginians took advantage of opportunities where they appeared and turned their backs on the Six Nations, at least concerning western affairs, while keeping up the politically useful fiction of a single, united Iroquois society. The colonies' actions after 1747 marked a turning point in the history of the Covenant Chain: Anglo-Americans began to look beyond Onondaga and the Mohawk Valley to the Ohio Country and the new council fire at Logg's Town. No one captured the prevailing colonial mood better than Pennsylvania's Richard Peters, who concluded that "our only game to play now is with the Ohio Indians" and their Piankashaw allies. Even William Johnson, whose own career as trader and frontier diplomat relied heavily on ties to the Six Nations, agreed, observing how recent events had proved that Iroquois "fame and power may in some measure exceed the reality."[51]

Peters's insistence that the high-stakes "game" in the Ohio Country be played with the region's inhabitants meant that, for the moment at least, Tanaghrisson and his Iroquois followers enjoyed considerable prestige and influence. The Ohio Iroquois' diplomatic offensive had yielded significant results: a new native-colonial alliance and trade, both orchestrated by Tanaghrisson. The impact on anxious outside observers was striking; the French watched with concern "a sort of republic" on the Ohio, "which is dominated by the Iroquois."[52]

The French description of what emerged by 1748 was more accurate than they could have imagined. Cooperation, not coercion, defined the natives' side of the alliance, based on a recognition of a superior Iroquois role in regional affairs. Piankashaws of La Demoiselle's village worked *through* the Ohio Iroquois, because the latter were in the best position to further Piankishaw goals and because at the moment Piankashaw and Iroquois interests coincided. The Shawnees who were present at Lancaster in 1748 were symbolically rebuked by the Ohio Iroquois for their role in Chartier's uprising three years earlier. Yet the Shawnees may have been willing to put up with some Iroquois rhetoric spoken at the behest of Pennsylvanians—and outside the public council—in return for reestablishing amicable relations with the colony. Less can be said about the several Delaware villages in the Ohio Country at the time. But as Weiser clearly indicated, they, the Senecas, and the Shawnees were given equal allotments of treaty gifts, and in subsequent meetings representatives of all three societies could be found in attendance, though Tanaghrisson or other Ohio Iroquois continued to orchestrate the agendas for several more years.[53]

The Iroquois' influence in the late 1740s and early 1750s was based on several things, including a superior claim to the region, numbers, and initiative. It was also based on native-centered concepts of clientage and reciprocity. Tanaghrisson maintained his position at the head of the Ohio Iroquois through his generosity as well as through political astuteness. Likewise Piankashaws, Delawares, Wyandots, and Shawnees *cooperated* with Tanaghrisson out of a sense of shared interests and because they expected that cooperation would be repaid both through access to desired goods and through continued peace and stability within the Ohio Country. No group surrendered its sovereignty in the natives' alliance; rather, each cooperated as reason and interest demanded, while allowing Tanaghrisson to take the lead and develop his now well-established ties to the colonies.

Taking the lead proved especially challenging for Tanaghrisson and the Iroquois in the months following the Logg's Town council. For though the Ohio alliance was based on a short-term convergence of native and British interests—antipathy toward the French and the desire to profit from trade—in the long run those interests diverged when the colonies sought to press their cheaply bought advantages in ways that threatened native autonomy and security as French traders and isolated garrisons never could. At the same time, French reaction to events on their vulnerable southern frontier pushed Tanaghrisson closer to the British and placed additional stress on his partnership with his native allies.

A French response came within a year of the Logg's Town council. Though Great Britain and France declared a truce in their decades-old conflict, the Treaty of Aix-la-Chapelle in 1748 did nothing to resolve intercolonial conflict in the Ohio Country. And for Canadians and Anglo-Americans alike, the Ohio Indians remained objects of solicitation and intimidation in the cold war that followed.

"Though at peace," outgoing governor-general Roland-Michel Barrin, marquis de La Galissonniere, urged, the French must be prepared to block "every attempt of the English to settle" anywhere west of the Alleghenies. Galissonniere's successor, Jacques-Pierre de Taffanel, marquis de La Jonquière, was prepared to do just that when, in summer 1749, captain Pierre-Joseph Céloron de Blainville, former commandant of Detroit, was dispatched with colonial regulars, Canadian militiamen, and native allies to take the measure of the recent Indian-British alliance and remind Ohio natives that the French were still a power to be reckoned with. Céloron's expedition from Montreal through the upper Ohio Valley to Pickawillany and Detroit was the most tangible measure of his superiors' concern about their continuing ability to control the middle west. All the interior posts remained intact, and though several dozen traders had been killed, injured, or temporarily detained by western warriors, the military regime was still in place. Fear nevertheless remained that France's grip on the middle west had been loosened and that the near disaster of 1747 was merely a harbinger of things to come unless control of the interior, and with it French prestige, was quickly restored.[54]

Had Céloron had any assumptions that a show of force would correct the political imbalance in the Ohio Country, they would have been quickly disspelled by his reception upon entering the Allegheny Valley from the Chautauqua portage. Instead of awestruck natives, the French were met by angry and alarmed Indians who reacted to their appearance by abandoning their towns "with so much precipitation" that they "left behind a part of their utensils, their canoes, and even their provisions." Such scenes were repeated from Buckaloons to Kittanning. When Céloron did manage to speak with local natives, he was met with equivocation and distrust. The natives' actions were in response to the large size of the captain's party and his insistence on referring to the Ohio Country as "my territories." The latter was made more troubling by his habit of burying lead plates claiming the region for Louis XV at major stream junctures. Meanwhile inhabitants of outlying settlements hurried downstream to Logg's Town, where on August 7 Céloron found "one of the most considerable villages of the Beautiful River," a multiethnic trading town inhabited by Shawnees, Iroquois, and Delawares as well as Nepissings, Abenakis, and Ottawas, all doing a brisk business with the Pennsylvania traders.[55]

Céloron's appearance in the Ohio Country clearly angered local Indians and fueled debate within Ohio Iroquois towns about the meaning of the Frenchman's journey and how to deal with the intruders. Céloron's demand that British traders be expelled from the region clearly upset natives, who countered by asking if the French were prepared to fill the void with their

4. Lead plate buried at the mouth of the "Rivière Chinodahichetha" (Kanawha River), August 18, 1749, by Céloron de Blainville. (Courtesy of the Virginia Historical Society.) The text of the plate reads: "The year 1749, in the reign of Louis XV, King of France, We, Céloron, commandant of a detachment sent by Monsieur the M[arquis] de la Galissonière, commander in chief of New France, to restore tranquility in some Indian villages of these districts have buried this plate at the mouth of the river Chinodahichetha the 18 August, near the river Ohio, otherwise Beautiful river, as a monument of the renewal of possession which we have taken of the said river Ohio and of all those which fall into it, of all lands on both sides of it as far as the sources of said streams, as enjoyed or ought to be, by the preceding Kings of France and as they have maintained themselves by arms and treaties, especially by those of Ryswick, Utrecht and Aix la Chapelle" (from Severance, *An Old Frontier of France,* p. 436).

own men and goods. The Iroquois and Delawares may already have known the answer since, as Céloron confessed in his journal, he replied "without making them any promises," their pointed request having "embarrassed me very much." Met and rebuffed on one tack, Céloron tried another, reminding the Delawares near Kittanning of their earlier dispossession by the Pennsylvanians and predicting that the same thing would soon happen on the Ohio. Though there is nothing in the captain's journal to confirm it, this brief history lesson and prophecy may well have struck a nerve, especially given the Frenchman's own persistence in declaring his country's ownership of territory that the Delawares and their neighbors were inclined to call their own. Meanwhile, the haphazard organization of Céloron's expedition became clear with his lack of an English interpreter. Thus his own warnings were lost on traders, who prudently withdrew only to return once the Canadians had drifted downstream. For his trouble, Céloron received equivocal answers, abandoned towns, and a sense that his mission was bound to fail.[56]

Thus the encounters at Logg's Town and, later, the Shawnee town at Scioto were charged with tension and distrust. Both the Indians and their uninvited guests prepared for the worst. Céloron, already concerned about his own untested soldiers, arrived at Logg's Town armed and ready for battle. He camped some distance from the town along the Ohio River, surrounded by guards, having, as he said, "no confidence in their [the natives']" good intentions. Father Joseph-Pierre Bonnecamps, the expedition's spiritual leader and a careful observer, shared Céloron's apprehension when he learned of the impending arrival of eighty warriors from Kuskuski "to aid their brothers and deal us a blow." No blows were struck. In fact, Céloron's arrival generated some confusion and indecision among the natives. The captain found three French flags flying over the lodges, and the one English banner in view was quickly removed by those who told Céloron they were "entirely French." The rival flags suggest some internal division over how to behave toward the French, with some apparently taking a more defiant stand than others felt prudent. The dissent may also have reflected a lack of effective leadership; throughout the brief and troubled encounter, the Iroquois insisted that they could not conduct council business in the absence of their chief men, and no mention was made of Tanaghrisson, Scarouady, or others. Consequently some among the Logg's Town Indians may have been sincere in their offer to abandon Pennyslvania traders if only the Canadians could sustain the trade. Short of that, however, the natives insisted that business continue as usual. Céloron soon left Logg's Town amid an atmosphere charged with distrust and suspicion.[57]

Céloron's reception at his later encounters with the Shawnees and Piank-ashaws matched the one he received at Logg's Town. Indeed, as news of the captain's progress raced ahead of his small flotilla, native apprehension increased. Once again the French armed themselves as they arrived on August 21 at the lower Shawnee town at the mouth of the Scioto River. Father Bonnecamps pointedly observed that "their reception was not gracious." Céloron's own account states that the natives "were frightened out of their wits." Even assuming that the captain inflated his own impact on his hosts during what had thus far been a decidedly inauspicious journey, it seems clear that the Shawnees expected an attack rather than a parley, in part owing to the rumors that spread ahead of the expedition as it moved down river. Yet Céloron was in no condition to act as the natives suspected he might. His concerns about his own men, most of whom were "recruits who had never made an attack" and who had earlier bolted at the sight of their own native allies, grew with each encounter. Moreover, his detachment was short of food, and as the end of August approached, Céloron was ever more anxious to complete his trip to Detroit and disperse his forces before winter trapped them at the outposts. The captain was therefore grateful when the Shawnees made an overture with "pipes of peace" and allowed him to render his now familiar harangue against the British while trying to assert French authority by "forgiving" the Indians for their initial reception. Yet here as before Céloron received noncommital replies from natives whose trust of Frenchmen extended no further than the captain's faith in his listeners.[58]

Céloron's reception at Pickawillany was decidedly less hostile or strident, yet in the end his confrontation with La Demoiselle was no more productive. To a large degree, Celoron's correct, even cordial, reception reflected La Demoiselle's control within his own town and the headman's self-confidence. Céloron was met while still some distance from the town by natives bearing calumets, and he entered into a formal dialogue with the Piankashaws that in the end proved fruitless. Using carrot and stick, Céloron urged La Demoiselle to return to his former townsite near the French, who would forgive all former hostilities. Céloron's insistence that at their former town the Piankashaws would "enjoy a perfect peace" carried the implied threat that no such peace could exist at Pickawillany. To illustrate his point, Céloron symbolically "extinguished" the natives' fire at Pickawillany and pointed them toward the warm glow of the pro-French Miamis' town on the White River. In response, La Demoiselle, with the same careful equivocation that had earlier frustrated Céloron, agreed to go to the White River *if* the winter's hunt proved successful but said that economic necessity prevented their moving before spring. In the meantime he hoped "to have the pleasure of making you a good speech in the spring"—a carefully chosen non-answer that enraged Céloron and ended the council on a sour note. Pickawillany remained to threaten the vulnerable interior of New France. French suspicions of La Demoiselle's duplicity seemed confirmed when his rival within the Miami Confederacy, the French ally La Baril, flatly told Céloron that "the Demoiselle is a liar."[59]

Though Céloron and his superiors found little to comfort them as they reflected upon their southern frontier, the expedition nevertheless made an impact on the Ohio Indians and reveals in retrospect the Ohio Country's marked volatility and the unstable nature of the Iroquois-British alliance. Much the greater portion of the hostility displayed at Logg's Town and Scioto grew from the fact that, although English and France were officially at peace, no such condition prevailed between Canadians and Ohio Indians. No one, least of all the Pennsylvanians, had taken the hatchet from the hands of Ohio warriors in council and urged them to remain at home. Thus, to use the Iroquois metaphor, the war kettle continued to simmer. Moreover, the Indians assumed that the French, like themselves, would be eager to retaliate for earlier attacks. This explains the concern reflected by natives at Logg's Town as Céloron approached with his Canadian Indian allies and the Shawnees' alarm when, in the midst of their council with Céloron at the Lower Town, news arrived—later proved false—that French-led Indians from Detroit were about to fall upon their town. Given the continuing hostile atmosphere that prevailed throughout the region, it is little wonder the French governor's demands, requests, and threats met only cold silence or equivocation; to the Ohio Indians Céloron's expedition was less a diplomatic mission than a hostile invasion.[60]

Yet rather than summarily destroying the intruders, as Céloron feared and Pennsylvania traders doubtless wished, the natives did choose to listen. That the French could mount such an expedition must have impressed more than a few onlookers, while others may have seen an opportunity to demonstrate forbearance as a first step toward peace. Though the presence of French flags at Logg's Town and natives' insistence that their "hearts were French" were efforts to deal with a large and potentially dangerous force, some among the Indians who met Céloron at Logg's Town may have genuinely sought to restore the balance of power in the region: trading with both Canadians and Pennsylvanians would be preferable to having one or the other gain too much influence. Such considerations were never explicitly stated. But in striking contrast to the orderly way La Demoiselle conducted business with Céloron, events along the Ohio suggest that among the Piankashaws' allies there was far more volatility and far less consensus. Céloron failed to identify one or more individuals he dealt with at Logg's Town and was told repeatedly that those he did meet were "young men" who "have no longer ancient chiefs" and that their current headmen were absent. If so, then the unsettled state of affairs that Conrad Weiser had found a year earlier appears to have persisted, and Tanaghrisson still did not enjoy absolute support at home but represented a consensus that shifted with the political currents that ran through the region. And given this situation, Céloron's greatest achievement may have been to push Tanahgrisson, Scarouady, and their followers closer to the British while preserving the fissures that persisted within the Ohio Indian alliance—gaps that could widen as external pressure grew.[61]

Céloron also introduced a far more sensitive issue into Ohio Indian affairs: native landholding and sovereignty. Though he attempted to wreck the alliance by reminding the Delawares of their earlier problems with British colonists, the captain's own words and deeds gave native onlookers no cause for comfort. The burial of lead plates from Buckaloons to the Miami River—plates the British were all too happy to translate and explain to the Indians—and Céloron's insistence on at least one occasion that the Ohio Country belonged to the French king were met by Indians who, at Logg's Town, "gave the French to understand that the land was theirs." At the Lower Shawnee Town they emphasized *their* sovereign rights by tearing down "and trampling underfoot with contempt" one of the several placards announcing French ownership that Céloron had attached to trees or posts along his line of march. Such words and actions were merely the earliest expression of what would soon become the most pressing issue for the natives as their homeland continued to attract outsiders.[62]

If the Ohio Indians anticipated decisive British countermeasures in the face of Céloron's advance, they were to be disappointed. Rather than confront the French, Pennsylvanians monitored Céloron's progress as best they could. Presents and traders continued to make their way to Ohio Indian towns, while diplomacy was placed in the hands of George Croghan, whose pragmatism and intimate knowledge of the western Indians allowed him to supplant Weiser as the colony's advance man on the Ohio. And though he expressed grave concern about French activity in the west, Governor Hamilton nevertheless continued to gather information that would help determine the feasibility of settlements west of the Alleghenies.[63]

five

"A Country Between"

The summer of 1752 was an especially crucial and troubling time for Tanaghrisson and the Ohio Iroquois. The Canadian French, undeterred by the reception given Céloron, stepped up pressure on both recalcitrant Ohio Indians and the British traders they entertained. Meanwhile, Virginians were applying pressure on the natives in order to secure ownership of lands west of the Allegheny Mountains. In both cases the rival colonies proved a serious threat to Indian autonomy.

Amid efforts to navigate the increasingly dangerous channel between rival empires, Tanaghrisson voiced the Ohio Indians' concerns that year. Reminding a French officer that the Ohio Country "belongs to neither one nor t'other" of the colonial powers, the headman also reflected that he and his neighbors "live in a Country between." In a few well-chosen words, Tanaghrisson expressed the central dilemma confronting the natives as their lands became, first, a prize in a high-stakes game of international politics and, ultimately, part of what the victors took as spoils.[1]

It was Virginia, rather than Pennsylvania, that brought the specter of British land hunger to the Ohio Country and thereby added considerably to the sense of crisis that spread among the region's natives. Virginia's means was the newly formed Ohio Company, composed of wealthy planters and speculators who saw profit in the ever-increasing migration of German and Scotch-Irish settlers into the Shenandoah Valley. The Company, officially organized in 1749 and numbering among its members the colony's new royal governor, Robert Dinwiddie, pinned its hopes on a large tract of land lying between the Blue Ridge and the Ohio River. The colony claimed the land through its sea-to-sea royal charter, but access was gained only in 1744 when, through the Lancaster Treaty, the Six Nations relinquished their claims east of the mountains.[2]

When news of the Virginians' interest in the Ohio Country reached the region's inhabitants, it arrived in the worst possible way: from ambitious and aggressive Ohio Company traders and agents. George Croghan attributed much of the natives' testy response to Céloron to "an alarm that Mr. [Thomas] Cresap and Mr. [Hugh] Parker Spread amongst the Indians Last fall [1748]" that the Ohio Company would soon settle the Youghiogheny Valley. Such important and disturbing news, arriving outside normal diplomatic channels, made the Virginians even more suspect. Moreover, the Ohio Indians, especially the influential Iroquois, had no use for Virginians in the best of circumstances. A generation of border friction had spawned deep Iroquois "resentment against the People of Virginia," whose traders, especially Hugh Parker, did business in ways that provoked violence and bloodshed.[3]

Official confirmation of the rumors was to arrive in 1750 in the shape of Christopher Gist, who during two trips into the Ohio Country between November 1750 and March 1752 served as the Company's advance man. His task, to "take an exact account of the Soil, Quality, and Product of the Land," would produce information on which the investors could stake their claim to western lands. Meanwhile, by observing "what Nations of Indians inhabit there, their strength . . . who they trade with and in what Commodities," Gist could offer guidance for the Company's plan to enter the trade as well as negotiations over the land itself. Above all else, however, Gist was to act as the Company's principal real estate agent, a role he found difficult to hide as he traveled west toward Logg's Town and the Muskingum Valley. Gist was beset by anxious natives who "began to enquire my Business" and who grew increasingly restive in the face of Gist's disingenuous responses. Indeed, so upsetting had his journey become that he found himself forced to "set my Compass privately . . . for I understand it was dangerous to let a Compass be seen among these Indians," who knew well enough what such instruments portended. Only by insisting that he was an ambassador was Gist able to safely complete his first trip into the west.[4]

There is little doubt that Gist's appearance, preceded as it was by rumors and comments from Virginia traders, had once more raised a powerful and sensitive issue among Ohio Indians. Land as a commodity meant far less to them than cultural and political security against grasping colonists. The region's history was itself an object lesson in what happened to people who were unable or unwilling to retain control of an adequate land base. Thus far the Delawares and Shawnees had avoided the worst effects of colonial expansion by moving west. Yet having moved before, the westerners were not inclined to repeat the process, as their barely veiled hostility toward Gist demonstrated. Moreover, there were other signs that the tide of Anglo-American settlement was surging closer to the Ohio Country. During his westward trip in 1748, Conrad Weiser reported that settlers had advanced up the Tuscaroras Path some fifty miles west of Aughwick Creek. Virginians also spoke of the "outsettlers beyond the Endless mountains," who were part of the southward migration of Germans and Irish from Pennsylvania that had produced homesteads along the Greenbriar River by 1745. Though few and still far from the Ohio River, they nevertheless represented an unauthorized intrusion onto native hunting grounds and reflected a process that Delawares, Shawnees, and some Iroquois understood all too well.[5]

Some Ohio Indians responded to the new threat introduced by Gist and the Virginians with verbal protests and requests that provincial governments exercise some control over their border settlers. Others made known their distaste for particular colonists by telling George Croghan that they did "nott Like to hear of there Lands being Setled over Allegany Mountain, and in particular by the Virginians." For still others, the threat of a new wave of settlements stirred up bitter memories of earlier frauds and dispossession. One Delaware headman, Nemacolin, told Gist that his father, Chickoconnecon, had been given title to his land by Pennsylvania officials only to see it appropriated by settlers. Nemacolin urged Gist to write to the king and ask him to order the colony to restore the land or render payment. Nemacolin's assumptions about power within the British world proved as ill founded as his trust in Gist, who wrote down the complaint only "to please the Indian." Most of the region's people, however, must have felt as beleaguered as the "Great Men" of the Delawares—Tamaqua and Oppamylucah—who "desired to know where the Indians' Land lay, for that the French claimed all the Land on one Side the River Ohio and the English on the other Side." It was a question Gist was unable to answer, but one that would quickly dominate the Ohio Indians' relations with Canadians and Anglo-Americans alike.[6]

Not only did the Ohio Company spark fear of a colonial invasion of the Ohio Country, it also complicated the Iroquois-Pennsylvania alliance by posing a direct challenge to Pennsylvania's influence in the region. Originally Virginia had been content with a modest role in the west, contributing £200 to the presents Weiser distributed at Logg's Town and accepting a decidedly subordinate place in the alliance system. A royal charter to western lands soon demanded a more independent, aggressive undertaking, however. In the meantime, as the Company opened its own trade along the Ohio, it confronted the entrenched interest of Pennsylvanians who, until 1749, enjoyed a virtual monopoly within the region. For their part, Pennsylvania's great men quickly saw the Ohio Company as a strategic and economic, as well as territorial, threat in a region whose colonial proprietorship was unclear. To the extent that Virginians and Pennsylvanians shared one goal—British hegemony over the middle west—their interests did coincide, especially as the threat of French retaliation grew. Weiser, for example, promoted the interests of both colonies in his shuttle diplomacy between Philadelphia, Albany, and the Six Nations. Yet animosity and friction most often prevailed. Richard Peters lashed out at "that vile fellow Cressup [sic]" who, he believed, had first broached the idea of Virginia trading posts in the west. The provincial secretary also assiduously kept his London-based proprietors informed of every detail of the Company's activities, hoping that Thomas Penn could nullify the Virginians' efforts by direct application to the home government. Meanwhile, George Croghan worried about the adverse impact the Virginians would have on trade, while Weiser, who knew better than most the damage such a move could cause to Indian relations, nonetheless suggested that Pennsylvania plant settlements along the Juniata River to secure the colony's western trade.[7]

The Virginians were no less eager to cast aspersions. Thomas Lee, the Ohio Company's principal correspondent with Pennsylvanians, complained that the latter's traders, whom Lee referred to as "rascally fellows," were spreading wild rumors about Virginia forts in the west designed to "bridle" the natives, and that the Company also planned to set the Catawbas on the Ohio Indians. And Thomas Cresap, the object of Richard Peters's wrath, put it mildly when he later observed that Pennyslvania's Indian agents and traders were "disaffected to us."[8]

This intercolonial squabbling could not have generated much confidence among the Ohio Indians. Just when French enemies seemed prepared to act with decisiveness, Pennsylvanians and Virginians seemed capable of doing very little. At the same time, rumors of forts, Catawbas, and conflicts between traders from colonies the natives viewed as symbolically bound together must have raised doubts in the minds of many natives about their British alliance while strengthening the hand of those who, from the beginning, had questioned Tanaghrisson's leadership and initiative. An alliance that was to secure the Ohio Country for its people and provide a bulwark against the French was already beginning to weaken as the colonial end of the chain of friendship showed signs of wear and stress.

Ohio Indians who took stock of their condition in 1750 and 1751 thus found little comfort or satisfaction. A French military expedition had been met by internecine squabbling on the part of colonial allies. At the same time, from Quebec, Pennsylvania, and Virginia came disturbing signs that native sovereignty was being challenged by colonists who barely hid their desire to possess the Ohio Country. To an extent that became alarmingly clear over the next three years, the region was being transformed from a haven for migrating societies into a center of conflict that placed the natives in the midst of the very turmoil they had sought to escape.

That transformation continued as natives and colonists met once again at Logg's Town in May 1751. It was an impressive gathering. A "great number" of Ohio Indians convened, including a delegation from Kuskuski led by Conagaresa as well as Iroquois from the "Head of Ohio"—the villages on the upper Allegheny River. Though there may have been some second thoughts by Shawnees and Delawares with regard to the alliance, the headmen and warriors met to hear a message from Pennsylvania's governor, delivered by Croghan and Andrew Montour. The local Iroquois continued to be the principal actors, and Tanaghrisson once again served as moderator. Croghan and Montour consulted at length with Tanaghrisson and others about the speeches to be delivered to the other nations; at the close of the council, the Iroquois leaders also "took great pains with [Croghan] in dividing [the present] amongst the other Nations that it might have its full force with them." Yet even among the Iroquois, evidence of a possible rift could be seen in the arrival of Philippe-Thomas Chabert de Joncaire, who had wintered among his adoptive Seneca kinfolk on the upper Allegheny and was escorted to Logg's Town by forty Iroquois warriors.[9]

Croghan, on behalf of his governor, urged the natives to remain true to the alliance and to resist the French and their increasing attacks on British traders in the disputed land south of the Ohio River. Joncaire responded by calling on the natives to drive out the British. In neither case was the message especially new or striking; what was different was the tone of Tanaghrisson's reply. Speaking "very quick and sharp with the Air of a Warrior," he startled Joncaire by reminding him that the land belonged to the Indians and "stamping on the Ground and putting his Finger to John Coeur's [Joncaire's] Nose," Tanaghrisson demanded to know by what right "has Onontio to our Lands" and unceremoniously ordered the Canadian to leave.[10]

The force of Tanaghrisson's direct, almost imperious, speech might be seen as grandstanding for the Pennsylvanians. Yet he made the clearest statement yet of the Ohio Iroquois' growing concern over their, and their neighbors', autonomy. Furthermore, when Croghan pressed them for a reply to an invitation by Virginia to meet at Winchester to discuss that colony's plans for forts in the Ohio Country, the Iroquois quickly set these newcomers straight about the region's power structure: they insisted that the proper meeting place was Logg's Town and told the Virginians that "*we expect* you will send our Father's [Dinwiddie's] Speeches to us here." Taken together, the brief but dramatic exchange conveyed one message: the Indians were determined to live unfettered by any colonial power, French or British.[11]

The Logg's Town meeting also marked the end of Pennsylvania's role in the west. Croghan returned to Philadelphia with a message from the Iroquois purportedly asking that a "strong House" be built "on the River Ohio." Governor Hamilton quickly informed the Assembly that the Indians, "so apprehensive of the Consequences of their refusing . . . the French Demands," wanted a British post in their midst. To the governor, as well as to like-minded expansionists, such a request was both timely and advantageous: it would strenghten the colony's ties with the Ohio Iroquois, and of greater importance, a fort would secure Pennsylvania's territorial claims in the west against both Canadians and Virginians. However, the Quaker-dominated Assembly saw darker implications and investigated the request. Having little reason to expect the truth from Croghan, they questioned Andrew Montour instead. Montour revealed what the Assembly doubtless suspected: that the Iroquois had not freely asked for the fort but were reluctant to make any such commitment, and that Croghan's version was of his own devising. Montour thus stood against his mentor Croghan and some of the colony's most powerful men. His kinship ties to the Ohio Iroquois and the trust they placed in him as an interpreter make it unlikely that his testimony was fabricated, though Montour may well have expressed the desires of only one Iroquois faction and may have personally welcomed colonial intervention. Furthermore, Tanaghrisson's oration at Logg's Town on behalf of the Iroquois makes it unlikely that he would have willingly embraced such a scheme, one that would have invited French retaliation.[12]

In the end Quaker principles outweighed the ambition of Croghan and other expansionists. The Assembly refused to vote funds for forts or any other projects that implied direct or indirect military involvement in the Ohio Country. Hamilton conceded as much but wondered whether the proprietor could obtain the needed funds from the home government. Any such hopes were shattered, however, when an exasperated Thomas Penn, in no need of new troubles from an already disputatious Assembly, directed the governor to suspend contact with the Ohio Iroquois "on any other foot than through the Council at Onondaga." With that Pennsylvania was, for the moment, removed from Ohio affairs, leaving the field to ambitious Virginians who quickly began to exploit native uneasiness and Tanaghrisson's growing vulnerability to exact further concessions for the Ohio Company.[13]

The Company, fully supported by Governor Dinwiddie, wasted little time securing a foothold in the west. With their suggestion that negotiations be held in the colony rebuffed, the Virginians once again sent delegates across the mountains to Logg's Town with the twofold purpose of clearing native title to the lands the Company claimed and obtaining permission to build their own "strong house" as proof of possession. It was a meeting that would prove the undoing of both Tanaghrisson and the Ohio Iroquois.[14]

The 1752 Logg's Town treaty council began inauspiciously and continued to be clouded by suspicion and a growing sense of impending crisis. The inept preliminaries by Colonel James Patton, a member of the colony's delegation, angered the Ohio Iroquois, who found his request for a council more in the manner of a threat and were so "generally affronted" that they paid little regard to Patton or his message. The result was that when the Virginians did appear near Logg's Town they were not met with the customary ceremonies "at the wood's edge," since the natives were never certain of the party's route or itinerary. Initial breaches of protocol were followed by delays that angered two principal Shawnee headmen, Big Hominy and Tamany Buck, who were on the verge of leaving when the Virginians—as the people who had called the meeting—addressed the gathering.[15]

From its beginning the Logg's Town treaty council was marked by Virginian duplicity and by considerable confusion on the part of the Ohio Iroquois as to the exact nature of the land claims in question. When presented with the Virginians' version of the 1744 Lancaster Treaty, Tanaghrisson and other Iroquois balked at endorsing such a sweeping—perhaps specious—interpretation, since they understood the Six Nations to have ceded land only to the "warriors' road at the foot of the Allegheny mountain." Temporarily stopped on this point, Patton and company tried a different approach, telling the natives that the gifts Weiser give them in 1748 had really been sent by the king as payment for the 1744 cession as defined by the colonists. To this Tanaghrisson replied by condemning Weiser as a liar and by returning the 1748 council wampum, thus demonstrating his belief in Weiser's duplicity. Having thus weakened the natives' faith in the Pennsylvanians, the Virginians pressed ahead and urged the local Iroquois to accept the Lancaster land cession and agree to a provincial fort in the Ohio Country. Much to the frustration of Ohio Company agents, Tanaghrisson continued to defer making a decision. Instead, the Seneca told them that while his people were willing to "confirm anything our council [at Onondaga] has done," they nevertheless "understood . . . that the lands then sold were to extend no further to the sunsetting than the hill on the other [east] side of Allagany hill," and therefore they could not respond further on the matter.[16]

The Iroquois did change their position in one important way: they asked the Virginians for a "strong house" well supplied with powder and shot. Even so, however, the natives made it clear that they were giving up ground only "sufficient for the fort to stand on" rather than agreeing to a territorial cession. Anticipating the Virginians' next move, Tanaghrisson added further that "*we* will take care that there shall be no scarcity [of provisions]"—the colony would not need fields and grazing lands. Yet within days of these remarks, Tanaghrisson and his followers among the Iroquois did capitulate to the Company's larger demands. Unable to move the issue in open council, the Virginians, "having drawn up an instrument of writing confirming the deed made at Lancaster," ordered their interpreter, Andrew Montour, to privately "urge the necessity of [signing] such a settlement and the great advantage it would be to them as to their trade and security." Under such pressure Tanaghrisson caved in and signed, giving the Virginians the necessary legal basis for their claims in the west. No one, however, bothered to take the measure of non-Iroquois observers at the treaty, natives who from long experience held a more jaundiced view of "instruments of writing."[17]

What additional pressure Montour brought to bear on Tanaghrisson is unclear, but by 1752 the headman's position clearly depended on the goodwill and largess of his colonial allies. Tanaghrisson was undoubtedly feeling increasingly beleaguered in the weeks and months preceding the Logg's Town Treaty; the French were stepping up their raids against British traders, and rumors were abroad that the western anchor of the anti-French coalition—La Demoiselle's Piankashaws—were themselves a French target. It is possible that, in the wake of their conference with George Croghan and the heated exchange with Joncaire, a growing number of Iroquois and the heretofore silent partners in the alliance, Delawares and Shawnees, were beginning to question both French and British intentions and the wisdom of a partisan alliance with the British. Such undercurrents would have placed Tanaghrisson in a most awkward and trying position, having to please colonial allies whose support was vital while confronting the growing

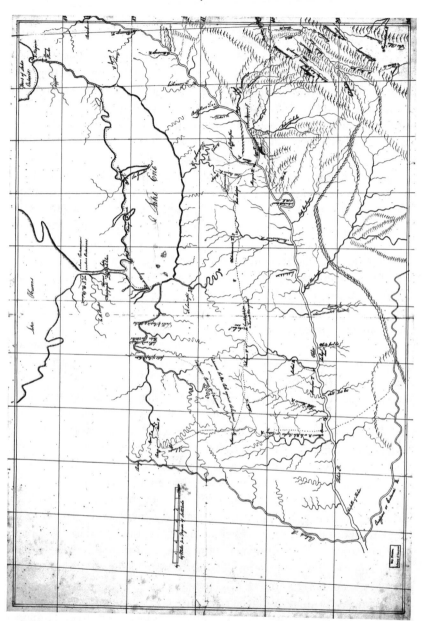

5. John Patten's 1752 map of the Ohio Country. (Courtesy of the Library of Congress)

distrust of his own Iroquois and of those other natives who looked to him and his people for leadership and protection.

At the same time, however, Tanaghrisson's ultimate willingness to overcome his own misgivings and cooperate with the Ohio Company may have come from the realization that, had he proved uncooperative, the Virginians would have abandoned him in favor of direct negotiations with local Delawares and Shawnees. His fears were well founded. The previous year, Croghan had asked the scattered and largely autonomous Delaware villages to select a "king" with whom the colonies could conduct business. At the signing of the Logg's Town Treaty Tanaghrisson managed to forestall direct contact between Delawares and Virginians by staging a ceremony during which he "gave" the Delawares a "king," Shingas, thus continuing the fiction of Iroquois authority over other native societies. Though Tanaghrisson appears to have taken in the Ohio Company's agents, the act had little meaning for the Delawares. Shingas had legitimate claims to leadership that were independent of the Iroquois or Tanaghrisson. At the treaty council Tamaqua, already recognized as a "king" or village spokesman, stood proxy for his brother, and the whole ceremony only confirmed for the Assembly a choice already made by the Delawares.[18]

Shingas's emergence marked another step in the process of Delaware unification in the west. Moreover, it underscored the increasingly important role the western Delawares played in regional affairs. Their efforts to distance themselves from the Ohio Iroquois and chart their own course arose from misgivings over the direction that Iroquois-British relations were taking. As a result, Shingas's emergence as a Delaware headman may not have been coincidental. He later attempted to secure native hegemony in the Ohio Country and, having been rebuffed, took up arms to defend the region against British expansion during the Seven Years' War.

Although Tanaghrisson managed to maintain his credibility with the Virginians, the Logg's Town Treaty intensified rather than lessened Indians' concerns about their security. Even as Tanaghrisson agreed in principle to the 1744 land cession and reflected on what it meant to be between competing empires, his companion Scarouady warned the colonists that "we intend to keep our country clear of settlements."[19]

The Logg's Town meeting had hardly ended before the imperial vise began to tighten. On June 21, as William Trent left Logg's Town bound for Pickawillany on behalf of the Ohio Company, French and Indian raiders from Michilimackinac (Mackinac, Michigan), led by Charles Langlade, fell upon the Anglo-Piankashaw settlement, destroyed the town and the trading posts, and killed La Demoiselle. The raid sent shock waves through the

Ohio Country; on his return from Pickawillany with some of the survivors, Trent found Shawnees at the Lower Town badly divided, with one faction hoisting a French flag only to have others tear it down. At the same time Piankashaw survivors, including La Demoiselle's young son, remained defiant and, joined by local Iroquois and Delawares, called upon Tanaghrisson and the British to honor the 1748 alliance and help them retaliate against the Canadians.[20]

If Tanaghrisson and others anticipated decisive British countermeasures, they were soon disappointed. Instead the Pickawillany raid proved to be only a hint of the possible response to what the French viewed as a dangerous turn of affairs in the west. Within a year, Governor-General Duquesne dispatched a much larger expedition into the Ohio Country and snatched control of the region from Indians and British alike while delivering the death blow to the already tottering Iroquois-British alliance.

Céloron's expedition confirmed what many in Quebec already suspected about the state of western affairs, and it triggered intense discussion of how best to regain the strategic initiative. Debate was shaped by the facts of continued native hostility and by persistent British expansion into the vacuum created by the loss of French influence during the 1744–48 war. Moreover, colonial officials based their plans and views on two continuing assumptions: that the upper Ohio Valley was a vital link in a proposed chain of forts and settlements that would bind Canada and Louisiana, and that the new Iroquois-British alliance in the west was growing ever more powerful and, if left unchecked, would ultimately destroy communications to the south as well as open New France to piecemeal reduction. Given these facts and perceptions, the question was not whether to seize the initiative, but how. By autumn 1751, French officials on both sides of the Atlantic concluded that there was "in fact, no other course to adopt than to drive from the Beautiful River any European foreigners who will happen to be there."[21]

The most obvious—as well as obnoxious—targets were La Demoiselle and those Pennsylvania traders using Pickawillany as a base of operations. La Demoiselle's people had kept up incessant guerrilla warfare against the Canadians since 1747 while ignoring every effort to bring them back into the French political sphere. Moreover, from the point of view of officials at Quebec, the renegade Piankashaws' efforts to extend their British alliance westward, beyond the Miami River, made them a greater immediate threat than Tanaghrisson and the Iroquois at Logg's Town. Therefore the first steps were to shatter that alliance once and for all while rolling back the tide of British peddlers and Indian agents. Thus, in 1750 and 1751 efforts to seize the traders were increased as raiding parties scoured the countryside as far south as Kentucky. At the same time, plans were laid for an attack on Pickawillany. Finally, in the wake of Céloron's expedition, a number of Canadians were licensed to trade in the Ohio Country to keep French interests alive and to offset British influence.[22]

Nevertheless, French colonials enjoyed no more unity of purpose than did the native-British alliance they hoped to smash. The raid against Pickawillany had to be postponed for months because the Ottawas, Ojibwas, and Potawatomis from Detroit showed considerable reluctance to play their assigned roles. Whatever ties bound them to the French could not completely outweigh their unwillingness to trigger an interethnic war against a people who had already put the Canadians on the defensive. The attack finally took place only when young Charles Langlade rallied his Ojibwa kinfolk and their neighbors at Michilimackinac and led them south against La Demoiselle. Closer to home, and of greater concern to royal officials, was a division within the colony over larger strategic aims. Accepting that raids, while temporarily intimidating natives and British foes, would not in themselves redress the balance of power, by 1752 metropolitan officials were determined to occupy the Ohio Country and build forts as a barrier to further British expansion and as a way to overawe local Indians with the might of the French king. Strategically the plan appeared sound enough, yet most Canadian merchants and their allies opposed any campaign that would divert precious resources in an effort to seize and hold a commercially unprofitable region like the Ohio Valley. Indeed, much to the despair of royal officers like Intendent François Bigot, the Canadians even conceded prior British rights to the region and argued instead that the Crown's efforts should be directed toward repairing Indian relations in the lucrative "pays d'en haut" beyond Detroit. In the end, however, metropolitan needs outweighed local interests, and in spring 1753 the new governor-general of New France, Ange de Menneville, marquis Duquesne, issued the final orders that sent Captain Paul Marin de la Malgue and nearly two thousand Canadians and mission Indians into the Ohio Country.[23]

The Ohio Indians had ample warning of Marin's movements and destination. As small parties of Canadians moved slowly past Fort Oswego and across the Niagara portage, word spread through the Ohio Country; as early as March local traders were aware of French activities, though the first of Marin's forces did not appear until late April. Yet despite the warning the natives remained cautious, in sharp contrast to their reception of Céloron four years earlier. Ohio Indians neither abandoned their towns and fled nor took a confrontational stand as the Canadians appeared. Instead the natives' response was more measured—not out of fear, but because much had changed at home since Céloron's passing. Then, in the immediate aftermath of successful attacks on French traders and the expectation of retaliatory raids, the Ohio Indians were more unified. Further, Weiser's visit to Logg's Town, with his promise of British aid, was recent enough to provide assurance to those willing to follow Tanaghrisson and the Iroquois' lead.[24]

Now, however, the facade of British unity had given way to a cacophony of accusatory and contradictory voices. Despite the din, however, one message did come through: Virginians and Pennsylvanians were every bit as eager to possess the Ohio Country as were Marin's troops. At the same time, although the French had just shattered the western end of the Ohio alliance chain at Pickawillany, their demeanor toward Indians in the Ohio valley had thus far been nonthreatening. The appearance of native unity, on which Tanaghrisson had built an alliance and his own prestige, was also beginning to crumble as local natives found themselves besieged by both British and French colonists who, they feared, "were going to divide the Land between them." Yet the rapid turn of events demanded caution as well as a careful assessment of the intruders' intentions and strengths and some indication of how the British would respond.[25]

Tanaghrisson, Scarouady, and their Iroqouis followers were clearly taken aback by the French invasion and "seemed much concerned at the News." Tanaghrisson canceled a planned trip to Pennsylvania and instead tried to rally support among the Delawares and Shawnees by calling a council at Logg's Town. At that moment the French were still some distance away; Marin's vanguard was busy building Fort Presque Isle (Erie, Pennsylvania)], while the bulk of the army was struggling with the Niagara portage and poor management. In any event, the Delawares and Shawnees failed to respond to the summons, claiming their headmen were too drunk to attend. For the moment Tanaghrisson could do little more than send messages to his Pennsylvania allies "in behalf of the Six Nations Indians at Ohio," asking the colonists to back their repeated pledges of aid with more substantial shipments of powder and lead.[26]

Tanaghrisson's early failure to rally other natives at Logg's Town was an indication that many Delawares and Shawnees, as well as Iroquois, were determined to shape their own more cautious strategies. By midsummer, as most of Marin's troops were inching their way south from Presque Isle toward John Fraser's smithy at Venango (Franklin, Pennsylvania), local Delawares, Shawnees, and Senecas began to appear at the portage camps, where, according to Marin, "they are very zealously assisting with *their* horses . . . in making" the exhausting but vital portage between Presque Isle and the recently completed Fort Le Boeuf (Waterford, Pennsylvania) at the head of French Creek. Noticeable among these native porters were Munsees from Custaloga's town near Venango. The presence of French troops clearly stirred debate within this town: William Trent reported that "the Delawares had chiefly left Venango, *one part of them* was gone to help the French." That faction, led by Custaloga, continued to chart its own independent course for years to come, one that often irritated other natives and the British alike. On this particular occasion Custaloga's people continued to portage and hunt for the French even after a warning from Tanaghrisson.[27]

Although it would be easy to assume that these natives acted out of fear, more calculated motives appear to have been at work. Marin was clearly delighted that the Indians brought their own horses; his own few draft animals were already giving out, and the natives easily observed both the captain's lack of progress and the scattered condition of his forces, stretching as they did from Venango back to Fort Niagara. Had they cared to, Custaloga's people could have brought the French advance to a standstill; indeed, it was already slowing as more and more men succumbed to heat, overwork, and short rations and as junior officers verged on mutiny. That the Indians chose otherwise shows that they had other purposes in mind, best met through accommodation. As British traders rapidly abandoned the upper Ohio Valley, the Delawares and others needed to establish economic ties to the French to ensure a supply of needed goods, especially with the autumn hunt approaching. This became clear when natives began demanding payment in advance for trips across the Presque Isle portage. Moreover, gunsmith John Fraser's establishment at Venango was now a French outpost, and the technological difficulties arising from Fraser's departure also made accommodation a prudent policy. Finally, aside from the Venango natives' penchant for independent action, the French supply trains were simply too tempting to ignore. By working on the portage, natives could pilfer with impunity, as did those Delawares who "set off with full Loads, but never delivered them to the French, which incensed them very much, being not only a Loss, but a great Disappointment."[28]

Not all Ohio Indians followed Custaloga's example, however. The Delaware "king" Shingas kept his distance, adopting a cautious approach to the invaders, one that neither British agents nor Tanaghrisson appreciated. Other Delawares, particularly Tamaqua, relied on long-standing reciprocal relations with the Iroquois, expecting the latter to take the initiative. Tamaqua represented yet another group within Delaware society, one that wished to uphold their people's respected position as "women": people who mediated disputes in return for protection from the Iroquois. The Shawnees likewise reflected the divisions appearing within neighboring societies, as well as the deliberately cautious approach being taken by most. Though in 1752 Shawnees at the Lower Town were prepared to retaliate against the French for their raid on Pickawillany, Canadian officers the following year could assure Marin that "the Cha8enons are not making much noise" and were not eager to endorse Tanaghrisson's actions. Some hostility remained, however, as the Scioto River villages continued to express antipathy toward the French while those Shawnees at Logg's Town took a less hostile position.[29]

Although the Ohio Indians' responses to the French invasion were restrained and diverse, tensions remained that fed suspicions of French goals while reinforcing the localized nature of native responses. Marin's Indian agent, Joncaire, conceded in early September, five months after the troops first arrived, that "all the Indians are murmuring a great deal about Onontio's [the French governor's] undertaking." The sources of the discontent were not hard to identify. By early autumn the French had completed a chain of posts from Presque Isle to Venango and made no secret of the fact that they would continue down to the Ohio in the spring. The significance of the forts was not lost on the Ohio Indians, who only a year earlier had bridled at similar plans advanced by the Virginians. Though the French invasion of the Ohio Country has usually been defined with reference to the British, by the autumn of 1753 the Ohio Iroquois and their neighbors were feeling the immediacy of that invasion far more than Virginians or Pennsylvanians, while the French forts confirmed suspicions that the European contenders would indeed divide the land between them.[30]

Moreover, Marin's army brought with it another unsettling element in the form of Ottawa and Caughnawaga (mission Iroquois) auxiliaries whom the Ohio Indians viewed as intruders. These northern Indians, as much as the Canadians themselves, added an unpredictable, potentially dangerous element to the invasion. Though Shingas's Delawares discounted the potential for conflict with Ottawa hunters, asking, "What need they care, had not the French sent them Wampum and it was all white," symbols of peace did not prevent a party of Caughnawagas from killing other Delawares. Such behavior, whether deliberate or accidental, embarrassed the French and further strained relations with local natives, whose country seemed fairly overrun with Caughnawagas, Ottawas, Potawatomis, and Ojibwas—including, perhaps, warriors who had destroyed Pickawillany.[31]

In the midst of the turmoil generated by Marin's appearance, Tanaghrisson attempted to regain the initiative. His role as principal spokesman for the Ohio Iroquois demanded some action designed to assert local Iroquois authority over the region while fulfilling his obligations to those other natives who looked to his people for guidance and protection. Therefore, between July and September Tanaghrisson personally, or through Scarouady, issued the Iroquois' traditional three warnings to the French to depart the region or face retaliation. The strategy was a bold one, especially since it revealed how much Tanaghrisson's own influence, and that of his followers, had declined since the ill-fated Logg's Town Treaty. The first two warnings were unproductive, owing in large measure to the Canadians' unwillingness to consider Tanaghrisson's speeches. Nonetheless Tanaghrisson persisted, a man now caught "between" expectant allies and defiant foes, the latter having already fixed their own council fire at Venango as a direct challenge to the Iroquois at Logg's Town.[32]

Having been twice rebuffed, which added little to his prestige, Tanaghrisson sought to rally British support while making a final effort to reason with Marin. As Tanaghrisson went to the French captain again, in late August Scarouady, accompanied by a number of Delawares, Shawnees, and Piankashaw headmen, left on a journey that carried them to Winchester and Carlisle. By the time Scarouady's party reached Carlisle for a meeting with Pennsylvanians, Tanaghrisson's mission had already failed.

Challenging the French king's title to the Ohio Country and the captain's plans to build more forts, the Seneca reminded Marin that "the river where we are belongs to us warriors," adding that "the chiefs who look after public affairs [i.e., the Onondaga council] are not its masters. It is a good road for warriors and not for their chiefs." Tanaghrisson's speech reflected not only the local Iroquois' own claims to the land, but also the increasing distance between them and the Six Nations. Unimpressed by such claims or by Tanaghrisson's reputed authority, however, Marin rejected the final warning, refusing even to touch the accompanying wampum. Instead he sent Tanaghrisson packing, convinced that "he has little repute among the nations," a conviction borne out when the French observed that local natives made no effort to second Tanaghrisson's remarks. The headman left the meeting broken and bitter; observers reported that he returned to Logg's Town shedding tears of frustration. His final attempt to assert authority had failed, and even his British allies were forced to concede that "this Chief who went like a Lyon roaring out destruction, came back like a Lamb."[33]

Scarouady's reception in Virginia and Pennsylvania was more cordial, but no more productive. The delegation consisted of a number of influential men, including Shingas, Tamaqua, Delaware George, and Pisquetomen for the Delawares and Nucheconner and Tamany Buck representing the Shaw-nees. Most of the these men had been, and would continue to be, active in try-ing to balance competing European forces in the west as the best way to pre-serve their own autonomy, a task they once more attempted in autumn 1753. By urging their colonial allies to assert themselves in the region, the natives hoped that the French and British might check each other. This version of the "play-off system" long associated with the Six Nations was a dangerous venture for people already being squeezed by land-hungry Virginians on one side and French armies on the other. At the same time, Scarouady carried the same message Tanaghrisson had delivered to the French: the Ohio Country ultimately belonged to its native inhabitants. Assistance would be wel-comed—but on Indian, not colonial, terms. Neither the Pennsylvanians nor the Virginians provided much encouragement, however. At both meetings the natives were urged to unite and maintain their contacts with the colonies; other requests were to be taken under advisement.[34]

Though urged to unite and speak to the French with one voice, Sca-rouady's embassy showed how deeply the Ohio Indians were divided. Although his companions were "some of the most considerable Persons" among the Ohio Indians, Scarouady was careful to emphasize that "all we who are here" were speaking with one mind; those who were not present or represented, including Conagaresa's Iroquois and Custaloga, had chosen a different course. And though Scarouady remained the spokesman for the assembled natives, it was nonetheless clear that what remained of the Ohio Iroquois' alliance was fast crumbling from within as groups that had for-merly accepted subordinate roles in return for Iroquois guidance began to distance themselves from a diplomatic process that now threatened the very security the alliance had once promised to maintain.[35]

Tanaghrisson's bold assertion that the Ohio Country belonged to the war-riors living there and was of no concern to the distant Six Nations would not have been well received by the Confederacy headmen whose authority he denied. Marin's invasion had not gone unnoticed in Iroquoia. Since the 1748 Logg's Town Treaty the Onondaga council had insisted that the Ohio Country belonged to the Confederacy and was not the exclusive preserve of those the Six Nations condescendingly styled "young and giddy Men and Children . . . childish People," who were in fact dangerous upstarts whose independence posed a direct challenge to the Six Nations' claims over the Ohio Country. Yet the French invasion revealed the same divisions and caution within the Confederacy as had appeared in the west. The concerns in each case seem to have been much the same, for the Six Nations were well aware that they too lived between two powerful and unpredictable colonial empires and that any new round of fighting would almost certainly take its toll on the Iroquois. Therefore, as French troops entered the Allegheny Valley, Confederacy headmen anxiously sought to maintain their neutrality while trying to keep the Ohio Country from becoming the next Anglo-French battleground. To the Pennsylvanians they emphasized that the Six Nations "love the English and . . . love the French," while urging both to "make up your Matters among Yourselves" away from the Ohio Country. At the same time, the Confederacy sent warnings of its own to the Ohio Iroquois "of the Preparations the French are making to attack them."[36]

None of the Six Nations went beyond such verbal responses, however. Though the Canadians were clearly worried about how easily the Iroquois could destroy their expedition at the vulnerable Niagara portage, no attack ever materialized. Instead the Senecas, through whose territory Marin passed, responded only by sending several matrons to the army to determine whether Marin "was marching with the hatchet uplifted" or came in peace. Having been reassured that they were not in harm's way, the Senecas agreed that they "would not meddle with" the army but "would look quietly on, from their mats." Marin also learned that the Senecas had rejected British efforts to enlist their aid against the army.[37]

The Six Nations' cautious response to the French, and the seeming contradiction between their claims to the Ohio Country and their timid actions, grew from suspicions and factionalism similar to those present among the Ohio Indians. British colonists who found the Six Nations' indecision a threat to their own western designs were initially at a loss to understand. But as Conrad Weiser learned, divisions within the Confederacy made a consensus on the Ohio Country impossible. When, for example, William Johnson sent a message through Iroquoia to the Ohio Iroquois urging them to resist Marin's advance, the "Senecas stopped it, and sent their own Message," one that counseled noninterference and coincided with the Senecas' own decision not to oppose the French.[38]

One reason for the internal dissension became clear in an exchange between Johnson, New York's premier Indian agent, and Six Nations headmen at Onondaga in September 1753. When asked if they had allowed the French to enter the Ohio Country, the Iroquois denied any such decision but shot back that "we don't know what you Christians *French and English together* intend." Their principal concern became clear when they pointed out that "we are so hemmed in by both, that we have hardly a Hunting place left," so much so that "if we find a Bear in a Tree, there will immediately appear an Owner for the Land to Challenge the Property, and hinder us from killing it."[39]

To make matters worse, the Six Nations' relationship with New York, the senior British partner in the Covenant Chain, was at an all-time low. Angered by the Yorkers' facile policy of exploiting Iroquois manpower in time of war while ignoring the Confederacy in peacetime, Mohawks angrily stormed out of a council at Albany in June 1753, declaring the Chain broken. For the colony's oldest and most loyal Iroquois allies to make such a declaration shocked British officials on both sides of the Atlantic and jolted an already divided Confederacy. By the time Marin's troops dug in for the winter, the Six Nations were internally riven and at odds with their own British allies. Little wonder, then, that in response to their renewed pleas for assistance the Ohio Iroquois and their neighbors received from the Six Nations only admonitions to "do nothing . . . but keep fast hold of the Chain of Friendship," whose links were rapidly rusting away. At the same time, it was easy for British colonists to question once again Six Nations influence along the vulnerable western border; as Pennsylvania's Governor Hamilton observed, the Confederacy's insistence that it alone controlled the Ohio Country amounted to little "from a People who are not at present in a Condition to defend themselves."[40]

The Six Nations' response was not what the Ohio Indians might have hoped for. And if Tanaghrisson and others anticipated strong British countermeasures in the wake of the French invasion, they were to be disappointed again. Instead, colonial assistance came in the form of the young Virginia aristocrat George Washington, first as a messenger to the French at Fort Le Boeuf, later as head of the Virginia "army" assigned the task of clearing the invaders from the Ohio Country. In both instances Washington failed, however, and his actions in the region helped bring down the curtain on the Ohio Iroquois alliance.

Washington's journey to Fort Le Boeuf in November and December 1753 revealed how a once promising Indian alliance had been shattered. Charged with delivering governor Dinwiddie's demand that the French withdraw from territory owned by Great Britain and Virginia, Washington sought help from Tanaghrisson only to find him desperately trying to rally support for himself and his colonial allies. Although Tanaghrisson still enjoyed support from Shingas, Tamaqua, and Scarouady, that support was based largely on the assumption that the British would quickly help the natives regain control over their land. Though some Ohio Indians were now ready to acknowledge the need for British forts, they still harbored misgivings about colonial motives. Shortly after arriving at Logg's Town, Washington was asked by the Iroquois about the real purpose of his mission, a curiosity that caught the Virginian off guard but that suggests lingering native doubts about whether the colonists were coming to assist or to dispossess them.[41]

That uncertainty, plus the contrast between aggressive French actions and the limited British response, encouraged other Ohio natives to distance themselves still further from Tanaghrisson. Though he attempted to impress the naive Washington with his influence by "ordering" Shingas to accompany the party to Fort Le Boeuf and Custaloga to return French wampum in his care, in fact Tanaghrisson's instructions were ignored. Shingas and the Delawares pointedly refused to participate in what they surely saw as another futile gesture, while Custaloga continued to keep his distance from events in Logg's Town. Tanaghrisson's effort to rally other natives to Washington and present the French with a united front thus failed, and in the end only a few Iroquois accompanied the Virginian to the French commandant, Captain Jacques Legardeur Saint-Pierre, who politely rejected Dinwiddie's and Tanaghrisson's demands that he withdraw.[42]

Meanwhile other natives at Logg's Town provided shelter and protection to French officers, and the survivors of the Pickawillany raid had finally made their peace with the French. The failed embassy to Fort Le Boeuf further strained Indian-colonial relations when the impetuous Washington angered Tanaghrisson by not following the older man's advice on how to conduct his mission. In his first encounter with Indians, Washington found little to admire in his hosts and convinced himself that Tanaghrisson was neither reliable nor entirely trustworthy.[43]

Governor Dinwiddie's belated decision to send an armed force into the Ohio Country seems to have restored the confidence of those Indians who counted on colonial assistance against the French. Shortly after Washington left the region, William Trent, trader and now captain in the Virginia militia, arrived at the Forks of the Ohio to build a fort on land Washington had selected during his trip. Trent's sometime partner George Croghan reported that, with the militia's arrival, the local natives were "in high sperets" and prepared to rally to any force sent by the Virginians. At the same time, however, Croghan was forced to lavish particular attention on the Shawnees from Scioto, who were convinced that they were a likely target for French raiders and therefore reluctant to commit themselves.[44]

What comfort some Ohio Indians took from the Virginians' arrival was fast disappearing by April as improving weather led to a resumption of the French advance down the Ohio. On April 17 Washington, now a lieutenant colonel and at the head of reinforcements marching to the Ohio, learned that Tanaghrisson and others were "very angry at our delay" in reaching the

Forks of the Ohio. On the day Washington received the message, the French extended their control of the region by overpowering a detachment led by Ensign Edward Ward and staking out the perimeter of what would be their headquarters in the Ohio Country, Fort Duquesne.[45]

The delay that so upset the Ohio Iroquois—Washington's force did not reach the Great Meadows (near Uniontown, Pennsylvania) until May 24—was largely due to the poor planning of the expedition sent by Dinwiddie. Just two weeks before Ensign Ward surrendered his troops, Washington, as second in command of the Virginia forces, had raised only 131 men. The unimpressive turnout reflected Virginians' suspicion that the campaign was a public effort to protect a private speculative venture, despite what Washington and others did to convince their fellow citizens that the Ohio Company's claims and imperial fortunes were really the same. Supply and manpower problems continued to dog Washington all the way to the Ohio, and his "army" was ultimately composed of "those loose, Idle Persons that are quite destitute of House and Home," marginal men from Virginia's western counties whose better sort were all too glad to be rid of them, and men of doubtful martial spirit. Certainly men who "press greatly for Cloathing . . . without Shoes . . . Stockings . . . Shirts" cut poor figures for their own officers and for native allies who had already seen and respected French troops.[46]

Indeed, the Ohio Iroquois appear to have been unimpressed with Virginia's small, ill-equipped force. Their concern was enough to compel Washington to invent an army where none existed, telling Tanaghrisson that his own party was "a small part of our army," one that included "large artillery" besides ample stores of ammunition and food. Coming from someone whose judgment he already had reason to suspect, the story may have comforted Tanaghrisson less than Washington hoped. Other Indians were surprised to learn that the leader of so mighty a host was so ill prepared to conduct business that he lacked the necessary wampum and gifts to hold councils. At one point Washington started a rumor that the French wanted to kill Tanaghrisson, hoping this would spur the Iroquois to action. And though the initial skirmish between Washington's men and a Canadian party under Ensign Joseph Coulon de Villiers de Jumonville was a success, it further poisoned Iroquois-Virginia relations, since Washington once again chose to ignore the advice of his native allies. As a result, during the battle Tanaghrisson and his warriors went their own way, no longer willing to trust a man who, by Scarouady's account, not only refused sound tactical advice from men who knew the country and the enemy, but also could not control his own troops, which fired "in great confusion."[47]

Disgusted though they were by Washington's high-handed behavior, Tanaghrisson and his followers had little choice but to remain with the Virginians in the hope that together they could still loosen the French grip on the Ohio Country. Having participated in the destruction of Jumonville's party, Tanaghrisson's people could expect little save retaliation from the nearby garrison at Fort Duquesne. By early June Tanaghrisson, Aliquippa, and some eighty Iroquois had joined Washington's camp, while Scarouady, at Logg's Town, was preparing to abandon that settlement and lead the remaining members of Tanaghrisson's following to the Great Meadows camp. Tanaghrisson made one last effort to rally other Ohio Indians, sending French scalps taken from Jumonville's men "to all the Nations of Indians in union with them." Yet by early summer that union was largely a fiction. Though Delaware headmen Shingas, Tamaqua, and Delaware George still favored a bold British attempt to drive out the enemy, none of their people answered Tanaghrisson's call; both the Delawares and the Shawnees preferred to keep their distance, many sending their families east toward the Susquehanna River, out of harm's way. And though Tanahgrisson and Scarouady still enjoyed support among the Ohio Iroquois, meaningful help was slow to arrive. Suspicions about French and British plans persisted and continued to divide the Iroquois, as some incessantly demanded to know from Tanaghrisson and Washington the latter's *real* purpose in advancing to the Ohio. Ohio Indians seem to have placed little faith in either of the colonial rivals, and most chose to await the outcome of the summer's campaign while some avoided the impending confrontation by leaving the Ohio Country altogether.[48]

By the time Scarouady burned Logg's Town in late June, the Ohio Iroquois' alliance and Tanaghrisson's ambitions were a shambles. The ever faithful "half king" managed to keep a handful of Iroquois warriors together at the Great Meadows, but it was hardly the native host Washington had anticipated. And even here Tanaghrisson's abiding suspicion of the Virginian's leadership compelled him to draw his people out of the new, and doomed, Fort Necessity to their own camp some distance away. As Tanaghrisson had foreseen, Washington's motley force, now reinforced by regulars from South Carolina, was trapped and forced to surrender on July 4, ending the campaign and forcing Tanaghrisson and his followers among the Iroquois into exile at Croghan's trading post on Aughwick Creek (near Mount Union, Pennsylvania), where on October 4 their leader died. Before his death, however, Tanaghrisson issued one final bitter indictment of his colonial allies, accusing Washington of being a man of "no Experience" who "took upon him to Command the Indians as his Slaves" while "by no means tak[ing] advice from the Indians" who were so evidently concerned about the indefensibility of a fort Tanaghrisson called "that little thing upon the Meadow." It was a situation so galling that Tanaghrisson "had carried off his Wife and Children[,] so did other Indians before the Battle began, because Col. Washington would never listen to them."[49]

Allowing for wounded pride and the frustrations that had dogged Tanaghrisson over the previous two years, his words nonetheless suggest how far the Ohio Iroquois' alliance, predicated on an assumption of common interest with neighboring British colonists, had disintegrated. Indeed, much had happened during the seven years since the Ohio Iroquois had begun to knit together an intercultural alliance. Then as later, they and their neighbors had actively shaped their country's history. Trade relationships with Pennsylvanians, a growing sense of their own importance, and regional interests led the Iroquois to seek British allies, to create a new center of power at Logg's Town, and to fashion their alliance into a force bent on maintaining their own autonomy in the face of rival colonies and the Six Nations. Through kinship ties, council experience, and perhaps links to Iroquoia, and by consciously allying himself with British colonials who were equally keen on expanding their influence in the west, Tanaghrisson had made himself a power broker in the Ohio Country.

Yet Tanaghrisson, the Ohio Iroquois, and the British approached their alliance with very different assumptions. The Indians' insistence that the land was theirs and their expectations of colonial help in maintaining that claim against the French after 1748 were met by provincials, especially Virginians, who gladly promoted the alliance and Tanaghrisson while using it to strengthen their own claims in the region. The one thing natives and colonists shared—a fear of French expansion—itself became a tool of British expansion and ultimately the Iroquois' undoing, as ambitious Virginians turned native fears into signatures on the Logg's Town Treaty. By the early 1750s the Ohio Iroquois and their neighbors found themselves having to assert their autonomy not only to distant Six Nations councils and French soldiers, but to their Pennsylvania and Virginia allies as those colonies attempted to extend their own imperial spheres westward. At the same time, by actively courting British aid against what they saw at the time as a more immediate French threat, Tanaghrisson and his followers guaranteed a French response that drove the Indians closer to the British; indeed, in Tanaghrisson's case his own influence by 1752 rested primarily on support from Virginia. Yet aid from outside the Ohio Country eventually cost Tanaghrisson and the Iroquois allies support from within the region. Delawares, Shawnees, and others who had initially deferred to the Iroquois distanced themselves from the Iroquois-British alliance and began to act for themselves. The choices available by 1753 were neither easy nor clear cut. For although Delaware and Shawnee leaders continued to encourage the British to help them regain control of their land, suspicions, rooted in long and often bitter experience, ran through native communities whose new homeland was rapidly being transformed into a battleground and whose autonomy and security were threatened.

Though they were clearly "very uneasy to see the backwardness of the English," which seemed to confirm French insistence that the British had no stomach for a fight, the natives who gathered at Aughwick in September 1754 continued to hope that their colonial neighbors could drive the French away and return the Ohio Country to its native inhabitants. Delawares and Shawnees joined Tanaghrisson and Scarouady in urging their allies to hold up their end of the compact. But circumstances had clearly changed. Tanaghrisson was in exile, Washington had fled the field, and Delaware, Iroquois, and Shawnee villagers lived in the shadow of French forts. Tamaqua best summarized the current situation when, at Aughwick, he noted that "things seem to take another Turn, and a high wind is rising." No one yet knew what that "high wind" would carry in its wake.[50]

six

A High Wind Rising

 On December 4, 1758, amid the ruins of Fort Duquesne, the Delaware "king" Tamaqua held a brief council with Colonel Henry Bouquet. The meeting was not unanticipated. Bouquet and some seven thousand men of General John Forbes's British army had been on the site since the French blew up and abandoned their principal Ohio Valley bastion on November 23. Tamaqua's Delawares and other Ohio Indians were fully aware of the army's mission and movements; some had attempted to stop Forbes's progress by attacking his supply base at Fort Ligonier in October and again just days before the French evacuation. In the meantime, Tamaqua and other Delaware leaders had negotiated at length with the general's emissary, Christian Frederick Post, and had agreed not to interfere with the army during its final drive to the Forks of the Ohio.[1]

Tamaqua's emergence as principal spokesman for this group is clouded, but his leading role in subsequent affairs was hardly coincidental. He had first come to the attention of Virginians several years earlier, first as a headman, then by standing proxy for Shingas at the Logg's Town Treaty. As a nephew of Allumapees, Tamaqua enjoyed the same legitimacy that evidently led to Shingas's being selected as "king" by the western Delawares in 1752. Yet other considerations may have played a greater part in Tamaqua's rising influence. Though Shingas led raids against the border settlements, Tamaqua consistently refrained from joining his brother. By remaining scrupulously above the conflict, Tamaqua could present himself to the British as a genuine man of peace, unstained by their countrymen's blood. Such a course seems to have had special appeal for Tamaqua, whose subsequent actions suggest a strong attachment to the ideals embodied in other natives' reference to the Delawares as "women," or peacekeepers. Tamaqua's growing influence among his own people is best revealed in that by 1758 he was being referred to by Delawares and British alike as "king"; by going to war Shingas had, in effect, abandoned the sachem's role for that of the warrior.[2]

The subsequent meeting between Tamaqua and Bouquet was significant less for any substantive results than for what their encounter symbolized. Over the ruins of the brief French occupation of their territory, local Indians confronted the armed might of another invader: not Washington's ragtag Virginia provincials but servants of the British government bent on centralizing and reshaping relations with natives throughout the middle west—natives who would soon be counted by Whitehall as residents of a greatly enlarged colonial empire. At the same time, power relations had changed within the Ohio Country. Where Tanaghrisson and his Iroquois followers had stood only four years earlier as partners of Virginians and Pennsylvanians, there now appeared Tamaqua, backed by a coalition of Delaware villagers, men and women far more cautious in their dealings with both French and British than their Iroquois neighbors had been.

As soldiers and sachems took each other's measure, each side faced new challenges created by their meeting. As they slowly destroyed France's new world empire, British armies presented their masters with a host of new possibilities and problems. From 1758 to 1762 meetings like the one at the Forks marked the entrance of soldiers, Indian agents, and traders into what had once been the "pays d'en haut." For British officials, however, the attempt to extend their sovereign's authority into newly acquired territory became a frustrating task of balancing conflicting colonial, native, and metropolitan interests along a cultural frontier that ultimately extended from the mountain fastness of the Cherokee towns in the southeast to Ojibwa fishing stations on western Lake Superior.

Although the British presence was new, for Indians familiar challenges remained. One European army had suddenly been replaced by another, but the goal of the region's natives stayed the same: to regain control of the Ohio Country while at the same time retaining the cultural and political autonomy they had gained by migrating into the region a generation earlier. Yet in one respect—one that neither Tamaqua nor anyone else could have anticipated—the challenge posed by the army and the imperial authority it represented was different, in magnitude if not in kind. Whereas the French had occupied the Ohio Country as a measure of military defense, and with only limited armed forces, British occupation would prove far more extensive. Royal authorities expected not only to impose their will and law in the west, but also to transform the region from alien territory into a province of an enlarged empire, a transformation in which the natives' role was anything but clearly defined. Moreover, the total collapse of New France by autumn 1760 meant that British efforts to occupy and govern the middle west would be free of the threat of French retaliation. Instead of dealing with the provincial authorities' haphazard efforts to control the Ohio Country, the natives now directly confronted an expanding imperial power as its armies arrived in the west.

In the weeks and months that followed Washington's surrender at the Great Meadows and Tanaghrisson's exile, many within the Ohio Country persisted in seeking a way to dislodge the French invaders. Foremost among these were the Delawares, led by Shingas and his brother Tamaqua. At George Croghan's post at Aughwick, amid a growing number of refugees from the Ohio Country, Tamaqua joined other Delaware and Shawnee headmen who tried to secure assistance from Pennsylvania while urging the Six Nations to help Ohio natives against the French aggressors. Reminding Conrad Weiser that they had followed the colony's advice "to be still and quiet," the Delawares and Shawnees now came hoping that their colonial neighbors would reciprocate by supporting them during the present crisis.[3]

Native expectations met with disappointment. In the aftermath of Washington's defeat, confusion, not purpose, gripped both the Aughwick camp and Philadelphia. Uncertain that any future campaign would be successful and not wishing to raise native expectations, Weiser was careful not to refer publicly to Virginia's plans to send another expedition to the west. Indeed, the provincial agent's best advice to his own people was to suggest that "large Belts" be sent to the Ohio, since, unlike powder and shot, "Wampum are cheap" and would, he hoped, be a suitable substitute for action.[4]

The Ohio Indians were unimpressed with such tokens and were, as Croghan reported, "very uneasy to see the backwardness of the English," an uneasiness that seems to have exacerbated growing tension within Delaware and Shawnee societies over the best course to take. Among the Delawares, suspicions and factionalism compelled Tamaqua to demand that the Pennsylvanians "take no Notice of any thing that will be said" contrary to his own words. Divisions within native ranks were made worse when the colony, through Weiser, told the Indians that their homes on the Ohio were viewed "as your hunting cabbin only"—not as permanent abodes. The implication that the colonists saw them as merely a transient population whose real homes lay elsewhere must have fueled the suspicions of natives

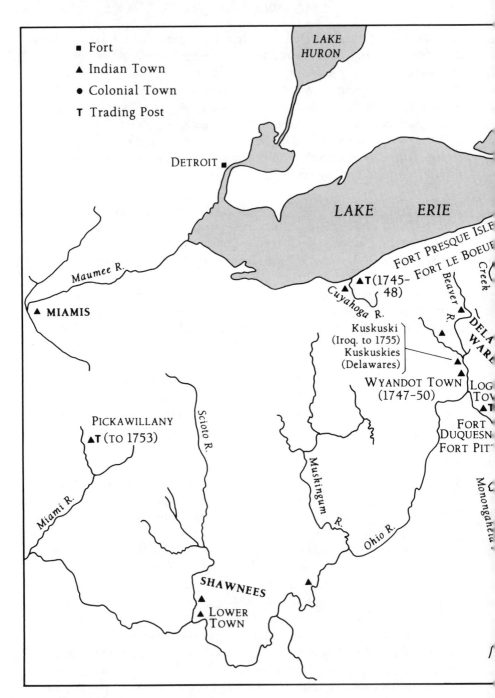

Map 4 The Ohio Country, 1747–1758.

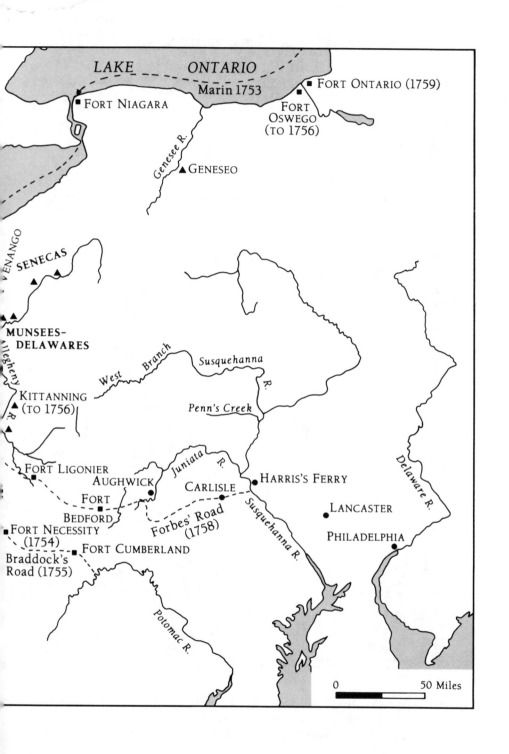

LAKE ONTARIO

Marin 1753

■ FORT NIAGARA

■ FORT ONTARIO (1759)

FORT
OSWEGO
(TO 1756)

Genesee R.

▲ GENESEO

VENANGO

SENECAS ▲

▲

MUNSEES-
DELAWARES

Alleghey R.

West Branch *Susquehanna*

R.

▲ KITTANNING
(TO 1756)

Penn's Creek

▲

Juniata R.

■ FORT LIGONIER

AUGHWICK ●

CARLISLE

● HARRIS'S FERRY

FORT
BEDFORD ■

*Forbes' Road
(1758)*

Susquehanna R.

● LANCASTER

Delaware R.

■ FORT NECESSITY
(1754)

■ FORT CUMBERLAND

PHILADELPHIA ●

Braddock's
Road (1755)

Potomac R.

0   50 Miles

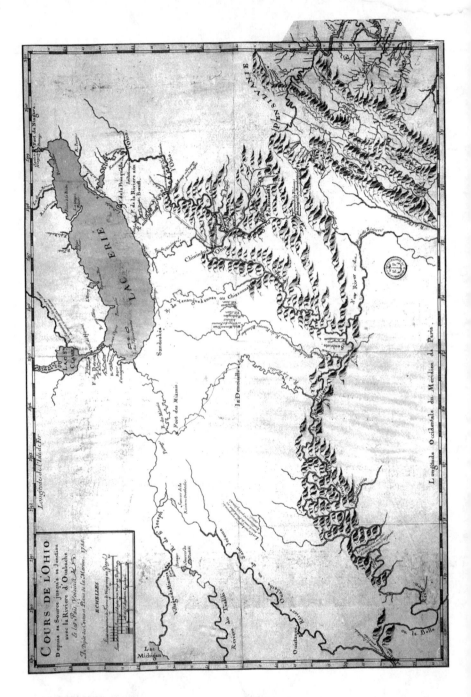

6. French map of the Ohio Country and the west based on Céloron de Blainville's 1749 expedition; it shows the chain of forts in the Ohio Country that was the culmination of the invasions of 1753 and 1754. [Jacques-Nicolas Bellin], "Cours de l'Ohio . . . 1755." The original is in Paris, Service Historique de la Marine, Recueil 67, No. 90; reproduced from a photographic copy in the National Archives of Canada.

who were coming to believe that all Europeans were equally a threat. Moreover, any expectation of leadership from their Six Nations "uncles" ended when the sudden death of Tanaghrisson plunged his followers into a squabble over his successor. Scarouady quickly emerged with the title "half king"—but he was a British agent without a following beyond the camp at Aughwick. Such confusion and lack of commitment weakened the already fragile bonds that held the Delawares and Shawnees to their Iroquois neighbors and Pennsylvania allies. Over the winter of 1754–55 factional divisions within the Ohio towns deepened, as Wyandot warriors sent message belts "underground" to avoid their being blocked by village headmen more inclined to accommodate to the French. Aside from Conrad Weiser and George Croghan, few colonials appreciated that the Ohio Indians viewed alliances as reciprocal in nature and were unwilling to risk themselves and their families without some tangible sign of support.[5]

Evidence of new British determination to confront the French arrived the following spring in the form of General Edward Braddock and two regiments from the Irish garrison. Braddock's arrival signaled a marked escalation of the Anglo-French conflict in North America: in place of intercolonial squabbling along distant frontiers, regular armies would now march to assert royal claims and to fix disputed boundaries. Indeed, the forces mustered at Alexandria, Virginia, represented only one of several ambitious British expeditions to be launched all along the arc of contested territory from Nova Scotia to the Ohio. Other armies would take Fort Niagara, seize control of the strategic Lake Champlain corridor, and remove French influence once and for all in the troublesome marchlands north of Halifax.[6]

For Ohio Indians still clinging to the hope that British forces would help them liberate their country, Braddock's arrival sparked renewed optimism. Meanwhile, provincial officials were lavish in their assurances to the Indians that Britain's primary aim was to "recover . . . what has been so unjustly taken from them [the natives] by the French." Yet such words were quickly followed by bitter disappointment. When Shingas approached Braddock with an offer of assistance in exchange for a pledge that the Ohio Country would be restored to the natives, the general's only response, albeit a candid one, was to assure Shingas that "No Savage Should Inherit the Land." Braddock's tactless statement cost him Delaware miliary aid, help that might have prevented the disaster that overwhelmed his army near Fort Duquesne. The general's words ultimately cost Pennsylvania, Virginia, and the Crown much more as lingering Indian doubts about British motives now seemed confirmed. This, and the failure of the Ohio campaign later that summer, forced many Ohio natives to reconsider whether the French with their forts or the British with their single-minded determination to grasp the Ohio Country presented the greater immediate threat. As the end of 1755 approached, many natives decided that British expansion was a far greater evil than French military occupation; by October Shingas and other Delawares joined Shawnees to, in the words of one informant, "proclaim war against the English" and, with the wholehearted support of local French garrisons, introduced Pennsylvanians for the first time to the violence of border warfare.[7]

The presence of French troops and their eagerness to offer material support no doubt made Indian attacks against colonial border settlements logistically possible. But, the native warriors who followed the paths leading east toward Fort Cumberland or Penn's Creek were not, nor did they view themselves as being, mere auxiliaries in a largely Anglo-French conflict. Shingas and others quickly recognized the necessity of establishing some rapport with the French, who could supply weapons and clothing for warriors as well as food and shelter for their families. Moreover, without Indian raiders the French could never hope to seriously threaten border settlements and divert British forces from other operations. What emerged was not a "French and Indian War" but a cooperative venture born of common need that allowed the natives to wage their own campaign against the threat of British expansion.[8]

The distinctiveness of the Indian-British war, one that eventually involved natives from the upper Susquehanna Valley, led by the eastern Delaware Teedyuscung, was underscored by the western Delawares' announcement that "We, the Delawares of Ohio, do proclaim War against the English." That declaration of war was based on a number of grievances that emerged from the natives' relations with their British neighbors. Even before Braddock's army met disaster on the Monongahela, Shawnees struck border settlers in the Carolinas. Their choice of targets was not a matter of chance. In 1753 several Shawnees had been jailed in Charleston for allegedly attacking settlers and Indians allied to South Carolina. This incident was only the latest in a series of collisions between peripatetic Shawnees and southern colonists, and Shawnee victims or their kin would have felt obliged to even the score. In much the same way, Ohio and Genesee Senecas carried the spreading border war into western Virginia. The immediate cause—the killing by border inhabitants of Senecas returning from a raid against the Catawbas—reflects the generations-old pattern of the "mourning war." Yet given the frequency of such violent episodes, stretching back over forty years, Senecas and other Ohio Country Indians similarly affected would have been only too happy to repay the Virginians with interest.

Delawares joined these attacks and offered another reason for their participation: the anger they felt at being blamed for Braddock's defeat by colonists who condemned them for abandoning the army.[9]

Yet beyond these more immediate concerns was the long-standing awareness that, given the opportunity, British colonists would possess themselves of as much Indian land as they could. Braddock's words only confirmed doubts that had surfaced earlier when Christopher Gist heard Delaware complaints about land frauds and found all his native hosts profoundly suspicious of inquiring strangers armed with compasses, maps, and paper. Moreover, Ohio Indians could look eastward to kinfolk living on the margins of a colonial society now fully in control of what had once been native land. It was an experience that few were willing to see repeated in the Ohio Country, whether they took the field or not. A generation of Delawares, Shawnees, and Iroquois had lived in the region, had grown to identify with it, and now acted according to regional interests, with less regard for kinfolk outside the Ohio Country. Thus westward-bound British soldiers and the Virginia surveyors and speculators who hoped to follow in their train were, to the natives, a serious threat, one the French quickly seized on to enlist Indian warriors. However, the natives' determination to keep the Ohio Country free of foreign armies and settlers extended to the Canadians as well; at the height of the war Pennsylvanians learned that "the Delaware Council is wholly for the Demolishing of the French Fort [Duquesne]." This desire to clear the region of European forces and political influence continued to shape the complex relations between Ohio Indians and the intruders for two decades after Braddock's defeat.[10]

Although they had numerous reasons for going to war, the Ohio Indians did not allow themselves to be stampeded into a new intercolonial conflict. Rather, they held back while the issue was debated in village councils. There was never complete consensus, though pressure from warriors appears to have mounted in the wake of Braddock's confrontation with Shingas. Rather than risk dividing their towns, village headmen bowed both to their warriors' demands and to custom and stood aside as their young men accepted war belts from the Caughnawagas and other French native allies. In the meantime those who did not support a war against the British, including Tamaqua and several Shawnees, patiently awaited an opportunity to restore peace.[11]

The Ohio Indians quickly followed their decision to fight with action. For three years following the first raid at Penn's Creek in October 1755, the once Peaceable Kingdom was a special target of Ohio Indian raiders. Added to the often vexatious demands placed on them by the imperial conflict, the colonists were faced with an Indian war that grew ever wider as upper Susquehanna Delawares and Shawnees, led by Teedyuscung, launched attacks against neighboring settlers who had heretofore enjoyed the fruits of the Walking Purchase and other fraudulent land deals. The last vestiges of William Penn's social experiment collapsed as colonists raised troops and mounted guard over a steadily retreating western frontier.[12]

Pennsylvania and its neighbors suffered both physically and psychologically from the border war. By spring 1758 Harris's Ferry and Carlisle represented the westernmost pockets of settlement in Pennsylvania: Cumberland Country was all but abandoned, its inhabitants now refugees in Lancaster and Philadelphia. Elsewhere small "private forts"—substantial houses surrounded by stockades—appeared, crowded with people who "geather in the greatest consternation" and fear of Indian raiders. To the south Winchester, at the northern end of the Shenandoah Valley, and Fort Cumberland on the upper Potomac stood alone, the small settlements beyond the Blue Ridge having been overrun or abandoned in the early raids. As the attacks continued, casualties and property losses mounted. Some four hundred captives from Virginia, Maryland, and Pennsylvania, later repatriated by the army, suggest the magnitude of the losses suffered. So complete was the devastation that the Canadian governor-general Pierre de Rigaud, marquis de Vaudreuil complained that raiders entering the Susquehanna Valley near Shamokin in mid-1757 found nothing to attack: the region contained only abandoned farms.[13]

Within months much of the Pennsylvania and Virginia border region had been transformed into a no-man's-land. Pennsylvania's governor Robert Hunter Morris spoke of "a vast Tract of Territory" laid waste by French and Indian raiders. Years later John Heckewelder, on his way to the new Moravian mission in the Ohio Country, passed through Carlisle and entered a "howling wilderness" where, in every direction, the "blackened ruins of houses and barns, and remnants of chimneys" confronted him. In Virginia's hard-hit Augusta County, Governor Dinwiddie confronted panic-stricken settlers who, unable to farm, demanded food from the government. Those who fled to larger, more secure, eastern towns and cities confronted hardships of another kind. Confusion, overcrowding, and filth became the hallmarks of wartime Lancaster and Philadelphia. And in the summer of 1757, smallpox appeared in both places, adding to the misery.[14]

The anxiety generated by this border war was reflected in a number of ways by colonists and their governments. For those under fire, exposed to death or captivity, fear turned to hatred that soon carried racial overtones. Although indiscriminate assaults on Indians were not new among border

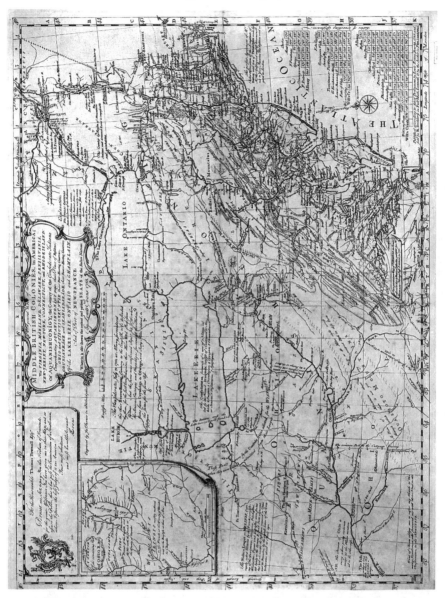

7. Lewis Evans's "A General Map of the Middle British Colonies in America" (1755), showing the location of principal Ohio Indian towns in the early 1750s. (Courtesy of the Library of Congress)

settlers—in Virginia they had been commonplace at least since Bacon's Rebellion—Indian hating began to infect Pennsylvanians for the first time by late 1755. In November of that year Conrad Weiser warned that survivors of early raids were demanding retaliation against Indians "without Distinction," an attitude that boded ill for the small number of natives still living in peace on the margins of colonial settlements. Far worse from the view of provincial officials was the equally infectious anger directed at eastern leaders as western farmers descended on the Assembly in 1755 demanding adequate defenses against the French and Ohio Indians.[15]

Responding to the public outcry, Pennsylvania's governor issued a formal declaration of war against his colony's Indian tormentors, an act that carefully excluded Indians living at peace within the colony but caught newly appointed royal Indian agents off guard and complicated their efforts to end the war through negotiation. More ominous was the scalp bounty appended to the declaration of war. In their efforts to encourage the reluctant to join hastily organized patrols and regiments, provincial politicians in Virginia and Maryland, as well as in Pennsylvania, offered cash bonuses for Indian scalps. The notion was not new or unique to these beleaguered colonies: bounties for Indians, dead or alive, had become increasingly common since the late seventeenth century, while General Braddock had offered a similar inducement to "any Soldier or follower" of his army. Appeals to hatred and self-interest did have their rewards. In 1758 Maryland's governor, Horatio Sharpe, was pleased to send General John Forbes fifty volunteers who had agreed to serve without pay in return for the privilege of keeping all the scalps they could take, trophies worth £50 apiece—many times a soldier's yearly wage.[16]

Yet the bounties carried with them practical problems that often threatened the very military operations they were designed to encourage. Virginia's newly arrived governor, Francis Fauquier, for example, discovered that his colony's bounty "was found to produce bad Consequences, by setting our people on to kill Indians whether Friends or Enemies," since, as many belatedly discovered, "It is impossible to distinguish the Nations of Indians." By late 1758 this fact led to the repeal of Virginia's bounty. In the meantime the damage had already been done as Cherokees and other nominal British allies fell victim to indiscriminate bounty hunters; this, in Fauquier's opinion, contributed to the Cherokee war that complicated British operations against Canada by diverting precious regular troops and supplies.[17]

Though they carried the war to their enemies, the Ohio Indians were no more immune to the costs of the struggle than were the settlers whose

homes and livelihoods the warriors ruined. In societies that did not dif-
ferentiate between young men who fought and stay-at-homes who fed and
maintained local communities, the growing participation of warriors in
border raids necessarily threatened the food supply at home. Both colonial
captives and British agents noticed that the natives had "neglected their
Corn planting" and experienced serious shortages. As the Anglo-French
campaign reached a climax in 1758, the situation deteriorated further;
British troops who appeared on the Ohio at the end of the year, for example,
discovered that many Delawares were nearly starving. Moreover, although
the French subsidized native war parties by feeding women and children,
the presence of large numbers of troops, French or British, and the building,
foraging, and off-duty hunting by soldiers may have contributed to the
problem by chasing away game. The natives continued to conduct autumn
and winter hunts, but they found success harder to come by as the war went
on.[18]

Living in close proximity to soldiers carried other risks far more severe
than occasional poor hunting or a decline in crop yields. By the autumn of
1757 smallpox again appeared in the west. The likely carriers were the
Ottawas, Ojibwas, and other Great Lakes Indians who had earlier taken part
in the siege of Fort William Henry. Canadian officers were alarmed at "the
great loss [the Indians] have suffered." Although there is no evidence of an
epidemic among the Ohio Indians, the western Senecas were affected, and
smaller, unreported outbreaks of the disease may have occurred elsewhere,
particularly in the small Scioto Valley towns where Ohio and Great Lakes
Indians often met to hunt, trade news, or recruit raiding parties.[19]

Casualties from disease or famine may not have been catastrophic among
Ohio Indians, but earlier losses from such killers, compounded by battle
losses, undoubtedly tore the social fabric of native societies. In this the
Indians shared a burden with their Anglo-American enemies. In the natives'
kin-based, oral societies, lost kinfolk threatened social continuity while
placing special obligations on survivors to replace the dead. This, and the
powerful emotions of grief and anger generated by death, fueled demands
for revenge. Thus, as time went on, raids across the mountains were driven
as much by the need to replace the dead with captives as by political or
strategic concerns.

For most of the war, however, the natives enjoyed immunity from the
brand of punishment they inflicted on their enemies. Scalp bounties and
martial ardor aside, the colonies were nearly incapable of mounting independent retaliatory raids and were relieved of the nightmare of the border
war only by Forbes's successful military and diplomatic campaign into the

Ohio Country. The singular exception was Colonel John Armstrong's destruction of Kittanning in September 1756. The Pennsylvanians' success,
which included killing their Delaware nemesis Captain Jacobs, stunned the
Indians.[20]

The Kittanning raid had a lasting affect on the Delawares. Kittanning and
other equally exposed towns east of the Allegheny River were quickly
abandoned in favor of more secure sites in the Beaver and Mahoning
valleys. Of greater significance was the gradual emergence, after the raid, of
a movement within Delaware society to open negotiations with the British.
The appearance of a group advocating peace reflected the continuing lack of
unanimity with Delaware towns and those of other Ohio Indians. By early
1757 Pennsylvanians had learned that many Delawares and Shawnees "who
have been hitherto Neuter" had left the Ohio Country altogether for the
upper Susquehanna Valley. Among the Senecas of the upper Allegheny
River, a lively debate ensued over whether the natives should resettle nearer
Fort Duquesne or remain in their villages. By the time of the Kittanning
raid, war and peace factions evidently had sometimes separated physically;
Kittanning held many of the raiders who made settlers' lives so miserable,
while the emerging peace group was located in the Beaver Valley at the
Kuskuskies towns. Similarly, anti-British Shawnees rallied at the Lower
Town on the Scioto River or at the site of Logg's Town, recently rebuilt by
the French for their native allies. Shawnees who opposed this moved east to
the Muskingum River or out of the Ohio Country.[21]

Negotiations toward ending the Ohio Indians' war with the colonies
began with Teedyuscung. Eager to conclude peace with their Indian neighbors, Pennsylvanians were attracted to Teedyuscung, who claimed to speak
for "ten nations" living in or near the Susquehanna Valley. At the same time,
Quaker politicians, inveterate enemies of their proprietors, were drawn by
the Delaware's apparent interest in exposing fraudulent land deals. At
preliminary discussions at Easton in 1756 and during a truce arranged the
following year at the same place, proprietary leaders and Teedyuscung were
able to agree on ways to end the Susquehanna Valley phase of the war. These
negotiations were watched with great interest by Ohio Indians, especially
the Delaware peace faction led by Shingas's brother Tamaqua.[22]

Contact between the western Delawares and the British resumed early in
1757 with a message from George Croghan, now deputy to the new royal
superintendent of Indian affairs, William Johnson. Croghan's first effort to
test Ohio Indians' receptivity to negotiations was received by Custaloga at
Venango and, according to one Delaware witness, the Indians "seem'd
desirous of Peace." Some may have been, but the natives' interest was

tempered with caution and skepticism. At the same time, Custaloga's powerful and experienced Seneca neighbors advised against making a reply. According to Garisages, a Seneca who knew Groghan, the message belts were "not proper Belts on this Occasion," not having "Men wrought in it for the several Tribes he [Croghan] wants to meet with (himself taking us by the Hand)," and "made of old [genuine] Council Wampum." War and peace were too important to rest on haphazard, garbled, or counterfeit messages.[23]

In the wake of the second Easton Treaty, another exchange between Ohio Indians and colonists took place. This time, however, the initiative came from the west when, in August 1757 "three Indian Men, and a boy" approached Teedyuscung with a message from Menatochyand (Delaware George) and Netawatwees (Netawatquelemond or Newcomer), "t[wo] of the Principal Men of the Ohio Indians." Eager to open contact with the natives, and doubtless encouraged by news that some of the Ohio Indians regretted the war, Pennsylvania's governor William Denny quickly responded through Teedyuscung. Though he could not have known it, Denny had made contact with the Delaware peace faction which, as early as that spring, had reached a consensus on negotiating with the British, one that awaited a favorable reply to their message. Indeed, Teedyuscung's son, who carried the governor's message west, found Menatochyand "waiting at Venango for a reply" that the future of the peace faction hinged on.[24]

This brief exchange bore fruit the following spring when Teedyuscung once again came to Denny, this time bearing calumets and council wampum from eight western nations who, according to Teedyuscung, had chosen him as their intermediary with the British. Teedyuscung, playing to the hilt his newfound role as Pennsylvania's favorite Indian, may not have held the expansive credentials he claimed. Whatever his precise relations with these western Indians, it is evident that the Delawares, at least, viewed him as a convenient messenger, someone the British listened to. One of the men who delivered the wampum and calumets to Teedyuscung was Gelapamund, Netawatwees's son. And the Delawares' absence from the list of eight western nations suggests that they preferred not to place themselves entirely in Teedyuscung's hands. At the same time, the leadership within the western Delaware faction continued to evolve and began to stabilize. Governor Denny's reply to the message Teedyuscung carried was received by Netawatwees, who thereupon carried it to Tamaqua, then living at the Kuskuskies (New Castle, Pennsylvania). By midsummer 1758 these men may have felt confident enough to dispense with additional mediation; from that point forward, they conducted direct negotiations with the British.[25]

The peace faction's success in maintaining contact with the British while expanding support at home rested in large measure on its members' persistence and skilled leadership in a divided society. Their ability to sustain peace negotiations that would embrace non-Delawares as well was also helped by growing Indian alienation from the French.

By the end of 1757 the marriage of convenience between western Indians and the French came close to divorce. Part of the problem arose from circumstances far removed from the Ohio Country or the Great Lakes: the British naval blockade of Canada that had reduced to a trickle the flow of supplies into the colony. The capture of Louisbourg in 1758 made the situation worse, and western garrisons were hard pressed to keep themselves supplied while providing the goods and services necessary to sustain the reciprocal relationship native alliances were built on.[26]

Growing native unrest took several forms. At the small outpost of Fort Rouillé (Toronto) "several drunken Mississaugas had threatened to destroy the fort," while Miamis began to express open contempt for French claims that they were driving back the British armies. The natives declared that "they were now resolved to turn the hatchet against" their onetime allies. Indeed, one French officer lamented that "great unrest [exists?] among the Indians of the Far West" and that relations with all the surrounding natives "are on the decline." The Ohio Country was no more tranquil than the pays d'en haut. Early in 1758 a Miami war party, refused food and liquor by a garrison on short rations, threatened to fire on Fort Duquesne, slaughtered some of the fort's livestock, and were themselves fired on by the troops. The commander's report suggests that such incidents were occurring with greater frequency. Earlier a Delaware told his British captors that many of his people would happily join British forces against Fort Duquesne, since "their Usage from the French is ready to make them strike." Moreover, General Forbes was pleased to learn that even the Shawnees were so "disobliged at the French" that they were "removing their wives and children" from Logg's Town up the Allegheny to the Senecas.[27]

The lack of supplies clearly contributed to the growing unrest. As French inventories dwindled so too did the ardor of native fighters, who found it increasingly difficult to fill powder horns and provide security for their families and who were in any event disinclined to fight for Frenchmen who could not reciprocate in customary ways for native assistance. At the same time, the war disrupted the normal channels of trade and diplomacy. Many Indians began to "complain for want of trade with the English," while others, including Indians in the Ohio Country, came to regret the French destruction of the New York emporium at Oswego. Moreover, warriors who were so often out hunting men had much less time to hunt game or clear new fields; the angry Miamis at Fort Duquesne may indeed have been in desperate straits, far from home in the dead of winter and faced with allies whose stinginess not only violated the Indians' concept of alliance but increased hardships as well. Compounding these problems were mounting casualties. On one occasion the Shawnees lost most of their war leaders in an accidental gunpowder explosion and had to "borrow" the Delaware Captain Pipe to lead them. Many western Indians may have had second thoughts about their role in the war, especially when they reflected, as did some Ohio Indians, "that so many of the Indians was killed, and so few of the French."[28]

For the Ohio Indians, disgruntled Shawnees and divided Delawares alike, these issues were compounded by yet another: the ongoing quest for regional autonomy. Those natives who had launched their war against the settlements did so to stem the tide of British expansion, deemed more immediately threatening than the French garrisons in their midst. Yet by 1758, as the captive Delawares suggested, the Indians were finding French "usage" as onerous as the threatened British occupation. The French seemed to have ignored the delicate and reciprocal nature of their relationship with the Ohio Indians while overlooking the fact that the natives had goals of their own that did not perfectly coincide with French claims to the region. Instead officers and Indian agents, according to returned British captives, "oblige their Indians to go to War . . . by threatening the Nations that Refuse with" retribution at the hands of other Indians. Such high-handedness, along with casualties, lack of necessities, and most of all the Ohio Indians' continued resolve not to be threatened by anyone, tipped the scales toward those who sought a solution that could rid the region of war and foreign armies while securing continued native autonomy.[29]

This continuing search for autonomy took an important turn in mid-1758 with the appearance in Philadelphia of Tamaqua's brother Pisquetomen, along with Keekyuscung. Their mission was to "see some of the Inhabitants . . . with whom we could speak . . . for we cannot believe all we hear, and know what is true and what is false." Specifically, they sought proof that the colonists were sincere in their desire for peace. In view of his army's impending march to the Ohio, General Forbes urged that nothing should stand in the way of peace with the Indians, and war-weary colonial officials agreed. Governor Denny assured Pisquetomen that the colony "and all others who held the Peace Belt" would gladly extend peace to the Ohio Indians and "that every Offense that has been passed shall be forgot forever." Denny reinforced the point by sending the Moravian missionary Christian Frederick Post back to the Ohio Country with the natives as a living token of

British goodwill. Post not only would encourage Delaware neutrality but would also act as an agent who could bring the fuzzy political world of Ohio Indians into sharper focus for his superiors.[30]

Post's journey westward reveals much about Delaware attitudes toward British peace overtures as well as the still-evolving nature of Tamaqua's coalition. Tamaqua, whose prestige undoubtedly rose with news of Post's impending arrival, was able to rally enough support to conduct negotiations with the envoy. Indeed, such talks were clearly anticipated and eagerly awaited by many of Tamaqua's allies; his brother Menatochyand (Delaware George), on meeting Post, told him that "he had not slept all night, so much had he been engaged on account of my coming." Yet the deep divisions within Delaware society and the fragility of Tamaqua's coalition were equally clear. As he approached Shingas's town at Saucunk (Beaver Falls, Pennsylvania), Post discovered that the "people of the town were much disturbed at my coming," and on closer inspection the missionary found "their faces were quite distorted with rage." Having heard Post assure Shingas that Pennsylvania would rescind its bounty for his scalp, Shamokin Daniel gave voice to Delaware suspicions when he interrupted, telling Shingas, "Do not believe him, he tells nothing but idle lying stories." In the face of Post's strong denials, Daniel's anger burst forth. "Damned you," he lashed back, "why do not you and the French fight on the sea? You come here only to cheat the poor Indians, and take the land from them." In the most dramatic way possible, Post was introduced to the crux of Delaware concerns, shared by Shawnees, Iroquois, and Wyandots.[31]

Though Post's reception at the Kuskuskies was far less hostile, the missionary found Tamaqua, Delaware George, and others no less suspicious. The Delawares began by making clear their expectations and by emphasizing their growing influence when they insisted that "all the Indians, from the sunrise to the sunset," who looked to the Delawares for guidance "should join in the peace" the Indians and British both desired. Meanwhile the march of Forbes's army reinforced the Delawares' belief that "you and the French continued to war to waste the Indians between you" and insisted that Post was actually an agent of this sinister design. Moreover, the Delawares knew that the army included several hundred Catawba and Cherokee warriors, the "Flatheads" the Ohio Indians had fought with for generations: their presence also suggested British treachery. None of this helped foster a climate of cooperation and trust, as Post learned when he was told pointedly that "if you had brought the news of peace before your army had begun to march it would have caused a great deal more good."[32]

Nevertheless, Tamaqua answered Denny's message and made the Delawares' own requirements perfectly clear to the British. To the Delawares and their neighbors, the principal issue remained control of the Ohio Country. On this the natives were uncompromising, emphasizing that "the land is ours, and not theirs [the British]," and they agreed not to assist the French only if "you will be at peace with us" and drop any plans to occupy or settle the region. To British demands that all captives be returned, the Indians were dismissive and not a little contemptuous, finding it "very odd and unreasonable," as Post observed, "that we should demand prisoners before their is an established peace, since an unreasonable demand makes us appear as if we wanted brains."[33]

The exchange between Post and his Delaware hosts did not lead to wholesale native acceptance of peace, but it did give each side a chance to hear and be heard. The Delawares' formal reply to Denny made no mention that peace had been concluded, but it did open the door to future discussions. The exchange at the Kuskuskies also revealed how far Tamaqua, relying primarily on kinship and friendship networks, had created a consensus on the issue of negotiations with the British. Significantly, the first name to appear beneath Tamaqua's on the Delawares' message was Shingas's. His alliance with the peace faction may have been crucial to its success, and it served as a powerful signal to the British that the Delawares were now willing at least to consider an end to the war. In addition, the message was carried east by Pisquetomen, yet another of Tamaqua's brothers and a man well known to provincials for over a generation. Moreover, the message to Denny was sent on behalf of men representing all the major western Delaware ethnic divisions. Finally, Post was able to report that, although they were initially hostile toward him, war leaders Coquetageghton (White Eyes) and Killbuck were decidedly less so by the time the council ended.[34]

Yet the fragility of this alliance of headmen and warriors was made quite clear in the Delawares' admonition to Post and his superiors to "make haste, and let us soon hear of you again." Indeed, as Pisquetomen and his companions traveled east with Post in tow, Ohio warriors, including some Delawares and Munsees, participated in the near annihilation of a British detachment near Fort Duquesne in September and were also part of the abortive attack on Forbes's base at Fort Ligonier a month later. At such a difficult time, when British signals appeared mixed and confused, and with native towns equally divided over the wisest course for the future, some clear sign was vital if Tamaqua and his allies were to continue their work of peace.[35]

Pisquetomen stopped briefly in Philadelphia and then went on to Easton, where in mid-October he arrived in the midst of the general peace con-

ference that brought together Crown Indian agents, Pennsylvanians, Teedyuscung's Delawares, and the Six Nations in a final effort to resolve the
tangle of differences between natives and colonists. Although royal and
provincial leaders hoped the results would induce western Indians to stop
fighting, the conference had not been called specifically for that purpose. In
fact, until Pisquetomen's arrival western affairs had hardly been mentioned
during the proceedings.[36]

Though the Easton Treaty subsequently proved to be a watershed in the
evolution of the Crown's Indian policy, its significance for the Ohio Indians
rested on three specific elements in the treaty. First, at the Crown's insistence, Pennsylvania gave back to the Six Nations lands between the Susquehanna River and the Alleghenies sold by the natives at Albany in 1754—
a purchase conducted in fraudulent circumstances and one that threatened
the security of the Ohio natives. Coupled with this was a pledge that no
attempt would be made to settle west of the mountains until the Crown and
native leaders could agree on reasonable cessions. Finally, the British agreed
to establish a fair and dependable trade in the west.[37]

It was this news that Pisquetomen carried west to his brothers and other
Delawares. Moreover, Pisquetomen's party was accompanied on this occasion by two Cayugas who would, the British hoped, lend weight and
credence to news of the treaty proceedings. At the same time, Governor
Denny's message urged the Delawares and their neighbors to enter the new
Covenant Chain forged at Easton, while he promised to "open the road"
between the natives and the colony.[38]

The reception the Delawares gave to the news from Easton is reflected in
notes kept by Post, who made the difficult trip west a second time in
November. No longer a diplomat at large, the Moravian had agreed to the
journey at the behest of General Forbes, whose tired and edgy soldiers—
many of them campaigning for the first time—needed accurate news of
French and Indian activities. Moreover, if an army its leader described as
"composed of raw undisciplined troops, newly raised and collected from all
parts of the Globe" was to avoid the logistical nightmare of being snow-
bound on the Ohio without completing its mission, Indian neutrality was
vital. Forbes trusted that the Easton Treaty, Cayuga sachems, and the
missionary's persuasive powers would help accomplish this.[39]

Post's observations reveal the continuing distrust that ran through Delaware village councils. Indeed, the continued advance of Forbes's army
intensified these feelings by juxtaposing British appeals for peace and the
presence of an armed host far larger than either the French garrisons or
Braddock's ill-fated army years earlier. It took little time for these concerns

to surface. Pisquetomen insisted that the natives be allowed to deal with the French in their own way—by withdrawing from the fight the Indians could render the French position untenable. A British army on the Ohio was neither needed nor welcome. Repeating once more the Delawares' conviction that "the English will take the land from us," Pisquetomen could point to the army's new road west from Carlisle as tangible proof, a road wide enough to accommodate settlers' wagons as well as gun carriages. Pisquetomen's suspicion was not lost on Post, who cautioned his own militia escort "to be careful how they argued with the Indians; and be sure to say nothing that might affront them," lest he and they once again face the hostility Post had found at Saucunk.[40]

Pisquetomen stressed how important control of the Ohio Country had become for the Delawares and their neighbors. Upon reaching Tamaqua's settlement at the Kuskuskies, Post noted that the Delawares "were afraid the English would come over the river Ohio" and that "they concern themselves very much about the affair of land; . . . and are continually . . . afraid the English will take their land." Having lived through one invasion of their Ohio lands, the Indians were now confronted with another as winter approached. Moreover, contradictory signals complicated the natives' decision whether to continue their own war or to stand aside, allow the British their victory over the French, and press for a peace settlement that would restore the Ohio Country to its native inhabitants. On the one hand, as the French prepared to abandon Fort Duquesne, the nearby Shawnees and many Delawares also began moving away from the Forks of the Ohio westward to new towns beyond reach of British troops. On the other hand, the Delawares had recently received messages of peace from both Forbes and Denny and admonitions from their Cayuga guests to "be still and quiet" even as the Anglo-American army prepared for its final assault on the French bastion—a drive that, correctly or not, many Delawares believed was directed at them as well.[41]

Pisquetomen's expression of Delaware concerns was confirmed at the Kuskuskies, where Post compounded an already complex and tense situation by arriving with his armed escort, something that endeared him neither to village leaders bent on talking about an armistice nor to the warriors. The cordial reception given Post earlier that summer was notably absent in the autumn. At the same time, headmen struggling to maintain some control urged Post not to "regard what the common people would say, but only hearken to the chiefs," and ordered him to make no attempt to converse with the many colonial captives then in the town, lest their exaggerated tales of ill treatment further poison the atmosphere. The Moravian's hosts were furious when his escort nevertheless attempted to question the prisoners.[42]

Although Post may have overstated the natives' "murdering spirit," his arrival and initial reception were anything but auspicious. What tempered the anger and calmed the general unrest caused by Post's arrival was the appearance of Tamaqua, Shingas, and the two Cauygas who had come with Pisquetomen. Isaac Still, one of Tamaqua's followers, took advantage of the Cayugas' arrival to silence the more vocal warriors in the town. Telling them of the Easton Treaty and of the Six Nations' participation, he challenged the still-suspicious warriors to "go tell them [the Cayugas] that they are fools. Go and tell the Cayuga chiefs so, and you will become great men." While dissent continued, Still's tongue-lashing brought an end to the bellicosity and allowed the meeting between Post and Tamaqua to continue.[43]

With opposition subdued for the moment, Tamaqua was able to make the peace faction's case for accepting British terms and withdrawing from the war. In this Tamaqua gained valuable help from the visiting Cayugas. Tamaqua's supporters and the Iroquois undoubtedly came to an agreement on how the ensuing council should unfold. Yet the meeting with Post was a Delaware affair, orchestrated by Tamaqua and his allies from several villages who looked on the Cayugas' position as decidedly inferior to their own. Tamaqua, for example, made it clear that the two Iroquois would "assist" and "help" him in his role as peacemaker in the Ohio Country. The Cayugas played their parts well, reminding the Delawares that the present war was the result of French and British greed and ambition and urging their audience to "let them [the Europeans] use it [the war hatchet] among themselves, it is theirs, and they are of one colour; let them fight with one another." These remarks and others led to a series of private meetings away from the council as peace advocates used their best powers of verbal persuasion to sway their opponents before making an answer to Governor Denny. Post was evidently impatient and anxious to report to Forbes, whose army had occupied the ruins of Fort Duquesne on November 25 as the deliberations at the Kuskuskies continued. Tamaqua, however, cautioned Post to remain easy, since peace "is a great matter, and wants much consideration."[44]

On November 28 the council reconvened as Tamaqua announced that the Delawares had reached agreement on a reply to the British message. Though the arrival of Forbes's army not many miles to the south undoubtedly helped determine the outcome of the private meetings, the Delawares did not allow themselves to be stampeded by British promises or troops. Instead they once again made their own position clear when they prepared a message warning the British that "not [to] settle here" in place of the French. A "chief counsellor," Ketiuskund, drove the point home privately by warning Post that "all the nations had jointly agreed to defend their hunting place at Allegheny, and suffer nobody to settle there," while hoping that with so many Delawares now "very much inclined" toward the British, the latter would not disturb the peace before it had fairly begun. It was a message also carried by Tamaqua when he later met Colonel Bouquet at "Pittsboro."[45]

Tamaqua's new role as Delaware "king" was also secured during the Kuskuskies council. He emerged as the most visible and energetic spokesman among the Delawares, having eclipsed even his brother Shingas. Tamaqua's role as a power broker at home and across the cultural divide was based on kinship and friendship networks at home and was enhanced when, in late November, 1758, he agreed to carry news of the Easton Treaty to Indians living beyond the Ohio Country. In so doing Tamaqua filled a power vacuum created by the rush of events on the Ohio during the previous summer and fall. For Tamaqua, however, the role would not have been the least out of character. Acknowledging himself a "queen"—a reference to his people's traditional role as "women" among neighboring societies—he took seriously his implied responsibilities as peacemaker. In this role Tamaqua appeared at the head of his own men as they confronted British warriors at the Forks of the Ohio. The meeting in early December was symbolic in another way, as yet little appreciated by natives or royal officers. On the Ohio the brief encounter of December 4 ushered in a new phase of Indian-colonial relations: less evident was the chatter of many provincial voices so familiar in the past; their place was being taken by those royal officials—often no more in harmony—determined to forge a new, imperial Covenant Chain stretching from London westward beyond the mountains into what would soon become part of a greatly enlarged continental empire.[46]

The arrival at the Kuskuskies of Cayugas bearing news of the Easton Treaty was an indication that the structure of intercultural relations was changing. Since the late 1740s, the Six Nations had kept their distance from events in the Ohio Country, condemning the behavior of so-called dependent peoples—"mere hunters"—more for the benefit of their colonial audiences than for that of Ohio Indians who, by the very act of resettling in the west, had placed themselves well beyond reach of the Covenant Chain that bound their eastern kinfolk. At the same time, many within the Confederacy had compelling reasons to avoid any entanglement in such a marginal area. The outbreak of a new intercolonial war found the Six Nations caught "between" as well, while competing European giants pulled and tugged at the nations and threatened Iroquoia with destruction.

The task of breathing new life into Six Nations–British relations was soon taken away from individual colonies and lodged in one of two newly created Indian superintendencies whose districts were divided by the Potomac and Ohio rivers. The Northern District, embracing the Confederacy and the Ohio Indians, was vested in New York land baron and provincial Indian agent William Johnson, whose temporary commission arrived with Braddock in 1755 and was confirmed a year later. Johnson—from November 1755 a baronet—had for a decade enjoyed a close relationship with the Mohawks, and through them he could exercise some influence at Onondaga and beyond. His appointment as Indian superintendent guaranteed both a vigorous effort to imperialize Indian affairs and a central place for the Confederacy in the renewed Covenant Chain. Under Johnson's regime, the Six Nations continued to enjoy the same prestige and influence that had characterized their relations with individual colonies; the superintendent quickly joined the ranks of those who, like Cadwallader Colden and James Logan, defined Iroquois power in native America in the most expansive terms and for the same ends: to legitimate and ease British westward expansion at the expense of France and of other native societies.[47]

Johnson's immediate responsibilities were threefold: to restore the Covenant Chain to its former luster; to end the border war that had errupted in Pennsylvania and Virginia; and to draw Indian support away from the French while at the same time increasing that given to his own government. Success, in Johnson's view, turned on the Six Nations, though in those circumstances the superintendent's task was daunting. The British rout on the Monongahela and subsequent defeats elsewhere did little to enhance British prestige or the British army's reputation.[48]

The Confederacy's reluctance to be dragged into the war extended to the volatile realm of Pennsylvania's Indian affairs as well. Two decades earlier Canasetego had conspired with James Logan to transform the Pennsylvania–Six Nations alliance into a tool of coercion. By late 1755 the victims of the Logan-Canasetego alliance were preparing for war, as were their kinfolk in the Ohio Country, and the colony was in desperate need of help. Governor William Shirley of Massachusetts, acting commander-in-chief of British forces after Braddock's death, attempted to enlist the Six Nations by reminding them that "the Indians the Delawares and Shawanese always lived under your Direction" and always "looked upon you as their Master." The Onondaga headmen could trade in myths too, and they agreed that they had "by a series of conquests" gained mastery over the Ohio Indians. The

Onondagas then exercised a conquerer's prerogative by deciding that "we always look'd upon the Delawares as the more immediate care of Onas [the Iroquois' name for Pennsylvania's governor], that they are within the circle of his arms" and suggested that since "he has not taken that friendly care of them as he ought to do," Onas could expect nothing but what his border settlers were already suffering.[49]

Between 1756 and 1758 Johnson ignored the Ohio Country in favor of resurrecting the Covenant Chain as an effective tool of imperial policy in the east. Success came at Easton in 1758, when Johnson and the Six Nations emerged as the principal architects of a peace agreement with the Susquehanna Indians that opened the road to the Ohio Country as well. Teedyuscung publicly acknowledged Six Nations leadership in regional matters, while Johnson was able to put his stamp on the proceedings through his commission as "colonel" and superintendent of the Confederacy. Equally important for the subsequent design of the imperial Chain were the promises given by Pennsylvania and ratified by Johnson and the Crown. The royal government's agreement to protect Indian lands, maintain open trade, and intercede in matters touching on native relations with the colonies presented Johnson with new challenges and new opportunities as the Seven Years' War came to an end.[50]

Johnson envisioned a London-based scheme of Indian affairs in the west that included three principal features. First, the expanded intercultural relations and especially the trade that would eventually follow upon the British victories in North America were to be centrally managed by the royal Indian Department and enforced by the police powers of the army. Next, to preclude any unified native resistance to the new British regime and to enhance his own importance, Johnson proposed the creation—or recognition—of several separate native confederacies. The purpose, as the superintendent explained it, was to "create a misunderstanding" between the Six Nations, Great Lakes, Canadian, and Ohio Indians "so as to render them Jealous of each other." Only such a scheme of divide and rule could guarantee the security of the empire's American frontier, for as Johnson never tired of stressing, "could [the Indians] arrive at a perfect union, they must prove very dangerous Neighbors." Finally, to further ensure peace along the border, Johnson proposed that a formal boundary between colonial and native territories be fixed as soon as possible, a concept that appealed to many within the home government for reasons having less to do with Indian affairs than with a growing concern for the implications of continued American expansion.[51]

In the Ohio Country Johnson's plan meant extending the Covenant

Chain across the mountains by once again resurrecting the now-familiar fiction of Six Nations conquest and Ohio Indian subordination. Some hint of this came as early as Post's second council with Tamaqua, when the missionary, reflecting decades of British mythologizing, reminded his Delaware audience that the Six Nations "are the chief owners of the land" and that "they will settle the affair" with regard to peace with the colonies.[52]

Yet buried in the Covenant Chain rhetoric was a new element that set the new system of Indian affairs apart from prewar relations. In the past the Six Nations had stood alone as the premier native allies of colonists from Massachusetts Bay to Pennsylvania. Now they were counted as merely first among equals as Johnson and his subordinates began direct treaty negotiations with natives as far afield as western Lake Superior and the Illinois Country. By the early 1760s Detroit, Michilimackinac, and Fort Pitt were fast replacing Onondaga and Albany as centers of Indian affairs in the east. The implications of this westward shift were not lost on the Iroquois. When in mid-1761 Johnson passed through their towns on his way to a major conference at Detroit, Confederacy leaders pressed their superintendent to explain the purpose of his going and told him they were "surprized to find you are going to call a Council at Detroit, as you know that the Chief, and the only Council fire burns at your house, excepting that which we have at Onondaga." Though Johnson tried to allay their concern, he did little to dispel the Iroquois' sense that somehow their superintendent was about to play them false.[53]

Though Johnson and Six Nations leaders once more engaged in the rhetoric of Iroquois conquests, the superintendent's plans had little immediate impact on the Ohio Indians. In the Ohio Country the complex realities facing both natives and the newly arrived British far outweighed bureaucratic proposals in shaping intercultural relations along this portion of America's frontier. And paramount among those realities was the need of all those in the region for a respite from years of costly, disruptive warfare.

Some measure of the circumstances and needs of Ohio natives and their British adversaries can be gained from the December 1758 meeting between Tamaqua and Bouquet. Although the news from Easton helped tip the scales in favor of a Delaware-British cease-fire in November and December, the treaty did nothing to guarantee Anglo-American military success. Nor did it establish peace between the Crown, the colonies, and the western Indians; indeed, peacemaking had only begun. Likewise, the approach of Forbes's army did not force natives to concede defeat. Tamaqua came to the Forks at Forbes's request, and the council was held because the army was all too painfully aware that most Ohio Indians were anything but awestruck by the redcoats. In fact the Delawares used the meeting to once again urge the British to "go back over the mountains, and stay there." As they had in the past, Tamaqua and his followers continued to base their actions on a clear understanding of the present situation as well as on a persistent desire to see the Ohio Country emptied of contending European armies and left to its native owners.[54]

Although the Delawares found the assembled troops an ample reminder of British military power, the army's success in 1758 was more apparent than real. As they prepared to occupy the Forks, Forbes's regiments had secured their immediate objective. However, French troops were menacingly close in the upper Allegheny Valley through much of the following year. Moreover, the general's forces were virtually in the midst of enemy territory: the French still held Fort Niagara, the Great Lakes, and the Illinois Country, and Forbes's communication with the eastern settlements and magazines was limited to two long military roads, each easily blocked by bad weather or the enemy. British control over the Ohio Country was therefore tenuous at best and would remain so for some time. If conquest was ever to be translated into effective possession, native cooperation was not only desirable but vital.

Thus the need to secure both the army and its conquests led to the meeting at the Forks and the reassuring, conciliatory tone taken by Forbes's deputy. Colonel Bouquet emphasized that the army's purpose was not to take possession of the land but only to drive away the French, whom he attempted to cast as the common enemy and the real threat to peace in the region. The troops could also protect the "large and extensive trade" promised once peace had been restored. And Bouquet once more cited the Easton Treaty as the foundation for all subsequent British-Indian relations in the west. The colonel thus painted an encouraging picture for his native audience, one shaped by several fair promises and hardly darkened by threats or demands: only once did Bouquet refer to captives still held by the natives, and he did not press an issue already raised by Post. Instead, Bouquet's speech was loaded with requests: for supplies and native help in protecting the small garrison to be left at the Forks; for timely intelligence of French activities; and for Tamaqua's help in spreading word of the Easton Treaty and his cooperation in bringing peace to the middle west.[55]

Tamaqua had good reason to cooperate with Bouquet, though his reply was cautious as well as encouraging. In fact Tamaqua and other native leaders might have found greater appeal in Bouquet's speech than the colonel could have imagined. Though by no means a defeated people, the

Delawares and their neighbors were feeling the effects of war and the recent British invasion. The Shawnees who had reoccupied Logg's Town in 1755 had recently abandoned the place and moved farther down the Ohio, nearer their departed French allies. At the same time, the Delaware relocation begun with the Kittanning raid continued as new towns were founded on the Mahoning and Muskingum rivers, though substantial numbers of Delawares remained close to the Forks and in the vicinity of the Kuskuskies. Although these removes were orderly and planned, they still entailed some short-term loss of crops. The abrupt departure of the French created a more serious problem, since gunsmiths, some foods, and hardware also disappeared.[56]

Three years of war made enviable reputations for Shingas, Captain Pipe, and their men, but at a price measured in the growing number of British Americans—once captives, now adoptive kin—residing in virtually every Ohio Indian town. The war had also cost the natives social harmony and political consensus as factionalism and openly competing interests surfaced. A responsible headman, Tamaqua was now in a position to give his people and their neighbors a respite from wartime turmoil.[57]

The Delawares near the Forks thus sought to follow a middle course between continued hostility and a hasty peace while persisting in their efforts to curb British and French hostilities that threatened native security and autonomy. This goal was neatly stated in the face of subsequent French efforts to enlist the Delawares in a campaign to drive out the small British garrison left at the Forks of the Ohio. Kuskuskies villagers refused, determined that "they would have no war in their Country." The presence of the British force, some two hundred men commanded by Colonel Hugh Mercer, had been agreed to by Tamaqua and his followers, who nonetheless cautioned the garrison at the Forks to remain within its walls and likewise warned Bouquet that a British force on the Ohio could only prolong the conflict. On Bouquet's request that he and the Delawares join forces to drive the French completely out of the Ohio Country, the natives remained noncommittal, preferring to shape their course to the Europeans' subsequent actions. Yet Tamaqua did agree to send messages westward with news of the Easton Treaty and the British interest in peace.[58]

Shared needs thus laid the foundation for cooperation between the Ohio Indians and the British. Unable to drive Forbes's army away, the natives accepted the reality of its presence. In practice this meant embracing the Easton Treaty and using British promises to curb further colonial expansion. The army and the Indian Department above all needed peace on the western frontier, both to weaken French resistance and to remove the terrors of border warfare from Pennsylvania, Maryland, and Virginia. As a result, accommodation began to supplant conflict as a strategy for both Ohio natives and their adversaries during the three years following Forbes's arrival at the Forks.

seven

Adjustment and Accommodation

The brief December meeting between Tamaqua and Bouquet— lasting just two days—defined the issues that would shape intercultural relations for the future. The encounter also confirmed Tamaqua's growing influence and his central place in Ohio affairs. By the end of 1758 he was, to the British as well as to many of his own people, the western Delaware "king": the man who stood as principal broker between his people and outsiders. As such, Tamaqua put his stamp on intercultural relations for several years. Moreover, his influence and that of the Delawares continued to grow as Tamaqua promoted peace among the nations living beyond the Ohio, including the Miamis and Kaskaskias. Thus, as Forbes's army began the long, cold trip back over the mountains, Tamaqua and the Delawares had begun to fill the power vacuum within the Ohio Indian world created by Tanaghrisson's departure in 1754.

The most visible signs of cooperation to emerge in the months and years after 1758 were the public councils at which Tamaqua and successive British commanders in the west attempted to make good on their commitments. Having accepted the role of mediator, Tamaqua energetically pursued negotiations with British officers and a growing list of native societies; in the process, he demonstrated much diplomatic skill and political savvy. As early as February 1759, Tamaqua was again calling on the British army. In a meeting with Colonel Hugh Mercer at "Pittsboro," Tamaqua reaffirmed his own commitment to peace. Yet he also made clear his people's expectation of reciprocal acts of goodwill: the headman arrived with several of his hunters, men eager to trade as soon as possible. Mercer, whose own men were then on short rations, could only promise once again that traders would soon arrive.

The fullest measure of Tamaqua's success, however, came with two summer councils at the site of the future Fort Pitt that culminated in a formal end to hostilities within the Ohio Country. At a preliminary meeting in early July, Tamaqua arrived not only with his loyal supporters from the previous year, but with Shawnees and Sandusky Wyandots, the latter commissioned to speak for eight other native groups from as far west as Detroit and the Miami River. It was an impressive gathering, including nearly five hundred natives. And it was Tamaqua's affair. The Wyandots quickly served notice that they had come "as was agreed upon in a Council held over the Lakes by the Beaver King with their Nations." As council spokesman for the assembled civil chiefs, Tamaqua also pressed George Croghan on the issue of peace: the headmen had come prepared to hear British conditions and clear the way for a more general meeting with war leaders to confirm the peace proposals first broached the previous winter.[1]

Tamaqua and other native leaders at Fort Pitt evidently did their work well; within the month, war leaders from the Delawares, Shawnees, Wyandots, Ottawas, Ojibwas, Kaskaskias, Miamis, and Potawatomis arrived to make peace by symbolically burying the war hatchet under the tree of peace, an act that had meaning only when performed by warriors. Once again Tamaqua and the Delawares led the way; White Eyes, a Delaware war leader, took the initiative in accepting responsibility for the fighting and in so doing was then able to "take the Hatchet" from the assembled warriors. After this, with a display of appropriate council wampum, he metaphorically buried the hatchet, hoping that it "may never be found more." Once again the Delawares, on behalf of those they acted for, let their British audience know that peace, like virtually every other relationship, was based on acts of reciprocity to which the army was expected to conform. In this instance White Eyes urged the warriors to "go hunting and travel this Road of Peace . . . and exchange your skins and furs, for Goods to clothe your Women and Children," a subtle reminder that peace and trade were but two sides of the same coin.[2]

Tamaqua's activities during the busy summer of 1759 serve as an example of what many men—and village matrons—must have experienced. In July the Ohio Indians were confronted with the first of many British demands that Anglo-American captives be released as a precondition for peace. Such insistence ignored the fact that many of those people, mainly women and children, were now adoptive kin of their former captors and that native societies had no means of forcing compliance with such a demand—one that struck at the very core of society. Nevertheless, rather than risk an end to negotiations before they had fairly begun, Tamaqua took the initiative by releasing two adoptees, women he referred to as "my Mother" and "my Sister"—a clear sign of the important place they occupied in his own lineage, something further illustrated when Tamaqua told the assembly at Fort Pitt that "I love them as well as I do my own Mother and Sister." The magnitude of his personal sacrifice may have been lost on the British, but it may have served its intended purpose as an example to others; in succeeding months increasing numbers of colonists were repatriated at Fort Pitt.[3]

Even before this dramatic gesture, Tamaqua had to cope with a threat from another quarter. In the midst of arranging the July council, Tamaqua was forced to rush off to Venango. There an eastern Delaware identified as Teedyuscung's son was attempting to stiffen anti-British resistance among the Munsees, Shawnees, and Senecas living in the upper Allegheny Valley. Fearing that such an effort would wreck peace negotiations, western native leaders urged Tamaqua to intervene. By dint of personal influence and perhaps that of friends and kin, the headman managed to quell the disturbance and ensure harmony at the forthcoming meeting at Fort Pitt.[4]

This challenge from Venango points out another element that complicated the search for peace. The councils at Fort Pitt and the behind the scenes wrangling that brought them about were all played out against a backdrop of continued fighting between British forces and western Indians whose villages had not yet agreed to end hostilities. In May and again in August 1759, vital supply convoys were ambushed, with loss of both escorts and materials. Less dramatic were the raids and ambushes carried out by small parties of warriors. Though the British capture of Fort Niagara in late July forced the French to abandon their remaining forts in the Allegheny Valley and thus lessened the intensity of attacks in the Ohio Country, Bouquet's troops at Presque Isle in 1760 were under constant observation and periodic harassment from Wyandots, Ottawas, and other western Indians.[5]

Attacks against British forces were only the most extreme example of continued, deep-seated native distrust of the army and of the society and powers it represented. This suspicion was reflected by other Indians, including Custaloga's people and many Wyandots, who either were singularly reluctant to confront British officials directly or were, in Croghan's words, "for Standing Neuter" as they awaited the outcome of the Anglo-French conflict. For an increasing number of natives, however, the invitation to discuss peace also provided a forum for stressing their own expectations and concerns. As a result, the Fort Pitt meetings helped highlight native interests. This began soon enough when Pisquetomen demanded to know "what the English of the General [John Stanwix, commander of forces in the Ohio Country after Forbes] meant by coming here with a great army," a demand that led Quaker trader James Kenny to conclude that the "Indians are very jealous of the English . . . they seem jealous of their lands being settled."[6]

Though the issue of autonomy remained paramount for the Ohio Indians, they also continued to raise two other, interrelated issues of considerable importance: trade and the creation of a proper relationship with the British. The Ottawas who had migrated into the Lake Erie basin, away from the French, reminded the British that "we have thrown away the French and must now depend upon you for Supplys." The dependency was real enough, but so was the expectation that *their* choice to give peace entitled the Ottawas to expect something in return. The same logic led Tamaqua to bring his hunters to Mercer's fort earlier in 1759 and ask that trade be reopened. In the natives' world of face-to-face encounters such reciprocity was essential, as were gifts exchanged at councils; these exchanges—which over time weighed heavier on Europeans than on natives—breathed life into relationships and symbolically quickened the personal and social ties that bound people across the cultural frontier. Peace could not be made and maintained in any other fashion.[7]

British responses to native peacemaking efforts, while encouraging, were often equivocal. When he faced the assembled nations in July 1759, Croghan insisted that "the English will never violate any of their Engagements to you or any of your Brethren of any other Nation, but hold fast the Covenant Chain." He also discounted native fears about the continued presence of army garrisons by insisting that the troops were only to build "strong houses" to protect the traders who, Croghan insisted, would soon appear in native towns. The implication, doubtless recognized by the agent's Indian audience, was that the removal of French forces would prompt the dismantling of British forts as well. The apparent sincerity of these and other encouraging statements was reinforced by the liberal distribution of gifts that punctuated each of the council meetings.[8]

The conciliatory tone of British officals during the early meetings on the Ohio reflected their own desire to secure peace with western natives as soon as possible, though for reasons that turned not on relations with regional societies, but on events beyond the Ohio Country. By the end of 1759,

Britain's campaigns in North America had reaped unanticipated dividends as the French were forced to surrender Quebec to General James Wolfe's army in September. The impending conquest of all of French America increased the problems already facing royal officials in the colonies as they attempted to manage affairs in the borderlands. The effort to end Pennsylvania's Indian war led the home government to accept direct responsibility for colonial-native relations and to make specific guarantees to Indian societies that had, by 1759, become the foundation for peace west of the Alleghenies.

Peace in the Ohio Country became imperative as the army and Indian Department faced the new responsibilities that arose with Canada's surrender in September 1760. Not only did more than 65,000 *habitants* and Canadian Indians have to be pacified and governed, but a vast and ill-defined territory west of the St. Lawrence Valley also had to be occupied and drawn into the British imperial orbit. The latter process began even before the final surrender at Montreal, when Tamaqua encouraged representatives of Great Lakes Indian societies to meet at Fort Pitt. Throughout these and numerous other encounters from Detroit to Michilimackinac and La Baye, British officers continued to use the Easton Treaty as the basis for the Crown's new relationship with dozens of trans-Appalachian Indian societies. This was especially true in the Ohio Country as the government struggled to redefine and more efficiently manage a greatly enlarged empire.[9]

The home government's failure to anticipate the administrative needs of its new western territories largely shaped the character of British efforts to manage the west while making at least a short-lived accommodation with the region's natives not only desirable but necessary. Along the ill-defined border between British and Indian America, the government left to its commander-in-chief Sir Jeffery Amherst and his subordinates the immediate task of pacifying and defending what Britain claimed by right of conquest. The result was a purely de facto arrangement, based on the Easton Treaty and influenced by the changing political and fiscal climate in both London and the colonies as well as by the shifting course of British-Indian relations. Given the Ohio Indians' clear assertion of *their* claims to the land—claims soon echoed throughout the Great Lakes basin—the years after 1758 saw an interregnum rather than a swift, complete transfer of effective sovereignty from vanquished natives to victorious British Americans. From the natives' perspective, of course, even "interregnum" had no meaning, since the only sovereign rights the Indians recognized were their own.[10]

In the absence of any civil authority in the west, the home government relied on Amherst, his regulars, and martial law to enforce the Easton Treaty and subsequent orders governing the new territories. This meant that Indian affairs would invariably be conducted in the shadow of army posts, whose commanders became in effect extensions of the Indian Department as well as leaders of a military police force. Though "garrison government" had been a feature of British expansion for generations, the army in America at the end of the Seven Years' War faced special challenges as it undertook to show the flag and establish effective royal authority west of the mountains.[11]

Amherst controlled some twenty thousand regular and provincial troops in the autumn of 1760, but that force rapidly disappeared after the surrender of Montreal. Few provincials could be induced to volunteer for subsequent campaigns, and many of the regulars were transferred to other active theaters, notably the West Indies, where in 1762 Spain entered the war as a French ally. Meanwhile, most of the forces remaining in North America were ordered to garrisons amid the Canadian population in the St. Lawrence Valley. Finally, for reasons of economy, the legal size of the army was twice reduced between 1761 and 1763; as a result, Amherst's seasoned infantry regiments saw their strength cut by half while the geographical and administrative scope of their responsibilities continued to expand. To this must be added chronic manpower shortages due to disease, desertion, and a drop in recruits. By mid-1763 the mighty host that had conquered Canada had been reduced to a skeleton force.[12]

This situation ultimately meant that few men could be spared for duty in the west; before 1763, garrison, police, and diplomatic responsibilities there were carried out by a single battalion—Bouquet's—of the Royal American Regiment, occasionally augmented by other troops such as specialists from the Royal Artillery. Bouquet's officers and men were for the most part seasoned veterans, having campaigned in the Carolinas and with Forbes. Nevertheless, the requirements of duty in the west stretched manpower, resources, and patience to the limit as the troops coped with conditions unlike those confronted during the war. Between 1758 and 1762 the army either reoccupied or built some thirteen forts ranging in size from massive Fort Pitt to the crude stockade at Ouiatanon, a line of forts extending from Bedford on Forbes's Road to La Baye (Green Bay) on Lake Michigan. So thinly spread were his men that garrisons typically numbered no more than an officer and fifteen to twenty men per post; only Detroit, Fort Niagara, and Fort Pitt, all key supply bases and centers of Indian diplomacy, held larger garrisons. Under such conditions the mantle of British authority lay very thin in the face of uncalculated numbers of natives and slippery colonial traders. No one was more painfully aware of this situation than Bouquet, who lamented that "we have detached officers more than 600 miles from here [Fort Pitt] and this poor battalion is divided and scattered throughout our immense conquests to the west."[13]

The vastness of the territory stretched Bouquet's crude supply system to the breaking point; troops were ill clothed and fed and devoted most of their time to moving stores and maintaining the vital river and portage routes that tied them to the outside world. That world must have seemed a universe away to soldiers trapped in small, often tumbledown garrisons surrounded by strange peoples, at the mercy of weather and the seasons, with little chance for leave or recall. Officers, many of them Scots and Germans, used to congenial conversation and the company of other gentlemen—and their ladies—bombarded their superiors with endless requests for fresh news, fresh food, and transfers. Their troops suffered more silently, only because they were less literate and had fewer opportunities to lobby on their own behalf. But among all ranks discipline eroded: soldiers drank, malingered, or deserted; officers drank, brawled, and faced courts-martial. Not even their colonel was immune; someone rifled Bouquet's quarters at Fort Pitt and made off with his personal funds and cash belonging to the army. Thus Britain's frontier force, composed of men who often had "Scarce Shirt, Shoe, or Stockings" and who were quarrelsome and seditious enough to address "Insolent letters" to their superiors, was poorly equipped to undertake the tasks forced upon it by the collapse the New France and the Crown's determination to fashion a new empire from the wreckage.[14]

Few were more aware of the army's limited capabilities than the junior officers charged with enforcing royal policies in isolated posts. Shortly after he assumed command of the important communication and trade center of Detroit, Captain Donald Campbell found that he did not know how to "behave in Indian affairs, as I have noe orders on that head." Even explicit instructions could not turn an army officer into a seasoned frontier diplomat and respected orator overnight, and Campbell and his comrades soon found themselves trusting their instincts and tested Indian agents such as Croghan, Alexander McKee, and the Canadian Jean-Baptiste de Couagne, all of whom took their orders from Sir William Johnson. In other matters, the army's problem was less want of experience than lack of a coherent program that would permit officers to deal with the king's subjects and Indians in ways that would lessen friction along the cultural divide.[15]

A "well regulated" trade had been promised at Easton, and both Johnson and Amherst agreed that only stringent licensing and regulation could curb the seemingly natural rapaciousness of traders while controlling natives' access to such dangerous items as rum, firearms, and gunpowder. Yet as often happened, traders acted more swiftly than their would-be governors and quickly outpaced the army's ability to monitor their activities. The elimination of French forces and rumors of fortunes in furs and hides piled high at Canadian fur posts drew merchants and peddlers into the west. The celebrating that followed Forbes's campaign had hardly abated before Johnson learned that the Pennsylvanians "are all running wild after the Indian Trade." Indeed, such claims seem only mildly exaggerated. Colonists held captive in the Ohio Country saw traders appear long before they encountered British troops. Lieutenant Elias Meyer's new fort at Sandusky was barely finished when that officer found himself providing for some twenty traders. So eager were traders to move west and beat the competition that they literally outdistanced the troops sent to protect and regulate them: two men were already in business at Fort Michilimackinac (Mackinac Straits, Michigan) when its new garrison arrived in 1761. Overwhelmed by numbers and by the constant demand for licenses, army officers, including Bouquet, succumbed to the pressure and began issuing passes on their own authority.[16]

The profits that lured traders into the west were not hard to come by; years of warfare had deprived Indians of opportunities to barter, and the arrival of men like Robert Callender and Alexander Henry allowed native hunters to replenish stocks of supplies for themselves and their families. The rush to trade amazed the French at Detroit, who insisted that they "never saw soe many [Indians] at this Place in former times," while the quest for quick profits led traders to abandon garrisoned forts in favor of native towns—in clear violation of hastily promulgated regulations. Such actions created further problems as liquor once more entered the market. Yet the meager garrisons could do little to stem the flow of peddlers or their rum, as Captain Campbell discovered when his efforts to enforce regulations merely drove local Indians to Niagara, where traders evidently operated under less restraint. On rare occasions violators were caught and prosecuted by courts-martial, but more frequently the traders merely winked at the rules, by-passed the forts, and went about business as usual, leaving the authorities frustrated by inadequate regulations and a military barrier that leaked at every turn.[17]

Trade management was also complicated by rivalries among the traders themselves. In the Ohio Country this grew from a trading post at Fort Pitt operated by the Friendly Association, a Quaker group led by Israel Pemberton that held a license from Pennsylvania to operate three such stores. In the process, however, their privileged position within the colony produced what independent traders, many of them border-dwelling Scots-Irish, saw as unfair competition. The result was periodic friction and recrimination, much of it born of the relations between the Quakers at Fort Pitt and Indian agent Croghan, with the bickering finally ending up in the lap of Bouquet or one of his long-suffering subordinates.[18]

But the arrival of colonial traders in the west was only one dimension of the larger challenge facing the army. Another was the continued interest of private speculators and provincial governments alike in the Ohio Country. In the midst of the Seven Years' War, Sir William Johnson recognized the threat to Indian relations inherent in the "Pestilential Thirst for Land, so Epidemic thro' all the provinces," which intensified once coveted western territories were finally taken from the French. Forbes's army was still at the Forks of the Ohio when Colonel George Washington wrote from camp urging his governor to "immediately" open a new road from Virginia to the Ohio so that the Old Dominion could stake its claims to land and trade well ahead of what Washington called "a set of rascally Fellows divested of all faith and honor"—Pennsylvania's ever eager traders. In their place, the colonel undoubtedly envisioned a better breed of men: himself and fellow members of the struggling Ohio Company. Robbed of their estate once by the French, the Company's men were determined to succeed in their speculative venture now that the Ohio Country was in British hands. Marshaling treaties, charters, and testaments, the Company once more prepared to stake its claim to the west against all comers, especially Pennsylvanians. The situation was exacerbated, as Virginia's lieutenant governor Francis Fauquier quickly realized, by the lack of a definitive boundary between the two colonies.[19]

Royal officials were quick to appreciate the threat that intercolonial rivalry in the west posed to peace along the border between British America and Indian America. In one of his last official reports, Forbes warned that Pennsylvania and Virginia "both are aiming at engrossing the Commerce and Barter with the Indians, and of settling and appropriating the . . . country," and he urged quick action to curb such expansion, "as the preservation of the Indians, and that Country Depends upon it." Forbes, like Johnson and other royal officers, took the Easton Treaty seriously; other Anglo-Americans did not, and the result was a growing conflict between the British Empire and the miniature empires that grew up along the Atlantic coast. Just as the Crown after 1758 appropriated to itself western lands taken in war and assumed the sole management of Indian affairs, so had colonies like Virginia earlier assumed similar powers under charters issued by the same monarchy. British imperialism and colonists' pretensions to empire within their own expansive borders collided in the Ohio Country.

For a decade and a half after the capture of Fort Duquesne, Crown and colonies would continue to compete for power in the west. In the meantime the army continued to act as the principal arbiter, but never with completely unchallenged authority.[20]

Army officers did receive help from the Indian Department in their efforts to maintain relations with western Indians while controlling expansionist colonists. Johnson, based on his own knowledge and information from a handful of subagents, would frame regulations and suggest policies that the army then attempted to enforce; its officer corps, meanwhile, augmented Johnson's network of deputies in the field. In practice, however, things never worked quite so efficiently. The Indian Department, like the army, developed its procedures through trial and error; not until 1764 could Johnson present to the home government a coherent plan for Indian affairs. In addition, the military consistently defined Indians as a threat, while Johnson and his subordinates often took a more conciliatory, if not always empathic, position toward the natives. Moreover, the Indian agents' views were based much more on a pragmatic assessment of real conditions than were those of army officers. Though Johnson and the army shared challenges, the military establishment itself—and the superintendent's role in it—posed additional problems for the fledgling Indian Department.[21]

Johnson, who had enjoyed much influence in New York's Indian affairs since the 1740s and had, after the Easton Treaty, gained control of Pennsylvania's Indian affairs as well, nonetheless found that a royal commission did not carry with it complete independence. In fact quite the opposite was true: Johnson's decisions were subject to veto from army headquarters, which also financed the Indian service through "contingency" funds controlled by the commander-in-chief. Under ideal conditions the army would be guided by Johnson's advice in the daily conduct of Indian affairs while army and Indian Department officers would work together to carry out policy. In reality conflict and distrust, rather than cooperation, shaped the relationship. During the Seven Years' War Johnson worked for a number of military leaders, one of whom, Governor William Shirley of Massachusetts, sought to monopolize Indian as well as military affairs during his brief tenure. The result was a near disaster as Shirley's clumsy efforts to cajole and coerce Six Nations warriors into joining the army threatened to destroy the uneasy alliance between Crown and Confederacy.[22]

Sir Jeffery Amherst, who led British forces in America from 1759 to 1763, was no Shirley, but neither did he hide his "very Contemptible Opinion of the Savages" or his determination to reduce them to what he viewed as their proper role as subjects of the king. Amherst and Johnson could agree that Indian policy existed to serve British, not native, interests and that foremost among those interests was a secure, peaceful frontier. Beyond this, however, the general and the superintendent parted company. Amherst's contact with Indians had been limited wholly to the battlefield, where Six Nations allies, disgusted with the general's method of campaigning, left him en masse in the midst of the 1760 Montreal campaign. From that moment "treachery," "villany," and "mischevious" were common terms in any Amherst discourse on Indians. Johnson harbored no illusions about noble savages, but twenty years of close contact with the Iroquois had given him a measure of appreciation for native values and traditions that Amherst would never enjoy. Moreover, though each man held a royal commission, each served different masters and interests. Amherst was far more sensitive to the political currents in London and was keenly aware that his career rested entirely on satisfying cost-conscious and results-oriented bureaucrats. Johnson, though accountable to both Amherst and the Board of Trade, had firm roots within the colonies, and his handling of Indian affairs was often an effort to balance imperial and local interests, including his own. Ultimately, however, Johnson could act only as far as the commander-in-chief allowed, a fact that boded ill as long as Amherst insisted on treating western natives like conquered peoples and the "savages" he knew them to be.[23]

The cultural frontier that defined the Indians' and Anglo-Americans' worlds was not rigid and impervious but was rendered more fluid by the lack of monolithic unity on either side. The variety of interests and lack of accord within either world gave rise to a degree of cooperation that lasted from the end of 1758 through 1762. Cooperation across the cultural divide took several forms. In some instances Indians attempted to develop a symbiotic relationship with Anglo-Americans by responding to the latter's needs in ways that could be turned to the natives' advantage. In other cases native interests happened to coincide with British policy goals to create what, on the surface, appeared to be mutually beneficial relations. In either case, from late 1758 through the early 1760s, many Ohio Indians actively pursued ties to the invaders, relationships that assured the natives some measure of control over the newcomers as well as access to information about British strengths, weaknesses, activities, and goals.

The efforts to bring peace to the region and the reopening of trade were themselves forms of intersocietal cooperation founded not only on the natives' needs and interests but also on their concepts of reciprocity. In a different arena, Ohio Indian participation in raids against the Cherokees after 1759 reflected a willingness to cooperate with the British against a common enemy. Yet as in other aspects of their relations, natives and royal officials were not "allies"; their distinct interests just happened to coincide to common advantage. From the point of view of George Croghan, Henry Bouquet, and others, Ohio Indian raids were a useful way of diverting and weakening the Cherokees while regular troops approached the Tennessee Valley towns from Charleston during two brief conflicts between 1759 and 1762. Moreover, intersocietal warfare, abetted by Crown agents, could prove a convenient way to discourage the pan-Indian alliances that Indian agents and army officers alike feared.[24]

Though British officers had good reason to promote Ohio Indian raids down the warriors' path, and certainly encouraged them through liberal gifts of munitions and other supplies, the success of such a scheme rested with Ohio warriors, for whom the traditional basis for warfare counted far more heavily than British power politics. The generations-old enmity that defined relations between Delawares, Shawnees, Senecas, and Wyandots, on the one hand, and Cherokees and Catawbas on the other was still very much alive; indeed, it had intensified during the Seven Years' War as British commanders, from Washington to Forbes, actively recruited southern Indians for service in the Ohio Country. The Catawba warriors who served with Forbes nearly wrecked negotiations with Tamaqua and his people, who repeatedly warned the British not to bring the Catawbas into their land while questioning the general's sincerity in asking for peace as he stood arm-in-arm with the Delawares' enemies. This intersocietal conflict transcended any wars involving British or colonial forces and was rooted in cultural values wholly alien to the Indian agents who encouraged Ohio warriors on their southward trek. British encouragement did make periodic raiding easier—and highly lucrative—for those involved. Moreover, from the warriors' perspective, British encouragement offered one more way to test the sincerity of treaty promises of trade and friendship. George Croghan, for example, soon found that Delaware and Shawnee warriors would delay any decisions regarding raids against the Cherokees until they "could be assured of our Friendship and Support"; assistance that Indian agents and garrison commanders were only too happy to provide to the increasing number of Carolina-bound war parties that passed through Fort Pitt in 1761 and 1762.[25]

Closer to home, Indian-British accommodation took yet another turn as natives became provisioners for army garrisons. That Ohio Indian hunters and British officers developed such an arrangement may at first glance seem curious, especially in light of deep-seated mistrust by warriors in both camps. The explanation lies both in the army's circumstances and in the natives' own recent experiences. General Amherst eventually hoped to obtain land near the larger forts so that the troops—or settlers—could produce food to augment the quartermaster's stores. Meanwhile, the western garrisons found themselves facing chronic shortages and having to make do with a completely inadequate system of transport. Unable to requisition supplies from the Indians, the army, through local Indian agents, encouraged natives to make up the constant shortfall in meat and meal. As early as December 1760, Croghan urged village headmen at Detroit to "Incourage your young Men to Hunt and bring their meat to me for which they shall be paid in Powder and lead." This invitation was soon followed by others as, during the next several years, Ohio Indians and natives in the Great Lakes region became a significant—often crucial—part of the British army's commissariat in the west.[26]

The Indians saw nothing unusual in the army's requests and found much to recommend meeting the troops' needs. In 1753 Ohio Indian hunters had provided much the same service for Marin's army, while also leasing much needed horses to the Canadians; for a much longer period, Senecas had operated the Niagara portage for the French, and Great Lakes natives had for generations worked as porters and canoemen for Canadian traders. Although there was nothing new about the proposed arrangements, the special conditions that prevailed in the Ohio Country may well have provided further inducements. For hunters and warriors, the prospect of a lucrative cash-and-carry provisions business offered an additional opportunity to replenish stocks of ammunition and other supplies, depleted during years of war. Moreover, the army's request did not require Indian men to deviate from normal work routines and seasonal hunts. Finally, the likelihood of conflict was somewhat reduced while the troops remained dependent on native supplies of venison and corn.

The provisioning business appears to have flourished. Praising the Delawares for their "zeal and fidelity," Colonel Mercer, at the makeshift post of "Pittsboro" in 1759, told Bouquet that "but for them our circumstances could scarcely have been made known to you, or supplies so readily attained." Two years later, military correspondence routinely contained references to food purchases, principally venison, from local natives. For some the language barrier initially proved troublesome. Lieutenant Elias Meyer at Sandusky complained that "the detachment suffers considerably" from the lack of a competent interpreter, especially since "in our present unfortunate position . . . we [have] need of them [neighboring Wyandots] both for the hunt and for Indian corn." Meyer apparently overcame this problem; a month later he had enough venison to feed his men for the winter. In the meantime, other officers found their Indian neighbors were now "supply[ing] us pretty well with venison," often "at Moderate Rates," while some commanders found that they could supply each other from the surplus corn they now enjoyed.[27]

While the trade in food grew, it was also being transformed into a cash enterprise. It is difficult to determine who was responsible for this: Captain Richard Mather, after meeting with Custaloga's people at Venango early in 1761, reported that "I told them they shod receive Ready Money [for venison] which pleas'd Them not a Little." While this suggests that Mather introduced the idea at his post, the Indians' response reflects an understanding of the value of cash and credit among the British, and their interest indicates that they may have first raised the subject. In either event, Munsees, Delawares, and other native hunters soon proved themselves adept at manipulating the market. Whereas the officially quoted price for venison was two pence per pound, there is evidence that officers were forced to pay more. Ensign Robert Holmes, at Fort Miami, found that local Indians brought little venison, "and what they Bring I have to pay an Exrequent [sic] price for." The Miamis may have been particularly tough bargainers: Sir William Johnson felt compelled to apologize to Amherst for the excessive accounts from Holmes's post, due in large measure to the purchase of food. Yet the strategy of withholding food until the price rose seems to have been widespread. The commander of Fort Sandusky was forced to pay over thirty-six shillings for a "small quantity" of venison. Adding to the woes of army officers who were short on both supplies and "ready money," Ohio Indians displayed a distinct lack of enthusiasm for credit transactions. Lieutenant Stair Campbell Carre at Venango, for example, had considerable difficulty persuading local natives to accept bills of credit drawn on Bouquet at Fort Pitt. In the Indians' world of trade and finance, the British army clearly enjoyed a less-than-perfect rating.[28]

The Ohio Indians' provisioning trade enabled the natives to coexist and profit from garrisons otherwise considered intrusive. At the same time, however, the trade may have exacerbated old problems and created new ones as well. The continued westward movement of natives into the Muskingum and Scioto valleys during the 1760s may have been tied to a growing shortage of deer in the Allegheny Valley. Military records yield only fragmentary information on the volume of meat purchased, though small numbers of Indian hunters could, in favorable circumstances, harvest impressive quantities of game. In 1769 Moravian missionaries reported that the Munsee town of Goschgosching, containing perhaps sixty to eighty hunters, killed 1,200 deer during the fall hunt. However, since 1763 most of the smaller army posts had been abandoned, with only Fort Pitt remaining in the Ohio Country; this, and the corresponding drop in demand for venison owing both to fewer troops and to an improved supply system, may have given the deer population a chance to recover. In the early 1760s renewed trade in deerskins, coupled with the arrival of hundreds of soldiers, workmen, and traders, may have to created local shortages of deer and other game by upsetting the previous balance between men and animals and disrupting local ecosystems. This may be reflected in the particular hostility Ohio Indians displayed toward colonial hunters, enmity that resulted in several deaths and other near-fatal confrontations. As game reserves fell, native hunters felt ever more threatened by these poachers. In one instance the focus of an attack on Virginia hunters was the interlopers' rifles, whose technology greatly increased the chances of a successful hunt. Purchase—or theft—of such weapons added to the natives' economic advantage while lessening that of the competition.[29]

While they supplied the forts with much-needed food, Ohio Indians were also able to take advantage of British needs in other ways. As messengers, porters, or scouts, local natives found their services in great demand by an army chronically short of transport, geographic knowledge, and woodcraft. Major Robert Stewart found Munsees and Senecas at Venango more than willing to extend a portage service once enjoyed by the French to the newly arrived Virginia militia, troops who marveled at the number and quality of the Indians' horses. Killbuck, a Delaware headman and close adviser to Netawatwees, could still find time to carry ammunition from Fort Pitt to Sandusky and Detroit, at the respectable wage of a dollar a day. Indeed, by 1761 army account books were filled with itemized expenses for services rendered by local natives; women as well as men rented out horses, furnished canoes, helped load and unload freight, and served as guides and messengers. These services, like the provisions business, provided additional income and further opportunities to test British promises of peace and fair treatment. These activities also not only permitted the Ohio Indians a glimpse inside forts, but let them assess the nature and quality of British forces, an intelligence opportunity they might otherwise not have enjoyed.[30]

Information on the British camp came from another quarter as well. Kept beyond their enlistments and deprived of adequate food, clothing, and shelter while isolated in small frontier posts, Bouquet's regulars deserted at an alarming rate, a matter made worse by the army's virtual inability to prevent woodcutters, sentries, or carrying parties from vanishing into the fastness of the Ohio Country. Moreover, the longer the troops were on duty the more familiar they became with the local rivers and paths, avenues that led many of them to Indian towns. At one point in 1762 no fewer than nine deserters from Fort Niagara were found among the Genesee Senecas; these same natives had earlier rescued six runaways "almost Dead with Fatigue and Hunger." Although these men in all probability were headed for eastern settlements, some deserters had other goals in mind, as suggested by the case of two soldiers from Fort Sandusky who "deserted *to* the Savages," or that of Lewis Trafield (Trefield) from Detroit, who was suspected of having gone "toward the Illinois with some Indians."[31]

These incidents suggest that here as elsewhere the frontier between Indians and British was far more permeable than might be imagined, owing largely to another convergence of needs. Deserters, assumed by their superiors to be terrified of Indians, nevertheless sought out native towns, near or far, as sanctuaries just as they might have done in the rural villages of Ireland, Flanders, or Hannover. That men like Trefield did so suggests they felt their chances of survival were good enough to risk the threat of draconian punishment if they failed. Close contact with local Indians may have revealed that the natives were not altogether averse to harboring runaways, any more than they opposed adopting colonial captives. Indeed, like the "white Indians" who were adopted and chose to remain, deserters may have been attracted by a way of life that offered far more security and companionship than could be found in the barracks. Nevertheless, the risks were very real. As the hapless deserters among the Senecas discovered, not all Indians were pleased to entertain fugitives, especially when bounties made returning such men a potentially lucrative trade for native hunters. In fact, among the Senecas at least, the only thing that prevented a more diligent search for deserters was the army's failure to pay the promised bounty money.[32]

For other Indians, however, promises of bounties could not overcome advantages represented by the deserters themselves. Faced at a critical time with uncertainties about British ambitions, strengths, and weaknesses, and no longer able to rely on Canadians for information on these and other matters, the natives saw deserters as a valuable source of information. Moreover, to the extent that they had any skills at all, fugitives could provide useful technical assistance of the kind once offered by blacksmiths and gunsmiths. Finally, many of the deserters carried with them weapons, ammunition, and other supplies, materials that could always find a place in towns plagued by war-produced shortages. For whatever combination of reasons, deserters and Indians shared interests that brought them together in circumstances that "transculturalized" some soldiers, who became bro-kers between two worlds. One such man was David Owen, who deserted during the Seven Years' War and lived among the Ohio Indians. He later served Bouquet, who, on meeting Owen in 1764, found that he "speaks the Delaware perfectly"—so well, in fact, that his former crime was forgiven and he was recommended to the Indian Department as an interpreter. For at least the next decade Owen remained in the Ohio Country as a guide, an interpreter, and a reminder of the constant fluidity of the western frontier.[33]

eight

"We Thought Your King Had Made Peace with Us": Defensive War

 Though the army's needs offered a basis for cooperation with Ohio Indians, the trade in venison and corn or the harboring of individual fugitives did not create a long-standing symbiosis on the order of the hide trade between colonies and natives. Food, unlike hides or furs, could eventually be obtained elsewhere, and as the army gradually put its logistical house in order it had less reason to rely on, and to accommodate, local Indians, who were overshadowed as provisioners by civilian contractors and settlers. Meanwhile, the larger problems of Anglo-American expansion became more acute as Indian and British goals in the Ohio Country began to conflict. Despite the example set by Tamaqua and other native leaders, mistrust continued to shape relations, while the cooperation that began at Fort Pitt in 1759 was jeopardized as the tone of British officials became more demanding and less compromising, as stipulations of the Easton Treaty were ignored or violated and as soldiers and Indian agents conspired to revolutionize relations with western Indians in ways that once again threatened the natives' autonomy and security.

Large-scale hostilities subsided in the Ohio Country by 1760, as the French either abandoned or surrendered their outposts and as Tamaqua and others who advocated peace gained influence within their own and neighboring societies. Nevertheless, even as trade in hides and food promoted cooperation, violence remained a fact of life, especially when native warriors found themselves near British troops. Mutual distrust, fear, firearms, and occasionally liquor together created a volatile atmosphere that often erupted in minor clashes between garrisons and their native neighbors. Indian assaults on soldiers grew for a number of reasons. Drunkenness contributed to the death of at least one soldier at Bushy Run in 1760, and three Iroquois and an unknown number of Virginians were injured in a drunken brawl at Fort Venango earlier the same year. Theft by Indians may also have led to the death of a Virginia corporal, Swain, whose rifle was later found among local Iroquois. More common, however, were incidents of the kind reported from Fort Presque Isle, near which an express rider was stopped and relieved of his weapons, ammunition, and provisions but was "otherwise used civily." The messenger's experience offers some insight into the motives behind such incidents; his food—and the means of acquiring more—was taken, but nothing else. Necessity is reflected in another incident on the path between Fort Venango and Fort Le Boeuf. Several Indians intercepted a group of soldiers, "felt their Napsacks for Provisions, found non and let them eskip without furder molestation." Yet another issue arose in a confrontation between a member of the Fort Le Boeuf garrison and three unidentified natives. The soldier, ordered out to hunt in the nearby woods, was accosted by the Indians, who "took away [h]is powder horn and bullets and told him not to come out there any more." By treating the soldier as a poacher, the natives asserted, in an unmistakable but nonviolent way, their sovereignty over everything beyond the fort's gate. Indeed, these incidents all suggest that specific goals lay behind natives' actions: efforts to establish or maintain boundaries or attempts to test the reactions of armed intruders in a way that would lessen the chances of large-scale retaliation. Violence for its own sake seems not to have been a motive.[1]

Natives' assaults on or harassment of the army also came in retaliation for their own similar treatment at the hands of soldiers. In this regard the troops seem to have missed no opportunity to trade blows or insults with Indians. An Ohio Seneca was shot and killed near Fort Venango, and Munsees living near the fort complained of being "Ill-used, by soldiers of [the] Garrison, and often Insulted by them" as well as by resident traders. Robbery, willful destruction of property, and physical violence were also part of the Ohio Indians' indictment against the army. What is striking, when one compares the acts committed by each side, is the controlled, largely nonviolent nature of Indian-provoked confrontations, whereas soldiers' actions, whether in reprisal or not, tended to result in more physical violence and vandalism, undoubtedly triggered by the isolation, the boredom, and the generally harsh regime at the small posts where most incidents occurred. Officers, more sensitive to the large native populations that surrounded them, tried to enforce order among their men and on occasion resorted to corporal punishment, though they admitted that their troops "Might at first have had the Right on their Side." As a result, at least two soldiers of the Royal American Regiment were flogged for acts of theft and vandalism committed against Indians. Perhaps believing they did indeed have right on their side, these soldiers doubtless harbored even more enmity toward their Indian neighbors—not to mention their own officers—after the lash than before.[2]

Horse theft by Indians was another common occurrence in the Ohio Country. Horses were already part of Ohio Indian life when the British army appeared and were a proven economic asset. Consequently natives seem to have gone to some lengths, and risks, to add to their stock from the region's biggest potential source: the army. For the warriors involved, horse theft was an undertaking that tested courage and skill, thus adding to personal prestige while at the same time testing the soldiers' strength and reactions and crippling their ability to move themselves and their supplies. The army clearly failed to meet the challenge, since theft of horses and other livestock reached epidemic proportions. Horse theft also served as yet another reminder both of the ease with which the army could be exploited and that the Ohio Country belonged not to the troops, but to the natives. This latter point was underscored by the Indians' appropriation of strays grazing in village cornfields. The army, however, quickly chose to respond according to its rules: orders were issued allowing soldiers to shoot on sight any Indian found with garrison horses or other stock. At Fort Pitt, at least, the order seems to have had some effect.[3]

Soon after traders reappeared in the Ohio Country, natives detected a serious difference between prewar and postwar prices as well as in the quality of the goods. George Croghan reported that the Indians "Complained of the price of strouds saying it was dearer than what they formerly gave the Traders for it." He also found both Delawares and Wyandots upset over the "Extravagent price" charged at the Friendly Association's trading store at Fort Pitt. In the meantime, the emphasis of Indians' complaints began to shift to the structure of the new trading system itself, especially when it appeared that British-implemented changes were not only an inconvenience but part of a larger effort to subordinate the Indians. As trade regulations issued by Johnson and Amherst became known, the level of native discontent grew.[4]

A special focus of native ire was the new requirement that trade be confined to a few forts, under the supervision of military officers and Indian agents. Veteran trader Robert Callender, who tried to adhere to the new rules, found his customers at Sandusky angry "because I would not sell them goods" in their towns as he had formerly done. Bouquet discovered much the same discontent at Fort Pitt, where he learned that local Delawares and Iroquois "do not complain of anything, except that the Traders are not permitted to go to their Towns." For Ohio Indians, the new British requirements spelled considerable inconvenience, since hunters and their families were now expected to make the long trip to army posts, where an uncertain reception awaited them. Moreover, few natives could have missed the larger impact of the new regulations. By attempting to confine trade to a few military posts, British officials seemed bent on removing one vital dimension of intercultural exchange from a native-controlled environment to an army-dominated one. Though such a design clearly impinged on native convenience and economic well-being, the larger implications were equally disturbing, as Shawnees made clear when they complained that the new orders made them think that the British "did not look upon them as brothers and friends."[5]

The Indians' suspicions of British motives were not entirely unfounded. General Amherst certainly lost no opportunity to remind the natives that, with the collapse of French power, the British were "the only People who can Protect" and provide for Indian needs, while both the general and his Indian superintendent spoke of "managing Indians" while "keeping them in Subjection." As Johnson realized, trade, properly maintained, could prove the easiest means of securing the west. The problem, however, rested as much with colonial traders as with the natives. Among the things the Indian Department and army wanted to eliminate altogether was the traffic in liquor. At the same time Amherst, ever distrustful of Indians and those who dealt with them, attempted to eliminate whole catagories of merchandise from the traders' stock, especially muskets, powder, and lead, but also "Scalping and Clasp Knives, Razors, Tomahawks, . . . Fowling pieces"—in short, anything that could be turned against his troops.[6]

Since few traders were under any sort of regulation—only Pennsylvania had enacted its own code—Johnson sought to control the trade by confining it to specific posts and limiting participation to those men who carried licenses issued by the superintendent or one of his subordinates, a system patterned after that previously used by the French. In theory the system would generate revenue through licensing fees that would help offset the cost of supervision while ensuring that no one could trade beyond the close scrutiny of military officers. In practice, Johnson's regulatory system was largely a failure. Army officers soon discovered how easy it was for veteran traders to slip past the forts as they struck out into familiar territory. In only a few instances, notably at Fort Pitt and Fort Sandusky, did the regulations hold for a time, and it was this that produced the Indians' complaints. Overall, however, concern about access to traders tended to subside as the army proved unable to stem the tide of men determined to conduct business as they had done in the past. By the time hostilities came again in 1763, the movement of traders throughout the Ohio Country and beyond had gotten completely out of control; a list of traders killed that year showed they had been in virtually every town west of Fort Pitt. In the meantime, Johnson was forced to admit that he was "at a loss what steps are to be taken" to regain control over the trade and, though it, the Indians.[7]

Indian problems with new trade regulations may have been partially offset by the ultimate failure of Johnson and others to regulate the peddlers' behavior. Nevertheless, from 1760 through the end of 1762 a growing chorus of complaints arose from Ohio Indians, who remained dissatisfied with British behavior and the direction that relations seemed to be taking. Not only were officers attempting to restrict trade while pricing needed goods beyond natives' ability to pay, but the British also suddenly dispensed with such time-honored protocols as gift giving and other signs of friendship and generosity.

   Along with his efforts to restrict the flow of liquor and weapons into the west, Amherst also insisted that the custom of treaty subsidies and periodic gift giving be severely curtailed. The general's decision was based largely on growing pressure from London to reduce contingency expenses as much as possible. Eager to please his superiors and convinced of the extravagance of Johnson's agents, Amherst was only too happy to lower the costs of Indian diplomacy. His prejudices against Indians made the decision easier still. Convinced that gift giving "only serve[s] to Encourage them in Idleness," Amherst insisted that what he variously defined as begging or bribery be ended at once. Moreover, the general believed that such a reform would produce two desired results. The end of gift giving would force natives to work for their supplies, and thus "Constantly Employed . . . they will have less time to Concert, or Carry into Execution any Schemes prejudicial to His Majesty's Interests." And by specifically proscribing weapons and ammunition, Amherst hoped to deprive natives of the "means of accomplishing the Evil which is so much Dreaded"—a full-scale border war.[8]

   What Amherst could never appreciate was the symbolic meaning that gift giving carried for natives. Objects—and sometimes people—served to animate and substantiate messages and agreements between societies, while the act of exchange itself created a bond between peoples. The reciprocal nature of gift giving, in effect, created a climate of peace. Colonists found it necessary to act on native terms in order to conduct business, and they also discovered that, once entered into, agreements needed to be renewed— reanimated—by the periodic rehearsal of the original treaty, a process known in the metaphor of the Covenant Chain as "brightening the chain of friendship." In the process reciprocity became a political tool and, over time, grew less symmetrical. Europeans found themselves providing the lion's share of what was exchanged during treaties, since the colonists more often than not initiated the treaty conferences and sought the alliances and lands that natives could provide. What Amherst defined as bribery was in fact protocol rooted in the reciprocal nature of eastern native societies, some- thing that generations of Anglo-Americans, royal officials and provincials alike, came to understand. Less obvious to colonists, but basic to the Indians' notion of reciprocity, were the assumptions of equality between the parties and the *mutually* binding nature of the exchanges that took place. The violation of reciprocal agreements by either party was in itself an act of war.[9]

It was this reciprocity that Amherst was prepared to ignore in his quest to both lower his army's expenses and reduce Indians to a docile peasantry. Others, closer to the realities of Indian relations, attempted to warn the general of the consequences of such action. Men like Johnson and Croghan feared their superior's "ill-timed Parsimony," which would enormously complicate diplomacy at a time when Britain's control of the west was anything but secure and depended heavily on native goodwill. That depen- dence was acutely appreciated by commanders of small, isolated garrisons, who discovered that Indians expected gifts of ammunition and other sup- plies as signs of friendship and because "it was the Custom" among them. Moreover, natives had a stronger reason for thinking that British generosity was their due since, as Senecas explained, the army had established itself without invitation "in the hart of our Cuntry and on the Warrers Road." Amherst's tight-fistedness only highlighted British intrusiveness while fail- ing to acknowledge native autonomy. Yet because of the constant presence of high-ranking officers like Bouquet, men who shared their general's assessment of gift giving, Amherst's injunction had a more telling effect in the Ohio Country than farther west, where distance and isolation de- manded greater discretion even at the risk of official reprimand.[10]

Ohio Indians were quick to recognize the contrast between the initial generosity displayed at Fort Pitt and the subsequent curtailment of gifts and other marks of friendship. Local Iroquois warriors upbraided George Cro- ghan for his stinginess, pointing out that "while the Warr between you and the french Seem'd Doubtfull you wore genrouse a nouff to all Nations," but now that the conflict had ended, "you Look on us as Nobody." The situation was made even less bearable in light of earlier pledges of generosity; now, it seemed, the British clearly "Spoke from [their] Lips and nott from [their] Harts." Warriors who had been encouraged with supplies to launch raids against the Cherokees discovered that such generosity was for the outbound trip only; others became "very uneasy" upon learning that they were not "being Alowed Amunision and Nessarys as they pas and Repass [Fort Pitt]." Moreover, local Iroquois asserted that British generosity was something they "had a Right" to expect "as being the Propreitors of the Land" on which forts now stood. The "Suden Change in our Generosety," in Croghan's opinion, would cause more harm than good, especially since Amherst's edicts, rigorously upheld by Bouquet, fell heaviest on native warrior-hunters; the very people Amherst attempted to disarm were beginning to "Loek on his Majestys Trupes with a Jelouse Eey."[11]

Indian warriors' "jealousy" surfaced as well over the question of colonial captives. Since the Easton Treaty, when royal officials linked peace with repatriation, the return of border settlers held by Ohio Indians had become a predictable topic at subsequent meetings. Initially discussions had taken a conciliatory tone as experienced hands like Croghan, fully aware of the status of such captives within native societies, insisted that "we do not think it practicable for you to deliver up at once, or in any Place, all our People." Such an approach soon bore fruit as Tamaqua's example at Fort Pitt in 1759 was followed, over the next four years, by a steady, if slow, trickle of captives into that fort and others. That any at all should have been returned was a mark of village leaders' patient lobbying, backed initially by British willingness to compensate those who gave up adopted kin. Moreover, what British authorities chose to see as foot-dragging on the issue was in fact the result of natives' having to deal with a demand that was not only extraordinary, but largely incomprehensible and not in the power of native headmen to order or enforce. Quaker trader James Kenny discovered that "notwithstanding what the head men may promise . . . its not in their power nor practice to force any-thing from the rest . . . without their consents." In these circumstances, obtaining the release of captives or adoptees was something that native leaders did at great risk to social harmony—their principal concern. Croghan, for example, learned that the Shawnees "are in the utmost confusion about [our] prisoners" and could not "agree amongst themselves to deliver the whole," a situation the Indian agent said required that British officers not press their demands too hard.[12]

Initial British generosity helped to relieve tension within native towns while providing incentives in the form of compensation to those who returned their adopted kin—a concept familiar to Indians who had historically employed gifts and ritual to "cover the dead" or otherwise replace losses within primary social groups. Gifts given to village leaders or other influential men often found their way to clan matrons, head warriors of lineages, and others as a means of securing the release of captives. Even then, parting with people who were the living embodiment of lost kinfolk was not easy, and many Ohio Indians were reluctant to take such a step unless others among them led the way. Such inherent difficulties were compounded both by Amherst's decrees governing gift giving and by the increasingly strident tone employed as the general, beset by relatives of the captives, insisted that Indians were not cooperating to the fullest extent. One British officer found himself under direct orders to "demand" that the Miamis immediately return all captives in their towns, while Johnson urged his Covenant Chain partners in Iroquoia to send messages to the Munsees on the upper Susquehanna "requiring" them "immediately to Set at Liberty all the English Prisoners remaining amongst them." However, the British learned that Ohio Indians "are not Willing to part With any [captives] Without Goods." This was especially true of the Shawnees, whom Indian agents and army officers alike found particularly uncooperative and whom Croghan later attempted to coerce by severing trade and other routine contacts. By then, in early 1761, many Ohio Indians may indeed have wondered, as did the Iroquois, whether the British spoke with their hearts or their lips.[13]

Discontent grew from another quarter as well. Though British garrisons provided a lucrative business for native hunters, the continued presence of forts in the Ohio Country further reinforced Indian suspicions that "the English has a Design of Cutting them of[f]," a belief founded not only in decreasing signs of friendship but in the fact that the British had "erected so many Posts in their Country." Native doubts were well founded: expansionists clearly saw garrisons as a way to "put a Bridle upon" uncooperative Indians. Moreover, British forts, and French posts earlier, were a constant reminder that the natives' sovereignty was too little respected and too vulnerable to European inroads. And though Amherst and others assured the Ohio Indians that the forts were only a wartime measure against the French, local natives soon learned that imperial realities clearly dictated otherwise. As Fort Pitt took shape amid the ashes of Fort Duquesne, Ohio Indians voiced concerns; Croghan reported that they were "very Jealous seeing a large Fort building here." The size of Fort Pitt may indeed have given natives additional cause for concern; the post was immense compared with its French predecessor; no mere "strong house," its size bespoke a permanence that clearly troubled its Indian neighbors.[14]

Indian concerns grew when, during the summer and autumn of 1760, the smaller French forts in the Ohio Country were reoccupied by British troops and new forts were constructed that lay athwart portages or, in the case of Fort Sandusky, along well-traveled paths. In addition, military construction continued even after the French had been driven from the area. Johnson was fully aware of the potential for trouble as the number of the garrisons increased, and he warned his deputy on the Ohio that the Wyandots would not find Fort Sandusky "agreable." Indeed, the natives found the place so offensive that they warned its commander early in 1762 that they would "have it burnt" the following spring. The fort stood for another year, but amid increasingly hostile Wyandots.[15]

Although few Ohio Indians were as vocal or as blunt as the Sandusky Wyandots, their actions left little doubt as to their feelings. The chain of outposts in the Ohio Country was the focus of most of the harassment, livestock rustling, and more violent confrontations that soured Indian-army relations. The reason is not hard to identify: throughout the Great Lakes and middle west, tiny British garrisons, isolated from each other and far from available reinforcements, posed no serious threat and were not a present danger. In the Ohio Country, however, though garrisons remained small, there were more of them, Fort Pitt with its much larger force of regulars was nearby, and given the strategic value of its waterways, the region was alive with military activity, as was the Niagara portage. Ohio Indians must also have often shared the suspicion expressed by a Mississauga headman at Niagara who asked Sir William Johnson "the reason for so many Men and so much artillery passing by." Neither Johnson nor anyone else offered any more honest answer than to insist that the forts stood for purely defensive reasons and as bases for traders, explanations that counted for little when the army's advance into the Ohio Country was overtaken by an invasion of far more alarming proportions.[16]

The advance guards of this colonial invasion of the Ohio Country were the hunters who entered the region to tap the rich supplies of game, for hides as well as meat. Precisely when these men, mostly Virginians, began to enter the region is uncertain, but judging from Indian reactions and army reports, by autumn 1761 this invasion had become impossible to ignore. From Redstone Creek Sergeant Angus McDonald reported "Crowds of Hunters" moving through the Monongahela Valley in October of that year. To the north, at Fort Pitt, Bouquet tried to cope with "repeated Complaints from the Indians" about hunters who were making the natives' fall hunt more difficult—and more dangerous. When Indians and Virginians met in the woods, more than insults or threats passed between them, and at least one group of would-be deerslayers was killed by Ohio Indians frustrated by trespassers and attracted by the hunters' superior weapons. Equally troubling to the army was the soldiers' virtual inability to do anything about colonial poachers: Sergeant McDonald complained that he could not "see them," nor "can I send after them," given the few men at his disposal. Despite the Easton Treaty's pledge to secure Indian lands—a pledge repeated often enough at Fort Pitt—it was becoming clear to Crown officers as well as any native who cared to reflect on the matter that the means simply did not exist to police such a vast territory.[17]

On the heels of Virginia hunters came squatters from the same colony, creating further consternation among Ohio Indians. In this instance, however, the army accepted the challenge of keeping the peace and securing native territory as best it could. Bouquet, having seen "these Lands . . . overrun by a number of Vagabonds" during the previous two years, finally issued a proclamation in the autumn of 1761 ordering everyone settled west of the Alleghenies to depart or accept the consequences. In the face of defiance, he backed words with deeds and sent troops from Fort Pitt to burn squatters' cabins along the Monongahela and Youghiogheny rivers and drive the occupants out of the region.[18]

Bouquet's was a singular act that immediately placed him at odds with the powerful gentlemen from Virginia who were already applying pressure on Virginia's new governor, Francis Fauquier, as well as on army officers like Bouquet to acknowledge the Ohio Company's claims in the west. Fauquier acknowledged the Crown's restriction on western settlement, soon to be embodied in a royal proclamation, but he nevertheless reminded Bouquet that the latter's own order on the matter "gives Rise to some Uneasiness," since it appeared to apply equally to "vagabonds" and the well-heeled members of the Ohio Company. Meanwhile the Company, through its agent Thomas Cresap, took a more direct approach, and in September 1760 it offered Bouquet a partnership and 25,000 acres of choice Ohio Valley real estate if he would overlook the Company's speculative schemes. Though ultimately sympathetic with the Company's goals, Bouquet refused the offer, at the same time telling Fauquier that any claims to land had to be approved by Amherst, who in this instance supported his subordinate.[19]

The significance of Bouquet's decision to stand his ground, however, rests on his insistence that the treaties negotiated by the Crown were binding on all the colonies and superseded any deals struck between individual provinces and neighboring Indians. Yet Bouquet's adherence to the letter of his instructions alone could guarantee neither the integrity of the Ohio Country nor the security of the natives living there. The colonel admitted that the squatters prevailed despite his punitive measures, while their numbers grew with the arrival of Pennsylvanians who came west along Forbes's Road, eager to stake new claims or reoccupy farms abandoned during the war. Moreover, while Bouquet was attempting to stem the tide of land grabbing in the west, Amherst was elsewhere permitting—indeed, encouraging— exceptions to the Crown's injunction against western expansion.[20]

Amherst appeared to endorse the Easton Treaty when he assured Ohio Indians that "I mean not to take any of your lands," a pledge endorsed by other officials who told the natives that troops had been sent west "without any design of settling those lands themselves." Yet the general soon made it clear that his promises were conditional and that those conditions had nothing at all to do with Indian territorial claims. To Governor James Hamilton of Pennsylvania, Amherst expanded on his statement to the natives by observing that "I mean not to take any of their Lands, except in such Causes where the necessity of His Majesty's Service obliges me to take Post where I must and will build Forts." It was a considerable exception and included doing more than merely "taking post." As a soldier and conquerer, Amherst well understood the value of a strongly defended, well-provisioned frontier, and soon a memorandum appeared suggesting the advantages of settling farmers near the forts and along the road from Pennsylvania to Fort Pitt.[21]

Amherst's plan for frontier forts sustained by colonies of farmers and tradesmen would have encouraged the very kind of invasion that Indians feared most and trusted Crown officials to prevent. In the meantime, the land beyond the ramparts of Fort Pitt took on the appearance of a settlement as implied by its original name: "Pittsboro." Far from the yeoman settlement Amherst may have envisioned, the clusters of shanties and tumbledown houses known as the "Lower Town," "Upper Town," and "Artillery" and their two hundred–odd inhabitants together composed what a beleaguered Bouquet once called "a colony sprung from Hell." Occupied by soldiers, traders, their women, and a handful of children, "Pittsboro" was more a collection of grog shops, traders' huts, and storehouses than a settlement, but to neighboring Indians the difference must have been insignificant.[22]

Genesee Senecas also balked at Amherst's attempt to "take post" along the Niagara portage. The general's need to control the strategic passage from the St. Lawrence Valley to the upper country led him to garrison Fort Niagara and to secure exclusive British control of the portage as well. One step in this direction was the creation of a boatyard at Navy Island near the Falls;

another was the posting of a small garrison at Fort Schlosser (Niagara Falls, New York), just above the Falls at the upper end of the old French portage road.

The road itself drew Amherst's attention; a settlement along the portage, he believed, would benefit the fur trade as well as local garrisons. Amherst quickly seized the opportunity to secure the road when, in April 1761, several former army officers and New York traders, led by Captain Walter Rutherford, petitioned for land at Niagara. Their plan to establish a portage operation and settlement met with Amherst's immediate approval and a grant of ten thousand acres, given contingent on government approval.[23]

Rutherford and company held other, barely concealed, ambitions beyond operating the portage. Their petition spoke of their having already dispatched workmen to the Falls to build houses, "also horses and oxen as well for farming as for the Conveyance of Boats and Goods." Moreover, protests filed later by traders suggest that the officers planned to turn their establishment to additional advantage by intercepting native traders before they could reach the officially sanctioned store at Fort Niagara. Sir William Johnson, who kept a particularly anxious watch over this activity, found during his trip to Detroit in July "some Carpenters at work, finishing a large house for one Stirling, near the Falls," a building soon joined by others.[24]

Such activity predictably angered the Genesee Senecas and nearby Mississaugas, who for more than a generation had earned a living on the portage road. Johnson warned that the appearance of buildings and heavy equipment "must greatly add to the Indians' discontent, being on the Carrying Place." Moreover, Johnson well understood that the natives would never surrender control over so vital a piece of land and the income it represented. Johnson warned that Rutherford's operation would only "confirm all the Nations in the opinion they have long had, of our desire to root them out of their Country." The concern was real, as was the Senecas' capacity to act accordingly: in 1763 their warriors moved quickly and effectively to close the road, killing dozens of soldiers in the process.[25]

In the complex interplay of interests that marked the west after 1758, the Senecas and Mississaugas found unlikely allies in other corners of the British camp as well. Major William Walters, whose garrison at Fort Niagara would supposedly benefit from Rutherford's establishment, joined the chorus of those who found the operation risky and counterproductive. Not only was Walters concerned about the Senecas' reaction to the portage settlement, he was especially worried about the supply and price of firewood for his troops, since the Rutherford grant embraced the timber stands the garrison normally used.[26]

Amherst's response to such criticism was characteristic. To the Senecas he repeated what must have seemed a hollow promise to respect their territory "unless the necessity of the service" demanded otherwise. Major Walters received much the same reply and was told that Rutherford's establishment was not a settlement but merely a portaging service, despite Walters's evidence to the contrary. The general proved unable to reply to complaints from New York fur merchants who protested that Rutherford's operation was "of the greatest prejudice to His Majesty's Interests," which in this instance meant free trade and unthreatened profits. Before he could respond to these latest charges, Amherst received orders from the Board of Trade to shut down Rutherford's business, a measure prompted in part by a petition received from the Yorkers. Amherst reluctantly ordered Fort Niagara's new commander, Major John Wilkins, to carry out the Board's order. However, Wilkins was expressly forbidden to "publish the orders to the Indians as that may be attended by bad consequences."[27]

British actions in the Ohio Country and on the Niagara frontier provoked a rising tide of Indian anger. During the summer of 1761 war belts circulated widely through the region, demonstrating that some natives began to see warfare, rather than accommodation, as the likeliest way to deal with the British invasion. The war belts originated with the western, or Genesee, Senecas and were readily accepted by their kin in the Allegheny Valley. A long-standing antipathy toward the British, sustained by close association with French traders and agents like the Joncaires, intensified with recent events along the Niagara portage as well as the continued presence of British troops throughout the Allegheny Valley. More important, information gathered after the British discovery of the Senecas' plan strongly suggests that the natives believed they were acting in self-defense. Angry because Amherst "[gave] away their Country to be Settled" and sensitive to the changes in intercultural relations brought on by the general's parsimony and imperious manner, the Senecas concluded that "the English had a mind to cut them of[f] the face of the Earth."[28]

Armed with this conviction and convinced that the danger was general throughout the west, Senecas who advocated a preemptive response to British aggression carried their message to neighboring societies. Their ambitious scheme aimed at nothing less than the total eradication of British forces west of the mountains. According to the plan represented by the war belts, the western Senecas and their neighbors in the Ohio Country would together destroy Fort Pitt and its outposts. At the same time, Indians at Detroit and across the Great Lakes would do the same to the forts in their midst.[29]

The Senecas' effort to galvanize western Indians' cooperation against the ever-troublesome British sheds additional light on Indian thinking. Though Quebec had fallen a year earlier and French forces subsequently removed from the west, the Senecas and others appear to have relied heavily on the assumption that their victory would hasten the restoration of French power and with it a valuable counterweight to British aggression. The Senecas who carried the war belts to Detroit later revealed that they and their people "expect[ed] a french Army to Retake Canada," a notion that may well have been encouraged by Canadians, who were themselves seeking ways to undermine the conquerers. One of the Seneca emissaries, Tahiadoris, was identified as the son of the influential Canadian partisan Philippe-Thomas Chabert de Joncaire. Furthermore, Ohio and Great Lakes Indians maintained regular contact with the French; the Shawnees were known to "Keep a constant correspondence with the Illinois," while Ottawas, Ojibwas, and others had only to visit Detroit, Michilimackinac, or numerous smaller posts to hear encouraging words from disgruntled Canadian traders and *habitants*, all of which may have helped shape an effort to turn back the clock to a more familiar and, for the natives, predictable time before the disruption brought by the Seven Years' War.[30]

By urging their neighbors to take up the hatchet against the British, the Genesee Senecas also revealed both their own growing identification with the nearby Ohio Country and the increasing gulf between the trans-Appalachian natives and their supposed overlords in Iroquoia. As Sir William Johnson hastened during June 1761 to gather the details of what he chose to call a "crime," he discovered that few among the Six Nations had— or at least were willing to share—any specific information about the Senecas' affair. Johnson persisted in his inquiry, however, and in frustration finally accused eastern Seneca headmen of duplicity. He found it impossible to believe that any Iroquois would "presume to undertake so dangerous an affair without your Concurrance and approbation," since he knew that "matters of the smallest importance are never agreed to without the consent of you all." Yet though the western Senecas were ultimately found to be the source of the war belts, Johnson's condemnation of other Iroquois appears baseless. The belts found their way into the Ohio Country and as far west as Detroit, but nothing suggests that any were passed *eastward*, through Iroquoia, though the Senecas seemed determined to unite "all the Indians from the Baye of Gaspie to the Illinois." One reason may have been an acknowledgment by the Genesee Senecas that their confederates to the east did not share the same concerns over affairs beyond the Alleghenies, a region traditionally central to the Senecas' interest.[31]

Moreover, Johnson may have greatly overestimated the influence Iroquois headmen enjoyed. The traditional division of male responsibilities into warmaking and peacekeeping had often led to collisions between village elders and warrior-hunters, each group seeking to maintain community integrity and personal honor through competing sets of values. By 1760 the contest between warriors and headmen had become a constant theme within villages caught up in lengthy wars during which rival Europeans made a habit of courting and promoting warriors, whose prestige mounted steadily as a result. One telling example came in 1762 when Seneca warriors, assembled for a meeting with Johnson, insisted that discussions begin despite the absence of village headmen, whose place it was to manage such events. The warriors brushed aside such protocol, however, insisting that "we are in fact the People of Consequence for managing Affairs," while their civil leaders were merely "a parcell of Old People who say much, but who mean and act very little"—a sentiment that echoed complaints by Ohio Iroquois warriors a decade earlier. Consequently, the 1761 plan for a preemptive war may well have originated with Seneca warriors, without the active participation or even specific knowledge of village headmen, though none of the surviving accounts specifically refers to the war belts as having passed "under the ground"—that is, outside formal councils and other lines of communication. Neither of the two men who carried the belts to Detroit—Tahiadoris and Kiashuta—were identified at the time as "chiefs" or "sachems," though their appearance in 1761 signaled a rising militancy among the western Senecas.[32]

The Senecas also attempted to enlist the Ottawas, Hurons, and Potawatomis living in the vicinity of Detroit. Yet the Senecas were apparently willing to go considerably further, even to calling for the inclusion of the Cherokees, traditional enemies of the peoples in the Ohio Country and lower Great Lakes basin. By casting their net so wide, the Senecas demonstrated the importance they placed on native unity in the face of an invasion that, indeed, was affecting virtually all Indians west of the mountains, though to greatly varying degrees.[33]

Fortunately for the handful of British regulars scattered throughout the middle west, the Seneca plan's greatest potential strength—ethnic unity—was also to prove its greatest weakness. Though some natives in all the towns near Detroit were willing to join the Senecas, few did so openly as the scheme foundered on the rocks of ethnic autonomy and long-standing mutual distrust. Crucial in this respect were the Hurons of Detroit, who both opposed the Senecas' efforts and exposed their plans to the fort's commander.

Captain Donald Campbell's subsequent investigation revealed that local issues played a major part in undoing the Senecas' design. The two emissaries initially expected to hold a general council at Sandusky in conjunction with the Wyandots there. Their invitations to the natives at Detroit were rejected, however. It appears that the Hurons, as titular head of a local alliance, the "Three Fires," were unwilling to let any initiative slip away to Sandusky. The Senecas pressed the issue to no avail and found that the Sandusky Wyandots would not "take up the hatchet without the Consent of the Nations [at Detroit]." Faced with the collapse of their initial plan, the Senecas reluctantly held a council at Detroit on July 3, in the shadow of the British garrison. There the "Three Fires" of Detroit rejected the call to war, warning the Senecas that if they attempted to draw others into their scheme "we shall look upon you as disturbers of the publick tranquility and restore peace and quiet again in the Land." The war belts went no farther, and when pressed by Captain Campbell and later George Croghan, both Seneca messengers revealed most of the details while attempting to allay British suspicions by pledging to "bury all bad thoughts and forget the injuries done against them by the English"—for the moment.[34]

Huron influence was not the only obstacle to pan-ethnic unity. Detroit Indians, who had clashed with Senecas and other Iroquois during the siege of Fort Niagara in 1759, were reluctant to cooperate with people they still considered enemies, who had made no effort to "cover the dead" and set the minds of bereaved kinfolk at ease. In addition, the Senecas may have encouraged powerful countervailing influences from another quarter. Campbell reported that Tamaqua was present at Sandusky, prepared to meet with the Seneca diplomats. Though no other source places him there, it is likely that the Delaware headman was in the vicinity in July; moreover, his previous activities on the Ohio make it likely that Tamaqua, had he been at Sandusky as reported, would most certainly have argued against the Senecas' plan.[35]

Finally, how deeply native societies felt the effect of British expansion helped shape their responses to the Senecas. Indians at Detroit were enjoying the fruits of trade for the first time since the shortages imposed by the war. Moreover, a small British garrison in the midst of a much larger native and Canadian population posed no immediate threat, certainly it did not change in any dramatic way the social or political patterns in the region. Farther west, Ojibwas and Ottawas had even less to fear from the puny garrisons and the handful of traders in their midst. As the Montreal-based peddler Alexander Henry quickly discovered, he and his fellows lived and worked at the pleasure of powerful local headmen, who made plain their contempt for the British. At the same time, the continued presence of numerous Canadian traders, agents, and settlers at Detroit, Michilimackinac, and smaller posts further lessened the impact of the recent British occupation; the natives assumed the French would return. Finally, even among the Ohio Indians who had been most directly affected by the sudden changes following Forbes's appearance, there was apparent reluctance to take up the hatchet. The influence of men like Tamaqua certainly played a part, but so too did the limited ways natives and soldiers in the region had found of accommodating to each other, arrangments that may have convinced local Indians they could still profit from these small forces yet snuff them out whenever they chose. That, and the as yet unclear extent of the British threat, may have induced many natives to continue their earlier decision to watch, wait, and take the full measure of the intruders.[36]

Although the Senecas' plan to rid the west of British intruders did not draw much support, the natives' warning about what would ultimately befall all western Indians should they fail to act proved prophetic. By the end of 1762 those, like Tamaqua, who urged caution and accommodation were losing ground before undeniable evidence that the British not only meant to overturn familiar patterns of intercultural relations but intended to destroy native sovereignty by laying exclusive claim to all the lands west of the mountains.

Though 1763—when native resentment and anxiety finally boiled over into open warfare—has been dubbed a "critical" year, the events of the preceding year were crucial in leading Indians from the Allegheny River to Lake Superior to conclude that only armed conflict could reestablish a proper balance between natives and intruders. During 1762 the friction and suspicion that met British efforts to rationalize control over the west not only intensified but became more widespread; as Amherst's regulations gradually took hold beyond the Ohio River, natives heretofore unaffected by changes in trade and patterns of reciprocity began to feel the pinch of British imperialism. Moreover native societies, heavily dependent on European technology but reluctant to confront the political and cultural implications of that dependence, searched for ways of accommodating tradition and innovation, a process that began among the Delawares but became a feature of trans-Appalachian Indian history for decades to come. Paralleling these tendencies were political changes as those who had argued for peace and cooperation found themselves challenged by others who offered different strategies to cope with events that, by early 1763, appeared to offer little choice beyond surrender or armed resistance.[37]

Trade continued to be a focus of Indian complaints. Credit arrangements, coupled with long-standing concern about prices, led one trader at Fort Pitt to observe that "there is dissatisfaction on both sides," a situation that quickly spread beyond the Ohio. At Detroit and its outposts angry natives railed against shortages of powder and ball, though they were as yet unaware that the scarcity was deliberate and was directly attributable to orders from army headquarters in distant New York.[38]

Meanwhile, Ohio Indians continued to face colonial settlers. Despite Bouquet's early efforts to curb both their speculative appetite and their search for homesteads, Virginians continued to turn up in the Monongahela Valley. The natives' alarm over the civilian invasion of the Ohio Country was reinforced by the army's failure to offer any compensation for lands now occupied by forts. By summer 1762 the Easton Treaty and all the assurances of limited, temporary occupation and pledges of friendship seemed designed only to dull Indian suspicions, as British leaders and their colonial subjects persisted in brushing aside native protests while they treated the region as their own. Ohio Indians whose earlier dispossessions were fresh in their minds could find much cause for unease as their new homes were now exposed to the same sort of invasion that had brought them to the Ohio Valley in the first place. Such thoughts may have shaped the Delawares' and Munsees' response to the appearance in the Muskingum Valley of Moravian missionaries Christian Frederick Post and John Heckewelder. Heckewelder found that many Delawares believed that "this missionary scheme might prove a mere pretence, in order to enable the white people to obtain a footing in the Indian Country," a suspicion seemingly confirmed when Post began to stake out a generous tract of land for his new spiritual sanctuary. He was forced into more narrow and, by native standards, more realistic limits by Kageshquanohel (Captain Pipe), who also urged the Moravians to conform to what the natives took to be the superior model of the French Jesuits, who made no claims to the land. Kageshquanohel ended his lesson with the warning that his people were determined not to be "driven further back, as has been the case ever since the white people came into this Country."[39]

Captain Pipe's own suspicions led him to war against the British less than a year after his encounter with Post and Heckewelder. Other Ohio Indians took more immediate action; the result was an increase in the level of theft and harassment that had marked Indian-army relations for the past several years. Horse theft at the outposts continued; meanwhile, war parties returning from the Tennessee Valley began to kill livestock belonging to the Fort Pitt garrison and nearby settlers. Robberies also continued; traders working among the Shawnees were plundered, and even the mustering agent for Bouquet's troops found himself waylaid by native hunters who relieved him of his rations and liquor but otherwise did him no harm. Others were less fortunate. Persistent disputes over prices and the now-predictable habits of colonial hunters and liquor-selling peddlers provoked confrontations that left traders William Clapman and William Newkirk and one other man dead. Clapman's killers included two of his Indian slaves, whose bid for freedom was abetted by Ottawas living near Sandusky. And in what was perhaps a sign of their disgust with Clapman and others like him, his killers destroyed his stock of goods rather than plundering them. Newkirk was killed by Genesee Senecas who then fled to Kanestio, a town on the headwaters of the Susquehanna that quickly became a haven for many of the anti-British Senecas and Munsees.[40]

Such incidents and the general increase in native concern about the future course of intercultural relations were further sustained by the convergence of other events peculiar to late 1761 and 1762. By autumn 1761 British officers were reporting food shortages among the Indians. As early as September, Ojibwas near Fort Michilimackinac expressed anxiety over food supplies for the coming months. A month later Captain Campbell reported that Detroit *habitants* and Indians alike had suffered poor harvests, while both the Six Nations and the Ohio Indians experienced a similar shortfall; in addition, the Ohio Indians' winter hunt was cut short by unusually severe weather. By spring 1762 John Heckewelder found that west of the mountains "there was famine in the land."[41]

Spring 1762 brought with it widespread sickness. Little is known about this malady; the British referred to it simply as the "sickness" or "severe sickness," though James Kenny identified it as the ague, from which many Indians died. The victims were from towns west of the Muskingum and south of the Great Lakes. The disease was unlikely to have been smallpox, which had struck the region as recently as 1757–58; however, it may have been a respiratory ailment, perhaps the influenza that appeared in the British colonies in 1761 and could have been carried west by any number of soldiers, traders, or other travelers. Whatever the source, the sickness lingered through the summer and brought death and hardship to a large part of the middle west, as British ensign Thomas Hutchins discovered. Sent by George Croghan to survey the state of Indian affairs and to compile cartographic data on the Great Lakes region, the future cartographer of the United States made his return journey to Fort Pitt by way of the lower Michigan peninsula and the Ohio Country. He first encountered the illness among the Potawatomis, who in August were still battling the infection and its consequences. Neighboring Ouiatanons, Piankashaws, Mascoutens, Kickapoos, Weas, and Shawnees were also stricken. At the principal Shawnee town on the lower Scioto River, Hutchins found that the "People were sick and are Dying every day."[42]

Hutchins also confronted widespread native dissatisfaction with the British response to their plight. From Michilimackinac to the Scioto Valley, Hutchins was berated and upbraided for his, and his superiors', marked lack of generosity. The ensign, who made his trip without a stock of the gifts normally expected of a colonial emissary, found the Potawatomis "greatly Surprised" at his inability to return their meager hospitality, especially since, laid low by sickness, they had expected that Sir William Johnson "woud send them some few Presents to keep their Women and Children from the cold" while the men, "afflicted with the Sickness," were unable to hunt or clear new fields for corn. Angry over this singular lack of regard for their welfare, the natives gave Hutchins a stern lecture on the principles of friendship and reciprocity as well as a thinly veiled warning of what might happen should British behavior not improve. The Ouiatanons and Kickapoos likewise condemned British tight-fistedness, contrasting it to the highly regarded generosity of the French, who were still close by in the Illinois Country.[43]

Hutchins and his superiors within the Indian Department got the message. To Croghan, Hutchins pointed out that whereas "during the Late War the french were Accustomed . . . to make these People great Presents," the Indians "think it very strange that this Custom should be so immediately broke off by the English," especially when traders were forbidden to carry needed ammunition to their towns "as to enable those Indians to kill game Sufficient for the support their families." This view was shared by Indians in the Ohio Country as well, where, even before Hutchins's journey, George Croghan confronted angry Iroquois who also complained that, while generosity "has allways been a Custom Long before [the Seven Years' War]," the British, having emerged the victors, "Look on us as Nobody." Widespread native anger forced the Indian agent to admit that "the Indians Seem Disapointed In thire Expectation of presents as useal and apear Very Sulky and Ill Tempered," especially the warriors who, faced with shortages and rampant sickness at home, were acutely sensitive to "this Suden Change in [British] Generosity to them."[44]

Some Ohio Indians and their neighbors confronted British imperialism with barely veiled hostility and verbal assaults. The western Delawares responded to the challenges posed by war and colonial expansion by attempting to bring their own world and that outside into greater harmony. The result was a nativist movement that, according to its adherents, would result in a better, more secure way of life.

The Delaware nativist movement emerged in response to the teaching of Neolin. Both the messenger and the message were rooted in Delaware culture; Neolin was only the latest in a line of prophets who had appeared among the Delawares and Munsees during the course of their struggle to cope with expanding colonial societies. Moreover, Neolin's message, which included the rejection of European technology and other aspects of colonial society and the ritual purification and revitalization of traditional Delaware culture on all levels, was more than a reaction to the stress created by widespread use of liquor, growing dependence on colonial societies, and the problems of being "in between" colliding empires. By identifying the newly arrived British as the greatest threat to native societies, Neolin's teaching also enjoyed popularity well beyond the confines of the Delaware towns. Great Lakes Indians, notably the Ottawa headman Pontiac, faced with the abrupt departure of longtime French allies and trading partners, also found Neolin's message appealing—especially since its anti-British theme reinforced the widespread belief in the lakes country that the British were unwelcome intruders threatening to upset a generations-old social and political order.[45]

Neolin's message also included a strong reaffirmation of Delaware culture. The prophet urged the Delawares to reexamine themselves and to adopt what he identified as a morally superior way of life. In this sense the prophet's teaching was as much "pro-Delaware" as it was militantly anti-British. Neolin's teaching did intensify the ongoing debate within Delaware society over how best to respond to new signs of British expansion, while the prophet's message encouraged other Delawares to challenge the accommodationist stand of men like Tamaqua, whose own influence waned in 1762 in the face of men who were willing to consider resistance an acceptable strategy—perhaps the only one that could preserve their society.[46]

Although John Heckewelder found Tamaqua still "favorably disposed" toward the British, the headman's cooperative demeanor was not shared by many of his people, whose earlier friendliness had, the Moravian found, "considerably cooled" as autumn approached. Neolin's preaching was clearly having an impact on the Delawares, as did events beyond the Ohio Country. In August, the western Delawares participated in yet another meeting with Pennsylvanians at Lancaster. A gathering whose purpose was to confirm peace between the colony and the Delawares quickly degenerated into a spectacle of political intrigue and recrimination that found Tamaqua caught in a verbal crossfire between proprietary authorities and Quakers who used the meeting to once again press eastern Delaware land claims. This in itself must have led Tamaqua and others to wonder about the sincerity of colonial peace overtures. However, the council also gave Pennsylvanians an opportunity to acquire greater access to the western tributaries of the Susquehanna River, ostensibly for trade. This move upset the western Delawares, who, "Imagening the Desire was to Setle thire Cuntry," vigorously resisted the governor's request. And to add insult to injury, the Delawares found that the treaty gifts had been distributed in an "unequal" fashion and were in any event mostly lost on the return to the Ohio Country when, according to George Croghan, the natives were "Robd of allmost all thire horses and other things."[47]

The Delawares thus returned from Lancaster "not so cheerful as befor." Some found temporary solace in drink: Kenny found several in Tamaqua's group "half Snow'd with Rum" when they reached Fort Pitt, but neither the numbing effects of the liquor nor fair words from British officers could prevent the natives from believing that their journey east had been a disaster. Consequently, Delaware willingness to cooperate in what now appeared to be a concerted drive to dispossess them declined precipitously, while the Lancaster Treaty's sorry outcome seems to have hastened Tamaqua's eclipse. Even before his departure for Lancaster, Tamaqua had begun to lose influence among his own people. James Kenny was told that the "Beaver never was made a King by the Indians, but by the people of Virginia," a reference to that colony's acknowledgment of Shingas and his family during the 1752 Logg's Town treaty negotiations. Made by a western Delaware, this declaration also reflected the less than unanimous support Tamaqua enjoyed at home. This point was impressed on Kenny when he learned from the same Indian that "Neat-hot-whelme" (Netawatwees or Newcomer) was, in 1762, recognized by many as the Delaware "king."[48]

Tamaqua's declining influence reflected the Delawares' growing rejection of their headman's advocacy of accommodation. Four years had produced few tangible benefits for the natives, while soldiers and Indian agents alike exhibited a marked inclination to threaten, withhold needed goods, and generally behave in a manner that completely contradicted fair words about peace and friendship. Indeed, that contradiction lay all about the Delawares in the shape of forts, once defined as temporary but now evidently intended to remain for purposes that seemed clear as squatters entered the region and colonial governments seemed bent on extending their borders at the natives' expense. Though their lands had been occupied by foreign armies for nearly a decade, the threat to the natives' sovereignty and security never seemed so immediate as in autumn 1762.

The Delawares were not alone in their growing distrust of British intentions. In November, army officers learned that the Ohio Iroquois were again urging their neighbors to war and had recently offered "a War Belt and Bloddy Tomahawk" to the Shawnees. The Shawnees readily accepted, even though they were besieged by the sickness then sweeping the middle west, which had already killed 100 to 180 people. The army dismissed the news, given the lateness of the season, though old hands among the traders, including Croghan, were convinced "that the Indians will Breake out again in War."[49]

Colonel Bouquet, sifting through reports from the field, wrote in November of the "pretended new conspiracy," which he believed embraced all the Ohio Indians. Yet from the natives' point of view the events of 1762 pointed just as clearly to a British conspiracy, one that few would have considered "pretended." The event that confirmed native suspicions was news of the Anglo-French peace negotiations. Word that France had ceded virtually the entire middle west to Great Britain spread quickly through Indian societies and caused widespread consternation bordering on disbelief. James Kenny, wintering at Fort Pitt, learned that Netawatwees "was Struck dumb for a considerable time" on learning of the Europeans' arrangement. Moreover, Indians in the Great Lakes region who previously had shown little concern about British expansion were equally stunned by the news. Whatever hope Ottawas and others may have had for the eventual return of the French were dashed as news of the peace treaty spread north from New Orleans. The year 1762 had opened amid suspicion, illness, and death; it ended with irrefutable proof not only of Britain's real objective in the west but of the singular duplicity of Europeans generally. As the Ohio natives were quick to point out, "They were never Conquered by any Nation" and therefore "the French had no right to give away their Country." As the new year approached, many natives, from the Genesee River to Green Bay, could have agreed with the Shawnees who concluded that the British had become "too great a People," a situation that seemed to allow no other choice but war.[50]

Although news of the Europeans' deal first reached western Indians between November 1762 and January 1763, armed conflict did not commence until May. Winter was a time when villagers in the west dispersed to hunting camps. Consequently, decisions about whether or when to attack the British outposts were necessarily deferred until spring.

Warfare came first not to the Ohio Country, but to the Great Lakes region. There elements of the "Three Fires"—the Ottawas, Potawatomis, and Hurons—under the charismatic leadership of Pontiac, attacked Detroit in early May, beginning a siege of that important post that lasted until October. Inspired by promises from local *habitants* of French assistance and hoping to resurrect the French king's more benign rule in the west, Pontiac and his followers began the first of a series of attacks that, taken together, have since been popularly known as the "conspiracy of Pontiac." Although the Ottawas' war leader undeniably commanded great influence in the vicinity of Detroit, a better name for the conflict—"the Western Indians' Defensive War"—has recently been offered by W. J. Eccles. Rather than a concerted pan-Indian uprising orchestrated by one man, the 1763 war was actually several local conflicts inspired by events at Detroit, the western Great Lakes, and the Ohio Country. Indeed, the one pattern that emerges from the Indians' Defensive War is the wide variability in native actions: some garrisons were wiped out, others were captured and their troops held captive, while the distant fort at La Baye (Green Bay, Wisconsin) was abandoned and its tiny garrison spared annihilation when the powerful eastern Sioux intervened on behalf of Ensign James Gorrell. In a broader sense, too, the war took on a distinctive regional character; those who rallied to Pontiac anticipated the restoration of French power in the region and a return to a more familiar pattern of intersocietal relations; the Ohio Indians fought for nothing less than control of their lands and their political and cultural autonomy.[51]

Detroit had been under close siege for nearly a month when Ohio Indians struck near Fort Pitt. Between May 27 and 29 a family settled near the fort was attacked, as were isolated parties of soldiers and traders. The more observant among the British garrison may have anticipated the attack, noting that several Delawares had arrived the previous week to trade but conducted their business with "uncommon dispatch" and with uncharacteristic disregard for the quality of what was offered for their deer hides. In the meantime, Munsees living in the upper Allegheny Valley had quietly "removed from their Towns, and carried everything with them, leaving their Cornfields open." The Munsees acted by choice, but the same words could have described the actions of dozens of squatters who fled to Fort Pitt in the wake of the Clapman Massacre and the attack on the fort's isolated sawmill.[52]

Not all Delawares and Munsees were bent on attacking the garrisons, however. Many, knowing what was to come, simply attempted to stock up on needed supplies before moving out of the line of fire. As in the Seven Years' War, the prospect of renewed fighting created divisions within Ohio

Indian towns or deepened factional conflicts already present. As early as January, some Shawnees admitted that their people "were much divided" over the appearance of new war belts from the western Senecas, saying that "one half of our Warroirs was for making War." Such divisions persisted. During the siege of Fort Pitt that summer, while numerous Shawnee warriors were sniping at the garrison, others appeared at the gates to assure the commander that traders living among them were safe and to inquire about events since the war began. This same party also told Captain Simeon Ecuyer that "the Capts and Warriors of the Delaware pay no regard to their Chiefs," who had tried in vain to persuade their young men not to accept the hatchet and encouragement offered by Pontiac's men.[53]

Delawares who had argued for peace lost much influence by late spring. Insisting that "all the Country was theirs" and furious that "they had been Cheated out of it" by the British and French, Delaware warriors took the field in large numbers, vowing not to rest "till they had burnt Philadelphia." In the face of such determination, Tamaqua and other headmen had little choice but to stand aside. By then Tamaqua's once far-reaching influence had all but vanished. Contributing to this may have been the sudden loss of kin and allies whose prestige had helped strengthen Tamaqua's own position. Tamaqua's brother, Delaware George died at Fort Pitt early in 1762. At about the same time, Pisquetomen, the able diplomat, disappears from the record—whether owing to advanced age and inactivity or to death is unclear. Finally Shingas, whose earlier support had been crucial to Tamaqua, lost his wife in 1762 and may have abandoned public affairs for a time.[54]

Meanwhile the Delawares' determination to strike the British before they themselves were destroyed was so widespread as to suggest near total repudiation of any policy of accommodation; a position that was evidently encouraged by the new, and popularly recognized, "king" Netawatwees. Information supplied by returned captives in 1764 indicates that settlers were held in at least half a dozen Delaware towns; traders were killed or plundered throughout the Ohio Country. Also, a large number of captives were held at Newcomer's Town, later the political center of the western Delawares. Finally, the eclipse of those who had earlier advocated peace and accommodation may have been partly self-imposed—as much the result of disgust with the recalcitrant British as of a shift in public opinion at home. On the eve of open warfare in the Ohio Country, Delaware headmen opposed to the impending conflict, including Tamaqua and Shingas, sent a warning to local traders urging them to leave the Delaware towns. The message reflected "the Friendship that formerly Subsisted between our

Grandfathers and the English," but it included a stern rebuke over recent affairs. Though "we thought your King had made Peace with Us," and though they had "Joined it heartily and Desired to hold it always good," the headmen made it clear that they had now become disillusioned.[55]

Nevertheless many of these men, eventually joined by Custaloga and others, also appeared at besieged Fort Pitt to declare that "they are for Peace" and were also prepared to use any means to stop the Ottawas' campaign against Detroit. In return, however, the Delawares expected the army to abandon Fort Pitt, since, as one British observer learned, "we by taking possession of their Countrey were the Cause of the War." The garrison was in no mood to entertain such notions, especially since it expected Bouquet's relief column at any time. Moreover, any prospects for negotiations were dashed when, during this meeting, the soldiers refused to return four rifles belonging to Shawnees in the delegation, whose peaceful demeanor was suspect. The Shawnee headman present, inclined to negotiate and doubt-less looking for a sign of goodwill, was "very much enraged" by Captain Ecuyer's behavior; the Delawares were also "very much irritated" and according to witnesses "would not shake hands with our People at Parting." It was an unfortunate gaffe: one of the Delawares present at the meeting was White Eyes, an influential war leader and eventual successor to Netawat-wees; another participant was the Munsee Wingenund, who remained an implacable enemy of the Anglo-Americans for years.[56]

Among the Genesee Senecas and their kin in the upper Allegheny Valley there was far more unanimity on the issue of war. Having first proposed a united assault on the British, the western Senecas were prepared to act when news of the Anglo-French peace reached them. The warriors found themselves "greatly mistaken" in their earlier willingness to believe British promises that their lands would not be threatened; that the "warriors *and* women were very uneasy" made a consensus much easier to achieve. Another powerful influence was a strong traditionalist element within the Genesee towns. As missionary Samuel Kirkland discovered in 1765, the traditionalists' "Aversion to the English" remained a powerful force among the Genesee Senecas. This deep-seated antipathy toward the British also drew on the close, generations-old contact between western Senecas and French Canadians. This and the western Senecas' strong westward orienta-tion made them powerful allies for natives living in the Ohio Country.[57]

French assistance, hoped for by Pontiac's followers and perhaps antici-pated by the Senecas, was limited to encouraging words and modest aid by Canadian traders in the west. Throughout 1763 and 1764 British officers received reports about French traders based in the Illinois Country, who

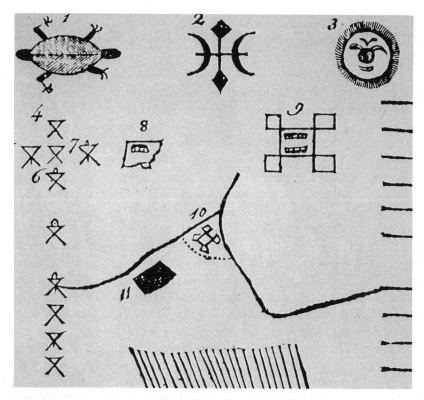

8. An Ohio Indian view of British occupation: map drawn on sugar maple bark by the Munsee Wingenund, interpreted by the Delaware headman White Eyes. The map identifies the British forts in and near the Ohio Country in 1762; nos. 10 and 11 are Fort Pitt and "Pittsboro"; no. 9 is Detroit. (Courtesy of the Hermon Dunlap Center for the History of Cartography, the Newberry Library, Chicago)

sent token gifts of powder and shot and lent moral support to their former Shawnee and Ottawa trading partners. Such help was welcomed by Ohio Indians, though a French restoration was not an issue among these natives as it was for those at Detroit. Moreover, by late 1763 Governor Louis Billouart, sieur de Kelérec of Louisiana, received instructions regarding the impending transfer of the Illinois Country to Britain and sent messages both to the *habitants* at Detroit and to Pontiac urging them to seek peace with their enemy, since no further assistance would be forthcoming. What few supplies continued to trickle into native towns came from Canadian traders whose own stocks had become badly depleted by war's end.[58]

Encouragement came to the Ohio Indians from other natives as well.

Soon after the first attacks on Detroit in May, "the Belt and Hatchet came from the Lake Indians to the Delawares at Tuskorrwas," who were urged to join in the struggle. Later that year the "Ottawa Confederacy"—Pontiac's force at Detroit—was again attempting to enlist the Ohio Indians in a more concerted effort to crush the last few garrisons in the west. Meanwhile, warriors from the Ohio Country and the Great Lakes managed to join forces on at least one occasion; in mid-June Fort Presque Isle fell to a native force that included Ottawas and Ojibwas as well as Wyandots and Senecas. Yet Ohio Indians fought their own war and would not be stampeded by outsiders. In October 1763 representatives of the Ottawas' "confederacy" became so exasperated with Shawnee foot-dragging on the question of a pan-native alliance that they "plucked the horns [symbols of chiefly office] from their [Shawnees'] heads"—by which they meant to remove "everything but War from the thoughts of [the Shawnee] Sachems." Yet the Shawnees, as well as the Delawares and Ohio Iroquois, held a distinctly local view of the conflict; Ohio natives and those to the west were fighting different wars, each directed at a different threat posed by the larger prospect of British conquest and expansion. Moreover, the historical ethnic friction that had shattered the Senecas' hopes in 1761 was still very much alive; Delawares who wanted a return to peace in their land proved willing to attack Pontiac's force at Detroit in order to secure that goal, while in 1764 British forces were able to enlist Ottawas and other western Indians in their campaign to end Ohio Indian resistance.[59]

Nevertheless, within the Ohio Country the war produced growing cooperation. Years of interethnic marriages produced bonds between societies, as was the case with the Wolf, whom the British identified as a Delaware who was "a son to Kickiuskum [Keekyuscung] but born of a Wyandot Woman." Kinship bonds like these became important as warriors sought allies in their attacks on British garrisons and traders. Cooperation did not end with kinship, however. Shared concerns about autonomy and security continued to bind together all natives within the Ohio Country. By October 1764 Shawnees, Senecas, and Delawares joined in sending their own war belts to the Miamis and to Pontiac's followers, urging them to continue the fight. And as Bouquet's army was nearing the Muskingum Valley in November, these Ohio Indians, joined by Munsees and Wyandots from Sandusky, were referring to themselves collectively as the "Five Nations of Scioto"—an alliance shaped in part by militant Shawnees who, in Croghan's opinion, had "More to Say with the Western Nations then any othe[r] [nation] this Way."[60]

Driven by a conviction that British expansion posed a grave, perhaps fatal, danger to their way of life, and encouraged both by events beyond the region and by growing cooperation closer to home, native warriors lost little time in destroying all British pretense of control over the Ohio Country. Between June 16 and 20, 1763, Senecas destroyed or forced the evacuation of Forts Venango, Le Boeuf, and Presque Isle; the Venango garrison was destroyed and the attacks dealt the army a serious blow by effectively cutting communication between Fort Pitt and the lower Great Lakes. An equally devastating blow came on September 14 when Genesee Senecas struck again, this time at the Niagara portage. Not only did they destroy a supply convoy and two companies of infantry, they also cut the portage road, further isolating those few western posts that remained in British hands. In the meantime Delaware, Munsee, and Shawnee raiding parties attacked Forbes's Road and the supply bases at Forts Ligonier and Bedford.[61]

Fort Pitt proved a more difficult target, much too large and heavily defended to be taken by storm or by surprise. The Delawares and Shawnees could not ignore the post, however, and their efforts to reduce it reveal a broad strategy that reflected both planning and coordination. When the fort was first attacked in late May, the warriors concentrated their efforts against the outposts that linked the fortress to its supplies and reinforcements. In swift attacks, warriors readily overpowered the token outpost garrisons, taking valuable supplies and weapons. Only then, in late June, did the Ohio Indians turn their full attention to Fort Pitt. Their larger strategy was made clear at a parley with the fort's commander on June 24. On that occasion the Delawares reminded Captain Ecuyer that "Fort Pitt was the last Fort [the British] had in their Country." Armed with clear knowledge that he was isolated, the natives hoped Ecuyer would abandon his post, and they promised "they would not Interrupt him nor his People in their March" to the eastern settlements. Isolation and fear of a prolonged siege would be the natives' principal weapons against large British garrisons, and the total elimination of these symbols of British military power remained the principal goal of Ohio Indian warfare.[62]

Though burdened with over five hundred people—half or more civilians, some with smallpox—Ecuyer refused the summons and held fast until reinforced by Bouquet later that summer. The Senecas' effort to apply similar pressure against Fort Niagara, although it produced a major tactical victory, fared no better, in part because of the natives' inability to block British reinforcements coming overland through Iroquoia to Oswego, then by water to Niagara. Yet throughout the summer and into late autumn, parties of warriors continued to punish the army whenever an opportunity arose, while keeping forts and roads under constant harassment.[63]

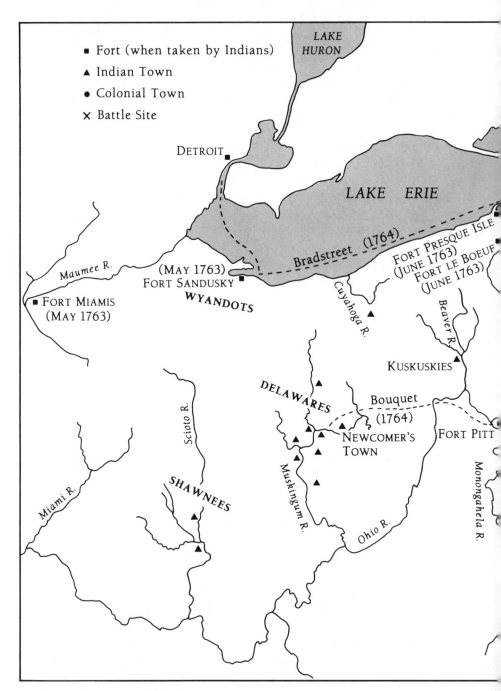

Map 5 The Ohio Country, 1758–1765.

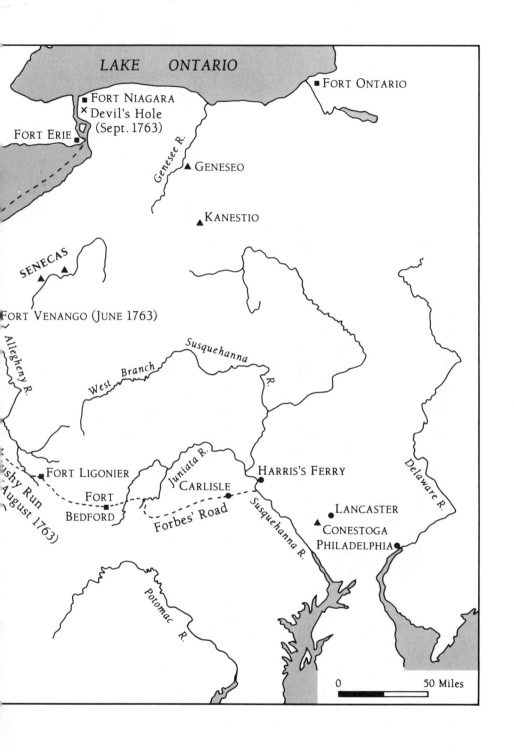

LAKE ONTARIO

■ FORT ONTARIO

■ FORT NIAGARA
✕ Devil's Hole
(Sept. 1763)

FORT ERIE ■

Genesee R.

▲ GENESEO

▲ KANESTIO

SENECAS
▲   ▲

FORT VENANGO (JUNE 1763)

Allegheny R.

Susquehanna

West Branch

R.

Delaware R.

■ FORT LIGONIER

Juniata R.

HARRIS'S FERRY ●

CARLISLE

●shy Run
August 1763)

FORT
BEDFORD ■

CARLISLE

Forbes' Road

Susquehanna R.

LANCASTER ●
▲ CONESTOGA
PHILADELPHIA ●

Potomac R.

0   50 Miles

Meanwhile Ohio Indians launched a new campaign against the other threat that confronted them: the colonial border settlements. In a series of raids Ohio warriors, joined by Senecas and Munsees from Kanestio, once more drove back Virginia and Pennsylvania settlers and brought these colonies face to face with the terror and political turmoil of border warfare for the second time in a decade. As early as mid-June 1763, Bouquet spoke of "a general Panick" in the vicinity of Carlisle as people abandoned farms only recently reoccupied after the Seven Years' War and fled to the security of eastern towns. The onslaught continued through the summer, diminished over the winter, but began anew the following spring. Meanwhile Virginia's western border came under attack "from Potowmack almost as low as the Carolina Line" as Shawnees and Delawares joined Ohio Iroquois warriors in attacks that, on one occasion, "penetrated . . . to within a few miles of Winchester."[64]

The Ohio Indians' raids against the border settlements produced not only panic but also a backlash of Indian hating and a widening rift between western settlers and eastern politicians. Neither race-based Indian hating not the east-west political division was new in 1763; each had roots in the destruction that marked the Ohio natives' first war against the settlements. At that time border settlers who were driven from their farms were less inclined to distinguish enemies from other natives who had no part in the war; to Scotch-Irish and German frontiersmen *Indians* were the problem, and a fear of some natives was, in the crucible of border warfare, transformed into racial hatred of all Indians.[65]

In the brief respite between Forbes's campaign and the outbreak of fighting in 1763, border settlers' attitudes had hardened. Pennsylvanians returning to pick up the pieces of wrecked homesteads and shattered lives were outraged that their government continued to deal with "savages," to "tamely cover" the bodies of hundreds of dead without demanding retribution, and to not only permit but encourage trade with Indians, all of which they held to be an outrageous "manifest Partiality in favor of Indians." Moreover, when attacks began anew in 1763, the provincial government that collected their taxes proved unwilling to protect border settlers. This, and the government's protection of Indians who were living within the colony, led to the Conestoga Massacre of December 14, 1763. Lashing out at Indian enemies and an uncaring government, frontiersmen murdered six Indians at the Conestoga town, and two weeks later they carried out another attack against Conestoga refugees who were being sheltered in the Lancaster jail. By February an army of embittered, vengeance-bent settlers, dubbed the "Paxton Boys," turned toward Philadelphia to attack Moravian Indians there and to force a showdown with the authorities. Though deprived of the chance to kill more Indians or to confront public officials like the reviled Israel Pemberton, whose Friendly Association promoted peace and trade with western Indians, the Paxton Boys nevertheless made their intense race hatred of Indians known to easterners. One observer found that the frontiersmen "in General, hates any Thing that Savours of the Name of an Indian," while others wished to "extirpate from earth this Savage Race." Such words, and the slaughter at Conestoga and Lancaster, were only the first salvos in a virulent, racially motivated campaign of Indian hating that spread through Pennsylvania and Virginia border regions during the 1760s and 1770s, carrying with it sectional animosity and distrust of provincial and royal authority.[66]

Although eastern Pennsylvanians were shocked by the indiscriminate violence the Paxton Boys displayed, the colony's leaders were also shaken by the idea of a western insurrection and were compelled to offer some protection to the border settlements. Falling back on earlier practices, in July 1764 the colony issued a new scalp bounty and once again used the promise of cash to induce westerners to enlist and see to their own defense. Perhaps in an effort to deny or dismiss the questionable practice of institutionalizing the sort of rampant violence that had produced the Conestoga Massacre, the bounty carefully distinguished between western Delawares and Shawnees, who were identified as enemies, and Six Nations Indians, Moravians, and other natives within the colony, who were to enjoy the full protection of the government. For enemy Indians, however, the province was prepared to pay 150 pieces of eight for each adult male captive and 138 for a man's scalp; women commanded 138 and 50 pieces of eight, respectively. The small difference between the price of a male captive and his scalp made it unlikely that anyone would go out of his way to take a prisoner, though the substantial difference for women served as an inducement to show mercy, as was the price of 138 pieces of eight offered for children taken captive. Given the mood on the border, however, it is unlikely that those who claimed the bounty bothered to consider the distinctions the government attempted to draw. Rather, the provincial bounty encouraged indiscriminate killing and contributed to the "open season" atmosphere that made the colonial border region increasingly treacherous for any Indians.[67]

The British army, expected to keep the peace and defend the western border, failed in both respects. Ill prepared to withstand the western Indians' aggressive style of warfare, the army struggled throughout the summer of 1763 to regain the initiative. In the process, the regulars proved no less vulnerable to Indian hating than the Paxton Boys. Amherst, who chose to discount earlier rumors of native unrest and the western officers' knowledge of war belts, still could not "think the Indians have it in their power to Execute any thing Serious against Us" as the first fragmentary reports filtered into his New York headquarters from Detroit and Fort Pitt. Later, finally convinced that he had an Indian war on his hands, the general continued to insist that he would readily punish the "Treacherous Behaviour" of people who, he said, cut a "Contemptible Figure" in the eyes of his army.[68]

As military reality intruded on Amherst's complacency, the general found himself hard pressed to place even a token force in the field; most of Amherst's American army was in the West Indies, and those few battalions that had returned were little more than collections of invalids stricken with tropical fevers and scurvy. Unwilling to denude the Canadian garrisons, Amherst collected malaria-ridden Highlanders and sent them to Bouquet in Philadelphia. Others, including recently discharged men pressed into service, were sent by way of Fort Niagara to Detroit, where at heavy cost they finally broke Pontiac's siege. In the meantime, with smaller outposts gone and without enough troops to hold Fort Niagara, Amherst's plan to regain control of the west rested entirely with Bouquet's motley collection of Scots, Royal Americans, and Pennsylvania militiamen, hardly five hundred in all, whose task was to move west on Forbes's Road, relieve Fort Pitt, then press on to Lake Erie and Detroit to deal the enemy a crushing blow. Amherst urged his subordinate to show no mercy, telling Bouquet that "I Need only to add, that I Wish to Hear of no Prisoners, should any of the Villians be met with in Arms." Bouquet concurred, but he wondered if precious manpower could be saved by "mak[ing] use of the Spanish Method to hunt [Indians] with English Dogs." which would, he thought, "effectively extirpate or remove that Vermin." Both men agreed that, in any event, every native town in the Ohio Country should be razed and its occupants scattered.[69]

Despite their aggressive tone, Amherst and Bouquet faced serious obstacles as they attempted to regain the west. The annihilation or capture of every western post save Detroit, Fort Niagara, and Fort Pitt left the few remaining regulars bottled up and almost isolated. So confusing and incomplete was the information coming from the west that Bouquet, pressed by Amherst to take the field, confessed that "We are yet too much in the Dark to form a Plan." Even after determining the course of his campaign, Bouquet found little immediate help in Pennsylvania and neighboring colonies and was forced to rely almost entirely on his two depleted battalions of Highlanders and his handful of Royal Americans. The march west from

Carlisle was slow and plagued with difficulties. Many of the troops were weak from malaria; those men who could march strayed from the road and became lost in the woods. Bouquet was finally forced to hire woodsmen to serve as flank guards, less to protect against ambush than to shepherd his regulars along the line of march. Supplying even a small force proved almost impossible; the army's quartermaster system was poor in the best of circumstances, and with outposts gone and magazines like Fort Ligonier undermanned and under attack, the western forces could expect little beyond what they could carry. Nine months after his march to the Ohio, Bouquet still labored "under great difficulties to Support Fort Pitt and the Communication" for lack of supplies and able-bodied men to escort what convoys could be provided.[70]

Given the enormous difficulties confronting the army's efforts to take the offensive, it is little wonder that Bouquet's encounter with Ohio Indians at Bushy Run was touted as a major—indeed, the only—victory in an otherwise dismal year. Bouquet's force came under attack on August 5 while on the last leg of its journey to Fort Pitt. Surrounded and forced to spend a harrowing night in the open and short of water, Bouquet's force survived only because its leaders devised a plan that allowed the troops, on August 6, to counterattack and scatter the enemy long enough to reach the fort.

Much was made at the time—and since—of Bouquet's tactical brilliance and his ability to complete his mission. Yet on closer inspection Bouquet's victory was far from the decisive encounter of the war. The army did reach Fort Pitt, thus ending the siege that had lasted since June. And though Bouquet was able to hold the fort and eventually evacuate civilians who had sought refuge with the garrison, these were only intermediate steps in a much larger plan that was to have Bouquet and his troops reestablish communications with Detroit and resume the attack against the natives. Bushy Run made this scheme impossible to carry out and guaranteed that fighting would continue at least into the following spring. The two-day battle cost Bouquet a fifth of his army, and by late August that tiny force was reduced to a mere 245 effectives. By then the colonel was talking less about offensive operations and more about putting his men into winter quarters. In the meantime Fort Pitt remained under periodic attack, and Bouquet continued to worry once more about being cut off, since he found that "our Communication will again be infested" unless additional troops could be sent west—not an easy task for an army headquarters that was scouring the hospitals in New York for any man who could walk.[71]

As to the question of Bouquet's battlefield triumph, Indian accounts and subsequent events both suggest something other than a crushing native defeat. Two years later the Delaware war leader Killbuck claimed that Bouquet was attacked by little more than one hundred warriors, whose losses were far less than the army's. The army's ability, on August 6, to drive off its attackers may have been enhanced by the Indians' own tactical objectives. Killbuck insisted that their object was to *delay* the regulars, not destroy them. It was a plan that made sense if, as appears likely, the warriors chose to maintain their grip on the fort while attempting to forestall reinforcements. Moreover, widely differing cultural values shaped each side's assessment of the battle. Bouquet's men were prepared to stand their ground and take heavy losses in the hope of victory, whereas such action was deemed foolhardy by Ohio Indians, who measured victory as much by their lack of casualties as by the damage they inflicted. Finally, as Bouquet conceded, his "victory" did little to tip the scales in favor of the army. Ohio Indians, instead of fleeing in panic, continued to "infest" the roads, "closely attacked" the fort, and harassed the garrison, all the while keeping the troops under accurate musket fire that even the colonel grudgingly admired. Bouquet's primary accomplishment was to guarantee the survival of Fort Pitt as a base for later campaigns; meanwhile, the army throughout the west remained on the defensive.[72]

Although in retrospect Bouquet's campaign appeared to have been a great victory, during the spring and summer of 1763 Amherst was unwilling to rely entirely on his depleted battalions to salvage Britain's western empire from a savage foe. The general and his subordinates were prepared, whether by desperation or by design, to enlist any ally, including pathogens, in their effort to improve the odds facing their troops and crush the natives' rebellion. As Amherst learned of the defeats being inflicted on his forces, he wondered in a memorandum to Bouquet, among others, if it could not "be contrived to Send the Small Pox among those Disaffected Tribes," since "We must, on this occasion, Use Every Strategem in our power to Reduce them." Amherst had clearly given some thought to what proved to be an early example of germ warfare by further suggesting that the Indians might be infected by giving them blankets from military hospitals. This, Amherst was certain, would "Exterpate this Execrable Race"—a notion that placed the general closer to that other savage rabble, the Paxton Boys. Of equal interest is the evident lack of any contrary opinion by Amherst's senior field commanders. In his reply to the memorandum, Bouquet pledged that, given the opportunity, "I will try to inoculate the [Indians] with Some Blankets," adding that he would "take Care not to get the disease" himself, an observation that suggests Bouquet recognized the practical limitations of germ warfare even if he chose to ignore its moral implications.[73]

The Amherst-Bouquet correspondence suggests how pervasive Indian hating had become by 1763 and how far British officers were willing to set aside their own soldiers' code when confronting the frustrations of frontier warfare. The actions of officers at Fort Pitt confirm that the army was all too willing to transform the language of racial warfare into action. During the parley held at the fort on June 24, the soldiers, as part of the expected exchange of gifts at such meetings, and "Out of our regard to them," gave the natives "two Blankets and an Handkerchief out of the Small Pox Hospital." William Trent, who had a hand in the incident, privately expressed the "hope it will have the desired effect." The fact that Ecuyer, Trent, and others were handing out disease-infested clothing while their superiors were still discussing the matter indicates not just the desperation of a garrison under siege—such tactics would never have been employed at Fort William Henry or Quebec—but rather the pervasiveness of the belief that fighting Indians demanded and justified actions not applied in conflicts between European enemies. It was a belief that tended to blur any moral distinction between frontier rioters and British officer-gentlemen.[74]

Ironically, British efforts to use pestilence as a weapon may not have been either necessary or particularly effective. Gershom Hicks, a trader turned "white Indian," told his British captors in 1764 that as many as one hundred Ohio Indians had died from smallpox that first appeared the previous year, though according to Hicks "it still continued amongst them." During autumn 1764, a Virginian reported that the natives were "Dieing very fast with the small pox" and were therefore unable to offer much resistance to Bouquet's army, then preparing to march into the Muskingum Valley. What little archaeological evidence remains from this period provides what may be physical evidence of the epidemic described by Hicks and Andrew Lewis. Yet there is evidence that the disease may have entered the Ohio Country by several means, and that the worst effects were contained by the natives themselves. Hicks indicated that the sickness first appeared in spring 1763; captive John M'Cullough understood that smallpox arrived in the Ohio Country when warriors assaulted an infected settlement; some of the natives died "before they got home, others shortly after," but the latter may have lived long enough to spread the sickness. More intriguing, however, is M'Cullough's statement that as soon as the infection appeared, the sick "were immediately moved out of town, and put under the care of one who had had the disease before," a not unlikely response among Indians for whom smallpox was by the 1760s a familiar, if still lethal, scourge. Moreover, the presence among the Delawares of "one who had had the disease" clearly implies that others were similarly immune. It thus appears that Trent and Ecuyer may well have represented only one source of smallpox and that however much they and their superiors may have wished to spark a pandemic, Indian knowledge of the disease and quick, intelligent action could have kept the death rate much lower than would otherwise have been the case.[75]

Despite their best efforts, smallpox did weaken the Ohio Indians. Killbuck reported that 149 Shawnee men "besides Women and Children" died during 1764, "as did Several of [the Delawares]." As 1763 ended, however, smallpox was only one of a number of forces that determined how far Ohio natives could continue the war. The need to harvest corn and begin the winter hunt meant that fighting would decrease over the autumn and winter; settlers at Carlisle found that as late as April 1764 "Fue or no Indians have Appeared in our Frontiers leatly."[76]

Diminished Indian activity into the new year was also the product of one inescapable fact of native life in the 1760s: a heavy reliance on firearms, not only for warfare, but for hunting as well. Traders, the principal source of muskets and munitions, either fled or were killed in the first weeks of the war. And though their plundered stocks, plus stores taken from captured forts, guaranteed a short-term supply, the end of trade and Amherst's belated restriction, in July 1763, on the sale in the west of any warlike stores ensured that, once exhausted, the Indians' supplies would be difficult to replace. British officers hoped as much and were convinced the natives must soon "disperse for want of Provisions," since "Ammunition and Supplys must be Soon greatly Exhausted." Such optimism seemed well founded when escaped captives confirmed that Delawares and Shawnees "had little Powder," some "none at all," and that over the winter "they chiefly used their Bows and Arrows in their Hunt," deciding to save powder and ball for use against the redcoats. By midsummer 1764, as Genesee Senecas met with Sir William Johnson to negotiate a cease-fire, they and Great Lakes natives in attendance spoke of their distress, including the "great Want of Cloathing."[77]

Conditions at home—sickness, battle casualties, and shortages of needed supplies—also reanimated those who had first opposed the war but had bowed to the prevailing mood and stepped aside. As early as October 1763, some within the Genesee towns had approached their eastern Seneca neighbors "requesting," as Johnson soon learned, "to be informed of our [British] present resolutions, and to know whether offers of peace . . . will be accepted or not." The Delawares and Shawnees held fast for several months longer, much to the irritation of the new commander-in-chief, General Sir Thomas Gage, but as Bouquet's army approached the Muskingum Valley in mid-autumn 1764, coupled with Colonel John Bradstreet's expedition then crossing the Great Lakes, Ohio Indians began to divide over the issue of war and peace. By mid-October, Bouquet found that Ohio Senecas led by Kiashuta, joined by Custaloga's people, "have offered me to separate from the rest."[78]

By the end of 1764 the Anglo-Indian war was drawing to a close; in the Ohio Country a combination of battlefield truces and ad hoc treaties brought an end to the fighting and paved the way for a formal peace the following year. For much of the year, however, fighting continued. A winter lull was followed by new Indian raids against border settlements. In response, the army and the Indian Department planned an offensive that was designed to beat down native resistance and restore peace to the border country. Two armies, led by Colonel John Bradstreet and Bouquet, were to move west; Bradstreet was to reopen communications through the Great Lakes, while Bouquet was invade the Muskingum Valley and crush Ohio Indian resistance. At the same time, Sir William Johnson would attempt to negotiate separate treaties of peace with the Senecas, Ohio Indians, and Great Lakes natives and to rebuild the imperial Covenant Chain.[79]

What proved to be the final campaign of the war quickly became costly for both sides and helped hasten the negotiations that followed. In mid-June, Shawnee warriors were able to keep up a six-hour fusillade against Fort Dinwiddie in western Virginia; by autumn such profligate consumption of ammunition was no longer possible, especially since the British army had kept its distance for much of the year, allowing no opportunity for warriors to replenish stocks from dead redcoats. But while troops continued to hold out at Detroit and Fort Pitt, it required a herculean effort by the army's new commander, General Gage, to scrape together the forces required to pacify the Great Lakes and Ohio Country. Increasingly factionalized and with limited means to resist, native societies faced British forces of impressive size but limited striking power. Given the circumstances, negotiations soon supplemented, then replaced, military action on both sides.[80]

Peace negotiations began in the spring when the Senecas met at Johnson Hall, Sir William Johnson's Mohawk Valley estate, to discuss terms. The Indians had been inching toward negotiations since January. At that time a delegation of Genesee Senecas approached the superintendent and disavowed any part in starting the war, though they still insisted that their "Liberty was at stake by the many Forts in our Country." Johnson responded by upbraiding them and insisted that peace could come only with "attonement," and he sent the natives packing without a "Penn'orth" (penny's worth) of gifts. Negotiations nevertheless resumed in late March. The Genesees then used the eastern, pro-British Senecas as intermediaries. At this second meeting Johnson set forth British conditions for peace, principal of which was a demand that the Senecas relinquish a four-mile strip of land on each side of the Niagara River. With Bradstreet's army scheduled to move through the vital passage, and with the Devil's Hole ambush still a vivid memory, Johnson and his superiors were eager enough to secure the portage that they continued negotiations with no further demands of "atonement" from the Senecas.[81]

The preliminary articles of peace signed at Johnson Hall were ratified at a much more impressive gathering at Fort Niagara in July and August. There some two thousand Indians assembled as peace factions from Detroit appeared to witness the Seneca-British treaty. Though Johnson boasted of the size of the gathering, he was obviously troubled by the conspicuous absence of the Ohio Indians, who chose to monitor British activities from the comparative safety of the Scioto Valley. Moreover, Johnson was later forced to concede that these and Pontiac's followers were "I believe[,] doubtfull of our sincerity." Meanwhile Johnson settled a peace with the Senecas, guided by the realization that they "are a people of great power and Influence and should be courted," since he was certain they would then draw other Indians to the British "interest." Indeed, although he publicly insisted that the Crown should exact its symbolic pound of flesh from the natives, privately Johnson urged Gage to consider employing the Genesees on the portage and recommended that fort commanders demonstrate all proper deference to the natives. No one wished to provoke a new round of fighting, least of all Colonel Bradstreet, who refused to budge from Fort Niagara until he received assurance that the newly fortified portage was really safe.[82]

The Senecas' reasons for seeking peace when they did turned in part on their increasing difficulty in sustaining their war beyond 1763. Internal wrangling may have played a considerable role. At the Niagara Treaty, Serrehoana was identified in the minutes as "chief of Chenussio." In fact, he and the six other headmen who signed the treaty represented only a faction within the western Seneca towns; others had chosen to stay away. Most conspicuous by his absence was Gaustarax (Augastarax), who until his death in 1770 or 1771 remained a staunch foe of British colonial expansion. And though Gaustarax did turn up the following year as one of the Seneca hostages left with Johnson to guarantee compliance with the treaty, he was identified as "the Chief Chenussio Sachem who was always for breeding Mischief." Nevertheless, for the moment the Genesee mischief makers were in the minority, and it was Serrehoana who ratified the treaty.[83]

Finally, the terms Johnson offered were not nearly as severe as the Senecas might have feared or as they might have at first appeared. The demand that prisoners and deserters be returned was met only insofar as the people in question were not adoptees; those who had become members of Seneca society were harder to locate and perhaps less valuable than runaway soldiers, indentured servants, and slaves. On the more substantive question of the Niagara portage, the Senecas agreed to the cession but made it clear that they were indeed giving what the British called "free use" of the portage "provided the Tract be always appropriated to His Majesty's sole use," which, put another way, meant that settlers would not be tolerated. As the Devil's Hole affair had demonstrated, the Senecas could readily close the portage road if the British did not live up to their end of the deal. And though they agreed to go to war against the Shawnees and Delawares, the Senecas pledged only twenty-three warriors—not an impressive commitment from the most populous of the Six Nations.[84]

Although Johnson could congratulate himself on ending Genesee hostility, the larger problem of reoccupying the west remained, with no peace negotiations yet possible. The Senecas chose to accept British terms, but the Ohio Indians had not. The Delawares, Shawnees, and Ohio Senecas kept up their raids through the spring and early summer while British troops remained confined to posts along Forbes's Road. By late summer, however, the balance began to shift as Bradstreet started to move beyond Niagara and as Bouquet labored to muster his forces at Fort Pitt. Militarily, the British scheme appeared simple: two armies would march into the west and converge on the hostile towns in the Scioto and Muskingum valleys, forcing the natives to accept whatever terms the army might wish to impose. In reality the 1764 campaign was more complicated, and it ended in an armed truce when the Ohio Indians once more launched a diplomatic offensive of their own.

The Indians' target was Bradstreet's army; many weeks ahead of Bouquet's force, it posed the most immediate threat to native security. Consequently, when Bradstreet's waterborne force landed at Presque Isle, it was met on August 12 by Shawnees, Delawares, Wyandots from Sandusky, and "what they call the Five Nations of the Plains of Scioto"—including Ohio Iroquois led by Kiashuta. The Indians insisted they had come to "beg for Mercy and Peace," had recalled their raiding parties, and were "empowered to Conclude, and Sign a Peace," one that "the Cheifs of the . . . Nations will ratify." With remarkable speed, Bradstreet obliged by setting forth terms not unlike those offered to the Senecas: the return of all captives, the surrender of hostages within a month, and the cession of lands on which British forts stood, as well as an immediate end to fighting. Bradstreet also went one significant step further by offering to forestall Bouquet's advance down the Ohio River in return for peace.[85]

Bradstreet's willingness to settle with the Ohio Indians grew both from his eagerness to attain his objectives, which included the relief of Detroit and the reoccupation of Michilimackinac, and from from knowledge that low water in the Cuyahoga and Sandusky rivers made an attack on the native towns to the south all but impossible. The Indians seem to have understood as much; certainly by striking a deal with the colonel they managed to free their vulnerable northern flank before Bouquet's force could strike down the Ohio. Moreover, in an effort to protect his own line of march, Bradstreet failed altogether to exact the proper "retribution" demanded by his superiors. Worse, the colonel negotiated not a *truce*, but a formal treaty. In doing so he ignored Johnson, the Indian Department, and the imperial Covenant Chain the superintendent was attempting to restore. Not surprisingly, therefore, when news of Bradstreet's negotiations reached army headquarters, he and his treaty were roundly condemned. Bouquet, whose own success turned on Bradstreet's aggressiveness, was particularly indignant and urged Gage not to confirm the treaty. The general, angered by hearing that Bradstreet had overstepped his authority, suggested that the colonel had been neatly duped by natives attempting to slow or stop the army's advance, while Johnson questioned the authority under which the Indians conducted their negotiations.[86]

Gage's suspicion that Bradstreet had been duped may have been correct. Certainly the Ohio Indians had much to gain by thwarting any part of the British invasion. Gage's evidence was the persistence of raids along the border after the treaty had been signed. However, another explanation lies in the inherently localized nature of Indian societies. Assuming that the natives did indeed want to make peace with Bradstreet, a treaty would have been binding only on those who participated in or supported the negotiations. The delegates spoke of representing all their headmen, but the assertion is vague. More properly, they represented those within their societies who wanted peace; those who did not remained away from the negotiations. Finally, the Indians at Presque Isle made peace with Bradstreet; Bouquet and the colonies were separate matters to be dealt with in turn. Indeed, it quickly became clear to the Indians that—despite Bradstreet's promise—peace at Presque Isle did little to stem the invasion of the Muskingum Valley. For the moment at least, the natives chose to exercise their own version of the enemy's timeworn strategy of divide and conquer.[87]

Affairs in the heart of the Ohio Country took a much different turn than did those at Presque Isle, if only because Bouquet was more determined to press the campaign to a decisive conclusion, while Bradstreet moved from one quick peace treaty to another at Detroit. Bouquet's army did not get under way until Bradstreet's force was returning from Detroit; it took Bouquet the entire summer to collect, organize, and equip his mixed force of regulars and provincials. The colonel's timing, though out of step with Bradstreet's march, did lessen the likelihood of battle. The most worrisome aspect of the Ohio Indians' resistance for the past year had been its constancy. Even though the Senecas and Pontiac's followers acknowledged the futility of their efforts to overrun strongly held bastions like Detroit and Fort Niagara, the Delawares and Shawnees had remained in the field, bypassing the few remaining garrisons along Forbes's Road to strike the border settlements. British leaders were frustrated as it became clear that nothing short of another costly campaign would end hostilities in the Ohio Country. General Gage was particularly hard pressed to understand why the Ohio Indians did not take advantage of negotiations opened with Pontiac at Detroit early in 1764; his frustration mounted when he learned that the natives had likewise avoided Johnson's treaty with the Senecas.[88]

By early autumn, Ohio Indian raids began to fall off. The reasons for the natives' willingness to treat with Bouquet rather than attempt another Bushy Run on a grander scale are not hard to identify. By September news of the Senecas' peace treaty and Bradstreet's negotiations with Indians at Detroit, left Shawnee and Delaware villagers isolated. Moreover, the lack of open French assistance intensified the growing supply problems as the second year of the war drew to a close. Shawnees continued to obtain munitions from French traders, yet nearby Delawares had been suffering shortfalls since the spring. By severing trade, the war hampered efforts to repair and replace firearms, clothing, and tools. Disease, including British-introduced smallpox, also hastened peace talks. Bouquet was to learn that the Shawnees had been "so Weakened by the War and the Small Pox, that they can do nothing without the Delawares." If so, then the Delawares' decision in October to seek a truce must have left their Shawnee allies little choice but to follow suit. Finally, Bouquet's army appeared during the harvest and stayed into the first snows of winter. Crops planted by villagers who were forced to move from exposed towns might not have been adequate and would have been endangered had fighting erupted in the Muskingum Valley. Having successfully carried fire and terror to enemy border settlements, the Ohio Indians had no desire to be treated in kind. And with winter came the hunting season; any hope that trade would follow peace ultimately turned on warrior-hunters' ability to amass deer hides for barter.[89]

Yet the natives had reason to believe they could reach an accommodation with Bouquet. Their own encounter with Bradstreet and that officer's equally lenient dealings later with Indians from Detroit were convincing proof that the army was as eager as the natives to avoid a showdown. At the same time, the Presque Isle "treaty" had reduced the opposing armies from two to one. Moreover, though they could never peer into British war councils, Ohio warriors knew firsthand just how badly they had hurt the regulars: every fort west of the Allegheny River save Detroit had fallen, and one relief expedition after another had been routed or badly mauled. Although the natives' confidence did not run as high as in the early days of the war, they could be satisfied that the enemy too had been hurt and that any negotiations would not have to end in surrender.[90]

Nevertheless, questions of war and peace continued to pit powerful interests against each other within Ohio Indian towns: council headmen trying to restore peace confronted warriors and women who urged continued resistance or pressed the need to replace the dead through scalps or captives. The appearance of Bouquet's 1,500 troops outside Tuscarawas in mid-October intensified the debate. Indeed, nearly three weeks before his overland march brought him to the upper Muskingum Valley, Onondagas and Oneidas, acting as intermediaries, warned Bouquet that "the Indians upon this river are now in a State of Confusion" and urged him to stop his march since, they insisted, "you do not see clearly what their Intentions are." The colonel's stubborn refusal added to the conflict within Ohio Indian towns, as Bouquet discovered after pitching camp at Tuscarawas.[91]

Although nothing of the debate and friction provoked by talk of negotiations escaped the Delaware towns to find its way into the historical record, the aftershocks indicate deep-seated divisions and intense feelings that continued for months, perhaps years. Ethnic divisions seem to have ruined the facade of native unity; those Delawares who urged continued resistance roundly condemned neighboring Munsees who were more willing to talk with Bouquet. George Croghan learned that the Delawares "called Custaloga an old Woman for agreeing to the terms, he did with Colonel Bouquet" and insisted that others were prepared to continue the fight and "would have cut off the Army" had Custaloga not betrayed them. Recriminations were not limited to verbal assaults. At the same meeting with Croghan at Fort Pitt in April and May 1765, "two Principal Warriors of the Delawares, differed in Council and stabb'd each other."[92]

The Delaware warriors, as was their custom, did make contact with Bouquet on October 14 and offered to make peace. Their efforts were exploratory but not insincere. The natives were willing to confirm Bradstreet's treaty with Bouquet and readily agreed to surrender their captives and give hostages as they had at Presque Isle. To underscore this, they offered a wampum belt symbolizing the "Chain of Friendship" between the Delawares and the British. Bouquet refused both the terms for peace and the belt, while moving his army closer to the Delaware towns at the Forks of the Muskingum. The colonel's demand that all captives be returned before peace terms could be discussed and his subsequent declaration that he was prepared to negotiate a truce and that only Sir William Johnson could offer a treaty set off a lengthy and complicated round of bargaining that culminated in an agreement between Bouquet and some, though certainly not all, Delawares.[93]

Some Delawares were angered by what appeared to them to be Bouquet's rejection of terms already offered by British authorities, but others, notably Custaloga and his followers, opened negotiations. During a busy week of councils, these natives were joined by Tamaqua and by Netawatwees's brother Keylappame. Absent was Netawatwees himself. His failure to appear, coupled with his known anti-British position, led to Bouquet's only effort to meddle in the internal affairs of the Ohio Indians. At a meeting on November 11, the colonel announced that he would depose Netawatwees, declaring that "from this Moment he is no more a Chief," and directed the Indians to select another, more cooperative "king." Another candidate, Tatpiskahong, was found, but Netawatwees continued, after a brief hiatus, as the leading headman and the western Delawares' king. Bouquet's imperious effort, like those of Tanaghrisson and the Ohio Company a decade earlier, meant little to the Delawares.[94]

The Shawnees proved to be far more reluctant participants at peace councils. Indeed, Bouquet found the Shawnees "very crabby"; he did not complete a truce with them until mid-November, by which time his negotiations with the Delawares were all but over. The Shawnees' reluctance— even defiance—was rooted in their complex relations with natives throughout the middle west that assured them at least token material support from French traders as well. In fact, Sir William Johnson subsequently learned that the Shawnees' tardiness in meeting Bouquet was due to the absence of many headmen, who were once again lobbying the Illinois French for aid; those who remained behind were "unwilling to take so much upon them in their Absence."[95]

By accepting Bouquet's offer of a truce, Delawares, Ohio Senecas, and Shawnees agreed to certain specific conditions: they would return their captives, even those already adopted; delegates were to be chosen to negotiate a final treaty with Johnson in the spring; and each nation would surrender hostages as an additional guarantee of compliance—six each from the Delawares and Shawnees, two from the Senecas. The greatest advantages gained by the Indians were that the truce spared their towns from British attack and that land cessions had not been demanded. As the councils drew to a close, both the army and its native enemies were content to stop the fighting.[96]

Though Bouquet had spelled out some conditions for peace, the Ohio Indians must have spent an uncomfortable winter as they reflected on what had passed and on the peace negotiations yet to come. The return to captives and adoptees was a painful experience made worse by the spectacle of adopted kin, as well as children born of captive women and native men, carried away, the women and older children sometimes trying to escape from the British troops and return to their Ohio Indian families. And though Bouquet's army returned to Fort Pitt without leaving garrisons behind, no one could know for certain when—or if—the army would reoccupy the chain of forts that had been a primary cause of the war just ended. Meanwhile, at Bouquet's direction the Delawares and Shawnees chose men to meet with Johnson and ratify a treaty of peace.[97]

Yet before the colonel had filed his official reports, new trouble arose when Shawnee and Ohio Seneca hostages fled Fort Pitt, the latter adding injury to insult by "stealing some of our best Horses." The hostages, among them the Shawnees Red Hawk and Cornblade (Cornstalk), had good reason for breaking their parole. At Fort Pitt a Maryland provincial delighted in showing the natives a scalp and boasting of the reward he would receive. The soldier's display suggested what might be in store for the hostages; not wishing to be murdered in their cells, the men fled. Their escape threatened to break the fragile truce as Bouquet angrily demanded that the escapees be returned or replaced.[98]

The uncertainty Ohio Indians felt was gradually dispelled as the new peace took shape during the spring and summer of 1765. The first indications of what the British would demand and what they would offer in return came at a meeting at Fort Pitt in early May with deputy Indian superintendent George Croghan. Croghan's arrival marked the beginning of British efforts to reach and occupy the ceded Illinois Country, a task made difficult because of the persistent hostility of natives living there and at Detroit. Croghan encouraged the Ohio Indians to abide by the truce and quickly send men to Johnson Hall to conclude a formal peace treaty. In return, the Crown agreed to protect their lands—not from French rivals, but from colonists who were even then pushing west over the mountains once more. When pressed by the large gathering of Delawares, Shawnees, and Seneca headmen, Croghan offered to reopen trade only when the natives formally ratified a treaty with the government. Meanwhile, the Indians could demonstrate their good faith by sending men with the Indian agent to act as intermediaries with the Illinois nations. Both the Delawares and the Shawnees agreed, though three of the Shawnees later paid with their lives for their people's cooperation when the party was attacked by Kickapoos and Mascoutens while traveling to Fort De Chartres.[99]

Croghan's effort to speed the departure of Ohio Indians for a meeting with Sir William Johnson was a measure of the continuing debate within native towns over the future of the Ohio Country. Efforts to arrive at a consensus and the bitter disputes that arose at the Fort Pitt congress were reasons why Johnson sat at his Mohawk Valley estate for weeks impatiently awaiting the arrival of the western Indians. Only Killbuck, who claimed to speak for all the Delawares, had appeared as planned by late February, and he was eager to return home.[100]

During the month-long congress that began on April 29, the natives accepted the peace offered them under the terms set down at Fort Niagara and on the Muskingum the previous year. More important for the subsequent history of the Ohio Country, however, was the proposal for a definitive boundary line that would separate native lands from colonial lands along the confused and troublesome Allegheny border. The boundary must have appealed to Johnson's audience even though, from the outset, the definition of the line and all subsequent negotiations to fix it by treaty were in the hands of the superintendent and the Six Nations. By May 6, representatives from Onondaga had established a line running from Owego in New York down the Susquehanna River, westward to Kittanning, and thence down the Ohio to the mouth of the Tennessee River. Johnson quickly endorsed the line, which was also accepted by the Delawares present. Under the tenth article of the peace treaty, they agreed that they would "engage to abide by whatever Limits shall be agreed upon between the English and the Six Nations" whenever the line was formally established. It was a stipulation agreed to by the Shawnees, the Ohio Senecas, and the remaining Delaware representatives who, at Croghan's insistence, arrived at Johnson Hall early in July to endorse the treaty.[101]

During the late summer and autumn of 1764 Colonel Bradstreet and Colonel Bouquet negotiated separate truces with Indians living at Sandusky and Detroit and natives in the Muskingum Valley—the "five Nations of Scioto." Although two small British armies were able to move far into the west, their ultimate success was due less to armed might than to the natives' acknowledgment that, however much they might punish the soldiers in specific encounters, their larger desire to drive the army and what it represented from the west was unobtainable. The problem was never a lack of battlefield skill or of a determination to fight. The year 1764 was punctuated by renewed attacks and new war belts from Senecas and Delawares calling on others to carry on the fight. Bradstreet had to maintain a strong force at his base at Fort Niagara just to keep the portage open amid Seneca raids that once again threatened to close that vital passage. And even after the negotiations with Bradstreet and Bouquet, numbers of Ohio warriors stayed in the field while Pontiac and his most loyal followers retreated inland from Detroit.[102]

The Ohio Indians' inability to sustain a conflict without a predictable supply of weapons and ammunition while at the same time providing for the economic needs of their towns and kin proved to be their greatest limitation. During the victorious summer of 1763 military stores were plentiful. By the following year such sources had given out. Amherst's replacment, Gage, appreciated as much early in 1764 when he predicted that renewed hostilities "will depend on the Condition" of the natives: not their willingness, something British officers no longer doubted, but their ability to renew the fight.[103]

But Gage's troops found themselves in a similar quandary. In addition to the chronic problem of collecting and moving supplies, manpower shortages continued to plague the army throughout 1764; both Bradstreet's and Bouquet's regiments were but a fraction of their authorized strength, while militia auxiliaries, including in Bradstreet's case a battalion of French Canadians, were untested and unreliable. Moreover, army officers were shocked at how quickly their forces were overrun and by the magnitude of their losses. And as Bouquet's 1763 campaign demonstrated, British forces still faced serious problems in their efforts to defeat their elusive Indian enemies.[104]

The result, by late autumn 1764, was a stalemate. Unable to drive out the dangerous and overbearing British, Ohio Indians could take advantage of the army's limited striking power to negotiate a settlement with Bouquet. The colonel, on entering the very heartland of Ohio native resistance, said nothing about burning towns and setting mastiffs on hapless savages. Rather, he was only too willing to talk with increasingly influential native factions who found bargaining preferable to fighting; neither side could win, and each for its own reasons was anxious about the coming winter. On the Muskingum and later at Fort Pitt and Johnson Hall, Ohio Indians and Anglo-Americans came to accept that neither could conquer the other. That realization would set the tone of intercultural affairs for the next decade.

nine

The Ohio Indians' World

 In the decades following the first Logg's Town council in 1748, the Ohio Indians confronted enormous challenges to their political autonomy and cultural integrity. Successive invasions by Canadians and Anglo-Americans turned what had been a haven into a battleground for over a decade.

Yet the struggle for control of the Ohio Country that began in the mid-1740s did not produce what Anthony F. C. Wallace has characterized as "disintegrating societies." Delawares, Shawnees, and Iroquois suffered losses on the battlefield, begrudgingly conceded the presence of British troops after 1764, and continued to absorb materials from an alien world. Nevertheless, the natives still fashioned strategies that challenged British efforts to impose royal sovereignty west of the Alleghenies. The Ohio Indians enjoyed considerable success in weathering two wars within a decade, fighting and talking their enemies to a standstill largely because the natives maintained a large measure of social and cultural stability and integrity. Beginning in the early 1760s, settlers and missionaries joined soldiers and the ubiquitous traders in threatening the Ohio Indians' culture and independence. Yet before the American Revolution these agents of cultural and political imperialism proved largely unsuccessful in their endeavors. Ohio Indians continued to face changes and challenges as they had always done: by creatively adapting to new situations, selectively adopting from outsiders, but always acting from within cultural frameworks that provided identity and order in an ever changing—and increasingly unpredictable—world.[1]

The Seven Years' War and the Defensive War of 1763 both led to considerable resettlement of Ohio Indian peoples. This migration within the Ohio Country was itself a defensive strategy. As Canadians and Anglo-Americans raced toward a showdown on the Ohio in 1758, few Indians were inclined to be caught in the crossfire. Moreover, the subsequent appearance of British garrisons, seen by many natives as a threat to their security, led to new removals in the early 1760s, which quickened with the resumption of hostilities in 1763. As a result, Ohio Indians tended to abandon the vulnerable Allegheny and Beaver valleys in favor of the Muskingum and Scioto valleys, trading distance for security as Delaware and Shawnee settlers had done a generation earlier.[2]

The Delawares were the first to feel the impact of wartime dislocation; after the attack on Kittanning in 1756 the natives pulled back to the Kuskuskies towns, Saucunk, and other settlements on the less exposed Beaver River. Two years later, in autumn 1758, the Delawares began another remove, one described by the captive Marie Le Roy. After the failed attack on Fort Ligonier in October the Delawares, anticipating the evacuation of Fort Duquesne, "brought their wives and children from Lockstown, Sackum [Saucunk], Schomingo [Shenango], Mamalty, Kaschkasching [Kuskuskies], and other places [in the Beaver Valley], to Moschinko [Muskingum]," which was to remain the center of Delaware settlements for the next twenty years. There, at Tuscarawas and Kekalemahpehoong (Newcomer's Town), the western Delawares established their homes and a new council fire. Not all followed the same route at the same time, however. The ethnically distinct Munsees led by Custaloga remained in the French Creek Valley, not joining the Delawares until the eve of the 1763 war. Characteristically, however, Custaloga's people remained in the Muskingum Valley less than a decade, returning to the Beaver River and the Kuskuskies in 1769 and 1770, thus reversing the tendency toward a westward movement of the region's people. Meanwhile, to the west a number of settlements were founded. When Bouquet's troops reached the Muskingum Valley in 1764 they found several "new towns," many of them only small hamlets and satellites of larger towns where influential headmen lived.[3]

The Shawnees too largely abandoned the eastern half of the Ohio Country by the end of 1758. Those who had occupied Logg's Town as French allies left the site at about the same time that their Delaware neighbors evacuated their Beaver Valley townsites, though the Shawnees' departure was more abrupt. Post found plenty of ungathered corn standing near the log houses built for the natives with Canadian labor. Smaller villages were also abandoned at the same time, and by November 1758, "between Sac-cung and Pittsburgh, all the Shawnas towns are empty of people."[4]

Social issues as well as fear of British retaliation and a desire to be far from the invaders also drew the Logg's Town inhabitants west. By 1755 a considerable portion of the western Shawnees were living in the lower Scioto Valley. Three years later the large "lower town" had moved to mid-valley where, as Chillicothe, it became the center of western Shawnee society. By the end of 1759 those at Chillicothe and surrounding towns had, according to George Croghan, dispatched messengers "to bring all their people who have lived several years amongst the Creeks, home." These Shawnees, remnants of Peter Chartier's band, were joined by a small but steady stream of immigrants from the Delaware and Susquehanna valleys. As a result, the Shawnees were to achieve a degree of unity that had not existed in living memory.[5]

The Senecas, however, remained in the upper Allegheny Valley, where they maintained contact with their Genesee kinfolk while offering a haven for Munsees from Pennsylvania. Downstream, below Fort Pitt, Senecas and other Iroquois founded new towns along the Ohio in a region "where they might have plenty of Game." These natives, identified with the Crow, Kiashuta, and White Mingo, were known to British officials as the "Ohio Senecas" to distinguish them from the Senecas of Iroquoia.[6]

Thus, by the mid-1760s the cultural landscape in the Ohio Country had taken on a new look. The Allegheny Valley, once the center of Ohio Indian life, was fast becoming a backwater as British forts and colonial settlements crowded in on the Allegheny and Monongahela valleys. The heart of the Indians' Ohio Country, with the notable exception of the Seneca-Munsee towns far up the Allegheny, was now along the Muskingum and Scioto rivers.

The westward relocation was an orderly one, reflecting the continued integrity of native communities rather than social decay or collapse. The Delawares, for example, quickly established a network of towns that looked to Newcomer's Town and the "king" Netawatwees for guidance. The relocation of Ohio Indian towns in the western half of the Allegheny Plateau also led to a more clearly definable pattern of ethnic territories as Shawnee and Delaware, as well as Seneca, villages tended to cluster together. This was the result of conscious design when, for instance, the Shawnees drew their kinfolk back from the Creek towns or when the Delawares were found, in 1759, to be "collecting their people together."[7]

Within this Ohio Indian world, the population continued to grow in the face of warfare, relocation, and army-induced epidemics. Precise population figures or rates of growth are all but impossible to obtain. Although a number of references to native populations exist, Canadians or Anglo-Americans who entered the Ohio Country left only incomplete, often impressionistic, sometimes contradictory comments about the number of Indians they met.

Despite these handicaps, the evidence that remains suggests that from 1730 to the mid-1770s the Ohio Indian population continued to grow, both from natural increase and because of a steady influx of natives from Pennsylvania and Iroquoia. In 1730 Pennsylvanians estimated between 1,200 and 1,400 Indians in the region. Nearly two decades later Conrad Weiser learned that 789 warriors, or perhaps as many as 3,000 to 4,000 people, lived in the Ohio Country; the figure given to Weiser may in fact be on the conservative side if we assume that only those natives allied to the Iroquois at Logg's Town were counted.[8]

The trend of rising population in the early years of native settlement seems to have continued. In 1766 missionary Charles Beatty found between 700 and 900 people in four Delaware towns; in addition, Newcomer's Town alone held some 200 warriors, or between 500 and 700 people. Fellow preacher David Jones estimated that some 600 Shawnees lived in several "small towns" in the Muskingum and Scioto valleys. Nevertheless, losses from warfare and disease must have slowed, or even temporarily reversed, population growth in the decade from 1754 to 1764. Hundreds of British colonial settlers and soldiers were captured during the wars; over 600 were *returned* to Fort Pitt and other outposts between 1759 and 1765. Given the natives' practice of adopting captives to replace dead kinfolk, such figures suggest a correspondingly high death rate among Ohio Indians during these turbulent years.[9]

The arrival of Munsee and Delaware emigrants from Pennsylvania in the 1760s and 1770s may have helped the region's population recover and slowly grow once more, as did the uncounted numbers of Six Nations Iroquois who continued to trickle into the Ohio Country. Yet by the late 1760s the native population may also have approached the limits set by the country's resources. Complaints about the scarcity of game and the Shawnees' belligerent defense of their Kentucky hunting grounds suggest increasing pressure on critical resources, made worse by rapacious colonial hunters or endlessly hungry garrisons. Thus, by the mid-1770s the region's Indian population could well have stabilized after several decades of growth.

The ebb and flow of the Ohio Indian population is one indication of the changes that helped shape the natives' world. Another element that gave definition to the Indians' way of life was the steady influx and incorporation of material goods from the European colonial world. After 1730, colonial traders carried into the Ohio Country not only familiar staples such as kettles, cloth, bar lead, and glass beads, but also European ceramics, jewelry of various sorts, toys, and hardware. Village sites associated with the Genesee Senecas, for example, have yielded artifacts that would have been recognizable to any Anglo-American. And by midcentury, silver in the form of brooches, buckles, gorgets, and other decorative items became increasingly popular. Indeed, silver and other decorative or cosmetic objects like vanity boxes, hair wires, and earrings constitute the bulk of the grave offerings at the Chambers Site, a cemetery associated with the Kuskuskies towns. Such a pattern attests both to native tastes and to the value placed on nonutilitarian objects by the 1760s.[10]

The limited archaeological record from the Ohio Country bears out the more abundant documentary evidence on the types and quantities of materials entering the region and the changes these goods wrought in native lives. The Indians' appearance was the most obvious sign of widespread adoption of European materials, especially to strangers taking their first look inside the Ohio Indians' world. By the time missionary David Zeisberger arrived in the late 1760s, cloth had all but supplanted buckskin as the preferred material for clothing. "Petticoats" made of "black, blue [or] red Strouds" were popular among women and were often adorned with red, blue, or yellow strips of cloth as well as the increasingly popular trade silver. David Jones, another missionary, was clearly impressed by one Shawnee woman, who had "near five hundred silver brooches stuck in her shift, stroud and leggins." Shawnee men, meanwhile, developed their own distinctive wardrobes, which included silk handkerchiefs worn as turbans. Men also adopted European clothing as much to confirm or assert their rank as to indulge personal tastes. Kiashuta, the influential Ohio Seneca headman, was seen "dressed in a scarlet cloth [coat] turned up with lace, and a high gold laced hat," attire that one colonist admitted "made a martial appearance"—undoubtedly the very impression Kiashuta hoped to convey.[11]

Personal appearance was not the only aspect of Ohio Indian life that continued to change. As references to crockery and other tableware in the archaeological record suggest, housewares were also taking on a culturally hybrid look, with creamware, tin-glazed earthenware, and the now common brass and iron kettles taking their place alongside spoons and dishes made "of the growths and knots of trees." Native dwellings where these goods were found also reflected much the same blending of alien and native forms and functions. Visiters to the Ohio Country found traditional housing standing alongside cabins hardly distinguishable from those of colonial border settlers. Newcomer's Town in 1772 was typical, consisting of houses "some of logs and others the bark of trees, fastened by elm bark to poles stuck in the ground and bent over at the top," in the fashion of traditional longhouses. The log houses were "well-built," boasted "stone chimneys, chambers and sellers," and were "well shingled with nails." In other towns the dwellings were made of "slabs or split wood Stuck in the ground and Standing up like a Stockade," a style similar to the Canadians' "piquet" style. As natives adopted colonial house styles, they found themselves, as Shingas did, confronting new needs. The Delaware headman sent a message to Colonel Bouquet in 1765 reminding him of an order he had placed for a handsaw, three hundred shingle nails, and a draw knife.[12]

While housewares and dwellings themselves continued to change in form, the meals served on ceramic plates at stone fireplaces also took on new appearances as Ohio Indians' tastes broadened to include new foods. This process did not begin in the Ohio Country at midcentury; contact with Europeans since the seventeenth century had offered many opportunities for natives to sample, adopt, and adapt elements of alien foodways. Yet items that had once been novelties at native meals were, by the mid-eighteenth

9. George I medal, bell, and thimbles, the last apparently used for decorating clothing, from the Chambers Site, a cemetery associated with the Delaware and Munsee Kuskuskies towns, 1756 to 1778. (Courtesy of the State Museum of Pennsylvania, Pennsylvania Historical and Museum Commission)

10. Engraved pendant from the Kuskuskies towns (Chambers Site). (Courtesy of the State Museum of Pennsylvania, Pennsylvania Historical and Museum Commission)

century, clearly standard fare among Ohio Indians. To the traditional "three sisters"—corn, beans, and squash—had been added cabbage, turnips, and cucumbers. Among the Delawares, visitors could enjoy a fine repast of these as well as "good veal," biscuits, traditional hominy, and "Indian-cake, baked in the ashes," washed down with milk and topped off with chocolate or a kettle of tea.[13]

The appearance of milk and veal attests to the growing importance of livestock among Ohio Indians. Although native horticulturalists could easily have mastered cucumbers or turnips, plants not so very different from native root crops and tubers, cattle and other livestock represented a more substantial change, not only in diet but in the nature of settlements and work. By the 1760s and 1770s, Indian towns sported fences as natives attempted to gain some control over rooting hogs, free-grazing cattle and horses, and the chickens that pecked amid corn fields and house lots.

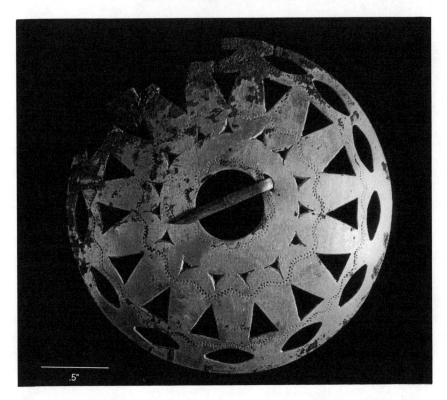

.5"

11. Silver brooch from the Kuskuskies towns (Chambers Site). (Courtesy of the State Museum of Pennsylvania, Pennsylvania Historical and Museum Commission)

Moreover, the Indians had evidently become "very fond of milk and butter," making the ownership of a least one or two cows a growing necessity.[14]

Along with clothing, housewares, crops, and cattle, Ohio Indians also continued to accept other elements of Anglo-American culture. Steel traps began to appear by midcentury and quickly grew in popularity. Firearms continued to be the mainstay of both commercial hunting and warfare; the constant requests for powder and shot received by garrison commanders attested to the natives' dependence on muskets, as did the Indians' fear of a British conspiracy to weaken them by withholding ammunition supplies after 1761. And though barter continued to shape trade between Ohio natives and colonists, the Indians were not shy about demanding cash in return for skins, meat, or services. According to one observer, the Delawares were particularly adept at casting accounts, using Dutch currency values— "stipel" (stiver) and "gull" (gulden)—as well as current sterling values.[15]

Although trade with British and, less frequently, French colonists remained the fundamental avenue through which European goods and their associated meanings entered the Ohio Indians' world, by the late 1740s other potential agents of cultural change began to appear. An increasing volume of materials became available as colonial diplomats began to arrive at Logg's Town, the Kuskuskies, and elsewhere, often with pack-train loads of merchandise intended to buy or sustain influence or renew agreements between natives and colonists.

The assimilation of alien materials and values into native towns was substantially augmented in the 1750s and early 1760s by large numbers of captives as hundreds of British-American men, women, and children found themselves in the midst of Delaware, Shawnee, and Seneca societies. We now know a good deal about the processes that transformed captives into "white Indians" and, often, into full members of adoptive families and clans. We can only speculate at this point about the ways captives contributed to the changes that marked Ohio Indian life in the middle of the eighteenth century, though it seems reasonable to assume that these "transculturalized" British-Americans had some impact, however subtle or limited. In the broadest sense, this may have included the accelerated adoption of English words by natives. It is clear that many Ohio Indians knew at least some English, though many—including, for example, Kiashuta—continued to

12. Iron jewel case and contents: glass beads and silver pendants and brooch, from the Kuskuskies towns (Chambers Site). (Courtesy of the State Museum of Pennsylvania, Pennsylvania Historical and Museum Commission)

insist on using interpreters as an additional assertion of independence or authority. How much of this language skill came from listening to colonial captives as well as traders is uncertain, but it is as likely as the opposite tendency for captives, missionaries, and diplomats to learn native dialects by listening, observing, and hard practice.

Beyond language, captives may have influenced Indian societies in two other ways, based largely on gender. Men and older boys would have carried with them knowledge of tools and technology that made the natives' adoption of European materials and houseways easier, if not more rapid. The appearance of colonial house styles, for instance, was partly the work of captive carpenters and joiners. Missionary David McClure, who visited the Ohio Country in 1772, found these houses and "was told [they] were built by the english captives, in the time of the French wars." Anglo-American women and their daughters may have wrought similar changes within the natives' dwellings. Foodways would have been exchanged between captives and clan matrons, whose work routines and interests were similar. Clothing styles may also have undergone subtle alterations as Indian women enjoyed rare opportunities to size up the attire of their colonial captives turned kinfolk.[16]

If the Ohio Country had been prized by men of the sword in the 1750s, during the following two decades the region's people themselves became the objectives of men of the cloth. Although missionaries had long been a part of the natives' evolving world in the northeast, Ohio Indians' encounters with French or Anglo-American preachers had not been common before the early 1760s; a mere handful of Jesuits at Detroit and Sandusky, and the chaplains who accompanied French and Canadian troops during their brief occupation, were available to instruct or otherwise influence the natives. This pattern quickly changed in the wake of the 1763 war. In 1766 Presbyterian Charles Beatty appeared among the Delawares' Muskingum Valley towns, bent on establishing a mission. Earlier still, in 1765, Samuel Kirkland, protégé of Eleazer Wheelock, sojourned briefly among the Genesee Senecas. From then until the mid-1770s, the Ohio Indians played host to an increasing number of hopeful missionaries: Moravians, Presbyterians, Baptists, and Quakers, all animated both by the theological groundswell of the Great Awakening and by the persistent urge to convert native peoples— spiritually and culturally.[17]

The so-called Moravian Indians—Delawares and Munsees from Pennsylvania who first arrived in the Ohio Country in 1768—like their own missionaries, also became agents of cultural change. By 1770 Friedensstadt had been founded near Custaloga's village at the Kuskuskies, and in 1772 two new towns were founded on the Muskingum: Schönbrunn and Gnadenhütten. These mission towns were one source of the livestock that visitors found throughout the region, and the "neat" and "regular" towns, composed of "neat log houses," may have served as models for the nearby Delawares and Shawnees. Moreover, at least some of the mission natives were "tradesmen, understanding farming and carpenter work," and thus were another potential source of skills and materials that led to well-shingled Delaware houses and village fence lines.[18]

The Moravian Indians also contributed to the diseases that periodically swept the Ohio Country. Missionary John Ettwein, who led one group from Friedensstadt to the Muskingum in 1772, kept an account of illness among his flock that included measles, dysentery, and malaria. These, added to the commonplace "festering sores," chills, fevers, and fluxes found among the Ohio natives, in addition to the venereal disease that often came in the wake of liaisons between native women and soldiers or traders, combined to give the Ohio natives one more element in common with settlers and natives to the east.[19]

Taken together, then, the native and colonial worlds were, at least in some respects, becoming more alike. Not only were Delawares, Shawnees, and their neighbors sharing a material culture drawn in large measure from colonial society, but trade, warfare, and other avenues for culture change had further blurred the physical distinctions between native and border settlements. The "well pailed gardens . . . fine fruit trees . . . herds of cattle, horses, and hogs" that John Heckewelder found among the Ohio Indians in the 1770s could have been found on the other side of the cultural frontier as well. And David McClure, who visited the Delawares in 1772, found that the "stone cellar, stairway, stone chimney and fireplace" and interior partitions of the prophet Neolin's house, as well as its "thrifty Peach orchard," gave the place "the appearance of an english dwelling."[20]

But appearances could be deceiving. Though the natives continued to *adopt* things that tended to "Europeanize" the outward manifestations of their societies, European objects, animals, foods, and ideas were also "Indianized"—*adapted* and endowed with the values and meanings of their native users. For example, Delawares began referring to their own healers as "doctols," a term the natives found appropriate given what they understood to be the equivalent functions of shaman and surgeon: to restore health and well-being through the use of prescribed rituals and devices. In the same way, the natives were resorting, by the 1770s, to "blood-letting and cupping" as part of their own curing rituals. Indeed, David Zeisberger found these practices quite popular among the Delawares. Yet there is nothing to suggest that European medical practice—much of it perhaps first demonstrated by traders or army surgeons—was used in any way other than to enhance the traditional process of diagnosis and healing.[21]

Ohio natives also managed to keep pace with European technology. They quickly recognized the greater accuracy and killing power of the Pennsylvania rifle, and as traders and others soon discovered, Indian hunters would "use no other than rifle-barrelled guns." Moreover, by midcentury the Indians were beginning to overcome their total dependence on colonists for repair and maintenance of firearms and other metal tools. In 1759 Andrew Montour found that Custaloga's people had meticulously picked through the ruins of the abandoned French fort at Presque Isle to salvage tools and ironwork. Although war-induced shortages certainly inspired such foraging, other evidence suggests that scrap metal was being refashioned by native artisans—perhaps routinely—by the 1760s and 1770s. Zeisberger found that some natives "who have been much with whites" had learned to forge iron and had "fashioned hatchets, axes, etc., right well." Indeed, the more skilled among them had become full-time craft specialists. Thus Zeisberger also discovered that, though gunsmiths were still in demand throughout the Ohio Country, the natives had "acquired considerable skill in making minor repairs when their weapons get out of order" and had learned to produce gunstocks "neatly and well made." Finally, Ohio Indians also continued to shape foreign technology to their own particular tastes and needs. One case in point was the use of metal traps. Larger furbearers like beavers were more frequently caught with metal traps, while smaller mammals like the marten and sable could be efficiently—and more economically—snared using traditional wooden traps. As in the case of kettles and bark vessels or muskets versus bows, decisions were based on what the natives understood to be reasonable trade-offs of cost, efficiency, and utility.[22]

Although the adoption or adaptation of foreign technology continued as it had for decades without creating serious problems, the appearance of domesticated animals and new crops borrowed from colonial societies might have posed a more serious challenge. Yet the scant evidence suggests otherwise. In fact, the widespread use of cattle, hogs, and horses indicates that livestock and Indians clearly learned to get along. The knowledge necessary to maintain such animals predated the natives' arrival in the west by many decades as Indians observed and learned from nearby colonial settlers. At the same time, domesticated animals were integrated into traditional patterns of labor within Indian societies. Though stock tending was men's work among colonists—or a task sometimes shared by men and women—in native towns cattle, identified with food raising and domestic labor, were tended by women. In the same way, horses were associated with men, a notion perhaps also borrowed from European societies, where horsemanship was a male skill and where soldiers, including frontier patrols, were sometimes mounted. Less can be said about such intangibles as tastes for certain foods, but observers commented that Indians were fond of butter and milk, that cabbage grew along with corn, and that pork may have replaced venison or fowl in some native stewpots. The Indians apparently had no greater difficulty in expanding their bill of fare than did colonists, who added roasted corn, boiled yams, and pumpkin soup to theirs, especially since foods borrowed from other cultures represented *additions* to the diet rather than substitutions for scarce or unobtainable goods.[23]

The "Indianization" of European goods was also reflected in ritual behavior. One Anglo-American found that Shawnees much enjoyed card playing. Zeisberger learned that in addition to dances and traditional games and tests of skill such as wrestling, the Delawares also enjoyed ninepins and card games, all of which "they have learned from the whites." What is revealing is not the source of playing cards or ninepins, but that these activities were included in an array of more traditional games whose purpose went beyond mere entertainment, serving an important role in social integration and the acting out of the reciprocal nature of community life. Games and contests could include members of other ethnic groups as well and thus helped to bind peoples together and reaffirm alliances. Lacrosse and bowl games had long served these purposes; bowling or card playing would easily have fit the pattern. Likewise, European livestock found its way into native ritual behavior; during a "spirits or ghost feast" observed in the 1760s, Munsees sacrificed hogs along with deer or bear.[24]

In much the same way, burials often included European materials yet lost none of their traditional meaning or value. Here as elsewhere, selected foreign objects "went native" as they entered Ohio Indian funeral rituals. By the middle of the century coffin burials were becoming increasingly common throughout the middle west, and archaeological evidence attests to their presence at the Kuskuskies and other sites in the Ohio Country. When she died in 1762, Shingas's wife was laid to rest in a wooden coffin, perhaps prepared with the help of local traders. Yet her kin took pains to shape the coffin to fit their own beliefs by placing numerous objects with the corpse: scissors, needles, thread, deer hide for moccasins, a bowl and spoon—objects "which she was fond of while living." Finally, the mourners made a hole in the coffin lid to allow the woman's soul to pass "until it found the place of its future residence." Meanwhile, warriors' graves continued to be marked by painted posts hung with scalps and other trophies belonging to the deceased, who were also buried with their weapons and other personal effects in preparation for the afterlife. And at funeral rituals patterns of reciprocity continued; only the goods exchanged revealed outside influences.[25]

Though Ohio Indians successfully absorbed foreign materials and re-fashioned objects, animals, and their associated meanings to fit native needs and values, not everyone accepted the merits of changes that brought more and more alien goods and ideas into their societies. Moreover, the apparent cultural threat of English cloth, cows, hardware, and house styles was made more compelling to some when considered in light of the real and immediate challenges posed by expanding colonial empires. The turmoil that accompanied French and British colonial invasions, added to the continuing dependence on foreign technology, produced crises of confidence within Ohio Indian societies.

The earliest efforts by Ohio Indians to regain control of their own societies amid rapid and unpredictable changes appeared among the Delawares in 1762, when the prophet Neolin began preaching his message of nativist revival. Neolin drew a clear distinction between Delaware and European cultures, finding the former morally superior and threatened by the corrupting influence of British outsiders. According to Neolin, this threat went beyond the simple adoption of foreign goods or the replacement of Delaware clothing and foods by their European counterparts. Europeans, specifically British Americans, posed a threat to native souls as well. This danger could be avoided, said Neolin, only by adhering to a strict regime revealed by the Creator; acceptance of this regime would be rewarded, while continued indulgence in the aliens' spiritual and material wares would lead to further decline in this life and eternal damnation in the next.[26]

According to Neolin, the Delawares' individual and collective salvation rested especially on their rejection of European culture and on the revitalization of "traditional" values. Thus, as trader James Kenny learned from his Delaware informant, Neolin's followers agreed that "all their Boys are to be train'd to the use of the Bow and Arrow for Seven Years . . . the Women and Antient Men may Raise and Eat Corn," and that "at the Expiration of Seven Years [they would] quit all Commerce with the White People and Clothe themselves with Skins." Captive John M'Cullough, living among the Delawares, described how converts, acting as "a company" of believers, isolated themselves from their unregenerate neighbors, "made no use of firearms," returned to the old practice of displaying friendship by shaking hands with the left hand, not the right—a European custom—and generally sought by their behavior to "purify themselves from sin." Even such mundane chores as fire making became symbolic tests of moral and cultural purity, since Neolin and his followers taught that "that fire was not pure that was made by steel and flint."[27]

These descriptions of Neolin's teaching and the behavior of his adherents shed important light on the concerns of the western Delawares. The prophet's appearance seems not to have been entirely accidental. By 1762 the combination of stringent British trade regulations, the expansion of garrisons, the appearance of squatters and hide hunters and the rumors that Britain and France were conspiring to divide the country between them filled natives with uncertainty and dread. Historically, at such critical junctures prophets had appeared offering new strategies for collective renewal and continued survival. The particular message spread by Neolin—that his people should shed the mantle of European-based materialism and instead clothe themselves in the dress and manners of their ancestors—seemed particularly apt to his audiences, since the aliens were already identified as the source of current political and security problems. Yet the call for revitalization based on nativist principles forced the Delawares to confront a perplexing conundrum: the promise of a better life was rooted in the rejection of materials and strategies that had allowed the natives not only to survive but to thrive in a colonial world. Moreover, the prophet's message came at a time when the Delawares were most threatened by the society that was the sole source of the materials that made everyday life possible.[28]

Neolin's ambitious call for cultural revitalization, while enjoying widespread popularity—one Delaware enthusiastically claimed that the prophet had been accepted by "their whole Nation"—failed to transform Delaware society. A new war against the British in 1763 interrupted the process of reform. Moreover, the outcome of the Defensive War—essentially a stalemate that permitted the British to remain in the west with all their influence—may have eroded Delaware confidence in Neolin's message. To the extent that it cast British Americans in a wholly unflattering light and identified them as an inherent threat to the cultural and moral well-being of the people, Neolin's message doubtless added to anti-British feeling among the Delawares, while the promise of a better future was clearly linked to the departure of foreign influence. If expectations ran high among the Delawares that the new war could lead to the total destruction of their enemies, the appearance of Bouquet's army on the Muskingum late in 1764 must have dampened much of the enthusiasm demonstrated for the prophet. Furthermore, leaders such as Shingas and Tamaqua, who were opposed to

the war and presumably to its spiritual underpinning, represented a countervailing force of some weight that may also have reduced the impact of
Neolin's teaching. Moreover, Neolin himself seems to have accommodated
to at least some of what the Euro-American world had to offer. His later days
were spent in a European-style house, though he continued to hold forth on
Delaware cultural and spiritual values.[29]

The Delaware nativist revitalization before 1763 was not an isolated
event. Throughout the Ohio Country during the troubled 1760s natives
continued to wrestle with the myriad threats posed by colonial expansion.
Though Neolin's movement collapsed during the Defensive War, efforts to
define, or redefine, Delaware society continued, as Moravians entering the
region in the late 1760s discovered. Both John Heckewelder and David
Zeisberger found a number of prophets active among the Muskingum
towns. The center of much of this activity was Newcomer's Town, the
residence of the Delawares' "king." Zeisberger found in 1768 that "they have
four Indian preachers, one building a meeting house" while actively promoting a nativist revival, which Zeisberger chose to see as a return to "pagan
customs and practices."[30]

To the east of Newcomer's Town, on the upper Allegheny among the
Munsees at Goschgosching, another prophet appeared. Wingenund was no
stranger to local Indians or the British; in 1763 he had been among the
native leaders who had tried unsuccessfully to persuade Captain Ecuyer to
abandon Fort Pitt. By 1767, however, Wingenund had earned notoriety of a
different sort as a nativist reformer whose rejection of British American
culture resembled Neolin's. The origins of Wingenund's career as a prophet
are unclear, though it is likely that his influence grew from his ability to
capitalize on the already divided Munsee community, whose factional lines
were more starkly drawn with the arrival in 1767 of David Zeisberger. The
Moravian came at the behest of one faction at Goschgosching but quickly
found himself competing with Wingenund for the loyalty of the villagers.[31]

The strong traditionalist position held by Wingenund and his followers
became clear at the outset as the natives confronted the Christian intruders.
Wingenund rejected the Moravians' advocacy of an inclusive brand of Christianity shared by natives and colonists alike. Instead, the Munsee "insisted
on maintaining that the Indians had a separate way upon which they would
come to God," one that did not include embracing Christian doctrine or
European culture. The exclusive, nativist position Wingenund staked out
found strong support among the "younger element," which, Zeisberger soon
discovered, "continued their heathen practices"—sometimes in defiance of
older men and women, though the factionalism was not based entirely on

age differences. Among the most vocal opponents of the missionaries were "the old women," who blamed the Moravians for a ruinous infestation of corn worms. The women and their daughters also prevented their younger children from attending the missionaries' services and lessons. This internecine contest for the spiritual and cultural identity of the Goschgosching villagers, including threats by traditionalists against those inclined to follow Zeisberger, was resolved only when the pro-Moravian faction departed to build its own mission town in the Beaver Valley.[32]

Concerns about the decline of spiritual and moral character that animated Wingenund, Neolin, and their followers appeared beyond the Delawares and Munsees, as did a belief that problems at home and Anglo-Americans were somehow closely related. Missionary Samuel Kirkland, on his first trip to the Iroquois late in 1764, arrived at the eastern Seneca town of Canadasegea only to find himself at the center of a dispute between traditionalists and those who held a more tolerant view of British missionaries and the society they came from. This dispute, pitting war leaders against village headmen, did not begin with Kirkland's arrival but was one reflection of a much larger conflict over how best to confront expanding colonial societies and their cultural baggage.

At issue were the very values that defined the Senecas as a people. Many, including the war captain Oniongwadekha, whom Kirkland identified as one of his "malignant Enemies," saw in the missionary the same threat to their people's spiritual and physical well-being that Neolin had earlier identified. Oniongwadekha also challenged those who somehow believed that the Senecas could preserve their own way of life while accommodating to the foreigners. Invoking Thaonghyawagon—the Creator, or "Upholder of the Sky"—Oniongwadekha warned against continued acceptance of Anglo-American culture and especially Christianity; to accept the missionary not only meant becoming like the "remnants of Tribes to the *East*" but would cause the Senecas to "soon loose the spirit of *True Men*." The debate on this particular occasion went against Oniongwadekha, though largely out of concern that someone might harm Kirkland and therefore invite British retaliation. Meanwhile, the impact of the Defensive War, and the more immediate fear of famine, continued to strengthen the traditionalists' position. Kirkland, however, would never discover the outcome of the debate: he left Canadasegea soon after his confrontation with Oniongwadekha, not to return for twenty-three years.[33]

The spiritual revitalization among the Delawares and Munsees was matched by a process of social consolidation in the Ohio Country. Indeed, the efforts of native leaders to draw their people together must be seen as

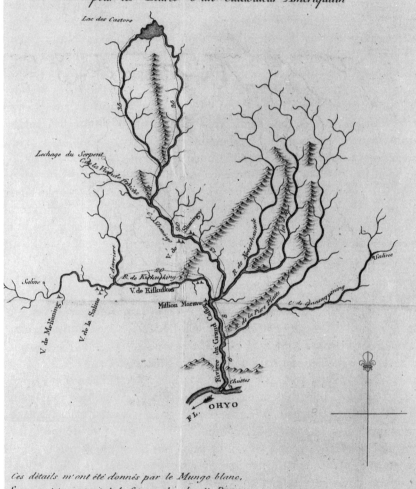

another dimension of the revitalization movement by peoples that did not recognize distinct spheres of "religion" and "society."

The creation of a Delaware nation in the west began with the early migrations of the 1720s. This process involved two groups of Delawares; one, perhaps the first to enter the Ohio Country, comprised followers of Allumapees. The other was composed of "Jersey" Indians—natives from the middle Delaware Valley. By the mid-1760s these groups had largely been reconstituted in the west and were undergoing a process of social and political coalescence that produced an ethnic alliance not unlike the one from which the Hurons of the west emerged in the late seventeenth century. At the same time, the ethnically distinct Munsees were also gathering in the Ohio Country under the leadership of Custaloga. Although they cooperated with nearby Delawares, notably during peace negotiations before 1758, the Munsees maintained their political independence throughout this period.[34]

Though shared cultural traits and close proximity made Delaware unity likely, it was the threat posed by French and British expansion that accelerated the move toward unification. Indeed, the years from Shingas's emergence as Delaware "king" in 1752 through the Defensive War of 1763 represented a critical period in the development of the Delaware nation in the west. This process was not conflict free, however. The paramount issues of war and peace after 1755 and the underlying threat posed by expanding colonial settlements sharpened differences between the principal Delaware groups. Tamaqua, drawing support from his own kin and followers among the former Schuylkill Indians, was able not only to disarm warriors after 1758 but also to reach out to Netawatwees and the Jersey Indians for support. Yet as British expansion continued unchecked in the early 1760s, an open rift appeared between the two Delaware societies that apparently arose from differences of strategy: Tamaqua's people favored accommodation while Netawatwees urged a more belligerent stand against the invaders. Thus ensued Tamaqua's loss of popularity in 1762 and the assertion by some Delawares—Jersey Indians—that Netawatwees, not Tamaqua, was the rightful Delaware "king." Moreover, throughout the Defensive War, Netawatwees and his followers were closely associated in British minds with the hostilities.[35]

Both Netawatwees and the process of Delaware consolidation drew

13. The Beaver River Valley, showing the location of Custaloga's Town at the Kuskuskies and the Moravian mission at Friedensstadt. From Hector St. John de Crevecoeur, *Letters from an American Farmer* . . . (London, 1782). (Courtesy of the John Carter Brown Library at Brown University)

strength from the revitalization movement. Neolin's message added to the ideal of a distinct Delaware society while it ratified the militant antiexpansionism represented by Netawatwees and his followers. It is perhaps no coincidence that Neolin drew much of his support from Newcomer's Town, a site subsequently identified by British Americans as the political center of the Delaware nation.[36]

Notwithstanding the emergence of Netawatwees as "king" of the western Delawares, the nation's constituent parts continued for some time to retain substantial independence; for example, each Delaware group selected its own headmen. In this regard Netawatwees was "first among equals" in the Delaware councils, and his role was not unlike that of his former rival, Tamaqua—that of an arbiter and moral leader whose example and wisdom helped guide his people. Yet his success and stature, both at home and among colonists, were enhanced by the growing inclination of once separate Delaware communities to cooperate and by Netawatwees's own moderating views toward the British Americans. Thus, to outsiders, Netawatwees, more than any other Delaware headman, was credited with enhancing his people's influence and prestige in the west.

Zeisberger, in the early 1770s, found that the Delawares' reputation among their neighbors had, "though the wise management of the Chief Netawatwees . . . amazingly increased" since the early 1760s. At the same time, Netawatwees actively sought to bring all the Delawares together on the Muskingum. In 1773, three years before his death, Netawatwees joined with other headmen in directing a message to New Jersey's governor, informing him that "they desired all the New Jersey Indians to move to their Country." Netawatwees also encouraged the resettlement of Moravian Indians led by Zeisberger, Heckewelder, and Ettwein, who founded two mission towns in the Muskingum Valley. These mission Indians, for the most part northern Delawares and Munsees, had entered the Ohio Country in 1768. They first moved to the Beaver Valley, there they joined converts from the bitterly divided Goschgosching villages; together the natives then moved on to the Muskingum.[37]

The Munsees' efforts to draw their people together in the west also turned on the presence of Moravian converts. Between 1762 and 1770 the Munsees who had lived in the vicinity of Venango had, like their Delaware neighbors to the south, resettled to the west, on the Walhonding branch of the Muskingum River, near the new Delaware towns. Though they lived in close proximity to the Delawares, ethnic differences kept the Munsees apart and may have helped shape their eventual determination to return east, where by 1770 they had taken up residence at the Kuskuskies.[38]

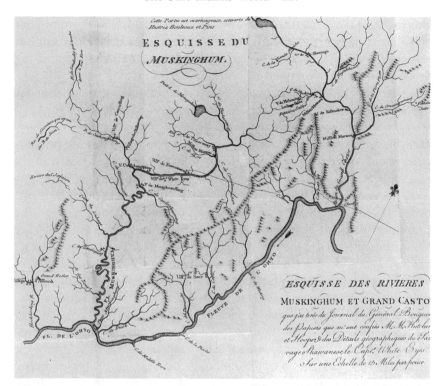

14. The Indian towns in the Muskingum Valley, showing Newcomer's Town and the Moravian missions founded in the early 1770s. From Hector St. John de Crevecoeur, *Letters from an American Farmer* ... (London, 1782). (Courtesy of the John Carter Brown Library at Brown University)

The effort to bring the Moravian converts from Goschgosching into their society was consistent with the Munsees' efforts to maintain their strength and independence apart from their neighbors. Custaloga must have kept an eye on the increasingly self-destructive character of the Goschgosching settlements. In the midst of the factional conflict there, as pro-Moravians led by their "blind chief" Allemewi decided to move away, a message came from Custaloga and his adviser Glikkikan, asking that the missionaries come to his people. Custaloga's reason was that the Moravians could teach his people how to make gunpowder, though the headman's interests were more territorial than technical. The Goschgosching natives had originally planned to resettle at Venango and soon found themselves the object of a tug-of-war between the Genesee Senecas and Custaloga's Munsees, each of whom laid claim to that portion of the Allegheny Valley. Custaloga used this issue to draw the converts to his town at the Kuskuskies. Such a move not only united many of the western Munsees under Custaloga's leadership, but also drew at least a portion of the Goschgosching settlement out of the Senecas' sphere of influence.[39]

Whatever hope Custaloga and the Moravians may have entertained about the benefits of resettlement at the Kuskuskies proved ill founded. In 1770 the converts built a mission town, Friedensstadt (Moravia, Pennsylvania), some distance south of the Munsee town. However, even separate communities could not prevent the reemergence of conflict between Christians and traditionalists and of factional disputes within the Munsee town itself. At issue once more was the perceived threat the newcomers posed to traditional ways of life. In the power struggle that followed, the traditionalist Custaloga faced his onetime friend and adviser Glikkikan, who quickly allied himself with the Moravians, was baptised, and took the name Isaac. Before the end of 1770 some Munsees were leaving their town, inclined to accept Moravian teaching and doubtless attracted by the relative calm and unity within Friedensstadt. At the Kuskuskies, meanwhile, conflict continued unabated. In 1772 Kiashuta learned that "one half of the Indians" in the town "were offended with the other for hearkening to" the Moravians. By then, however, the missionaries had concluded that since the "emnity of the greater part of . . . Kaskaskunk and other savage neighbors rather increased," their only choice was to accept the Delawares' offer of sanctuary on the Muskingum and to use Friedensstadt only as a way station for the anticipated arrival of more Christian natives from Pennsylvania.[40]

The invitation from the Delawares was also the product of much debate over the wisdom of accepting the strangers. Traditionalists had earlier attempted to blunt the Moravians' effectiveness in the west by sending a shaman to Goschgosching to challenge Zeisberger and his theology. Yet between 1768 and 1772 the conflict over the Moravians was carried on primarily within the council house; none of the Delaware towns appear to have been torn apart as Goschgosching and the Kuskuskies had been. On one side of the debate were older village headmen and councilors, notably Netawatwees and, until his death in 1769, Tamaqua, men who favored offering sanctuary to the Christians. Facing them were traditionalists and aspiring headmen, led by the younger Killbuck. Thus Zeisberger discovered that "King Beaver [Tamaqua] and his tribe [sic] . . . were locating a separate town, building a church, and arranging to have an English minister come among them." How completely these or any other Delawares were actually willing to separate from neighbors and kin is unclear, though Charles Beatty found some potential converts when he visited the Delawares earlier, in

1766. This secession movement came to nothing, however, having been blocked by traditionalists and those who sought a compromise.[41]

Two issues finally resolved the conflict in favor of the Moravians. One was medical and spiritual, the other, social. As disease once more swept through the Ohio Country in the early 1770s, many Delawares seem to have accepted the notion that they could add to their store of spiritual power by admitting the Christians. Heckewelder, for instance, learned that the Delawares had decided to confront the "epidemical disease by embracing Christianity." In doing so, the natives were not capitulating to outsiders but rather were augmenting their own collective powers against dangerous forces; even Heckewelder acknowledged that the natives saw conversion as a "remedy."[42]

At the same time, however, the Delawares sent their invitation to the Moravians on behalf of their "great council" and told the missionaries that the natives had agreed to accept the Christian Indians as members of the Delaware "nation." This desire to unite Delaware peoples as part of a single "nation" eventually transcended differences over the Moravians and permitted the converts to remove to the Muskingum Valley in 1772. The key was an apparent compromise that permitted the Moravians to settle among the Delawares, but in their own towns and presumably with their own local councils.[43]

Thus, though colonial expansion and imperial wars continued to threaten the autonomy of Ohio Indians, those forces did not break native societies but, rather, provided a catalyst for cultural renewal as scattered, largely autonomous villages banded together under the guidance of charismatic prophets or respected headmen. That process is clearest among the western Delawares; less detail is available about the Delawares' Shawnee or Seneca neighbors. Yet on one level consolidation seems to have been widespread. More than in earlier decades, the Ohio Country of the 1760s and 1770s reflected a regular pattern of ethnic territories as villages drew closer to each other. Clearly defined ethnic territories certainly did not suddenly emerge in 1760 or 1770—better reporting by colonial observers after 1760 makes territoriality easier to define. Nor were ethnic frontiers rigid and impervious; like every other aspect of Ohio Indian life, these territories emerged over time. The reunification of the Shawnees on the Scioto plains and the emergence of a western Delaware nation suggest, however, that outside pressure helped forge a new sense of ethnic identity and unity at the same time that colonial expansion led to efforts to forge an interethnic alliance.[44]

Neither the French nor the British were able to impose their will on Ohio Indians during the turbulent years from 1748 to 1764. Indeed, the French chose not to try for fear of alienating potential allies. British efforts to transform their assertion of ownership of the Ohio Country into political reality after 1758 failed repeatedly owing to native resistance, colonial recalcitrance, and ministerial instability. And Bouquet's march into the Muskingum Valley and the subsequent treaties that ended the Defensive War notwithstanding, British authority in the west was no greater in 1765 than it had been in 1758.

The physical distance between Ohio Indians and colonial society permitted the natives to develop their own strategies in the face of continued challenges from outside the region. This flexibility had been enjoyed for generations with respect to European material goods. The continued vitality of Ohio Indian societies can also be seen in their response to missionaries and their spiritual wares.

In nearly every case, the would-be saviors were forced to retreat. Most were overcome by what David Zeisberger called the "proud and haughty" character of native audiences and the persistence of traditional practices that were not easily dislodged by preaching and admonition. Yet the Indians' inner strength lay not in outward ritual behavior but in a firm belief in their own superiority. According to Zeisberger, although the natives readily admitted that the "whites are very ingenious, because of their ability to manufacture a great variety of things," the Indians nevertheless regarded the colonists' way of life as "wearisome and slavish as compared with their own."[45]

Against such convictions, missionaries could make little headway. Charles Beatty, for example, appeared at Newcomer's Town in 1766 eager to work among the Delawares. Though he "heard" that numerous Delawares, including Netawatwees and Neolin, were impressed with his preaching, Beatty's hopes were dashed when the village council returned the wampum by which he requested permission to continue his mission. Likewise, in 1767 other divines learned that "a considerable Number of Indians . . . are well disposed to Christianity" and had therefore decided to assemble on the Muskingum "with a View to hear and attend upon the Gospel." Yet both David McClure and David Jones, who sought to exploit native interest, suffered the same rejection experienced earlier by Beatty. McClure was invited to preach to the Delaware council in a test not unlike that faced by prospective ministers to New England congregations. McClure's efforts proved inadequate, however; the Delawares thanked him for the sermon but told him, "Brother, you will now return home."[46]

The natives' response once again reflected their own strong sense of cultural identity and a good idea of what conversion meant. In rejecting his effort to preach among them, the Delawares told McClure that "the white people, with whom we are acquainted, are worse, or more wicked than we are, and *we think it better to be such as we are than such as they are*." At the same time, the warriors were uninterested because "if we take your religion, we must leave off war, and become women." Baptist missionary David Jones was also rebuffed by the Delawares and found that "the king was not much for [Jones's remaining]"—a formidable rejection in itself. Worse still, Jones's one attempt to carry his message to neighboring Shawnees nearly cost him his life. His actions evidently so outraged traditionalists that they planned to kill the intruder. Only timely aid from a local trader allowed Jones to escape unharmed.[47]

The missionaries failed for other reasons as well. Long exposure to Jesuits, Moravians, Congregationalists, and others had allowed the natives to devise appropriate strategies in the face of persistent Christians. By the 1770s, Canadian mission reserves, Moravian towns, and border settlements all provided windows onto the preachers' methods and ideologies. One lesson readily learned was that on the other side of the cultural divide there were substantial differences of doctrine and sectarian politics that natives could turn to their advantage. Thus the Delawares were able to put off Presbyterian McClure in part by telling him of the Quakers' insistence that they alone should manage mission affairs in the west.[48]

Christian Frederick Post's failure to do more than arouse Delaware anger and suspicion in 1762 grew from the natives' association of Christian denominations or men more with territorial ambitions than with peace and salvation. The Delawares' rejection of Post and his hasty departure from the Muskingum—Tamaqua planned to take the missionary with him to the Philadelphia treaty council in 1762 and to "tell [the governor] to keep him at home"—grew less from the Moravian's preaching than from the fact that, on his only other trips into the Ohio Country, Post had come as a political emissary and agent of an army and empire the natives had good reason to distrust. Indeed, those who met Post at the Kuskuskies in 1758 with sour looks and clenched fists doubtless took special delight in later ruining his effort to preach among them.[49]

Post's was not an isolated case, however. Charles Beatty's failure to remain among the Delawares grew in part from the natives' tendency to identify Presbyterians with border violence. As Killbuck explained years later, the Delawares rejected Beatty and his companions because Presbyterian "ministers went to war against them, and therefore [the natives] did not like to be taught by them now, who were before for killing them." And David Jones, with whom Killbuck spoke in 1773, also found among the Delawares and their neighbors "a jealousy, lest we should have some design of enslaving them," a fear that was perhaps justified, since Jones made little secret of his desire to remove his own congregation to a new settlement in the west. Even the Genesee Senecas, far removed from border settlements, were demonstrably hostile to Zeisberger and his followers, both because the Moravians threatened to remove Munsee dependents and because many Senecas were inclined to view the missionaries as the forward edge of a general colonial invasion.[50]

Yet for all the suspicion, latent hostility, and cultural superiority Ohio Indians displayed toward missionaries, the Moravians managed to persist and succeed where others, even the pacific Quakers, had failed. The Moravians' success was due in part to circumstances as well as timing. By arriving in the Muskingum Valley with Delaware converts, the missionaries inadvertently furthered the efforts by local headmen to consolidate their people. And by the mid-1770s many aged Delaware headmen—Netawatwees among them—had softened their earlier objection to missionaries and were now urging their followers to, in Tamaqua's words, "listen to the Moravians and believe what they tell you."[51]

Nevertheless, the history and character of the Moravian mission itself contributed most to the ultimate success of men such as Heckewelder and Zeisberger. In this regard Post's experience is instructive: he alone among the Moravians was identified by the natives as a political partisan. By contrast, other men, arriving later, were listened to because the Delawares recognized correctly that the Moravians, in David Jones's words, "never fought against them" and that "therefore they might receive them." But the Moravians' methods also played a crucial role. David McClure could only admire men who "appear to have adopted the best mode of Christianizing the Indian." That mode demanded that the Moravians "go among them without noise or parade, and by their friendly behaviour conciliate [the Indians'] good will." And unlike the less well initiated for whom conversion meant hard preaching, the Moravians would "join them in the chace, and freely distribute to the helpless and [thereby] gradually instil into the minds of individuals the principals of religion." It was a method reminiscent of that used by the Jesuits in an earlier time, one that Ohio Indians clearly used as a yardstick as they sized up would-be missionaries. In a world fraught with difficulties, in which Ohio natives continued to fashion strategies for keeping the Anglo-American world at bay, the Moravians' "friendly behaviour" as well as their worldly skills and materials made them a welcome exception to the more general pattern of intercultural relations in the turbulent years following the Defensive War.[52]

ten

The Struggle for Sovereignty

 The movement of two British armies into the west in 1764 hastened negotiations that, within a year, brought a formal end to the fighting in the Ohio Country. For the next decade peace would be the official condition west of the mountains. In point of fact, however, the years after 1764 were punctuated by continued violence, death, and misunderstanding.

The stark difference between peace declared and a cultural frontier that grew ever more violent was one measure of the continuously evolving nature of British–Ohio Indian relations. In 1764 British officers were prepared to forcefully assert their sovereign's authority over the west and its native peoples. A decade later no British regulars stood along the Ohio, and distant Indian superintendents and generals could exercise little influence over a region that had become a strategic and political backwater as attention shifted to the rebellion within the older colonies. Moreover, by late 1774 the Ohio Indians were no longer fighting the British empire in the west but confronted the vanguard of a rising American empire.

Ohio Indians who had successfully held their own against invading armies found themselves increasingly exposed to a massive Anglo-American invasion that by 1774 had pushed colonial borders to the Ohio River itself and, for the first time in the fifty-year history of the Ohio Indians, threatened to breach the Ohio barrier.

By the summer of 1765, British-Indian relations had already become linked to a much broader effort by Crown and Parliament to rationalize a vastly expanded empire. From the outbreak of the Seven Years' War through the Indian war just ended, the home government and its agents had hammered together a rough program for Indian affairs, often shaped by unforeseen events and needs. However, no sooner had the Treaty of Paris been ratified than the Crown moved to substitute a thoroughgoing policy for wartime expediency, a change made more compelling by the transfer of Canada, the middle west, and the Floridas to Great Britain. The Indians' Defensive War underscored Britain's incomplete control over the most volatile portion of the ceded territories and the need to create an Indian policy that would at once satisfy imperial demands for peace along the western border, colonial territorial and commercial ambitions, and the natives' need for security within their own lands. It was a tall order. For a decade after 1764, efforts were made to provide such a comprehensive policy. Though ultimately unsuccessful, British attempts to devise a frontier policy nonetheless helped shape the course of events in the Ohio Country.[1]

Efforts to impose order on the west and on colonial-Indian relations first emerged at the height of the Defensive War. Issued in October 1763, a royal proclamation represented the first attempt to assert royal jurisdiction over the west as well to as bring order to colonial expansion and thereby enhance prospects for peace with the natives. The method in this case was a decree stopping all settlement at the crest of the Appalachians until a comprehensive boundary treaty could be negotiated and regulations for governing Indian affairs enacted.[2]

Many of the specific elements that might be included in a more comprehensive Indian policy had existed for nearly a decade before the 1763 Proclamation. Royal Indian agents, the primacy of Crown over colonial interests in Indian affairs, and the use of the army to enforce trade regulations had all emerged since the Albany Congress of 1754, though strictly ad hoc. What remained, as the American commander-in-chief General Thomas Gage recognized, was to establish a "settled, uniform, System for the Management of Indian Affairs"—a system made more necessary since "Our Concerns with Indians are now greatly extended by our Acquisitions in the late [Seven Years'] War." Gage's view was fully shared by Sir William Johnson, who gladly responded to the Board of Trade's inquiries by submitting a comprehensive scheme for Indian affairs. Johnson's plan included the licensing of all traders by their colonies and trade that would be conducted against exchange rates set by Indian superintendents. Johnson also called for a western boundary line as soon as possible, believing it was the only sure way to preserve the fragile peace with the natives. To oversee these and other matters, Johnson also advocated the creation of an independent

Indian service, a suggestion that reflected his own ambitions as well as the frustrations of being financially hamstrung by cost-conscious military officers who, with Amherst as an extreme example, seldom appreciated the demands of Indian diplomacy.[3]

Johnson's plan, portions of which were eventually incorporated into government policy, rested on the Crown's role as arbiter between natives and colonists, which had emerged since 1754. The plan also emphasized reliance upon the Indian Department rather than the army as the proper instrument for enforcing Indian policy. In Johnson's view the army's role in the west would be secondary to that of his own department, since he was convinced that no amount of force could prevail against the numerous western Indian societies. In fact, according to Johnson, only two options were open to the government if it wished to enjoy de facto as well as de jure control of its western territories: either destroy the natives—something the superintendent doubted the army could do—or retain their friendship and cooperation through diplomatic means. Any officer, including the commander-in-chief, who had been involved in the 1763 war would have agreed that only the latter course offered a reasonable chance of peace along the border. Moreover, neither Gage, Johnson, nor subordinate officers suffered any illusions about the army's ability to occupy so vast a territory. By scattering his few troops throughout the middle west, Amherst had invited their destruction in 1763. Gage, determined to avoid a similar catastrophe, decided not to reoccupy the small outposts overrun during the war, but to concentrate what men he could spare in larger forts that would also serve as the regulated trading posts Johnson advocated. Gage's superiors agreed, and both they and the general hoped that the reduced presence of redcoats west of the mountains would "ease the Jealousy of the Indians."[4]

Neither the Covenant Chain nor the Six Nations was mentioned in Johnson's otherwise comprehensive blueprint for Indian affairs. Subsequent events made clear, however, that the superintendent—and his superiors—continued to view Iroquois influence and the Covenant Chain as the dual bases of Indian relations in the northeast. Moreover, the rhetoric of Confederacy power, conquest, and hegemony continued to serve as a convenient tool in a continuing attempt to simplify and regularize Indian relations west of the Appalachians, an effort that paralleled the Crown's campaign to better regulate its provinces in eastern America. The new Indian world that Johnson envisioned took its form from the superintendent's earlier efforts to impose regularity by creating several "confederacies," all equally dependent on the Crown. In such a scheme—which never existed in fact as much as in officials' minds and rhetoric—the Ohio Country would continue as an extension of Iroquoia, its people still identified as "dependents" of the Confederacy.[5]

By the late 1760s, Johnson's particular instrument in the Ohio Country was the Ohio Seneca, Kiashuta. The onetime anti-British advocate reemerged after 1763 as the principal intermediary between Johnson, the Confederacy, and the Ohio Indians. Although Kiashuta's influence among the widely dispersed and independent Ohio Senecas is unclear, Johnson was quick to promote Kiashuta as "a man of universal influence," "a great Chief" who was "sensible [and] prudent" and "much esteemed by the several [nations]." Such comments suggest that, like Tanaghrisson's before him, Kiashuta's influence was based largely on a close relationship with British officials, supplemented in this instance by his role as messenger for the Confederacy council at Onondaga. In this capacity Kiashuta quickly emerged as the principal Six Nations figure on the Ohio in the decade after he helped orchestrate the truce between the Delawares and Bouquet.[6]

The grand, if nonetheless subordinate, role assigned to the Six Nations continued to be at variance with reality. The Confederacy remained divided over how to deal with the changes and challenges ushered in by the French defeat and the 1763 war. In particular, the western Senecas continually "seemed adverse to anything [the Confederacy] proposed." These Senecas, their leader Gaustarax, and their Ohio kinfolk would remain a thorn in Johnson's side for the rest of his career. During the 1763 war only the Mohawks and Oneidas actively supported British forces, though with some effect; Oneidas led by Andrew (Henry) Montour razed the Seneca-Delaware town at Kanestio. Yet the Six Nations played a distinctly subdued role in subsequent peace negotiations. Moreover, time and distance continued to erode the bonds linking the Six Nations with those Iroquois who had moved to the Ohio Country, and even Johnson was forced to concede that "the Senecas here [New York]" have "no more influence or Authority [over] the Senecas of Ohio who have resided in that Quarter for some Generations" and who were not inclined to follow the New York Senecas' lead in making peace in 1764. Nevertheless, British rhetoric of Confederacy authority, the base metal of the Covenant Chain, remained a fundamental ingredient in the Crown's formula for postwar Indian affairs.[7]

Johnson's recommendations first found their way into British Indian policy at the Johnson Hall treaties in 1765. When Johnson affirmed the Crown's commitment to a comprehensive boundary line, he made it clear that the line would be negotiated with the Six Nations acting on behalf of the Delawares and Shawnees, who would "engage to abide by whatever Limits shall be agreed upon." Yet beyond this early assertion of royal—and

Covenant Chain—dominion in the Ohio Country, Johnson's grand scheme began to encounter serious difficulties. A major problem was money: to pay for the regular renewal of treaties, to fund an enlarged corps of Indian agents, and to keep even the reduced force of regulars on station in the west. Although officials in London and the colonies understood the necessity of financing such programs, the urgent need to control an expanded empire was at odds with the alarming state of public finance as the government struggled to find a way to meet new expenses while paying the enormous national debt.[8]

Only months after the Johnson Hall treaties, General Gage informed his Indian superintendent that their superiors "seem much tired of the Expense of Supporting Forts" and other trappings of frontier security. Both Johnson and Gage understood the source of the discontent: by year's end the entire eastern seaboard was alive with vocal, sometimes violent, protest against the Grenville ministry's first effort to finance American defense and Indian affairs through American taxation. The urban unrest that followed passage of the Stamp Act and land riots on Hudson Valley estates forced the home government to shift more troops and money from supervision of the west to police duties in the east.[9]

The course of British American protest and the constitutional crisis that emerged over the Stamp Act had a direct bearing on the Crown's efforts to fashion a western policy. The inability of the government to generate sufficient new revenue from the mainland colonies, coupled with the growing need to shift troops to volatile seaboard cities, led to a gradual military evacuation of the west and a growing belief that the colonies themselves could better manage trade regulation. By 1768 Johnson's superintendency had thus been reduced to the status of a frontier diplomatic corps. In the meantime Johnson's hope for a powerful, independent Indian service vanished as cost-conscious ministries became less willing to increase Indian expenses; both northern and southern superintendencies remained what they had been since their creation, an advisory and diplomatic arm of the army, subordinate to the American commander-in-chief.[10]

Yet money was not the only source of British difficulties in the west. The chronic instability of the home government between 1765 and 1770 had an equally corrosive effect on western affairs. The government first attempted to prevent, then later supported, trans-Appalachian colonization while at the same time shifting a greater share of western management to the colonies themselves. The army, discovering anew how difficult it was to police the middle west, began to wink at those who violated Johnson's trade regulations and at the land speculators who entered the region. Taken together, the closely related issues of fiscal demands, colonial protest, and ministerial instability created a paralysis in British-Indian affairs and encouraged the substitution of stopgap measures for a coherent, consistent policy. It would be a mistake to assume that the day-to-day encounters between Ohio Indians and British Americans after 1765 were dictated by far-off events and abstract constitutional principles. Nevertheless, declining British influence in the west did affect intercultural relations, if only by removing a countervailing force to rampant provincial expansion.[11]

While the British government wrestled with frontier policy, the Ohio Indians continued to face familiar threats to their sovereignty. The urgency with which the natives spoke of trade at treaty congresses reflected continued material dependence. Yet after 1765 the greatest challenge once more came from settlers and speculators drawn west by the promise of cheap land both along the Ohio River and in the Illinois Country. Squatters had appeared before; after 1765, however, they came in greater numbers until the Allegheny Mountain barrier that had helped protect native societies was at last effectively breached.[12]

Meanwhile, other voices began to be heard in the Ohio Country. By spring 1765 the Delawares were losing some of their earlier influence among their neighbors. At Fort Pitt that spring Croghan noticed that Delaware headmen, among them Tamaqua and Netawatwees, "intended to be Mediators" but withdrew after "finding that would not take." In this instance Kiashuta once more stood as moderator, especially since he appeared to have "a Great Sway Amongst the Shannas." Yet while Croghan chose to assign the influential role to Kiashuta, it seems more likely that the Seneca's "great sway" grew from his association with "a very proud and high Sperreted pople" who "has More to Say with the Western Nations then any othe[r] this Way." Throughout the following decade, the Shawnees played an increasingly important part in regional affairs, serving as a focus for rising discontent over colonial settlements. Croghan well understood the source of the Shawnees' influence: their widespread bonds of friendship and kinship with nations from the Tennessee Valley to the Wabash and the upper Mississippi. As early as 1765 Johnson learned that "all the Western Nations often hold their Councils" at the Shawnee towns along the Scioto River. Croghan also identified what may have been another potent element in the Shawnees' rising influence in the Ohio Country: a strong attachment to French traders who still operated from the Illinois Country and from Louisiana and who nursed the Ohio Indians' distrust British Americans.[13]

If any among the Ohio Indians anticipated that peace would bring stability and security to their world, those hopes were soon shattered. Months before peace had even been ratified—and in violation of military decrees—merchants sent their men west against the moment when the rich and previously forbidden Illinois Country should be opened. As early as March 1765, some £20,000 to £30,000 worth of trade goods were hauled from Philadelphia to Fort Pitt in anticipation of a crush of deerskin-laden Indian customers. Traders were a familiar, predictable bunch and seldom came looking for trouble. Squatters and hunters were another matter; by mid-summer the eastern fringe of the Ohio Country was again the object of an invasion by border settlers, in defiance of the royal proclamation.[14]

Only a month after Croghan's Indian congress at Fort Pitt, Senecas living downriver demanded that the British live up to *their* treaty obligations by removing "several white Families [who] are settled on Red Stone Creek, and have planted Corn," even though the colonists were settled near a Mohawk family—perhaps hoping this would shield them from native complaints. For their part, the Senecas were willing to be generous. Insisting that "we do not desire they should lose their Labour," the Seneca headman Ogista expected that "when [the squatters] have reaped their Corn, we hope they will be removed." Ogista was far less generous toward numerous Virginia hunters, "who we desire may be Ordered to return immediately." Consideration might be extended to hardworking, if foolish, squatters, but not to poachers who spoiled native hunting and who were more than willing to waylay and murder the first Indians they encountered.[15]

The arrival of Virginia hunters "who had like to have killed" any natives they came across was only one sign that the virulent and largely indiscriminate Indian hating that had surfaced east of the mountains at Conestoga and Lancaster was spreading west on the tide of British Americans pressing westward after 1764. The fear and anger generated by nearly a decade of war and the isolation in alien territory that came with homesteading or hunting encouraged deep-seated suspicion and antipathy toward Indians. The provincial scalp bounties added profit to the motives for colonial attacks on Indians. Shortly after Ohio Indians accepted Bouquet's offer of peace, a Maryland soldier presented a scalp at Fort Pitt, clearly expecting a reward. He was only one of a number of current or recently discharged militiamen who "were out in the Woods" determined to raise extra cash by lifting Indian scalps on the long trek back home.[16]

Throughout the late 1760s a mounting tally of attacks and retaliation appeared in reports from the west. By mid-1766, Sir William Johnson lamented that "every Week brings me fresh Complaints from the Indians," made all the more alarming because the victims included not only distant

Shawnees and Delawares but Six Nations people as well. Earlier that year a Mohawk had been found murdered on the road between Fort Cumberland and Bedford, and Johnson's comment followed the news that four Onondagas and several other natives had been killed near Fort Pitt. Violence spread south of the Ohio as well, where Cherokees found themselves no more immune from attack than Indians to their north. The "Augusta Boys" from southwestern Virginia killed several Cherokees, ostensibly when those natives were unfortunately misidentified as Shawnees and Delawares—"enemy Indians." Yet the excuse pales against continued attacks on Cherokees and Creeks by the Virginians' version of the Paxton Boys, who, like their northern counterparts and border settlers generally, continued to live in a state of war with their native neighbors. Moreover, as squatters and long hunters appeared in greater numbers, the opportunities for conflict increased as almost any encounter—over land, game, or a native's prized rifle—could end in death and open the door to a bloody cycle of retaliation.[17]

The natives did not stand by passively in the face of violent outsiders. Some, like Ogista, lodged complaints with military authorities and Indian agents. Ogista immediately seized the moral high ground in response to the army's demand that Senecas accused of killing a colonist be given up for trial in a British court. The headman reminded Colonel John Reid of the recent murders of *three* of his people and wondered aloud about British promises of equal justice for Indians and settlers. In such encounters, Indian requests that the British control *their* wild young men carried an effective measure of irony.[18]

Others, impatient with the army's obvious inability to curb indiscriminate violence, struck back in kind. In the spring of 1767 seven Virginia traders died at the hands of Cherokees whose own people had fallen victim to the Augusta Boys. In all, some eighteen Virginians died in retaliation for six Cherokees killed within the colony. Ohio warriors also collided with provincials, on one occasion in a bloody fracas during which "some were killed and more wounded on each side." During the latter half of 1767 alone, at least thirteen provincials died in the Ohio Country and Great Lakes basin, many of them traders who became the hapless victims of hatred inflamed by others in a region where violence was becoming endemic.[19]

The increased level of violence and the unrestrained invasion of their lands soon made Ohio Indians fear a renewed British effort to destroy them. In fact, although murders and assaults were the most visible signs of Indian-colonial friction, the natives' persistent fear of dispossession most influenced their responses to British Americans. Indian agents found Ohio warriors "very sulky and much disturbed" by the rising tide of squatters. By 1767 only the natives' "love of peace" and their belief that the king would eventually take charge of his people prevented a new border war. The natives' forbearance must have been doubly difficult given other signs suggesting that the British meant to dispossess them. Stories, some undoubtedly spread by settlers themselves, told of colonial plans to "cutt off" the Delawares. And given the behavior of Virginians since 1764, the rumors seemed to the Indians to ring true. The Delawares made a point of reminding Virginia's governor Francis Fauquier that he had not "yet shook hands with us and brighten'd the Chain of Friendship" since coming to the colony. The lack of such symbols of peace gave a more sinister cast to other actions taken by the governor's subjects. Meanwhile, the Genesee Senecas found cause for alarm when a retired army officer began to graze draft animals and raise corn on part of the Niagara portage. It took quick action by both Gage and Johnson to allay native suspicions that a settlement was planned for the portage.[20]

As Indians' concern for their security continued to mount, so too did efforts to channel that concern into a concerted effort to redress the balance of power between natives and colonists. In an effort reminiscent of those of the early 1760s, natives from throughout the middle west considered discussing a new pan-ethnic alliance at the Shawnees' principal town on the upper Scioto River (Chillicothe, Ohio); the town's central location astride well-traveled paths and the Shawnees' own extensive relations with neighboring peoples would make them the central participants at any such councils. The call went out to at least a dozen native societies from the Genesee Senecas to the Miamis. Their responses reveal just how widespread native unrest had become. Although the Indians' official explanation for the council was that it was called to settle differences between the nations, later reports reveal that the driving force was a groundswell of anti-British feeling. Miamis were especially angry because British agents had not formally reopened trade with them as they had done with surrounding nations. Worse, the army was bending every effort toward driving French traders from the Illinois Country. Little wonder the Miamis and others living along the Wabash River believed that "the English dispise them." The Genesee Senecas, who advocated a regional congress, raised once more the central problem of unchecked colonial expansion, arguing that the squatters in the Ohio Country were clear evidence that the British "were Robbing them of a tract of Country" west of the mountains. And though the Senecas and other western Indians welcomed a clearly defined boundary, they doubted British sincerity and their willingness to maintain such a line.[21]

British justice (or rather the lack of it) also found a place on the natives' bill of indictment. Delawares later expressed their anger over the way assaults and murders were handled and drove home their point by warning that "the Nations over the Lakes were making a great complaint to their Allies" because, whereas Indians were summarily punished for acts committed while drunk, traders and their servants were rarely apprehended for their misdeeds—drunk or sober. The Delawares continued to hold forth, condemning their British audience by asserting that "we could never obtain justice from you" despite fair promises. When veteran Indian agent George Croghan used "every Argument in my Power to Convince them" that the Indian Department would take extraordinary steps to guarantee equal treatment, he was rebuffed by natives who told him, "We thought you had Laws for that purpose."[22]

For all the anger and frustration exhibited during the natives' efforts to assemble a regional council, no such meeting was held on the Scioto in 1767. Those living toward the Illinois Country could not attend a meeting that might seriously interfere with the harvest and the fall hunt. Moreover, latent distrust stretching back a decade may also have inhibited participation. The Hurons and others living near Detroit never received official invitations, perhaps a reflection of their role in betraying the Senecas' war belts in 1761 and of their lukewarm support for Pontiac two years later. Nevertheless, the Miamis and Senecas were determined to press ahead with a campaign to rid themselves of the British menace. They told their neighbors that they were "determined to Strike the English in the Spring" and called upon the Delawares and Shawnees to join them. In so doing, the Senecas, especially, reaffirmed their growing westward orientation and urged other Ohio Indians and those farther west to join together "so that we become One People." The 1767 efforts, though not wholly productive, did mark the beginning of a renewed search for unity and a strategy that could stop the threat to Indian sovereignty posed by unchecked British American expansion.[23]

Unkown to the Senecas, their call for united action provided British officials with one more piece of evidence that their scheme for managing the west was proving a failure. So low had Indian relations sunk that, even before the reports of the planned Scioto congress reached New York, General Gage was found "in Great Distress for fair [sic] of an Indian Warr." Subsequent news added to his concern. For two years the army and Indian service, following Johnson's recommendations, had attempted to regulate trade and colonial settlement. At every turn their efforts failed.[24]

The civil unrest that engulfed the eastern towns and countryside and drew British resources from the west appeared earliest in Pennsylvania when settlers calling themselves the "Black Boys" attacked a convoy of treaty gifts destined for Fort Pitt. The attackers learned that private traders were using the government convoy to circumvent trade restrictions by smuggling goods into the west, an attempt the Black Boys feared would rearm native enemies. The border settlers did more than stop a shipment of Indian trade goods at Sideling Hill in March 1765; they also attacked its military escort, fired on Fort Loudoun's garrison of regulars, and made it clear that they would not condone what amounted to trade with the enemy by anyone, British or provincial.[25]

The Black Boys may have been right in suspecting collusion between George Croghan and private traders; certainly the circumstances surrounding the shipment are open to question, and the owners—the trading house of Baynton, Wharton, and Morgan—subsequently played a major role in the Illinois Country trade as well as supplying western garrisons. Once reopened, however, trade west of the Ohio was anything but the regulated business envisoned by the army and the Indian Department. Cutthroat competition between traders meant that regulations limiting trade to Fort Pitt or other garrisons were largely ignored. The Ohio Indians also played an important part in undermining efforts to regulate the trade. Natives as well as British authorities had a stake in a regulated trade, but the two sides differed over what "regulated" meant. The Indians found it inconvenient to travel long distances to the forts, where they frequently met with abuse at the hands of soldiers and local civilians. The natives favored efforts to stem the flow of liquor into the Ohio Country, but they wanted the structure of trade to adhere to the older pattern common before the wars. Colonial traders, eager to satisfy customers and their own creditors, happily complied. By 1767 commercial regulation was a shambles as traders easily avoided Fort Pitt and entered Indian towns. Neither Indian agents nor the army's warning that the peddlers were vulnerable to attack had much effect as traders and their merchant suppliers hurried to stake their claims to the newfound opportunities in the west.[26]

The limits of royal authority in the west were also tested by the ever increasing number of would-be settlers in the Ohio Country and the speculative ventures organized to carve out new colonies from trans-Appalachian territories. Such pursuits ran counter to the government's desire to restrict settlement to the mountain watershed, but the British response was far less effective than even Bouquet's limited actions years earlier. Officials on both sides of the Atlantic understood that disputes over land had spawned one

Indian war and could well spark another. Nevertheless, army and Indian service leaders could do little to stem the tide. So frustrated was the commander-in-chief that he could "Sincerely Wish that the Indians had killed" squatters who had attacked a hunting party, as a lesson to "such Execrable Villians." Yet name calling and wishful thinking were no substitutes for action, and Gage's frustration mounted as he realized that the small force of regulars in the Ohio Country could do nothing to stop the surge of invaders. In fact, the army found itself on questionable legal ground when it faced the squatters. Uncertain western boundaries made Gage cautious about precipitating a confrontation with Virginians who could claim they were within their charter bounds.[27]

Frontier violence, unchecked trade and settlement, and the seeming failure of efforts to establish royal authority in the west reinforced the opinion among Crown officials that western affairs were becoming too costly—to political reputations as well as to the treasury. The failure to secure an adequate American revenue added to the problem, as ministerial opponents in 1766 and 1767 demanded that garrisons and Indian expenses be cut. Consequently, by 1768 western policy was altered once more as the home government sought to retain its authority over the west as well as to meet its treaty obligations to Indians living there. Regulation of trade was returned to the colonial governments, which presumably would understand that their own economic and security interests were best served by maintaining tight regulations. Meanwhile, in response to new evidence of native unrest, the Crown did try to make good its pledge to establish a boundary line that could reduce future conflicts over land and resources. In this light the Fort Stanwix Treaty, so crucial to subsequent events in the Ohio Country, was one of the last acts of a frustrated search for order in the west rather than a culmination of any consistent British "program" for the trans-Appalachian region.[28]

As 1768 began no people were more eager than the Ohio Indians to see a definitive boundary line. The lack of boundary negotiations since 1765 was interpreted by the Indians as another sign that royal officials really did wish the destruction of Indian societies. Moreover, any lingering doubts on either side of the ill-defined frontier about the necessity of a clear border between Indian and colonial worlds must have vanished in the wake of the murders, in January, of ten Delaware, Shawnee, and Iroquois men, women, and children near Penn's Creek by Frederick Stump and his servant John Ironcutter. The enormity of the act—the victims had been scalped and their bodies hidden under the ice of the creek—shocked Indians and provincials who had lived for years with the endemic violence of the border. Worse, the victims had kinfolk living in the Ohio Country, and as word of the crime raced west, the Shawnees, at least, interpreted the murders as an act of war, since the victims had been scalped.[29]

Stump's and Ironcutter's actions could not have been more badly timed. The murders increased border tensions just as Johnson was laying the groundwork for a general congress later in the year to settle the boundary line. The superintendent and the governor of Pennsylvania, John Penn, acted quickly to calm the Indians. The condolence council, held in late April and early May at Fort Pitt, was intended to cover the dead and persuade grieving kinfolk not to retaliate and thus threaten the fragile peace along the border. To that end, Six Nations representatives, including Kiashuta, added their voices to those calling for restraint. However, the council quickly moved in another direction as Ohio Indians took the opportunity to once more raise long-standing grievances and assert their claims to the Ohio Country.[30]

At the height of their efforts to rally other natives to stand against the colonial invasion, the Genesee and Ohio Senecas reminded their Shawnee and Delaware neighbors that "those lands [along the Ohio] are yours as well as ours." Now, in the spring of 1768 the Indians set forth their claims and began to draw their own line against colonial expansion. Tamaqua reminded George Croghan that "the Country lying between this River [the Ohio] and the Allegheny Mountains, has always been our Hunting Ground." But it was the Shawnee faction led by Nymwha that took the most aggressive position at the council. Nymwha pointedly blamed the British for the violence along the border by reminding his audience that the army had ignored warnings to demolish their remaining forts and keep settlers out of the Ohio Country. The headman also demanded that settlers and hunters be prevented from moving downriver into Kentucky, the Shawnees' principal hunting territory and a land soon to become the focus of Indian-colonial conflict. Nymwha ended his speeech by asserting that the Ohio Valley "is the Property of us Indians."[31]

Nymwha's aggressive defense of Shawnee territorial claims was not shared by all of his people. A second faction, led by Kissonaucththa, took a far more conciliatory tone. Yet this group also asked that the army evacuate Fort Pitt. For George Croghan, the nearly universal Ohio Indian call for the British to keep troops and settlers out of the west presented a challenge that could not go unanswered. Forewarned of the natives' agenda, Croghan came to the council prepared to face down Nymwha and anyone else who elected to challenge superior British sovereignty. In response to the Shawnees, Croghan lectured the natives, while Kiashuta conveniently produced a written text of the Bradstreet "treaty" to refute claims that the army had promised to leave the region. Croghan also reminded the Shawnees that the Six Nations had agreed that the western forts should remain. Faced with what must have seemed a fait accompli, Nymwha backed down. Nevertheless, the Ohio Indians' position had been clearly stated. Also clear was that remaining goodwill and trust between natives and Crown officials was fast evaporating.[32]

Although Croghan could not ignore the Indians' assertive claims to the lands they occupied, his superiors continued to dismiss them as unfounded or irrelevant. A year earlier, Johnson had once more made the Crown's position clear when he declared that "the Northern Confederacy"—his term for the Ohio Indians and other midwestern natives—"have no just claims to lands South of the mouth of Ohio," including Kentucky. Indeed, Johnson asserted that those lands were held exclusively by the Six Nations as a result of earlier "conquests."[33]

Johnson's position reflected the now-standard British interpretation of Indian affairs in the northeast. Moreover, by transacting business with the Six Nations, Johnson maintained his own preeminent position as sole manager of Indian affairs in the north while greatly simplifying difficult—and potentially lucrative—negotiations. Neither Johnson nor his Six Nations allies could afford to have the Ohio Indians directly involved in boundary negotiations; Nymwha's outburst made it clear that, given an opportunity, the Ohio natives might choose to contest rather than accept a boundary line that came too close to their own domain. Worse, they might elect to transact business with colonial governments directly, thereby challenging the Crown's—and Johnson's—authority. Thus the boundary negotiations were to be conducted only by the Six Nations and the superintendent.

Nevertheless, the Six Nations' image as the principal force in the Ohio Indians' world was more than a little tarnished. The Ohio Country had been of crucial interest to the whole Confederacy only to the extent that colonial rivalries there threatened to explode in warfare that could easily spread to Iroquoia as well. Since the early 1750s, Six Nations involvement in the region had been sporadic and largely rhetorical, with direct involvement limited to Senecas and others with immediate interests in the area. Although Mohawk and Oneida warriors razed Kanestio in 1764, neither they nor other Six Nations fighters ventured beyond the Alleghenies. Indeed, the Confederacy had carefully avoided becoming ensnared in the Ohio thicket from the moment Canadians and Virginians exchanged gunfire in 1754. And as much as the Six Nations may have welcomed a boundary line as a way of shedding an increasingly tenuous title to a clearly volatile land, their headmen were nonetheless careful in staking and asserting claims west of the mountains. In autumn 1767, for example, Six Nations headmen met with Johnson and complained about Virginians' encroachments in "their Country" west of the Alleghenies. Yet at the same time the natives admitted that "all the western Tribes and Senecas were as much or more concerned" with the boundary treaty, an acknowledgment that implied a superior, but by no means exclusive, claim to the lands east and south of the Allegheny and Ohio rivers. The vague references to the Ohio Indians' interest in lands east of the Allegheny River suggests what the natives had made manifestly clear two years earlier—a claim to the land based on use. In 1765 Delawares and Shawnees, joined by neighboring Wyandots, agreed—without consulting the Six Nations—to George Croghan's request for a land cession to compensate traders for losses during the recent war. The natives agreed to cede some land on the *east* side of the river—land so near the expanding Virginia settlements that "it was now, of no use to them for Hunting Ground." Moreover, the nature of the Six Nations' claims in the west was emphasized when Delawares and Shawnees refused even to discuss selling land to Virginians in the Monongahela Valley, saying that "it was none of their Business, that the Lands belonged to the *Senecas*"—not to the Six Nations collectively.[34]

Although the Six Nations' claims to land west of the mountains were open to interpretation, so was their much-vaunted authority over those whom British officials chose to identify as client, or dependent, peoples. The Confederacy's limited influence among the Ohio Indians had been revealed during the 1740s and 1750s as divergent interests and distance guaranteed that, though Ohio natives might defer to the Six Nations when circumstances required, reciprocity and equality—not dependency—shaped intersocietal relations, a fact of life the Six Nations came to appreciate. During the condolence council at Fort Pitt in April 1768, Six Nations headmen "forbade" their own people to attack border settlers along the southern war road. However, these men "desired" the same from the Delawares and Shawnees, who were addressed as "brothers" rather than by the diminutive "nephew" metaphor. Moreover, the New York Iroquois found it impossible to manage their people in the Monongahela Valley, who were encouraging neighboring settlers to stay in the area rather than depart as the army, Indian Department, and Six Nations demanded. Here the localist tendencies of Iroquois society continued to erode bonds between the Confederacy and emigrants to the Ohio Country. Taken together, the Six Nations' role in the region, in the eyes of the natives living there, was that of adviser—"as the door . . . to their Country and Channel by which they

[Ohio Indians] might receive the Surest intelligence concerning the design of the White people." It implied a reciprocal relationship: in return for information and guidance, Ohio natives would continue to acknowledge a superior, though not exclusive, role for the Confederacy as intermediary between natives and colonists. It was a position that carried with it a heavy burden of responsibility as Ohio Indians agreed to trust the Confederacy's judgment; any breach of that trust could terminate the relationship and rob the Six Nations of any influence in the west.[35]

As the conflicts between natives and colonists increased west of the 1763 Proclamation line, in October 1767 Six Nations headmen once again urged that the boundary line be run as soon as possible; in their opinion it seemed the only way to avoid a war that would surely follow the unchecked invasion of the Ohio Country. Moreover, the Onondagas and, by implication, others in the Confederacy made it clear that they could not be counted on to march into battle with the British should a new war errupt. The Onondagas' declaration was sobering for Johnson and his superiors. In the meantime, London finally provided Johnson and his southern counterpart, John Stuart, with authorization to run the line from Iroquoia through the Carolinas. By April 1768 Johnson was issuing the necessary instructions and invitations for a general congress of the Six Nations and their "dependents" to be held that autumn at the abandoned Fort Stanwix (Rome, New York) at the head of the Mohawk River.[36]

Johnson quickly made it clear that the Ohio Indians' role at the congress was quite secondary. He readily conceded that "thou[gh] dependents" of the Six Nations, the Delawares and Shawnees ought to be shown some small consideration because "some [of those] lands actually belonged to them formerly," but more importantly because "their Vicinity to *Pennsylvania* and *Virginia*, makes their perfect agreement necessary." Yet though the superintendent was willing to make a place for the Ohio Indians at the council, that place was defined as neither participatory nor crucial. Johnson shrugged off news that Shawnee delegates would be delayed because of their discussions with the "Misisipi Nations," pointing out that since they had agreed to accept any Six Nations–negotiated treaty, "I cannot think their presence very necessary." Only observer status awaited any Ohio Indian delegates to the treaty.[37]

Fort Stanwix soon became a rendezvous for men other than royal Indian agents and Six Nations sachems, however. The impending negotiations were a tailor-made opportunity for a number of colonial interest groups who also found in Johnson a powerful and willing ally. Speculators who had long been unsuccessfully pursuing grants west of the Proclamation line

Map 6 The Ohio Country and the borderlands, 1765–1774.

sought to have their claims included in the cession that would inevitably be a part of any boundary treaty. Among these men were the Philadelphia trading partnership of Baynton, Wharton, and Morgan and deputy Indian superintendent George Croghan, representing a group of "suffering traders" who asked for confirmation of an earlier agreement with the Ohio Indians for war reparations. The governors of New York, Pennsylvania, and Virginia also sent representatives not merely to witness a treaty but to ensure that coveted lands would fall within British territory. Virginia's interest was especially keen, since both this and the planned boundary treaty with the

Cherokees could secure the colony's access to vast territories long claimed through royal charter. And in the background were individual speculators, including the royal governor of New York and, rounding out the cast of players, Congregationalist missionaries who were bent on protecting what they saw as the rights of their Oneida followers and whose dissenting, blatantly anti-imperial demeanor irritated Johnson throughout the proceedings.[38]

Far from being overpowered by the irresistible might of merchants, governors, and land jobbers, Johnson acted consciously and carefully on their behalf. As historian Peter Marshall has pointed out, Johnson's motives were complex and were shaped by personal interests as well as by what he perceived to be unwelcome changes in royal policies governing the west. Long before he set the Fort Stanwix negotiations in motion, Johnson had agreed to assist those men whose investments and futures rested in the trans-Appalachian territories. On behalf of the "suffering traders," their merchant creditors, and the speculators who eventually bought their claims, the superintendent pledged to "procure an Advantageous Grant" as part of the boundary treaty. Likewise, Johnson found in the boundary line a way to satisfy numerous interests while adhering to the official mandate of securing a border that could be maintained without fear of a new Indian war. Indeed, on the eve of the treaty congress, Johnson candidly observed to New York's governor Henry Moore that "it was my Intention to Obtain as Much Land as I possibly could, and agreable to such Boundary as would be most Advantageous to the Province, and agreable to the Indians." In fact, Johnson had already ensured "advantageous grants" by accepting the Confederacy's expansive claims to all lands east of the Ohio River as far as the mouth of the Tennessee River. Johnson's superiors, however, had more modest, and politically acceptable, gains in mind when they agreed to the mouth of the Kanawha River as the end of the northern half of the line. The difference was significant: Johnson's acceptance of the Six Nations' 1765 proposal would place virtually all of Kentucky within British America and open the region for settlement—the very land that Nymwha had warned the British to avoid. Whatever Johnson may have thought of the Shawnee warning, it did not prevent him from quickly ignoring his instructions to end the line at the mouth the Kanawha River and accepting the cession originally put forth by the Six Nations. Johnson, the Confederacy, and the speculators could rest easy with the result; only the Ohio Indians and the home government were ignored.[39]

The treaty congress, which finally opened on October 24, must have been an impressive gathering. It was one of the largest assemblies of its kind: over two thousand natives occupied the lowlands around Fort Stanwix, far more than Johnson had wanted or than cost-conscious superiors could afford, a gathering that eventually cost the government £13,000. Amid this impressive assembly the Shawnees and Delawares were a distinct minority. Only Benivissica officially represented the Shawnees, while Killbuck and Turtle Heart appeared on behalf of the western Delawares. The opening of the congress was repeatedly delayed while Johnson awaited late arrivals, notably Senecas whom the superintendent suspected of conspiring en route. Nevertheless, the negotiations proved satisfactory to both the superintendent and the colonial representatives.[40]

Three issues dominated the congress: the Confederacy's claims south to the Tennessee (Cherokee) River; the Penns' quest for the lands at the Forks of the Susquehanna River; and the northern limit of the boundary line, which would be run through Iroquoia. Johnson quickly accepted the Six Nations' supposed conquest of Kentucky, and the Pennsylvanians were willing to offer the Confederacy additional compensation for a westward adjustment of the line through their province. The question of the boundary line's northern terminus posed a more difficult problem because the Oneidas, who also wanted a definitive line between their lands and the onrush of colonial settlement up the Mohawk Valley, "gave great obstruction to the business" until they received the proper guarantees. There was hard bargaining for several days, much of it "in the bushes"—carried on in an unofficial way, usually at night, away from the council. These discussions were made more difficult by what Johnson called "some busy persons"—missionaries—but were in fact complicated by the Oneida headmen's delicate negotiations with their own warrior-hunters, whose interests could not be ignored. Finally, through "Sir Williams solicitations," which may have included a few bribes, he and the Oneidas came to terms and eliminated the most serious obstacle to a final boundary settlement. The Fort Stanwix Treaty was signed on November 5.[41]

The Oneida problem that confronted Johnson was precisely the sort of assertiveness that the superintendent was determined to avoid with the Ohio Indians. By declaring in advance that their interests would be looked after by the Six Nations, Johnson all but excluded the Shawnees and Delawares from the proceedings. Moreover, Johnson made it clear from the outset that the Ohio Indians' presence at Fort Stanwix was required only to guarantee that, as witnesses, they could not muddy the waters later by claiming ignorance of the treaty's content. What remains unclear is how far all Ohio Indian interests were represented by Benivissica, Killbuck, and Turtle Heart. Killbuck, who later succeeded Netawatwees, may have represented the Delaware king and the council at Newcomer's Town. Given the factionalism among the Shawnees in 1767 and 1768, it seems unlikely that Benivissica represented all of his people then living in the Scioto and Muskingum valleys. It appears more likely that only those Delawares and Shawnees who were inclined to accept Johnson's invitation and a negotiated boundary were represented, while others, through indifference or distrust, stayed away.

The Six Nations left the treaty with the satisfaction of knowing that they had collectively gained a great deal at little cost. The Oneidas obtained the northern extension of the boundary line that would, they hoped, prevent them from being overwhelmed by settlers as had already happened to their Mohawk neighbors. The centerpiece of the treaty—the extensive cessions beyond the Susquehanna River and Allegheny Mountains—contributed to Confederacy prestige, sustained their role as Britain's principal native allies in the northeast, and of equal importance, allowed the Confederacy to shed responsibility for an increasingly dangerous region. For those Iroquois who continued to use the Ohio Country and Kentucky, access was unimpeded while responsibility for keeping the peace there would now fall entirely on the British. It seemed a good exchange in return for a fixed boundary that was to be enforced and that guaranteed the integrity of Iroquoia itself.

The Fort Stanwix Treaty would prove to be Sir William Johnson's last great accomplishment as Indian superintendent. Even though his other plans for a comprehensive approach to Indian affairs had been either ignored or carried through as half-measures, a central element of Johnson's vision—a fixed boundary between colonists and natives in the north—had come about through his work. Moreover, faced now with diminished responsibility and authority, Johnson had successfully met the needs of myriad provincial interest groups by adjustments to the original treaty line that gave ample room for expansion in both Pennsylvania and Virginia.

Yet an air of pessimism hung over the proceedings. Johnson may have hoped that the individual colonies would enforce the boundary provisions, but more than two decades of experience must have told him otherwise. His superior General Gage issued his own prophetic opinion when he observed that boundaries, though useful, could work only "if they could be inviolably preserved," something that colonial self-interest and declining royal authority made unlikely. Furthermore, Gage expressed particular concern about the "Frontier People," who were "too Numerous, too Lawless and Licentious ever to be restrained" by any authority. And if self-doubt and the lack of enthusiasm of his immediate superior were not enough, Johnson soon found himself facing criticism from angry superiors in London who had learned that their agent had ignored his instructions.[42]

Johnson accommodated provincial speculators and governments by radically altering the original boundary proposal in two places: he pushed the line west so that much of the upper Susuqehanna Valley would fall within Pennsylvania's jurisdiction; and to the south the line was once more pushed west, this time from its intended end at the mouth of the Kanawha River to the mouth of the Tennessee River. In this way Johnson not only extended colonial borders up to the Ohio River itself but placed Kentucky within reach of the Virginians. The prospect of a new wave of uncontolled migration into the west was only one concern of royal ministers as they examined Johnson's work. The other was the now disjointed nature of the line. John Stuart had run the southern half of the line at the Treaty of Hard Labor—a line that should have joined Johnson's at the Kanawha. What worried Stuart and his superiors was how the powerful Cherokees would react if asked to renegotiate based on the new Iroquois cession to the Crown. Though Johnson initially justified his actions on the grounds that the Six Nations claimed Kentucky and insisted on ceding it, few outside the Mohawk Valley—least of all the Confederacy's frequent enemies, the Cherokees— were willing to accept such a spacious, and specious, claim. Johnson's negotiations became a formula for disaster.[43]

The secretary of state for the colonies, Wills Hill, earl of Hillsborough, lost little time in calling Johnson to account for the "improper conditions" found in the Fort Stanwix Treaty. Yet after more deliberate reflection, the government was reluctant to scrap the boundary settlement altogether. Rather, Hillsborough instructed Johnson to arrange a retrocession of the Kentucky lands that would place them once more under Six Nations control and secure the southern boundary line. Johnson balked at the idea, however, insisting that such a move would insult the Confederacy and cause more serious trouble if, in the meantime, colonials moved into the region. As it happened, the Kentucky cession remained, while the southern portion of the line was redrawn in a new series of negotiations as the home government tried to put the best face on a bad situation by declaring the lands below the Kanawha off limits until further notice.[44]

Johnson defended himself by pointing out that, since colonial expansion was in any case inevitable, he believed it was necessary to "get as extensive a cession as was practicable," a view he insisted was shared by "everybody"— certainly the speculators whose needs Johnson served so well. The superintendent's logic turned on the conviction that in order to forestall border conflicts the colonies should be given the greatest amount of land in which to expand, territory sufficient to preclude the need for new cessions in the near future. In November 1772 Johnson again justified his actions at Fort Stanwix by citing the Virginians' continued expansion as one of the "material considerations which principally induced" him to "extend the purchase *a little farther* down the Ohio," a task made easier by the Six Nations' willingness to sell. However, Johnson's statements reveal broader assumptions that all but guaranteed future conflict in the Ohio Country. First, Johnson concluded that peace could last only if Indians and settlers were kept apart—but at the expense of natives whose lands would become colonial buffer zones in the west. And the superintendent conveniently dismissed the Ohio Indians, relegating them to the status of political nonpersons who were not considered materially concerned with any "minor" adjustments in the boundary line. In the process he all but guaranteed that the new border between natives and settlers would remain a dangerous flash point.[45]

eleven

"A War Will Be Inevitable"

 From the perspective of the Shawnees, Delawares, and Iroquois living in the Ohio Country, the Fort Stanwix Treaty was hardly an advantageous adjustment in the Anglo-native frontier. The Ohio Indians were willing enough to accept the idea of a fixed boundary; indeed, as the people most affected by the unchecked invasion of the west, the natives welcomed an effort to impose limits on colonial expansion. It is equally clear that the Ohio Indians were aware of the serious doubts about the forthcoming treaty held by some of the Genesee Senecas, who openly predicted that "a war will be inevitable" should lands immediately east of the Allegheny River be surrendered by the Confederacy. The Senecas may well have strengthened Delaware and Shawnee suspicions that some of the Six Nations might be willing to give away too much. Nevertheless, the Ohio natives were willing to accept a role secondary to that of the Confederacy. The reasons were rooted not in the acceptance of "tributary" or "dependent" status but in the reciprocity that bound these societies together. As senior members of an extensive alliance system that secured them an influential voice in British councils, the Six Nations assumed the responsibility of negotiating for Delawares and Shawnees as well as for themselves. The Shawnees and Delawares agreed to accept arrangements hammered out by the Confederacy's headmen provided the outcome proved beneficial to all concerned. This arrangement was best summed up by the Shawnee Red Hawk, who later explained that his people had acknowledged the Six Nations as their "elder Brother" and agreed to follow their lead "while we found their advice good" but who quickly added that "their *power* extends no further with us."[1]

The Ohio Indians' sense of betrayal became clear as news of the treaty came west with Killbuck and others. Not only had the Six Nations headmen acted "without asking their Consent and Approbation," but the Ohio Indians' deputies had never been called to the private meetings during which the final boundary arrangements were made. The outcome was even more infuriating than the treaty process itself. The Delawares and Shawnees quickly discovered that, according to the treaty, "their Hunting Ground down the Ohio" had been given to the British. The cession *might* have been accepted by some had not the Confederacy added insult to injury when they "shamefully" took "all the money and goods to themselves" rather than sharing with the Ohio Indians as compensation for the loss of land and resources.[2]

The Delawares and Shawnees were quick to grasp the implications of the Fort Stanwix Treaty. Angry that valuable hunting territory had been bargained away while colonial borders moved even closer to their towns, and infuriated that the Six Nations not only had sold the land but had selfishly walked away with the purchase price, the Ohio natives redoubled their resolve to chart their own way through the thickets of intercultural relations while ignoring the Six Nations guides, who were no longer trustworthy. The treaty had driven the wedge dividing the Confederacy and the Ohio Indians ever deeper, making an already wide gulf unbridgeable. Joining the Delawares and Shawnees were the Ohio Iroquois and the Genesee Senecas. The Shawnees set the tone, telling Cherokees in 1770 that though "their Lands had been Sold to the English" without consultation, yet "luckily, One Village only of that Nation, paid any Attention" to the British and to the Confederacy elders who struck the deal. Some natives entertained a far different strategy. In 1771 Netawatwees politely informed Pennsylvania's proprietor that he intended to travel to England and speak directly with the king. Netawatwees's purpose was to ask that the Ohio Indians be given their own superintendent. Despite Governor Richard Penn's insistence, Netawatwees ignored the Covenant Chain rhetoric and persisted in his request for assistance, though to no other end than to alarm Sir William Johnson, who correctly saw the scheme as a means of emphasizing the Ohio Indians' independence from the Covenant Chain. Such was the westerners' level of distrust of both Johnson and his Six Nations allies.[3]

Netawatwees's request was not the only evidence of a continuing decline of Six Nations and British influence among Ohio Indians. In 1770 continued border violence and fear of settlers led the Shawnees once more to seek a pan-ethnic alliance, this time by soliciting the Miamis and Illinois natives. In response, Johnson persuaded the Oneida Thomas King to lead a Six Nations delegation to the Scioto River towns to thwart the Shawnees' efforts while also deflecting any attempt by the Ohio Indians to make common cause with nations south of the Ohio River. British observers were satisfied with King's success the following year, crediting the Six Nations' intervention for ruining Shawnee plans. Yet ethnic jealousies also played a role, as did divisions within the Shawnees. King was unable to deliver his messages to Indians living on the Wabash, who refused to meet him. Moreover, a similar effort in 1772 met with even less success. Western Indians simply ignored the Confederacy's mission; Six Nations messengers were forced to leave their message belts with the Shawnees for later distribution.[4]

Although the Ohio Indians could keep the Six Nations at arm's length, the natives still had to confront the consequences of the Confederacy's deal with Sir William Johnson. On one level, very little changed with the Fort Stanwix Treaty: squatters, long hunters, and traders appeared as before, bringing the same troubles in their wake. In another way, however, the treaty did fundamentally alter long-standing aspects of Indian-colonial relations in the Ohio Country. Previously, though armies and garrisons came and went, the region had remained largely secure to its native inhabitants. The land that separated border settlements from native villages provided security for the Ohio Indians. By placing Kentucky and much of the land east of the Allegheny and Ohio rivers within colonial jurisdiction, the Fort Stanwix Treaty robbed the natives of their most effective bulwark against colonial expansion. In effect, the four-decades-old territorial barrier had been removed as the treaty encouraged the ambitions of speculators and settlers.

The lands south of the Ohio River, already home to numerous squatters from Virginia, quickly became the target of speculators from that colony. Meanwhile Benjamin Franklin, Sir William Johnson, and George Croghan were among those with plans for western colonies that, had they taken root, would have virtually enveloped the Ohio Indians and their western neighbors in colonial settlements. The Ohio natives could not have known the plans of ambitious men in London, Philadelphia, or Albany, but the Indians grasped the larger implications of what had passed at Fort Stanwix. Less than a year after the treaty, General Gage learned that "those Indians will not allow us to Settle on the ceded Lands."[5]

In retrospect, any determination by Ohio Indians to forestall occupation of their Kentucky hunting grounds and other borderlands seems a futile gesture at best. By the time the Fort Stanwix Treaty was signed, Pittsburgh had been transformed from a military post to a garrison town of several hundred people, and Virginians continued to pour into the Monongahela Valley. Moreover, as colonists scrambled to seize lands quickly claimed by their governments, the army abandoned its remaining posts south of the Great Lakes and gave up all pretext of being able to patrol or govern west of the mountains.

The violence that was the hallmark of the native-colonial border continued without interruption through the late 1760s and 1770s. Although they had caused a sensation on both sides of the frontier, the Stump-Ironcutter murders were unusual only in their number and in the widespread kinship ties of the victims. Ohio Indians were killed by soldiers at Fort Pitt as well as by civilians along Redstone Creek and the Ohio River. Senecas "cut off" five boats belonging to traders, apparently in retaliation for the killing of two Senecas by a deserter from one of the western posts. Traders murdered natives, as did settlers in the "back parts" of Virginia. At the same time, the border regulators variously known as the Paxton Boys or the Black Boys reappeared, seizing goods belonging to a trader at Fort Pitt while "threatening all who shall attempt to go a Trading" with Indians the mauraders viewed as mortal enemies. The pattern of violence came to resemble nothing so much as the natives' own "mourning war" as one death or injury demanded retaliation in kind in a spiral of violence. In fact, a state of war existed along the borderlands as settlers and others attempting to penetrate the region were met by force in a struggle that was all the more vicious as the battle lines hardened into "Indian" against "white." This chronic violence produced alarms and widespread fear on both sides that threatened to explode into another full-scale conflict. When, for example, Iroquois warriors collided with Virginians, fearful Pennsylvania settlers abandoned their homes "out of fear of assaults by Indians." Yet as Pennsylvanians prepared to bolt, Virginians resolved to avenge the insult by razing an Iroquois town on the Ohio River.[6]

Added to Indian-colonial conflict was the persistent raiding across the Ohio River borderlands between Ohio Iroquois and Six Nations warriors and the southern nations. The Ohio Valley continued to serve as the main thoroughfare for such raids; George Washington, inspecting his western landholdings in 1770, found three score Six Nations warriors gathered at a town on Cross Creek, preparing for a raid against the Catawbas. To the west the Miamis and others living along the Wabash River were engaged in their own campaign against the Cherokees. This latter conflict was quickly seized upon by royal officials as a means of keeping western Indian societies divided, hence less threatening. Cherokee solicitations to the Six Nations for help in striking the Wabash natives were met with interest by the army and Indian Department, and in 1773 Chickasaws and Cherokees attempted to make a pact with the Ohio Indians against the Miamis, adding yet more volatility within the Ohio Country.[7]

Raiders on their way south inevitably passed up the Monongahela Valley or through Kentucky, in the process confronting the ubiquitous Virginia hunters. Both areas, especially Kentucky, were marked by conflict. To the Shawnees these hunters continued to pose an immediate economic threat, while the inveterate Indian hating these men displayed guaranteed that encounters with natives would end in bloodshed. Eastern colonists were no less disposed to condemn the character and livelihood of the long hunters than were Indians; missionary David McClure decided that "the whites on the extensive frontiers of Virginia, are generally white Savages," subsisting almost entirely by hunting. Yet his observation that "Murders between them and Indians, when they meet in hunting, are said sometimes to happen" was an understatement. Indians as far west as the Illinois Country were seen with scalps and pack horses lifted from Virginia hunters in the Cumberland and Greenbriar valleys, while Cherokees warned of similar consequences when they complained about "Vagabonds who Steal their Horses and insult them," as well as about the "daily Encroachments of the White People and their killing the Deer."[8]

Yet it was the Shawnees who found themselves most often in competition for resources in Kentucky, especially in the early 1770s, as the region became the center of Virginians' attention. McClure noted euphemistically that several men had been killed by the Indians "down the Ohio," while traders and border settlers also fell victim to Shawnee raids. However, on occasion the natives did display considerable restraint, as in the case of Shawnees who relieved several Virginia hunters of their horses, weapons, and 1,100 deerskins. Although colonists called such behavior robbery, the Shawnees would have labeled it just compensation for poachers who had themselves robbed native hunters of their livelihood.[9]

If the Virginia hunters, prone to violence and destructive of game, represented a major challenge to Ohio Indian security and border peace, so too did settlers. Indeed, so widespread and rapid was colonial occupation of lands east of the Ohio River that contemporaries could do little more than guess at the number of people involved. As early as 1766 Charles Beatty found at least eighty families along the track that followed the Juniata River into the west. A year later, merchants estimated that there were four hundred families living in the lower Monongahela Valley alone. By 1771 those traveling in the west claimed that the "Country beyond the Laurel Hill as fare as Redstone" was already "full of People." George Croghan, attempting to be more specific, reported that some 5,000 families, perhaps 20,000 to 25,000 people, lived west of the mountains. Ligonier, for example, was already a town of 100 families in 1772, and Pittsburgh had long since broken out of the confines of the garrison. So quickly had people moved into the Ohio Valley, and in such numbers, that the local subsistence economies were unable to support the crush. David Jones found "many thousand inhabitants" but also discovered that some "were near a famine, occasioned by the multitudes lately moved into this new Country." George Rogers Clark also found that rising demand had driven up the price of corn as well as other foods.[10]

The story was much the same in Kentucky. By the mid-1770s Grave Creek and Wheeling were already well settled. During his 1773 trip down the Ohio with Indian converts bound for the Muskingum Valley, John Heckewelder was struck by the number of settlements on the south side of the river. He wrote that "Here and there . . . we saw more houses belonging to white men" and, occasionally, settlements inland of several hundred people. Heckewelder and others from the east might have imagined themselves in the Susquehanna and Delaware valleys rather than in the west.[11]

Homesteaders all along the ill-defined border were in some ways little different from the roaming hunters and liquor traders who infested the borderlands. The entrenched hatred of Indians was certainly present, as the Moravians discovered when they and their native flock encountered settlers who wished the Indians "ten thousand times farther" away than their destination on the Muskingum and who were only slightly less hostile upon learning that the natives were Christians. Others characterized the settlers as "white savages," going half-naked while scratching out a meager living from the woods and meadows. Indeed, equipped with the barest necessities, these border settlers had little to distinguish them from the Indians they despised, until hard work began the gradual process that imposed a more "ordered" British American landscape on the borderlands.[12]

Despite the rapid transformation of the eastern margins of the Ohio Country into parts of British America, the lands west and north of the Ohio—now the heartland of Ohio Indian settlement—still remained in native hands. In spring 1772 David Jones found only "one house inhabited by white people" west of Fort Pitt. There were doubtless others, occupied by traders, but Jones found nothing that remotely resembled the frenzied clearing and building that occurred to the east. Nevertheless, the Ohio Indians were less secure in the Muskingum and Scioto valleys than they had been even five or six years before Jones appeared. With settlers flooding into newly ceded lands, native hunters found game more difficult to take, and smaller, outlying towns in the path of the invasion were abandoned. And knowing what was happening across the Ohio River gave the natives reason to fear for the future. As early as autumn 1771 George Croghan found that the Indians "do not think themselves safe even on the West side of the Ohio," even though they understood the river to be the new boundary between their world and that of the settlers. Not content to passively watch the invaders roll over their hunting grounds and threaten their towns, the natives searched anew for ways to stem the tide.[13]

As he approached Newcomer's Town in October 1772, missionary David McClure met Delawares who made no secret of their growing anxiety. McClure confided in his journal that "some of the warriors had expressed to me their extreme resentment at the encroachments of the white people, on their hunting ground." Four years earlier David Zeisberger discovered that the Genesee Senecas had "become very angry" with neighboring Munsees; the Senecas feared that any Moravian mission among those natives would soon be followed by settlers who would, the Senecas were convinced, "build a city and take the land." Zeisberger and McClure thus learned firsthand of the Ohio Indians' escalating concern about their security and sovereignty as the frontier was dramatically altered first by treaty, then by a virtually uncontrolled invasion that pressed beyond what the natives understood to be the proper limits of the Fort Stanwix cession. Even before the 1768 treaty, royal officials understood that "the affairs of Lands are more immediately interesting and alarming to the Indians than anything else."[14]

Although officials spoke in broad terms about "affairs of lands" their dispatches tended to gloss over three specific native concerns often buried in the larger debate over ownership and control of the borderlands. First, the Ohio Indians made little secret of their distaste for the Six Nations' ways of handling land transactions and quickly challenged the legitimacy of the Fort Stanwix Treaty, choosing instead, as George Washington discovered, "not [to] scruple to say that *they* must be compensated for their Right if the People [colonists] settle thereon, *notwithstanding the Cession of the Six Nations*." It was an issue that speculators like Washington, or imperial agents like Johnson, chose to ignore. From the natives' point of view, however, no compensation meant no sale. Nevertheless, the mounting pressure from colonial—especially Virginian—expansion after 1768 led to a de facto transfer of long-disputed territories in the Monongahela Valley from Indian to provincial sovereignty as the few natives still living near the border prudently withdrew.[15]

Next, though the natives reluctantly conceded colonial control of the 1768 cession, they continued to insist that it covered only the land, not its resources. As warriors explained to David McClure, "When you white men buy a farm, you buy only the land. You don't buy the horses and cows and sheep. The Elks are our horses, the Buffaloes are our cows, the deer are our sheep, and the whites shan't have them."[16]

To ownership of the land and control of its resources the natives added a more fundamental and pressing concern: their sovereignty. For decades Ohio Indians had consistently held that the land belonged to them. This was especially true of warriors, whose labor and risks had tamed and defended the region and had given their societies legitimate claims to the lands they held and used. By ignoring those claims and four decades of Ohio Indian history, the Fort Stanwix Treaty posed a threat to the natives' independence.

Though angry at the Six Nations' duplicity and lack of reciprocity, the Ohio Indians had accepted the treaty in hopes that the cession would satisfy the British appetite for native lands. Yet the next three years provided no evidence that settlers were willing to stop at the new border. In 1771 the Delawares, Munsees, and Mahicans from the Muskingum Valley towns jointly addressed their colonial neighbors, reminding them that the natives had never sought a confrontation but had accepted land cessions and promises of peace even though the ceded lands "were the property of *our* Confederacy"—a not so subtle slap at the Six Nations. Now, however, patience was wearing thin as the invasion continued. So badly had relations deteriorated that some natives anticipated a war; some Delawares decided to run up large accounts with traders, believing a new round of fighting would effectively cancel their debts, while headmen warned that their warriors could not be restrained forever.[17]

For all their frustration and pointed warnings, the Delawares ultimately avoided any confrontation with the colonists or the army. But the Genesee Senecas and their kin in the Ohio Country did not, and by 1770 they were once more attempting to organize a resistance movement that could stop the oncoming British Americans. As in 1760, the Senecas cast their net wide, reaching out to the natives of the Wabash and Illinois country as well as those closer to home. The Senecas' task was made easier by continued widespread dissatisfaction with British policies and with provincials' behavior.

The substantial number of Senecas already living in the Ohio Country meant that the Genesee towns could count on ready support for any plan to confront British expansion. The Genesee Senecas continued to be among the most defiantly opposed to the changes overtaking the west. "Insulted where-soever they went" by parsimonious fort commanders and ill-disciplined troops, and angered by unbridled colonial expansion, the Senecas began a campaign that included "Killing Cattle, Stealing Horses, and in short plun-dering every House and field" they could in the vicinity of Fort Pitt, attacking traders along the Niagara portage, while boycotting Six Nations–British councils.[18]

The driving force behind renewed Genesee Seneca hostilities was Gausta-rax. During the years just before his death in 1771, Gaustarax took every opportunity to blunt British expansion and power in the west. He signed the Fort Stanwix Treaty, perhaps because he was unable to convince a majority of Genesee Senecas to withhold their approval, perhaps to help ensure consent to a document that later provided him with ample ammunition in his campaign against the British. He was also thought to have used the treaty council to secretly rally Shawnee and Delaware support: the headman later declared that he would "remove the [western] door of the Six Na-tions . . . down to Scioto plains" to the heart of the Ohio Indian settlements. It was to counter Gaustarax's influence over the Ohio Iroquois that Johnson relied upon Kiashuta after 1768.[19]

The message and accompanying wampum sent by Gaustarax to the Ohio Indians and those living in the Wabash Valley reveal that the Genesee Senecas had hardly been cowed in 1764 and that the Niagara cession continued to be a sensitive issue. Gaustarax used this and the mounting violence along the border to rally support among his own people and the western Indians in a campaign that may have begun as early as 1765. He also offered his own interpretation of the Fort Stanwix Treaty, telling the west-erners that the Six Nations "had not sold the Lands on the South Side of the Ohio" but that "the English had forced or Stolen them and was encroaching into their Country." Gaustarax also sent his messages in the name of the "Six Nations," which tended to lend weight to declarations considered so inflam-matory by British officials that Johnson was still trying to get the council wampum recalled in 1773, two years after Gaustarax's death. Moreover, Gaustarax's messages, with their references to settlers' threats to hunting territory, village security, and the southern war road, carried an especially strong appeal to the Ohio warriors—so strong, in fact, that the local British Indian agent reported a growing breach between village headmen, who seemed "Rather afread of a Warr than Desiering itt," and warriors, whose views ran to the opposite extreme by 1770.[20]

Gaustarax found a willing audience among western Indians after news of the Fort Stanwix Treaty began to circulate. In the meantime, Sayenqua-raghta's peace faction among the Genesee Senecas found itself hard pressed to keep wampum belts, which threatened to spread a "Spirit of Discontent" from circulating throughout the west. Moreover, by addressing their frustrations to the western Senecas, Ohio Indians revealed that they too saw these people as distinct from an otherwise untrustworthy Iroquois Confederacy. By pledging to move the western door of the Confederacy to the Scioto, Gaustarax once more stressed the western orientation of his people. Johnson's habit of referring to, and dealing with, the Genesee Senecas as a nearly separate nation within Iroquoia mirrored circumstances already recognized by the natives.[21]

Within the Ohio Country itself, rising anti-British feeling found its greatest expression among the Shawnees. By 1770 these natives were working hard to overcome the many obstacles to a broad alliance that would draw a new, Indian-defined barrier between the invaders and the native west. The Shawnees' effort went beyond even the Senecas' ambitions a decade earlier, as the natives reached out to southern Indians as well as to those in the middle west.[22]

Their history and location, as much as their determination not to surrender Kentucky to the Virginians, made the Shawnees well suited to be the linchpin of a new pan-Indian movement. The Shawnees' wide-ranging contacts within Indian America were respected even by the British, who, in rebuilding relations with western Indians after 1764, found they could best do so by working through Shawnee mediators as George Croghan did in 1765 and again two years later. Geography played a role as well. So important was the location of the Shawnee towns that Gaustarax had pointed to the Scioto as the preferred "western door" of the Six Nations. Finally, after 1768 the Shawnees found themselves quite literally facing the colonial invaders pressing west beyond the mountains. Of all the Ohio Indians, the Shawnees knew best what those settlements meant to native security and sovereignty.[23]

The Shawnees, like Gaustarax and his followers, were able to tap widespread native discontent. They and their Delaware neighbors were so unsettled by the growing struggle for Kentucky that they believed the British were planning yet another war against them. Indeed, by 1770 feelings ran so high that many Shawnees, Delawares, and Ohio Iroquois were prepared to abandon the Ohio Country for a safer haven to the northwest. And Captain Pipe warned Pennsylvanians that "this difference between the Governor of Virginia and the Shawnees gives us all great uneasiness."[24]

As they labored to knit together an alliance that could stop British expansion, the Shawnees found their task easiest among the nations to the west. The Miamis and their neighbors had already forged an alliance acknowledged by local Indian agents, who spoke of the "Wabash Indians" or the "Confederacy." By 1769 shared interests, rooted in historical suspicion of the British, drew these westerners into closer cooperation with the Ohio Indians. In that year George Croghan learned that the Senecas, Shawnees, and Delawares had "held a Council with the Tweetwees [Miamis], Waweattenas [Ouiatenons], Pyankeehy [Piankashaws], Musquetomeys [Mascoutens]," and Kickapoos. On that important occasion the natives had agreed "that in Case any Diferance Should hapen between any of them and any other Nation that the whole Should Rise up as on[e] Man." Such an alliance was reinforced by a history of cooperation that extended back to the 1740s. Then the Ohio Indians had been joined by Piankashaws and others of the Miami Confederacy against the French, and after the Pickawillany disaster of 1753, survivors had found refuge among the Shawnees. Now, in 1769, the Shawnees once more took the initiative to strengthen the bonds between Ohio and Wabash natives.[25]

The Ohio Indians were able to create a defensive alliance with the Wabash nations with little apparent difficulty. The story was different, however, when the Shawnees attempted to extend that alliance southward to the Cherokees. As they crossed the Ohio River, the Shawnees found themselves confronting a wholly different political landscape in which historical animosities, not cooperation, shaped interethnic relations. Continuing warfare between the Cherokees and the Wabash Indians led the former, in 1769, to take the important step of seeking peace and alliance with their other northern foes, the Six Nations. The Cherokees' reasons became clear when, at German Flatts, New York, in July 1770, they and the Confederacy confirmed their new alliance before Sir William Johnson. Peace with the Six Nations would secure the Cherokees' northern flank as they planned retaliation against the Miamis and their allies.[26]

The Cherokee–Six Nations peace had created a dilemma for Johnson and his superiors: to encourage close cooperation would be to create a native alliance perhaps too powerful for the British to control, one whose aggressiveness against native foes could threaten the Anglo-native border as well. To discourage the Cherokee bid for peace, however, would guarantee the continuation of north-south feuding that often involved border settlers as well. In such circumstances, Johnson continued to follow the dictum of "divide and rule." He urged that, instead of joining Cherokee raids, the Six Nations send a warning to the Wabash Indians telling them that they should remain at peace or face the combined wrath of Iroquois and Cherokee warriors. Such a course reinforced the influence of the Confederacy head-men and forestalled military cooperation between two powerful native peoples. Johnson's suggestion would also weaken the worrisome Ohio-Wabash alliance.[27]

The Shawnees nevertheless continued to work toward their own Cher-okee alliance while undercutting that with the Six Nations. Taking advan-tage of their own recently concluded peace with the Cherokees, the Shaw-nees launched a diplomatic offensive in 1770 and 1771. They urged the Cherokees to cooperate in confronting the shared threat of colonial expan-sion. Southern Indian agents anxiously reported initial Shawnee success in this regard. John Stuart learned of increasing unrest among the Cherokees and of the difficulty village peace factions had in maintaining their influ-ence. "All this," Stuart declared, "is the Effect of the Shawnese Machina-tions." Stuart may have felt relieved when he subsequently learned how difficult the Shawnees' task had become. Only after they had exacted a promise of Ohio-Wabash Indian aid against their Chickasaw foes would the anti-British Cherokees listen to Shawnee plans "to Strike the white People." Other southern Indians responded with coolness when they were later approached by "Western Indians"—the Wabash nations. Ethnic hostility, reinforced by recent raids and retaliation over control of Kentucky, made the Shawnees' grand scheme hard to translate into effective action.[28]

The Shawnees continued to enjoy success on their own side of the Ohio, however. At a large council at their principal town on the Scioto in late summer 1770, the Shawnees managed to convince the Wabash Indians to put aside their differences with the Cherokees and seek an alliance with the southern nations. This would create precisely what British Indian agents and army officers feared most: an alliance that could threaten the western border while more than balancing any possible retaliation by Britain's Six Nations allies. Johnson worried that the natives were meeting to "form Confederacys, for very bad purposes," while General Gage reluctantly ad-mitted that the Shawnees had accomplished far more than anyone had anticipated and further conceded that the Scioto council had been "a nota-ble piece of policy." Johnson and Gage could only hope that somehow Thomas King and the messages he carried from the Onondaga council could alienate the Shawnees from their new allies.[29]

Despite their best efforts, however, the alliance envisioned by the Shaw-nees and encouraged by the Genesee Senecas failed to materialize. This latest attempt, like those of 1760 and 1763, collapsed in the face of fac-tionalism within native societies and deep-seated suspicions that drew on years of ethnic friction, to which Johnson added his own brand of divisive diplomacy. Although decades of interethnic warfare between northern and southern nations made an alliance between them unlikely, within the Ohio Country itself differences between peoples also eroded regional unity. The British learned early in 1771 that the Shawnees were again rallying their neighbors but had specifically excluded the Delawares from a planned conference later that year. This, according to reports, "created great Jealousy between theas tow Nations." Netawatwees later confirmed this when he notified Governor John Penn of the congress, by noting that the Shawnees "have not as yet invited us to their Council"; indeed, Netawatwees knew nothing for certain about the agenda. The reasons for excluding the Delawares in this instance are not clear. One explanation may lie in the Delawares' increasing inclination to avoid further confrontations with British Americans. Another might be these natives' acceptance of Moravian missionaries. Recalling the betrayals of 1760, the presence of Europeans among the Delawares may have convinced the Shawnees that their neighbors were a poor security risk. Finally, the early 1770s saw considerable changes in Delaware-Munsee leadership as older men, including Netawatwees and Custaloga, stepped aside in favor of younger kinsmen. This process was complete by 1774, but it may have caused a good bit of internal debate earlier that precluded closer attention to outside affairs, though the borderlands remained an issue and perhaps influenced the final choice of successors to elder headmen.[30]

At the same time, factions dedicated to maintaining peace appeared among both the Cherokees and the Shawnees themselves. In the latter case it was the peace element that acted in concert with Thomas King in 1771, carried his message belts to the Wabash, and "upbraided" the Indians there "with their past Conduct," thereby assisting in efforts by outsiders to divide would-be allies and lessen the danger of war.[31]

King's mission contributed to the divisiveness working against an alliance rather than alone decisively crushing it. Though he missed the Scioto council, King, with Shawnee help, was able to send Six Nations messages west. He, like subsequent Confederacy messengers, was compelled to use Shawnee mediation with natives to the west, who were less inclined to deal directly with the Six Nations. To the Ohio Indians King offered a thinly veiled threat of Six Nations and, by implication, Cherokee and British retaliation should they carry through their planned alliance. The Shawnees' subsequent difficulty in rallying their neighbors was compounded by King's words. Of greater significance was the unreliability of the Delawares, as well as division within Shawnee ranks and among the Ohio Iroquois, where Kiashuta continued to encourage his own Senecas to return to Iroquoia.

This and the unlikely combination of Ohio, Wabash, and southern Indians rendered the Genesees' and Shawnees' plans moot.[32]

Although Johnson was able to report that the "Indians Settled about Ohio, shew plainly their disappointment," native hostility remained very close to the surface for the next several years. Shawnees, fighting with squatters for Kentucky, continued to attract British attention, especially when in 1772 yet another "Great Congress" was held on the Scioto, followed the next year by one attended by "some thousands" of Indians. Johnson once more mused about turning the Six Nations' warriors loose on the Potawatomis and others in the Wabash Valley while continuing to blame the Illinois French for instigating native unrest. The superintendent's London superior, the earl of Hillsborough, had his own view of events, however. Studying dispatches from the colonies, Hillsborough realized that "Every day discovers more and more the fatal policy of departing from the [boundary] line prescribed by the Proclamation of 1763; and the extension of it on the ground of a cession made by the Six Nations."[33]

It was into this volatile atmosphere that Pennsylvanians and Virginians brought an acrimonious jurisdictional dispute over the lands near Pittsburgh. Had the conflict remained confined to the colonists themselves, it might have been only a minor footnote in the long history of native-colonial encounters in the Ohio Country. However, in their bid to forestall the Penns' own expansive claims, Virginians—including the royal lieutenant governor, John Murray, Lord Dunmore—rushed to stake their claims to as much of the west as possible, a strategy that placed them on a collision course with the Shawnees.

The Pennsylvania-Virginia dispute arose from the vacuum created by the reduction of royal jurisdiction over western affairs and, in 1772, the evacuation of Fort De Chartres and Fort Pitt by regular troops. Faced with the urgent need to concentrate all his forces in the east to confront political unrest, General Gage ordered Fort De Chartres dismantled and Fort Pitt abandoned after government stores had been safely removed to Philadelphia. Thereafter only a token force of some fifty men would remain at Kaskaskia in the Illinois Country.[34]

Reaction on both sides of the cultural frontier to the evacuation of these last signs of British authority was mixed. To some Indians who had chafed under the virtually unregulated trade and settlement during the military regime, the evacuation was hardly a watershed. Others, especially warriors, "could not conceal their joy" on learning that Fort Pitt was to be abandoned. Still others, who took a moment to reflect on events, were glad to be done with the redcoats but worried about who could now stop the unbridled invasion that threatened to engulf the Ohio natives.[35]

This same mixture of apprehension and elation swept the border settlements. At a time when race hatred and competition for resources had turned the Ohio borderlands into a powder keg, settlers were "greatly alarmed" as the Fort Pitt garrison prepared to depart. The sudden feeling of losing even this token force and the authority and succor it represented added to the anxieties of the more isolated settlers. For others—hunters, traders and, especially speculators—the troops' departure was anything but cause for alarm. What little remained of the Crown's authority in the west departed with the regulars and gave virtual free rein to those bent on quickly incorporating the Fort Stanwix cession into their colony's domain. Within two years of the army's departure Virginians seized the opportunity—and Fort Pitt, which was renamed "Fort Dunmore"—and declared the surrounding lands westward to Kentucky to be part of the county of Augusta in Virginia.[36]

Led by Dr. John Connolly, the Virginians asserted their colony's claim on the Ohio to block similar claims by the Penns. Pennsylvania settlements had moved steadily westward since 1763; Arthur St. Clair, a principal figure in the intercolonial squabble, had been among the first to settle the Ligonier Valley in 1764. Since then the colony had gradually extended its authority westward as well, pushing the jurisdiction of Cumberland County to the Ohio and then, in 1773, reorganizing the western lands as Westmoreland County, with St. Clair one of several new proprietary magistrates. By creating Westmoreland County, the Penns announced that their colony's proper western boundary was the Ohio River. That assumption, unsupported by charters or surveys, brought them into direct confrontation with Virginians.[37]

Opposition to the Penns' effort to control the upper Ohio Valley came almost at once, from several quarters. Virginians who had earlier settled the Monongahela Valley were loath to pay taxes to Pennsylvania agents when they believed themselves to be legally residing in their own colony. By late summer 1771, "resolves" were circulating through the Virginia settlements, challenging Pennsylvania's authority. Virginian defiance was fueled by men like Michael Cresap, who told his neighbors that the Penns had no jurisdiction west of the mountains. Others had different economic interests to protect. Speculators, among them George Washington, stood to lose vast estates and revenues should the Penns make good their claims. These men found a powerful ally in Lord Dunmore. Dunmore made a point of consistently disputing his northern neighbors' claims in the west.[38] Matters were also complicated by negotiations in London between the Crown and the Grand Ohio Company for a tract of land encompassing much of the Fort Stanwix cession below Fort Pitt. The petitioners hoped to create a new colony—"Vandalia"—from the grant. This scheme appealed to those in the home government who searched for a way to extend civilian government over the west. Others, including the secretary of state of the colonies, Lord Hillsborough, remained opposed to any interior expansion, but Hillsborough's resignation in 1772 offered renewed hope to the Grand Ohio Company and other speculators. Meanwhile, those with ties to the Vandalia project continued to dispute the Penns' authority in the Ohio Country. Reflecting recent history, George Croghan pointed out to Arthur St. Clair and the home government that Pennsylvania's refusal to confront the French in 1753 and 1754 was proof that the colony's claims in the west were specious and that Virginia had better grounds for claiming the Ohio borderlands on the basis of its role in defending the region.[39]

This jurisdictional conflict continued indecisively until early 1774, when Connolly, as Dunmore's agent, seized Fort Pitt, called out the recently organized militia, and declared the Forks of the Ohio and surrounding lands part of Virginia. Connolly also appointed civil magistrates—later confirmed by Dunmore—all to the consternation of Pennsylvanians. Arthur St. Clair unsuccessfully attempted to have Connolly arrested, while settlers on both sides took up arms as their governments tried to negotiate an end to the dispute. Then in April 1774 events down the Ohio sparked a war that allowed Virginia to tighten its grip on both the Forks and Kentucky at the expense of the Penns, the Shawnees, and the local Iroquois.[40]

While Connolly and St. Clair waged a verbal war over which of their governments could rightfully claim—and tax—the borderlands, Ohio Indians continued to face the larger consequences of the British Americans' invasion. Had they been privy to the rancor at Pittsburgh, the natives might have found it ironic that colonists were now fighting each other over lands that Shawnees, Delawares, and local Iroquois had steadfastly defended for decades.

The defense of the Ohio Country continued to shape discussion and debate within Ohio Indian towns during 1773 and 1774. By then the areas of contention with colonists had been reduced to one: the lands west of the Kanawha River in Kentucky. The principal users of this land, the Shawnees, now faced an invasion that had, in the estimation of Governor Dunmore, put upward of 10,000 people onto the lands south of the Ohio River.[41]

Throughout the winter and spring of 1773–74 native complaints con-

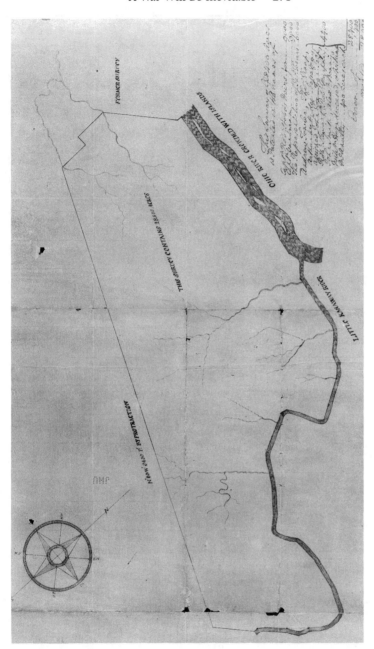

15. Virginians' encroachment on the Ohio Indians' borderlands: "Plat of the Survey [of] the Little Kanawha 28,400 Acres Made in 1773," by George Washington. (Courtesy of the John Work Garrett Collections of the Milton S. Eisenhower Library, The Johns Hopkins University)

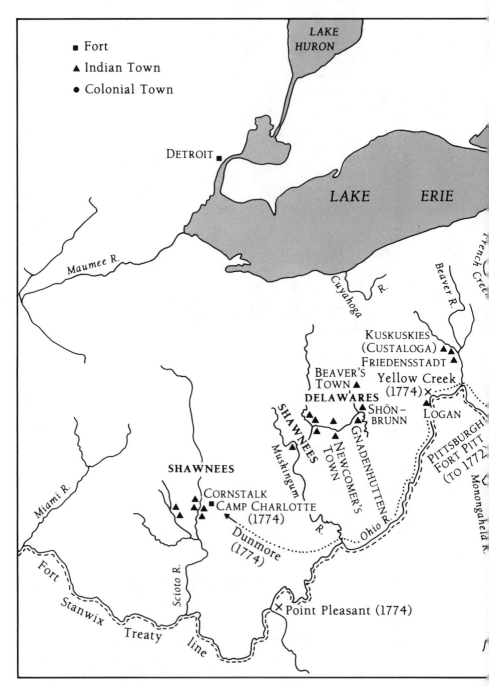

Map 7 The Ohio Country, 1765–1774.

tinued to pour into the Indian agency at Fort Pitt. In October 1773 Alexander McKee, who had a Shawnee wife and enjoyed close contact with her people while serving as Indian agent at the fort, reported that "none of the Indians, Tho' never so well disposed to the English can relish the Settlements making down the Ohio." What worried McKee was knowledge that not only were hotheaded young warriors fed up with the invasion, but even "the most reasonable [people] that I have mett with amongst them are extreamly irritated" by the magnitude of the Virginians' invasion beyond the Kanawha Valley. By the following spring the Ohio Valley below Pittsburgh had become so critical that Sir William Johnson planned to call the Ohio Indians to a council in an effort to keep the peace. Yet during this trying time, the natives continued to display restraint. Henry Jolly, who witnessed the events of 1774, later recalled that "the Indians had for some time before . . . thought themselves intruded upon by the long Knife [Virginians]," but he insisted that, despite such provocations, the natives "had refrained from resisting" until colonial actions left them no choice but to take up arms. Jolly's recollection suggests that the continuing struggle within native towns finally, in some instances, tipped decisively toward those advocating war in the face of subsequent actions by the Virginians.[42]

Hostilities began with nearly simultaneous attacks by two parties of Virginians on April 27, 1774, one led by Daniel Greathouse, the other by Michael Cresap. Of the two, Greathouse's attack was the more sensational, if only for its cold-bloodedness. According to reports, Greathouse's men, mostly hunters and others looking for trouble, lured an Iroquois hunting party to their camp at the mouth of Yellow Creek, where the natives were set upon and nine were killed. In the meantime, Cresap's group struck a party of traders escorted by Shawnees, killing at least one Indian and wounding a Pennsylvanian.[43]

The attacks by Greathouse and Cresap capped a winter and spring marked by rumors of war on both sides of the Ohio River. Border settlers as far south as the Clinch River were increasingly anxious about the prospects of a new Indian war. In the meantime, word circulated that Shawnees had "cut off" families living west of the Kanawha River, and McKee learned that some members of that nation were once more attempting to raise their neighbors against the Virginians. The Shawnees did stop a Virginia survey party and ordered it out of Kentucky, after which native headmen once more warned McKee of the consequences should settlers continue to invade their lands.[44]

Nevertheless, tension had run high for years without major incident, and rumors or survey parties alone cannot be held responsible for the hostilities that followed. Greathouse, Cresap, and their followers were looking for trouble. Consisting of men with no love of Indians or of any who would supply them, these groups were on patrol, looking for natives and traders. Greathouse and his men in particular were reminiscent of the Paxton Boys of a decade before. Cresap's men were patrolling the river and later discussed plans to attack a Shawnee town on the Scioto.[45]

The brief conflict that followed the Greathouse-Cresap attacks has been called "Dunmore's War" after the Virginia governor who orchestrated the final campaign and dictated the peace that followed. The war might better be called the "Connolly-Dunmore War," since from the outset the governor's local representative did all he could to create a full-scale war from incidents that might otherwise have been resolved. A week before the Cresap-Greathouse episodes, in fact, Connolly had raised the alarm over the possibility of Shawnee attacks, a fact Cresap later used to justify his own actions. And once the shooting started, Connolly lost no time in proclaiming a state of war and raising a militia that even fellow Virginians declared to be "all the hunters, men without families." Less charitable Pennsylvanians believed the force consisted of "men without character and fortune," animated more by Indian hating and the prospect of scalp bounties than by concern for hearth and home. Yet Connolly was able to raise a group that was prepared to clear Kentucky of native competitors as well as challenge Pennsylvania's title to the Ohio borderlands. In this regard it is worth noting that Connolly carefully singled out the *Shawnees* for special mention and, through vague references to "several murders" allegedly committed by that nation, to put the blame for the war—and the anticipated territorial retribution—squarely upon the natives.[46]

Unfortunately for Connolly, the Shawnees and Ohio Iroquois refused to cooperate by staging a general uprising. In the aftermath of the Greathouse-Cresap attacks, kin of the slain Iroquois, led by John Logan (The Great Mingo), sought revenge in the tradition of the mourning war, limiting the number of colonial victims to the number of their own people killed at Yellow Creek. Logan then declared that he was willing to end his campaign. However, subsequent events led to ever more hardened Iroquois resistance to the Virginians.[47]

Given the provocation of murdered kinfolk, compounded by the taking of their scalps, the Shawnee headmen especially went to some lengths to demonstrate their people's desire to remain at peace. Nevertheless, those Shawnees whose kinfolk had died in the April attacks likewise took up arms, as did other warriors bent on taking advantage of the Virginians' attacks to even the score in Kentucky. Some Shawnee headmen complained that they were losing control of their young men, reporting in May that "Our People at the Lower Towns have no Chiefs among them, but are all warriors." Yet not all the towns seemed in favor of retaliation; David Zeisberger, among the Delawares at Schönbrunn, learned in mid-May that anti-Virginia sentiments ran highest at Wakatomica, presumably because some or all of the Virginians' victims had lived there, but that the other Scioto Valley towns "were peaceable yet, and would have no war," and that the Shawnees "are far from being unanimous for War."[48]

Indeed, Shawnee behavior during late spring 1774 stood in stark contrast to the bellicosity of local Virginians. Taking advantage of the lack of consensus at home, Cornstalk and other Shawnee leaders made it clear that though their people and the Ohio Iroquois were "very much Aggravated" by the recent murders, the natives would nonetheless work to keep the peace and "likewise request that . . . Captain Connolly of Pittsburgh, will do his endeavour to stop such foolish People" from committing hostile acts "for the future." In another message, Cornstalk also attempted to school Connolly on the reciprocal nature of peace. Responding to word from the Virginian urging the Indians to take no notice of the actions of a few men, Cornstalk told Connolly, "We desire you likewise not to take any notice of what our young men may now be doing." The Shawnees also guaranteed the security of all traders in their midst and provided armed escorts for these men all the way to Pittsburgh, escorts that included Cornstalk's own kinsmen. By early June, as the traders began the journey to Pittsburgh, observers were able to report that the "Shawnees are now quiet," with village headmen once more able to prevail over headstrong warriors.[49]

Warfare might have ended at this point but for the Virginians' determination to strike out at their Indian enemies. Connolly continued to press for retaliation, insisting both to Dunmore and to local settlers that the natives were to blame for the hostilities by pointing to recent mourning-war raids—without reference to Greathouse's or Cresap's earlier deeds. Then in late June, animated both by Connolly's inflammatory rhetoric and by widespread fear of a major new Indian war, the Pittsburgh militia attacked the Shawnees who had just arrived with colonial traders. The attack, in apparent retaliation for an earlier Shawnee raid, shattered what little goodwill and trust remained among the natives; by mid-July raids were once more being reported at Pittsburgh as Dunmore began preparations to carry the war directly to the Shawnee towns.[50]

Dunmore, who arrived at Pittsburgh in September to take command of military operations against the Shawnees, may have been led astray by Connolly's reports of events during the summer. One observer learned that, upon arrival, Dunmore was upset to discover that circumstances were not what he had been led to believe, and Indian agent Alexander McKee told the governor that the fighting had been started by the Virginians and not, as Connolly would have it, by the natives. Nevertheless, Dunmore did nothing to bring the conflict to a speedy and equitable end; instead he drew up elaborate plans to march two militia armies into Shawnee territory that autumn. The opportunity presented by Connolly's actions was evidently too good to ignore.[51]

Faced with the choice of maintaining an uneasy status quo or securing absolute possession of disputed territory in the face of native owners and Pennsylvania claimants, Dunmore chose the latter course. He later justified his actions by pointing to the manifest need for peace along the volatile frontier. Others believed they saw another motive in Dunmore's decision to strike the Shawnees. One witness to events at Pittsburgh enthusiastically predicted a rise in speculators' stock once Kentucky was cleared of Indians, while the governor's opponents within the colony insisted that his only motive was to grab Kentucky and preempt any effort by the Penns to assert jurisdiction over the Ohio Country. Certainly Dunmore's actions left little doubt that he was bent on military conquest; his signals to peace-seeking Indians were mixed at best. While he spoke of peace, he mustered his forces—actions that led the natives to doubt both his sincerity and his good sense.[52]

Though Dunmore chose to campaign against the Shawnees and Ohio Iroquois, others continued to search for ways to end the fighting, or at least contain it. The British army at far-off Detroit and Fort Niagara rejected out of hand Connolly's call for material assistance. Meanwhile, Sir William Johnson convened a council of Six Nations headmen in July and urged them to intercede with the Shawnees and to persuade other western nations to stay out of the fight. Johnson collapsed and died in the midst of the congress, and it was left to his nephew and successor Guy Johnson to prevail upon the reluctant Iroquois to send messages west. It was not an easy task; the Six Nations feared a general war and roundly condemned the Virginians, pointing out, in an ironic twist, that the border settlers were easily as ungovernable and just as dangerous as their own young warriors. Moreover, the Confederacy was not eager to see itself once more mired in Ohio affairs now that the borderlands belonged to the British. The assembled headmen agreed to help keep the peace—from a distance—only after demanding that the *real* problem, Virginia's land grabbing, be stopped.

However, both the Six Nations and Guy Johnson continued to worry that the longer Dunmore's militia remained in the field, the greater was the threat of a general war.[53]

Kiashuta, as emissary of Guy Johnson and the Six Nations, proved largely successful in convincing Indians in the Ohio Country and beyond that their best course was to remain neutral. Even before the Confederacy sent him "a private instruction" in late summer, however, Kiashuta had been hard at work on behalf of Sir William Johnson, moving from town to town in the Ohio Country trying to undercut efforts by militant Shawnees to raise allies in the wake of Connolly's treachery at Pittsburgh. Kiashuta's task must have been physically exhausting even as it taxed his respected diplomatic and oratorical skills. British army officer Augustine Prevost met the Seneca at Sideling Hill at the end of August as Kiashuta hurried east to confer with Guy Johnson. His role as roving ambassador for the Six Nations and the Indian Department also carried considerable personal risk. One measure of Kiashuta's success was the anger he generated among those Shawnees at Wakatomica who were determined to fight on. Guy Johnson observed only that Kiashuta "has rendered himself obnoxious to the Shawnees." It was an understatement; on at least one occasion the Seneca narrowly avoided a Shawnee ambush as he traveled to the Wabash River. Undeterred, Kiashuta continued his mission, one that helped limit the war as western natives agreed to follow the Six Nations' advice and remain quiet.[54]

Notwithstanding his own efforts, Kiashuta received valuable, perhaps crucial, assistance from another quarter. Since early May, Delawares, Munsees, and their Moravian Indian neighbors had been working steadily to keep the peace. These natives had no immediate stake in the war; the Kanawha Valley and Kentucky belonged to the Shawnees, and many of the victims of the spring attacks were Shawnees. Moreover, Delaware headmen realized that they could not hope to gain from renewed hostilities and, judging from Virginia's demonstrated aggressiveness, had much to lose. Beyond practical considerations, however, lay the Delawares' role as "women," and it was in this spirit that Delaware headmen, foremost among them the aged Netawatwees and his successor White Eyes, as well as Captain Pipe and the venerable Custaloga, embarked on their own diplomatic mission during the spring and summer of 1774. In the meantime Dunmore's insistence that the Shawnees be punished for starting the war, coupled with his amateurish martial display at Pittsburgh, did little to enhance his esteem in the eyes of Delaware leaders. One of them, after watching the governor muster his troops, was amused enough to ask, "What old little man is that yonder playing like a boy[?]" In Delaware eyes, Dunmore's rash choice of war rather than the wise man's path of statesmanship marked him as much less than a responsible leader. This was especially so since the Delawares also believed that Virginia's aggression, not the Shawnees', was behind this latest threat to regional peace.[55]

By the end of July the Delawares found it impossible to keep the Shawnees and Virginians apart, and they announced that they and their Munsee and Moravian neighbors would stand aside. A few agreed to serve with Dunmore, however, hoping to "enable [the Virginians] to make a proper distinction between" friend and foe. The pro-war Shawnees were by then largely isolated. Guy Johnson learned in mid-August that few Iroquois beyond the kin of those slain in the April ambushes would take up arms, while the Onondaga headman Bunt contemptuously threw aside Shawnee belts that accompanied messages asking for help. Meanwhile, Cornstalk and other Shawnee headmen continued to seek ways of speaking with Dunmore in order to avoid a showdown. Yet the governor's determination to cross the Ohio River and attack the Scioto Valley towns may have undermined such efforts and hardened Shawnee determination to resist Viriginia's aggression. Nevertheless, throughout the fighting the Shawnees, more than their border militia foes, were careful to distinguish friend from enemy by refusing to molest Pennsylvania traders or settlements as their warriors continued attacking Virginians.[56]

Efforts to negotiate an end to the fighting having failed, Dunmore's forces pushed on to the Ohio. The Virginians, marching in several columns, reached the Ohio River and, in early October, established Camp Charlotte near the main Shawnee towns while hastily burning smaller Iroquois villages nearby. Though some Shawnees, especially village headmen, urged peace, most warriors from the Scioto towns struck back. Selecting the more exposed portion of Dunmore's army, they attacked Colonel Andrew Lewis's force at Point Pleasant and bloodied the Virginians, even though they were unable to overrun the camp. In the aftermath, Cornstalk and other Shawnees succeeded in meeting with Dunmore and accepted the governor's terms. By the Treaty of Camp Charlotte the Shawnees agreed to return all their captives. More important, they also agreed to remain north of the Ohio River, thus surrendering Kentucky to the colonists.[57]

conclusion:
after dunmore

Though neither the Shawnees nor Governor Dunmore could have understood its full implications, the war that ended at Camp Charlotte represented a fundamental turning point in the history of the Ohio Indians. In
two immediate ways Dunmore's War was clearly significant: it was fought
almost exclusively on the Ohio Indians' home ground, and it resulted in the
first direct cession of Ohio Country territory by the local Indians. In a larger
sense, however, the war heralded a new age for the Indians.

During the fifty years before Dunmore's invasion the Ohio Indians had
demonstrated great success in meeting myriad challenges to their independence. Confronted with the potential of French retaliation for attacks during King George's War, the Ohio Iroquois sought allies among the Pennsylvanians and Virginians whose commercial interests had already bound
them to the natives. Although Tanaghrisson's alliance ultimately turned the
Ohio Country into an imperial cockpit, the Indians were nevertheless able
to face changing conditions. They could easily adapt to a French military
invasion in 1753, especially since the French deliberately courted their
goodwill, a task made easier because the natives faced a growing threat from
expanding British settlements. That threat, more compelling than French
forts, led to an Ohio Indian war against British expansion between 1755 and
1758. Moreover the Ohio Indians, led by the Delawares, sought ways of
exploiting Anglo-French hostility to resurrect the "play-off" strategy of the
1740s in the hope of removing all intruding armies from the west.

The Indians' efforts, which led to the unchallenged arrival of a British
army on the Ohio and the hasty departure of the French, represented—as

did Tanaghrisson's alliance a decade earlier—a calculated gamble. The Ohio Indians could have little understood the broader implications of a British advance into the west, and the conquest of New France robbed the natives of a European counterweight to renewed British expansion. Nevertheless, the Indians were not wholly dependent on rival Europeans for their survival. During the decade and a half after 1758, native-British relations were shaped by efforts at accommodation based on a momentary convergence of interests and needs. Although the British viewed the west as a conquered province, the Crown had also undertaken to guarantee the security of native lands as the price of peace with the Ohio Indians. The Indians, though never conceding that they had been conquered or that their lands belonged to Great Britain, sought ways to control an army of occupation while they constantly reminded the Crown's representatives of their obligations under the Easton Treaty. The brief and costly war of 1763–65 made it clear that neither side could crush the other and that therefore accommodation represented the best—indeed the only—path for both Ohio Indians and the British government.

What neither the Indians nor the Crown proved able to effectively confront was the one frontier problem they shared: the rising tide of border settlements that, after 1765, threatened to engulf Kentucky and other parts of the Ohio Country. For the next decade the Ohio Country became the scene of an increasing cycle of violence as settlers from Virginia staked their claims in the west. Their moves were encouraged by declining imperial authority as the few troops in the west were sent to confront incipient rebellion in the east. Moreover, the Virginians carried into the west not only an insatiable appetite for land but virulent Indian hating and a territorial dispute with Pennsylvania that made another war all but inevitable by 1774.

Dunmore's War proved merely a harbinger of things to come. The political revolution that drove the royal governor into exile a year after his victory on the Ohio also unleashed the full force of aggressive American expansion. Between 1775 and 1815 the Ohio Indians were periodically able to slow, but never to stop, an American invasion animated by a powerful ideology that linked republicanism with territorial expansion. And unlike what had prevailed during the earlier French and British invasions, the Indians were given no role in the new American empire in the west. Instead, the new contest for the Ohio Country after 1774 turned on only one issue: exclusive control of the land itself. The Americans' violent pursuit of land included a singular quest for total victory animated by the same brand of Indian hating that had first surfaced in the 1760s.[1]

In their efforts to block the American invasion, the Ohio Indians fell back on the strategies developed against earlier threats, though never with the same success. Attempts to use the British as a counterweight to the Americans were repeatedly frustrated by the Crown's unwillingness to entangle itself in a protracted frontier war over lands that, after 1783, ceased to be part of the empire. This, and a demonstrated willingness to abandon native allies as international politics required, left the Indians increasingly isolated.[2]

Meanwhile the Shawnees under Tecumseh once more attempted to rally surrounding nations and weld them into an alliance that could defeat the American advance. Yet by the time Tecumseh died fighting the American army at the Battle of the Thames in 1811, the Ohio Country had been irretrievably lost. The Treaty of Greenville in 1795 ended the first phase of the American invasion with a land cession that left the natives in tenuous possession of only the northwestern portion of Ohio; by the time of Tecumseh's death, all the lands north of the Ohio River had long since become part of the Northwest Territories of the United States.[3]

Amid the change and turmoil that punctuated Indians' lives after 1774, however, native societies persisted. From the crucible of a fifty-year struggle for independence came new collective identities: from scattered lineages and bands had emerged Delaware, Shawnee, and Seneca nations. These new nations, each held together by shared rituals and a common history, helped guarantee the survival of societies and cultures faced with renewed aggression and dispossession. Thus Delawares, Shawnees, and Senecas who surrendered the last of the Ohio Country in 1795 were not shattered peoples. Shawnees and Senecas experienced new cultural revitalizations led by Tenskwatawa and Handsome Lake, and the Delawares and Munsees carried their cultural heritage with them to Canada, Kansas, and the plains of Oklahoma, where they were joined once more by Shawnees, much as their ancestors had once jointly pioneered the Ohio Country. In the continuing search for security, the natives had moved west once more.[4]

Notes

Pa. Archives   Pennsylvania Archives
Pa. Council Minutes   Samuel Hazard, ed., Minutes of the Provincial Council of Pennsylvania
SWJP   James Sullivan et al., eds., The Papers of Sir William Johnson
WO   Great Britain, Public Record Office, War Office Records, Series 34, Sir
                      Jeffrey, First Baron Amherst, Official Papers

Introduction

1   Recent studies of Indian societies facing colonial-imperial expansion in the eighteenth
    century include James H. Merrell, The Indians' New World: Catawbas and Their Neighbors
    from European Contact through the Era of Removal; Colin G. Calloway, The Western
    Abenakis of Vermont, 1600–1800: War, Migration, and the Survival of an Indian People;
    Barbara Graymont, The Iroquois in the American Revolution; Anthony F. C. Wallace, The
    Death and Rebirth of the Seneca; Richard Aquila, The Iroquois Restoration: Iroquois Diplo-
    macy on the Colonial Frontier, 1701–1754.
2   Lawrence Henry Gipson, The British Empire Before the American Revolution, vol. 4, Zones
    of International Friction: America South of the Great Lakes Region, 1748–1754, chaps. 6–9.
3   See Francis Parkman, Montcalm and Wolfe, passim, and Gipson, British Empire, for
    examples of the traditional approach to Indian participation in the era of the Seven Years'
    War. A notable exception is Randolph C. Downes, Council Fires on the Upper Ohio: A
    Narrative of Indian Affairs in the Upper Ohio Valley until 1795. Downes's book, now some
    fifty years old, was the first attempt to cast events in the upper Ohio Valley from an Indian
    perspective, though it suffers heavily from the same assumptions of "civilization" and
    "savagery" and of inevitability that marred other standard frontier histories. A recent
    revisionist study of the Seven Years' War is Francis Jennings, Empire of Fortune: Crowns,
    Colonies, and Tribes in the Seven Years' War in America. On the problem of Indians and
    colonial history, see the important article by James H. Merrell, "Some Thoughts on
    Colonial Historians and American Indians." Merrell's study of the Catawbas, The Indians'
    New World, is the best example of how to merge these two artificially separated halves of
    early American history.
4   Francis Jennings, The Ambiguous Iroquois Empire: The Covenant Chain Confederation of
    Indian Tribes with English Colonies; Wallace, Death and Rebirth of the Seneca; Daniel K.
    Richter, "Ordeals of the Longhouse: The Five Nations in Early American History," in
    Richter and Merrell, Beyond the Covenant Chain.
5   Dorothy V. Jones, License for Empire: Colonialism by Treaty in Early America, chap. 6 on
    the Revolution as a fundamental watershed in Indian relations in the West.
6   On the play-off system, see Wallace, Death and Rebirth of the Seneca, 111–14.
7   Michael N. McConnell, "Peoples 'in Between': The Iroquois and the Ohio Indians, 1720–
    1768," in Richter and Merrell, Beyond the Covenant Chain.

Chapter One

1   George P. Donehoo, A History of the Indian Villages and Place Names in Pennsylvania, 82–83.
2   Carl W. Albrecht, Jr., "The Peaceable Kingdom: Ohio on the Eve of Settlement"; Law-
    rence Henry Gipson, Lewis Evans, 172.
3   Lois Mulkearn, ed., George Mercer Papers relating to the Ohio Company of Virginia, 10–
    12, 33–35.

4 James Smith, "An Account of the Remarkable Occurrences in the Life and Travels of Colonel James Smith," in Washburn, *Narratives of North American Indian Captivities*, 55:181, 185, 188–89, 217.

5 Robert Rogers, *Journals of Major Robert Rogers*, 233–36.

6 Gipson, *Lewis Evans*, 15. The literature of the pre-European history of the upper Ohio Valley has grown considerably in recent years, much of it in the form of site reports and field surveys. Useful general studies of the region and its numerous cultures include William J. Mayer-Oakes, *Prehistory of the Upper Ohio Valley*, and James B. Griffin, "Late Prehistory of the Ohio Valley," in Trigger, *Northeast*. On the sixteenth century and the subsequent interethnic warfare see Bruce G. Trigger, *Natives and Newcomers: Canada's "Heroic Age" Reconsidered*, esp. chaps. 2, 3, 5; Daniel K. Richter, "War and Culture: The Iroquois Experience." Marian E. White, "Erie,"in Trigger, *Northeast*; Philip R. Shriver, "A Large Seventeenth Century Historic Contact Interment in the Cuyahoga Valley: An Iroquoian Piece in the Puzzle of What Happened to the Whittlesey Focus?"

7 On the history of the Delawares see C. A. Weslager, *The Delaware Indians: A History*; Paul A. W. Wallace, *Indians in Pennsylvania*, chaps. 3–11; recent studies utilizing a wider array of sources include Ives Goddard, "Delaware," in Trigger, *Northeast*, 213–29, and Herbert C. Kraft, *The Lenape: Archaeology, History, and Ethnography*. On early coastal encounters, see T. J. Brasser, "Early Indian-European Contacts," in Trigger, *Northeast*.

8 Weslager, *Delaware Indians*, chaps. 1–6; Donald H. Kent, ed., *Pennsylvania and Delaware Treaties, 1629–1737*, 2–3.

9 Marshall J. Becker, "The Lenape Bands prior to 1740: The Identification of Boundaries and Processes of Change to the Formation of the 'Delawares,'" in Kraft, *Lenape Indians*, esp. 20, 24, 28; idem, "Native Settlements in the Forks of Delaware, in the Eighteenth Century: Archaeological Implications." This and subsequent discussions of Delaware society in the Ohio Country draw heavily on Becker's recent work. My thanks to him for clarifying points on early Delaware history and group identities.

10 Weslager, *Delaware Indians*, 174–79; William A. Hunter, "Documented Subdivisions of the Delaware Indians," 21 –23.

11 August 11, 1733, deed to settlers on the Schuylkill River, Logan Letterbook 11 (Indian Affairs), HSP.

12 Hunter, "Documented Subdivisions," 23–25; "Bishop A. G. Spangenberg's Journal of a Journey to Onondaga in 1745," in William Martin Beauchamp, ed., *Moravian Journals relating to Central New York, 1745–66*, 8; on the Tulpehocken Indians at Shamokin see Francis P. Jennings, "Incident at Tulpehocken"; idem, *Ambiguous Iroquois Empire*, chaps. 16, 17; idem, "Brother Miquon, Good Lord!" in Dunn and Dunn, *World of William Penn*, 195–214.

13 Hunter, "Documented Subdivisions," 31–32.

14 Logan to Lt. Gov. George Clarke (N.Y.), August 4, 1737, Logan Papers, 4:7–8, APS; Conrad Weiser to Richard Peters, April 22, 1749, Indian and Military Affairs of Pennsylvania, HSP; deposition of Brandywine Indians concerning violations of their land rights (1725), Logan Letterbook, 11 (Indian Affairs), HSP; on Logan's role in Delaware dispossession see Jennings, *Ambiguous Empire*, 262–68, 271–74. These Delaware migrations—and the real reason for them—remained embedded in the natives' corporate memory; see John Heckewelder, *An Account of the History, Manners, and Customs of the Indian Nations*, 79–80.

15 Evelyn A. Benson, "The Huguenot Le Torts: First Christian Family on the Conestoga,"

96–97; Jennings, *Ambiguous Empire*, 196–99; *Dictionary of Canadian Biography*, s.v. "Bisaillon, Peter"; Robert Callender, "Shawnees" in Trigger, *Northeast*, 630; Logan to Lieutenant Governor Clarke, August 4, 1737, Logan Papers, 4:8–9, APS; Logan Papers 10:58, HSP; R. David Edmunds, *Tecumseh and the Quest for Indian Leadership*, 1–4; idem, *The Shawnee Prophet*, 7–8.

16 *Pa. Archives*, 1st ser., 1:213 (Conestogas), 223, 228, 329–30; such incidents seem to have led the Iroquois to send an emissary—Schickellamy—to the Susquehanna Valley to sort out affairs between the colony, the Conestogas, other Indians supposedly dependent on the Confederacy, and the Shawnees. See also James H. Howard, *Shawnee! The Ceremonialism of a Native American Tribe and Its Cultural Background*, 10, for Shawnee-Swiss land disputes in the Pequa Creek area.

17 *Pa. Archives*, 1st ser., 1:229–30, 329; New York Indian Commissioners, reel C-1220, 1:203–4; *NYCD*, 9:1013; Beauharnois to Minister of Marine, July 21, 1729, in Reuben Gold Thwaites, ed., *Wisconsin Historical Collections*, 17:64.

18 On this phase of Iroquois history see Jennings, *Ambiguous Empire*, chaps. 9–10; Richter, "War and Culture," 528–59; and Richard L. Haan, "The Problem of Iroquois Neutrality: Suggestions for Revision."

19 Aquila, *Iroquois Restoration*, chap. 7; Richter, "War and Culture," 557–58; Francis Jennings, "Iroquois Alliances in American History," in Jennings et al., *History and Culture of Iroquois Diplomacy*, 38–40; for a southern Indian perspective see James H. Merrell, "'Their Very Bones Shall Fight': The Catawba-Iroquois Wars," in Richter and Merrell, *Beyond the Covenant Chain*.

20 Barry C. Kent, *Susquehanna's Indians*, 58, 59, 62; William N. Fenton, "Problems Arising from the Historic Northeastern Position of the Iroquois," 241; Thomas S. Abler and Elizabeth Tooker, "Seneca," in Trigger, *Northeast*, 507.

21 *Pa. Archives*, 1st ser., 1:301–2; *Pa. Council Minutes*, 3:274–75; New York Indian Commissioners, reel C-1220, 1:159a, 164a.

22 On the French establishment at Niagara: *NYCD*, 9:885, 1057; Peter Kalm, *The America of 1750*, ed. Adolph B. Benson, 2:696. The best analysis yet of the contest for Niagara is Richard L. Haan, "The Covenant Chain: Iroquois Diplomacy on the Niagara Frontier, 1687–1730" (Ph.D. diss.), esp. 115–24, 210–18; see also Daniel K. Richter, "The Ordeal of the Longhouse: Change and Persistence on the Iroquois Frontier, 1609–1700" (Ph.D. diss.), 438–83, 571.

23 Peter Wraxall, *An Abridgment of the Indian Affairs . . .* , ed. Charles Howard McIlwain, 116, 119, 130; New York Indian Commissioners, reel C-1220, 1: 115 (emphasis added); historical antecedents of eighteenth-century Seneca divisions can be traced at least to the sixteenth century; see Charles F. Wray, et al., *The Adams and Culbertson Sites*, 1–5.

24 Wraxall, *Abridgment of Indian Affairs*, 187–90.

25 New York Indian Commissioners, reel C-1220, 1:160, September 7, 1726.

26 Craig MacAndrews and Robert B. Edgerton, *Drunken Comportment: A Social Explanation*, 149–56; James Axtell, *The European and the Indian: Essays in the Ethnohistory of Colonial North America*, 257–58; Bruce G. Trigger, *The Children of Aataentsic: A History of the Huron People to 1660*, 1:76–77, 81–84; Wallace, *Death and Rebirth of the Seneca*, 30–38.

27 Wraxall, *Abridgment of Indian Affairs*, 160–61, 183; New York Indian Commissioners, reel C-1220, 1:114a, October 20, 1724; 2:124, January 2, 1737–38.

28 Wraxall, *Abridgment of Indian Affairs*, 120 (1716), 187 (smallpox), 221, 224 (famine); Thwaites, *Wisconsin Historical Collections*, 17:172–73 (smallpox), 337 (famine); *Pa.*

Council Minutes, 3:512 (smallpox); famine among the Senecas was not unique to the eighteenth century, see Wray et al., *Adams and Culbertson Sites*, 241–42.

29   Pa. Council Minutes, 5:357–58 (Weiser on Iroquois migrations); *NYCD*, 9:885 (Iroquois porters at Niagara, 1718).

30   On the Senecas and French traders: Wraxall, *Abridgment of Indian Affairs*, 243 (October 1745); on the Iroquois' assimilation of defeated peoples see Richter, "War and Culture," 189. and Trigger, *Natives and Newcomers*, 273–74.

31   Hamilton to Governor Ogle, September 20, 1750, *Md. Archives*, 28:490.

32   Richard Peters to Thomas Penn, October 25, 1750, Penn MSS, Official Correspondence, 5:74, HSP.

Chapter Two

1   *Pa. Archives*, 1st ser., 1:301–2.

2   Ibid., 299–302; Logan Papers 9:27, HSP. I have used a warrior-to-dependent ratio of 1:1, taken both from the Ohio Country lists and from information supplied by John Bartram during his 1745 journey through the Six Nations, found in John Bartram, *Observations on the Inhabitants, Climate, Soil, Rivers, Productions, Animals, and Other matters Worthy of Notice . . . in His Travels from Pensilvania to Onondago, Oswego, and the Lake Ontario, in Canada*, 23.

3   *Pa. Archives*, 1st ser., 1:301–2, 305, 549; on Kakowatchiky see *Pa. Council Minutes*, 4:643, 747; Wraxall, *Abridgment of Indian Affairs*, 203–4; Logan to Lt. Gov. George Clarke, August 4, 1737, Logan Papers, 4:8, APS; Paul A. W. Wallace, *Indian Paths of Pennsylvania*, 151; on other Shawnee migrations see Howard, *Shawnee!* 10–11.

4   *Pa. Council Minutes*, 3:330.

5   *Pa. Archives*, 1st ser., 1:301–2.

6   Mulkearn, *Mercer Papers*, 16; Donald H. Kent, *The Iroquois Indians*, 1:208–11; Helen Hornbeck Tanner, ed., *Atlas of Great Lakes Indian History*, 43–44.

7   Joseph François Lafitau, S.J., *Customs of the American Indians Compared with the Customs of Primitive Times*, ed. and trans. William N. Fenton and Elizabeth L. Moore, 1:69–70, on women in Iroquois society; Anthony F. C. Wallace, "Women, Land, and Society: Three Aspects of Aboriginal Delaware Life," 6, 9, 11, on Delaware women; Howard, *Shawnee!* 42, and Callender, "Shawnee," 624, 627, on Shawnee women.

8   Lafitau, *Customs of the American Indians*, 2:70.

9   *Pa. Archives*, 1st ser., 1:300–301; A. A. Lambing, ed., "Céloron's Journal," 341, 350; "Bishop A. G. Spangenberg's Journal . . . 1745," in Beauchamp, *Moravian Journals*, 18; "Diary of J. Martin Mack's, David Zeisberger's and Gottfried Rundt's Journey to Onondaga in 1752," in ibid., 114; Bartram, *Travels*, 14, 40–42.

10   "Diary of the Journey of Br. Cammerhoff and David Zeisberger to the Five Nations from May 3–14 to August 6–17, 1750," in Beauchamp, *Moravian Journals*, 60, 69; Bartram, *Travels*, 42; Wallace, *Death and Rebirth of the Seneca*, 22.

11   "Scheme of an Expedition to Kittanning" (ca. 1755), Miscellaneous Manuscript Collections, APS.

12   Ives Goddard, "Delaware," in Trigger, *Northeast*, 220; *Pa. Archives*, 1st ser., 1:301–2; *Pa. Council Minutes*, 4:443.

13   *Pa. Archives*, 1st ser., 1:301–2, 395, 425, 551 (Nucheconner); *Pa. Council Minutes*, 4:641 (Missemediqueety); Howard, *Shawnee!* 26.

14 Delawares to Lt. Gov. Francis Gordon, August 8, 1732, *Pa. Archives*, 1st ser., 1:341; see also ibid., 300–301, 255, 265; *Pa. Council Minutes*, 4:443–47; Logan Papers, 9:27, HSP.

15 On Nucheconner: *Pa. Archives*, 1st ser., 1:329–30, 395, 425; on Kakowatchiky: *Pa. Council Minutes*, 3:309, 315, 330, 643; see also *Archives of Maryland*, 28:300.

16 *Pa. Archives*, 1st ser., 1:551.

17 On "wandering Indians," see Wallace, "Women, Land, and Society," 2; the foregoing discussion has been based on Fredrik Barth, "Introduction," in Fredrik Barth, ed., *Ethnic Groups and Boundaries: The Social Organization of Cultural Difference*, 9, 16, 18–19, 32–33; T. J. C. Brasser, "Group Identification along a Moving Frontier"; Robert A. Levine and Donald T. Campbell, *Ethnocentrism: Theories of Conflict, Ethnic Attitudes, and Group Behavior*, chap. 2, esp. 86–87; on the spatial distribution of native societies in the Ohio Country see Tanner, *Atlas*, map 9: "The French Era, 1720–1761"; Mulkearn, *Mercer Papers*, 16.

18 On Mesquakies. see chap. 1, above; on Conestogas see Francis Jennings, "Susquehannock," in Trigger, *Northeast*, 204–5, and Laurence M. Hauptman, "Refugee Havens: The Iroquois Villages of the Eighteenth Century," in Vecsey and Venables, *American Indian Environments*, 128–29; on Catawbas see James H. Merrell, "The Indians' New World: The Catawba Experience," 537–65; on the Shawnees see Edmunds, *Shawnee Prophet*, 7–8.

19 *Pa. Council Minutes*, 3:97.

20 Morton Fried, "On the Concept of 'Tribe' and 'Tribal Society,'" in Helm, *Essays on the Problem of Tribe*, 3–20; William N. Fenton, "Locality as a Basic Factor in the Development of Iroquois Social Structure," in Fenton, *Symposium on Local Diversity in Iroquois Culture*; Fenton, "Cultural Stability and Change in American Indian Society"; Fenton, "Factionalism in American Indian Society," 330–40; Goddard, "Delaware," in Trigger, *Northeast*, 213; Howard, *Shawnee!* chaps. 6–7; Jack Campisi, "The Iroquois and the Euro-American Concept of Tribes"; Anthony F. C. Wallace, "Political Organization and Land Tenure among the Northeastern Indians, 1600–1830"; Wallace, *Death and Rebirth of the Seneca*, 30–39; Melburn D. Thurman, "Delaware Social Organization," in Kraft, *Delaware Indian Symposium*. A fine study of Iroquois leadership is Mary A. Druke, "Structure and Meaning of Leadership among Mohawk and Oneida during the Mid-Eighteenth Century" (Ph.D. diss.).

21 Fred Gearing, "Structural Poses of Eighteenth Century Cherokee Villages"; Thurman, "Delaware Social Organization," passim.

22 Marshall D. Sahlins, *Stone Age Economics*, chap. 4, 193–211; the classic work on exchange and reciprocity is Marcel Mauss, *The Gift: Forms and Functions of Exchange in Archaic Societies*; on reciprocity and trade in the Northeast, see Bruce G. Trigger, *The Huron, Farmers of the North*, 42–43; idem, *Children of Aataentsic*, 1:50–51, 66–68.

23 Trigger, *Huron*, 29–31, 48–49; Kraft, *Lenape*, 131–32; Nancy Bonvillain, "Iroquoian Women," in Bonvillain, *Studies in Iroquoian Culture*, 47–58; Wallace, *Death and Rebirth of the Seneca*, 29; Archer Butler Hulbert and William Nathanael Schwarze, eds., *David Zeisberger's History of the North American Indians*, 51; Heckewelder, *History, Manners, and Customs*, 154–55.

24 Sahlins, *Stone Age Economics*, chaps. 4–5; Wallace, "Women, Land, and Society," 13; Wallace, *Death and Rebirth of the Seneca*, 28–30; Hulbert and Schwarze, *Zeisberger's History*, 16, 81–82, 92, 93; Lafitau, *Customs of the American Indians*, 1:69–70; Howard, *Shawnee!* 43; Judith K. Brown, "Economic Organization and the Position of Women among the Iroquois"; Bruce G. Trigger, "Iroquoian Matriliny."

25 Smith, "Life and Travels," 188, 190–91, 193, 195, 197, 198, 202, 204; Wallace, *Death and Rebirth of the Seneca*, 50–59; Goddard, "Delaware," 216–17, 226.

26 *Pa. Council Minutes*, 5:348 (sleeping places); "Cammerhoff and Zeisberger," in Beauchamp, *Moravian Journals*, 68 (Indian bridges); on trail systems see Wallace, *Indian Paths of Pennsylvania*.

27 Heckewelder, *History, Manners, and Customs*, 71–75.

28 Ibid.; Francis Jennings, "The Indian Trade of the Susquehanna Valley," 406–7; Carolyn Gilman, *Where Two Worlds Meet: The Great Lakes Fur Trade*, 1–4.

29 James Axtell, *After Columbus: Essays in the Ethnohistory of Colonial North America*, 144–81; Trigger, *Natives and Newcomers*, 172–225; James H. Merrell, " 'Our Bond of Peace,' " in Wood, Waselkov, and Hatley, *Powhatan's Mantle*.

30 Charles F. Wray and Harry L. Schoff, "A Preliminary Report on the Seneca Sequence in Western New York, 1550–1687." See also James W. Bradley, *Evolution of the Onondaga Iroquois: Accommodating Change, 1500–1655*, for this process among other New York Iroquois.

31 The literature on Indian-European trade has grown large and diverse in recent years, but representative of the effort to see trade in the broader context of native societies are Bradley, *Evolution of the Onondaga Iroquois*, esp. chaps. 3–5, and Christopher L. Miller and George R. Hamell, "A New Perspective on Indian-White Contact: Cultural Symbols and Colonial Trade." This discussion is also based on an inspection of Seneca material from seventeenth- and eighteenth-century sites housed in the Rochester Museum and Science Center; much of this material evidence is summarized in Wray and Schoff, "Preliminary report on the Seneca Sequence in Western New York," 53–61. On the issue of native dependence on European technology, see also Axtell, *European and the Indian*, 253–62; Merrell, *Indians' New World*, chap. 2.

32 Smith, "Life and Travels," 196.

33 Ibid., 197; Livingston quoted in Thomas Elliot Norton, *The Fur Trade in Colonial New York, 1686–1776*, 116.

34 On the pan-Indian trade culture see George Irving Quimby, *Indian Culture and European Trade Goods*, 140–41. On the consumer phenomenon in Anglo-America see James Deetz, *In Small Things Forgotten: The Archaeology of Early American Life*, chap. 2; Timothy H. Breen, "An Empire of Goods: The Anglicization of Colonial America, 1690–1776."

35 *Pa. Council Minutes*, 3:274; *Pa. Archives*, 1st ser., 1:243–44; though French agents visited the upper Ohio Valley in the 1720s and 1730s, their role in the region's developing trade was limited.

36 For Pennsylvania traders active west of the Alleghenies see Charles A. Hanna, *The Wilderness Trail, or The Ventures and Adventures of the Pennsylvania Traders on the Allegheny Path*, 2:326–43; William A. Hunter, "Traders on the Ohio, 1730"; on Logan and his traders see Jennings, "Indian Trade of the Susquehanna Valley," passim; *DCB*, s.v. "Bisaillon, Peter"; Albright G. Zimmerman, "The Indian Trade of Colonial Pennsylvania" (Ph.D. diss.), is still the most complete study of the Pennsylvania trade, though it is based entirely on the activities of provincial merchants and their traders.

37 *Pa. Archives*, 1st ser., 1:255.

38 Kent, *Susquehanna's Indians*, 60–68; Fred W. Kinsey III and Jay F. Custer, "The Lancaster Park Site," (36 LA 96): Conestoga Phase; Lambing, "Céloron's Journal," 353, 357, 366; the Cuyahoga River is referred to in Beauharnois and Hocquart to Minister of Marine, October 7, 1743, *NYCD*, 9:1099–1100.

39 Nicholas B. Wainwright, *George Croghan: Wilderness Diplomat*, 5; one noteworthy early colonial resident of the Ohio Country was gunsmith and trader John Fraser; see William A. Hunter, *Forts on the Pennsylvania Frontier, 1753–1758*, 27.

40 "Spangenberg's Journal of a Journey to Onondaga in 1745," in Beauchamp, *Moravian Journals*, 12, 18; Kent, *Susquehanna's Indians*, 63–65; for inventories of goods carried to Ohio Indians see Kenneth P. Bailey, ed., *The Ohio Company Papers, 1753–1817, Being Primarily Papers of the "Suffering Traders" of Pennsylvania*, passim; *Pa. Archives*, 1st ser., 1:265.

41 "Journey of Cammerhoff and Zeisberger . . . 1750," in Beauchamp, *Moravian Journals*, 64–65 (tea); Smith, "Life and Travels," 217–18 (swearing).

42 *Pa. Archives*, 1st ser., 1:261, 265; Zimmerman, "Indian Trade of Colonial Pennsylvania," 265; James Logan's web of credit and debt is discussed in Jennings, "Indian Trade of the Susquehanna Valley," 410–20; on the problems of debt confronting one well-known trader see Wainwright, *George Croghan*, chaps. 1–3.

43 Bailey, *Ohio Company Papers*, 67, 69, 98, 120, 129.

44 *Pa. Archives*, 1st ser., 1:261, 309, 328; ibid., 2d ser., 2:531–32; Mulkearn, *Mercer Papers*, 9–10 (Gist).

45 *Pa. Council Minutes*, 4:445; Mulkearn, *Mercer Papers*, 11 (Gist).

46 *Pa. Council Minutes*, 4:680–84; for a similar earlier incident, ibid., 3:285–86.

47 On Hart and Robeson, *Pa. Archives*, 1st ser., 1:254–55; on Indians killed see Julian P. Boyd, ed., *Indian Treaties Printed by Benjamin Franklin, 1732–1762*, 67 (1744 Lancaster Treaty).

48 *Pa. Archives*, 1st ser., 1:254–55, 262–63; Boyd, *Indian Treaties*, 57–58, 67.

49 *Pa. Council Minutes*, 3:275–76; on the ability of Indians to obtain liquor despite colonial laws, see Beauharnois and Hocquart to Minister of Marine, October 12, 1731, in Thwaites, *Wisconsin Historical Collections*, 17:145; on trader and Shawnee petitions, see Shawnees to Lieutenant Governor Gordon, April 24, 1733, *Pa. Archives*, 1st ser., 1:394–95; same to same, May 1, 1734, ibid., 425; the traders cited as acceptable to the Ohio Indians included Le Tort, Cartlidge, Peter Chartier, and Jonah Davenport—all of whom worked for James Logan.

50 *Pa. Archives*, 1st ser., 1:549–50, 551; ibid., 265 (Mohawks trading rum in the Ohio Country).

51 *Pa. Archives*, 1st ser., 1:549–50; cf. Logan Papers, 9:27, HSP.

52 *Pa. Archives*, 1st ser., 1:551–52.

Chapter Three

1 *Proceedings of the Council of Maryland*, 28:300, for Iroquois terms for Delawares and Shawnees; see also Boyd, *Indian Treaties*, 130, 131 (Carlisle, 1753).

2 *Pa. Council Minutes*, 3:93; Richter, "War and Culture"; James H. Merrell, "'Their Very Bones Shall Fight,'" 116–18; Merrell, *Indians' New World*, 41–43.

3 *Pa. Archives*, 1st ser., 1:213, 223; *Pa. Council Minutes*, 3:99–100.

4 NYCD, 9:886, 892; Wallace, *Indian Paths of Pennsylvania*, 27–29; Jennings, *Ambiguous Empire*, 294–98, on the 1722 treaty (Spotswood); Le Tort to Governor Gordon, May 12, 1728, *Pa. Archives*, 1st ser., 1:216, on clashes between warriors and settlers.

5 Dinwiddie to Catawbas, February 4, 1754, in R. A. Brock, ed., *The Official Records of Robert Dinwiddie, Lieutenant-Governor of the Colony of Virginia, 1751–1758*, 1:60; same to Cherokees, April 19, 1754, in ibid., 132–33; New York Indian Commissioners, reel

C-1220, 1:159a, September 7, 1726; Governor Glen to Governor Clinton, July 7, 1750, *NYCD*, 6:588, on raids against the Catawbas from both the Ohio and Susquehanna valleys. On Kentucky as a borderland between Ohio Indians and the Cherokees, see Henry Timberlake, *Lieutenant Henry Timberlake's Memoirs, 1756–1765*, ed. Samuel Cole Williams, 113–14.

6   Merrell, "'Their Very Bones Shall Fight,'" 14; John Lawson, *A New Voyage to Carolina*, ed. Hugh Talmage Lefler, 50, 174–75; William L. McDowell, Jr., ed., *Documents relating to Indian Affairs, May 21, 1750–August 7, 1754*, 421–29, 432–33, 442, 463; on Captain Hill and Shannopin, *Pa. Archives*, 1st ser., 1:24; *Pa Council Minutes*, 4:447; quotation on Catawbas from Smith, "Life and Travels," 190; see also Thwaites, *Wisconsin Historical Collections*, 17:280–81, for southern Indian raids against Indians at Detroit.

7   Louise Phelps Kellogg, ed., *Narratives of the Old Northwest 1635–1699*, 168, 170, 186–87; *NYCD*, 9:1057; [Bonnecamps], "Account of the Voyage on the Beautiful River Made in 1749, under the Direction of Monsieur de Céloron," by Father Bonnecamps, 409; Sylvester K. Stevens and Donald H. Kent, eds., *The Expedition of Baron de Longueuil; W. J. Eccles, The Canadian Frontier, 1534–1760*, 128. The reason for limited French understanding of the geography and people of the Ohio Country can be understood by reference to "The View from Sault Ste. Marie," in Tanner, *Atlas*, 36, which illustrates how the east-west axis of the Great Lakes dominated French thinking.

8   Eccles, *Canadian Frontier*, 141; W. J. Eccles, "A Belated Review of Harold Adams Innes's *The Fur Trade in Canada*," 442; Yves F. Zoltvany, "New France and the West," 305–7; idem, "The Frontier Policy of Philippe Rigaud de Vaudreuil, 1713–1725."

9   Haan, "Covenant Chain," chap. 5, on Niagara and Oswego; Zoltvany, "Frontier Policy," 243–45, 249–50; Eccles, *Canadian Frontier*, 142–43; quotation: Intendent Giles Harquart to Maurepas, October 7, 1737, Thwaites, *Wisconsin Historical Collections*, 17:265; see also New York Indian Commissioners, reel C-1220, 1:136–37, June 19, 1725; Thwaites, *Wisconsin Historical Collections*, 17:131–32; Beauharnois to Maurepas, May 1, 1733, ibid., 173, 281; see ibid., 214, for French trade ordinances (1735).

10   *NYCD*, 9:886; Beauharnois and Hocquart to Maurepas, October 25, 1729, ibid., 1016; [Bonnecamps], "Voyage on the Beautiful River," 404, on the lack of furs in area; W. J. Eccles, "The Fur Trade and Eighteenth Century Imperialism," 356–58; idem, "Belated Review," 420–22; idem, *Canadian Frontier*, 128.

11   *NYCD*, 9:1013; Beauharnois to Maurepas, July 21, 1729, Thwaites, *Wisconsin Historical Collections*, 17:64.

12   On Cavelier, see Hunter, *Forts on the Pennsylvania Frontier*, 11; *DCB*, s.v. "Chabert de Joncaire, Philippe-Thomas."

13   Thwaites, *Wisconsin Historical Collections*, 17:178; Tanner, *Atlas*, map 9: "The French Era, 1720 to c. 1761."

14   Beauharnois to Maurepas, October 7, 1734, Thwaites, *Wisconsin Historical Collections*, 17:210–11; same to same, October 12, 1736, ibid., 242–43; same to same, September 24, 1742, ibid., 417.

15   Beauharnois to Maurepas, October 1, 1740, ibid., 331.

16   Jennings, "Brother Miquon, Good Lord!" 195–207.

17   Gordon to Shawnees, December 4, 1731, *Pa. Archives*, 1st ser., 1:303–4; quotation from Gordon to Delawares, December 4, 1731, ibid.

18   On Governor Keith's concerns for the west (1718): Logan Papers 11 (Indian Affairs), HSP; *Pa. Council Minutes*, 3:99–100; *NYCD*, 5:602, 604, 619–25; Joseph E. Johnson, ed.,

"A Quaker Imperialist's View of the British Colonies in America, 1732," 103–4 and passim; Jennings, *Ambiguous Empire*, 285–87; Pennsylvania traders on French activities: *Pa. Archives*, 1st ser., 1:300–301, 305–6, 327–28; quotation from ibid., 309–10; on the importance of trade: Stephen Cutcliffe, "Indians, Furs, and Empires: The Changing Policies of New York and Pennsylvania, 1674–1768" (Ph.D. diss.), 150–51, 183; Zimmerman, "Indian Trade," 267–68; on efforts to regulate trade: Gordon to Ohio traders, October 4, 1729, *Pa. Archives*, 1st ser., 1:243–44; Logan to traders, October 6, 1729, ibid., 245; quotations: ibid., 243–44; Cartlidge to Gordon, May 14, 1732, ibid., 327–28, and *Pa. Council Minutes*, 4:445.

19   Francis Jennings, "The Constitutional Evolution of the Covenant Chain"; idem, "Iroquois Alliances in American History," 37–65; Mary A. Druke, "Linking Arms: The Structure of Iroquois Intertribal Diplomacy," in Richter and Merrell, *Beyond the Covenant Chain*.

20   Jennings, "Constitutional Evolution of the Covenant Chain"; idem, "Iroquois Alliances in American History," 37–65; Druke, "Linking Arms"; Richter, "Ordeal of the Longhouse," chaps. 10–12.

21   Jones, *License for Empire*, chap. 2, for a discussion of the Iroquois mystique; Richard L. Haan, "Covenant and Consensus: Iroquois and English, 1676–1760," in Richter and Merrell, *Beyond the Covenant Chain*; it is worth noting that the French, on the other hand, seldom took expansive Iroquois claims seriously; recent history, especially the Peace of 1701, had given the French a different, more realistic view of Iroquois capabilities and intersocietal relations.

22   Jennings, *Ambiguous Empire*, chaps. 13, 14, 16, on the 1722 negotiations and the evolution of the Covenant Chain in Pennsylvania.

23   Jennings, "Incident at Tulpehocken," Francis Jennings, "The Scandalous Policy of William Penn's Sons: Deeds and Documents of the Walking Purchase."

24   *Pa. Council Minutes*, 3:442; Jennings, *Ambiguous Empire*, 313.

25   Historically, each of the Six Nations took particular interest in and responsibility for territories and peoples nearby, but there appears not to have been a Confederacy "policy" toward regions beyond Iroquoia; see *Pa. Archives*, 1st ser., 1:231.

26   Delawares to Gordon, August 8, 1752, *Pa. Archives*, 1st ser., 1:341; Shawnees to Penn, March 20, 1738, ibid., 551; Abraham Wendell (New York trader) to Gordon, July 29, 1732, ibid., 454; *Pa. Council Minutes*, 3:608–9.

27   Delawares to Governor Thomas, August 24, 1744, *Pa. Council Minutes*, 3:747.

28   Delaware to Gordon, April 30, 1730, *Pa. Archives*, 1st ser., 1:255; Allumapees quoted in council at Philadelphia, September 15, 1718, Logan Papers 11 (Indian Affairs), HSP; Francis Jennings, "The Delaware Interregnum." Jennings suggests that with Allumapees's death in 1747 the Delawares were leaderless until the appearance of Shingas as "king" in 1752—this presupposes a political unity between eastern and western Delaware bands and assumes that there could be only *one* headman at any given time; the records clearly indicate otherwise and show that continuity, not discontinuity, marked Delaware society during the 1720s to 1750s.

Chapter Four

1   For Ohio Indian messages see Ohio Indians to Pennsylvania, April 20, 1747, *Pa. Archives*, 1st ser., 1:737–38; Indians to Pennsylvania, May 16, 1747, ibid. 741–42; see also George

Croghan to Richard Peters, Cuyahoga, May 26, 1747, ibid., 742; Peters to Conrad Weiser, June 13, 1747, ibid., 748–49; Weiser to Peters, June 21, 1747, ibid., 751; Croghan to Thomas Lawrence, September 18, 1747, ibid., 770; Peters to Weiser, September 26, 1747, ibid., 771; Logan Letterbooks, 4:132, August 18, 1747, APS.

2   Quotations from Boyd, *Indian Treaties*, 103–5.

3   Shawnees: Delawares to Governor Thomas, August 24, 1744, *Pa. Council Minutes*, 4:747; Iroquois: Beauharnois and Hocquart to Minister of Marine, October 10, 1743, *NYCD*, 9:1099–1100; the French referred to the Cuyahoga as the "Rivière Blanche"—White River.

4   For details see Thwaites, *Wisconsin Historical Collections*, 17:279–88; Richardie to St. Pé, August 26, 1740, ibid., 328; Beauharnois to Maurepas, October 9, 1744, ibid., 440; this discussion of the Detroit Hurons draws on recent work by James A. Clifton, especially "The Re-emergent Wyandot: A Study of Ethnogenesis on the Detroit River Borderland, 1747," in Pryke and Kulisek, *Western District*, idem, "Hurons of the West: Migrations and Adaptations of the Ontario Iroquois, 1650–1701," unpublished draft study for the Canadian Ethnology Survey, National Museums of Canada. My thanks to Professor Clifton for providing copies of these important publications.

5   Thwaites, *Wisconsin Historical Collections*, 17:326–27; Beauharnois to Maurepas, October 1, 1740, and Richardie to St. Pé, June 10, 1741, ibid., 331–33, 339–40, on Wyandot factions and French involvement; Chevalier Beauharnois to Beauharnois, August 2, 1741, ibid., 353–55; Richardie to Fr. Jaunay, December 1741, ibid., 370; Beauharnois to Maurepas, September 15, 1742, ibid., 414; Wainwright, *George Croghan*, 6.

6   Beauharnois and Hocquart to Maurepas, October 10, 1743, *NYCD*, 9:1099; Thwaites, *Wisconsin Historical Collections*, 17:326–27; Beauharnois to Maurepas, October 12, 1742, ibid., 429; Beauharnois to Maurepas, October 25, 1744, ibid., 445–46; Longueuil to Beauharnois, July 28, 1745, ibid., 446–47; Eccles, *Canadian Frontier*, 151.

7   Galissonnière to Maurepas, October 22, 1747, in Theodore Calvin Pease and Ernestine Jenison, eds., *Collections of the Illinois State Historical Library*, vol. 29, *Illinois on the Eve of the Seven Years' War, 1747–1755*, 38; Beauharnois to Maurepas, October 8, 1744, *NYCD*, 9:1105; Beauharnois to Maurepas, November 7, 1744, ibid., 1111; G. A. Rawlyk, "The 'Rising French Empire' in the Ohio Valley and Old Northwest: The 'Dreaded Juncture' of the French Settlements in Canada with Those of Louisiana," in Elliot, *Contest for Empire*.

8   Beauharnois to Maurepas, October 28, 1745, *NYCD*, 10:20; Beauharnois to Maurepas, August 28, 1746, ibid., 37.

9   *NYCD*, 10:119, 128–29.

10   On Chartier: Beauharnois to Maurepas, October 28, 1745, Thwaites, *Wisconsin Historical Collections*, 17:448; *Pa. Council Minutes*, 4:756–57; Wilbur Jacobs, ed., *The Appalachian Indian Frontier: The Edmund Atkin Report and the Plan of 1755*, 65–66.

11   War belts and British actions: Beauharnois to Maurepas, October 28, 1745, *NYCD*, 10:20; ibid., 142; Orontony: ibid., 83–84, 114–15, 138–39; lack of trade goods: de Longueuil to Beauharnois, July 28, 1745, Thwaites, *Wisconsin Historical Collections*, 17:446–47; Beauharnois to Maurepas, October 28, 1745, *NYCD*, 10:21; Galissonnière to Maurepas, October 22, 1747, Pease, *Illinois on the Eve of the Seven Years' War*, 38. Gary Clayton Anderson has shown how the erosion of kinship ties and traditional forms of cross-cultural relations led to conflict between the eastern Dakotas and the United States, a process suggestive of what may have happened in the less well documented 1740s; see

Anderson, *Kinsmen of Another Kind: Dakota-White Relations in the Upper Mississippi Valley, 1650–1862,* esp. 75–76, 257–58. My thanks to Richard Haan for bringing this to my attention.

12 On trade relations: *NYCD,* 10:150; Beauharnois to Potawatomis of St. Joseph, July 22, 1742, Thwaites, *Wisconsin Historical Collections,* 17:395; James A. Clifton, *The Prairie People: Continuity and Change in Potawatomi: Indian Culture 1650–1704,* 91, 94.

13 *NYCD,* 10:123; ibid., 142; Thwaites, *Wisconsin Historical Collections,* 17:488; *NYCD,* 10:139.

14 Weiser to Logan, October 15, 1747, Logan Letterbook, 4:134, APS; *NYCD,* 10:150.

15 Ohio Indians to Pennsylvania, April 20, 1747, *Pa. Archives,* 1st ser., 1:737–38.

16 Ohio Indians to Pennsylvania, May 16, 1747, ibid., 741–42. For another version of the events in the Ohio Country during the late 1740s, see Jennings, *Empire of Fortune,* 27–36.

17 *Pa. Archives,* 1st ser., 1:737–38.

18 Croghan to Peters, May 26, 1747, *Pa. Archives,* 1st ser., 1:742; Weiser to Logan, October 15, 1747, Logan Letterbook, 4:135, APS.

19 Cuyahoga Indians to Pennsylvania, May 16, 1747, *Pa. Archives,* 1st ser., 1:741–42; Ohio Iroquois to Pennsylvania, April 20, 1747, ibid., 737–38.

20 Peters to Weiser, June 13, 1747, *Pa. Archives,* 1st ser., 1:748–49; Weiser to Peters, June 21, 1747 (reply), ibid., 750; Croghan to Thomas Lawrence, September 18, 1747, ibid., 770; *Pa. Council Minutes,* 5:72; Peters to Weiser, October 26, 1747, *Pa. Archives,* 1st ser., 1:771; Logan Letterbooks, 4:132, August 18, 1747, APS.

21 Weiser to Logan, October 15, 1747, Logan Letterbooks, 4:132–37, APS.

22 *Pa. Council Minutes,* 5:146; Boyd, *Indian Treaties,* 103–4; on council protocol see Michael Foster, "On Who Spoke First at Iroquois-White Councils," in Foster, Campisi, and Mithun, *Extending the Rafters,* 183–208.

23 Boyd, *Indian Treaties,* 104.

24 Ibid.

25 Ibid., 105–6.

26 Ibid., 106–8.

27 *Pa. Council Minutes,* 5:289.

28 *NYCD,* 10:140–41; Raymond to La Jonquière, September 4, 1749, Pease, *Illinois on the Eve of the Seven Years' War,* 105; Raymond to La Jonquière, September 5, 1749, ibid., 110; Raymond to La Jonquière, January 5, 1750, ibid., 149; Benoist de St. Claire to Raymond, February 11, 1750, ibid., 163–64; Thomas Cresap to [?], December 1751, *Calendar of Virginia State Papers,* 1:245–46; see also R. David Edmunds, "Old Briton," in idem, *American Indian Leaders,* 1–20; *NYCD,* 10:157.

29 Palmer to Assembly, August 24, 1748, *Pa. Archives,* 4th ser., 1:82.

30 Alfred T. Goodwin, ed., *Journal of Captain William Trent from Logstown to Pickawillany, A.D. 1752,* 105; *Pa. Council Minutes,* 5:308; ibid., 309–10; on the metaphors of Iroquois diplomacy and the structure and meaning of alliances see Druke, "Linking Arms."

31 *Pa. Council Minutes,* 5:310–11, 312–15.

32 Weiser to Logan, October 15, 1747, Logan Letterbooks, 4:135, APS; Weiser to Richard Peters, March 28, 1748, ibid., 138; Weiser to Peters, July 10, 1748, *Pa. Archives,* 1st ser., 2:8; James Hamilton to Thomas Penn, November 18, 1748, Penn MSS, Official Correspondence, 5:89, HSP.

33 Peters to Penn, October 25, 1750, Penn MSS, Official Correspondence, 5:73, HSP; Hamilton to Penn, November 18, 1750, ibid., 89; Peters to Proprietor, October 15, 1750,

ibid., 73; Peters to Penn, October 24, 1748, ibid., 4:163; Penn strongly endorsed Weiser and objected to all attempts to treat directly with the Ohio Iroquois: Penn to Peters, June 9, 1748, Peters Papers, 2, pt. 2:105; and Peters to Penn, December 8, 1749, Penn MSS, Official Correspondence, 4:265, HSP.

34   *Pa. Council Minutes*, 5:290–93; ibid., 197: the inventory of goods taken west to Logg's Town suggests that no one was to be overlooked; in addition to cloth, shirts, kettles, medals, pipes, powder, and lead, there were "jointed Babys." See also "Invoice of Goods Sent to John Harris's on Account of the Government of Pennsylvania" (September 17, 1748), George Groghan Papers, sec. 29, Cadwallader Collection, HSP.

35   *Pa. Council Minutes*, 5:349; *Pa. Archives*, 1st ser., 1:737; Pease, *Illinois on the Eve of the Seven Years' War*, 919; *DCB*, s.v. "Tanaghrisson"; Lois Mulkearn, "Half-King, Seneca Diplomat of the Ohio Valley."

36   *Pa. Council Minutes*, 5:349–50, 358.

37   *Pa. Council Minutes*, 5:351–52: 307 Iroquois, Including 163 Senecas, 74 Mohawks, 35 Onondagas, 15 Oneidas, and 20 Cayugas; 165 Delawares; 162 Shawnees; 100 Wyandots; 40 Mississaugas; and 15 Mahicans.

38   *Pa. Council Minutes*, 5:353–54, 357.

39   Ibid., 478.

40   Beauharnois to Maurepas, August 28, 1746, *NYCD*, 10:41; ibid., 94; Weiser to Logan, October 15, 1747, Logan Letterbooks, 4:132–33, APS; Weiser to Logan, September 29, 1744 (on neutrality); *Pa. Archives*, 1st ser., 1:661–62.

41   *NYCD*, 10:23, 94; ibid., 6:239.

42   On the origins of factionalism among the Six Nations, see Richter, "Ordeals of the Longhouse," 17–26.

43   *NYCD*, 10:123; *Pa. Council Minutes*, 5:480.

44   Ibid., 471, 480.

45   Hamilton to Clinton, September 20, 1750, *NYCD*, 6:593–94.

46   *Pa. Council Minutes*, 5:439.

47   On the influence of locality in Iroquoian society: Fenton, "Locality as a Basic Factor in the Development of Iroquois Social Structure"; George Snyderman, "Concepts of Land Ownership among the Iroquois and Their Neighbors," in Fenton, *Symposium on Local Diversity in Iroquois Culture*; Haan, "Covenant and Consensus"; the Six Nations' lack of any coercive power over constituent or nominally dependent groups is revealed in a conference between La Jonquière and Cayugas in 1750: La Jonquière wanted the Six Nations to *remove* the Ohio Indians; the Cayugas give no firm answer, but they point out that the abundance of game keeps their people in the west, as does the presence of French and British traders; see *NYCD*, 10:206; for the Onondagas' particular interest in the Susquehanna Valley, see, for example, Weiser to Onondagas, September 21, 1750, *Pa. Council Minutes*, 5:479.

48   Boyd, *Indian Treaties*, 104; *Pa. Council Minutes*, 5:637 (emphasis added).

49   *Pa. Council Minutes*, 5:438–39 (emphasis added).

50   Snyderman, "Concepts of Land Ownership," 25.

51   Peters to Thomas Penn, December 8, 1749, Penn MSS, Official Correspondence, 4:265, HSP ; Peters quoted in Carl Van Doren, "Indian Affairs in Pennsylvania," in Boyd, *Indian Treaties*, lxiii; Johnson to Clinton, March 12, 1754, *SWJP*, 9:127; see also *Pa. Council Minutes*, 5:521; Peters to Thomas Penn, October 25, 1750, Penn MSS: Official Correspondence, 5:73, HSP, on the fiction of the Six Nations' supremacy in the west.

52 Maurepas to Vaudreuil, February 23, 1748, Pease, *Illinois on the Eve of the Seven Years' War*, 49.

53 Thwaites, *Wisconsin Historical Collections*, 18:47; on interregional relations: Lambing, "Céloron's Journal," 345; Wyandots and Piankashaws to Pennsylvania, September 20, 1750, *NYCD*, 6:594–96.

54 *DCB*, s.v. "Céloron de Blainville, Pierre-Joseph"; Galissonnière to Chev. de Longueuil, October 1748, *NYCD*, 10:161; Galissonnière to Rouille, June 26, 1749, Pease, *Illinois on the Eve of the Seven Years' War*, 97; Galissonnière had reason enough for concern: British returns from Oswego in 1749 reveal that seventy-eight canoes loaded with pelts had arrived that year manned by Potawatomis, Menominees, Ojibwas, Mississaugas, and Miamis—all ostensibly French trading partners—as well as several Canadian traders; *NYCD*, 6:538.

55 Lambing, "Céloron's Journal," 339, 341–46, 352, 353, 357, 359.

56 Ibid., 345–48, 351, 359–60.

57 Ibid., 352–58; [Bonnecamps], "Voyage on the Beautiful River," 406.

58 [Bonnecamps], "Voyage on the Beautiful River," 407; Lambing, "Céloron's Journal," 364–70.

59 Lambing, "Céloron's Journal," 371–76; when offered the pipes by La Demoiselle's emissaries, Céloron's weary and pleasure-starved Canadians, "worn out for a smoke, would have wished that the ceremony had continued longer"; ibid., 372.

60 Ibid., 358, 364–65, 369; [Bonnecamps], "Voyage on the Beautiful River," 406; Hamilton to Clinton, October 2, 1749, *NYCD*, 6:531.

61 Lambing, "Céloron's Journal," 358; Peters to Penn, January 30, 1751, Penn MSS, Official Correspondence, 5:121, HSP: reference to reports from Croghan suggesting that "some Six Nations" continued to meet with French agents.

62 Clinton to Duke of Bedford, November 22, 1749, *NYCD*, 6:533; Raymond to La Jonquière, January 13, 1750, Pease, *Illinois on the Eve of the Seven Years' War*, 155.

63 Hamilton to Assembly, October 16, 1750, *Pa. Archives*, 4th ser., 2:235–36; ibid., 1st ser., 2:47–49 (instructions to Lewis Evans, 1750).

Chapter Five

1 Tanaghrisson quoted in Mulkearn, *Mercer Papers*, 23.

2 On the Ohio Company see Alfred Proctor James, *The Ohio Company: Its Inner History*; Kenneth P. Bailey, *The Ohio Company of Virginia and the Westward Movement, 1748–1792*; on the 1744 Lancaster Treaty see Jennings, *Ambiguous Empire*, chap. 18, esp. 356–63; see also Thomas Lee to Weiser, February 13, 1748, Logan Letterbooks, 4:137, APS; Thomas Lee to Weiser, May 14, 1748, ibid., 140; Thomas Lee to Weiser, December 11, 1748, Peters Papers, 2, pt. 2:115, HSP.

3 Croghan to [?], July 3, 1749, *Pa. Archives*, 1st ser., 2:31; Weiser to Governor Thomas, January 26, 1743, ibid., 4th ser., 1:822–23.

4 Mulkearn, *Mercer Papers*, 9–10; see also Jennings, *Ambiguous Empire*, chap. 1.

5 Weiser to Peters, August 15, 1748, *Pa. Archives*, 1st ser., 2:15; Peters to Thomas Penn, May 16, 1749, Penn MSS, Official Correspondence, 4:213, HSP; Edmund Jennings to Weiser, August 29, 1750, Peters Papers, 3:13, HSP; Bailey, *Ohio Company*, 66, 68, 304.

6 *Pa. Council Minutes*, 5:440–41; Weiser to Peters, August 15, 1748, *Pa. Archives*, 1st ser., 2:15; Croghan to [?], July 3, 1749, ibid., 31; Mulkearn, *Mercer Papers*, 34, 39.

7   Thomas Lee to Thomas Penn, November 22, 1749, Penn MSS, Official Correspondence, 4:257, HSP; Peters to Thomas Penn, July 28, 1748, ibid., 143; Peters to Thomas Penn, July 5, 1749, ibid., 219 1749; Croghan to [?], July 3, 1749, *Pa. Archives*, 1st ser., 2:31; Weiser to Peters, May 8, 1749, Weiser Papers, 19, HSP.

8   Lee to Thomas Penn, November 22, 1749, Penn MSS, Official Correspondence, 4:257, HSP; Lee to Weiser, December 11, 1748, Peters Papers, 2, pt. 2:115, HSP; Cresap to [?], December 1751, *Calendar of Virginia State Papers*, 1:246.

9   *Pa. Council Minutes*, 5:530–34; Croghan to Thomas Penn, June 10, 1751, Penn MSS, Official Correspondence, 5:147, HSP.

10   *Pa. Council Minutes*, 5:535–36.

11   *Pa. Council Minutes*, 5:537–38; these speeches were delivered on behalf of *all* Ohio Iroquois headmen including Tanaghrisson and Conagaresa.

12   Hamilton to Assembly, August 13, 1751, *Pa. Council Minutes*, 5:528–29; Hamilton to Thomas Penn, September 24, 1751, Penn MSS, Official Correspondence, 5:173, HSP; Hamilton to Penn, November 20, 1751, ibid., 193.

13   Hamilton to Penn, June 27, 1751, Penn MSS, Official Correspondence, 5:157, HSP; Peters to Penn, [1751], ibid., 199.

14   Dinwiddie to Cresap, January 23, 1752, Brock, *Official Records of Dinwiddie*, 1:18.

15   Cresap to Weiser, February 20, 1752, Peters Papers, 3:54, HSP; "The Treaty of Logg's Town, 1752," 158; Mulkearn, *Mercer Papers*, 56.

16   "Treaty of Logg's Town," 161, 168; Mulkearn, *Mercer Papers*, 56–57, 64.

17   "Treaty of Logg's Town," 168, 169–72; Mulkearn, *Mercer Papers*, 56, 62–65; Dinwiddie to Cresap and Trent, February 10, 1753, Brock, *Official Records of Dinwiddie*, 1:23; Dinwiddie said that at Logg's Town, the Indians gave the colony "full power and propriety to settle all the lands."

18   *Pa. Council Minutes*, 5:533, 536; Mulkearn, *Mercer Papers*, 161–62; "Treaty of Logg's Town," 167–68; Jennings, *Ambiguous Empire*, chap. 3.

19   Scarouady quoted in Gipson, *British Empire before the American Revolution*, 4:284.

20   Goodwin, *Journal of Captain William Trent*, 90–99; French version found in Duquesne to Minister of Marine, October 25, 1752, Thwaites, *Wisconsin Historical Collections*, 18:128–31; see also R. David Edmunds, "Old Briton," in idem, *American Indian Leaders*, 14–18.

21   La Jonquière to Rouillé, September 20, 1749, in Sylvester K. Stevens and Donald H. Kent, eds., *Wilderness Chronicles of Northwestern Pennsylvania*, 27; NYCD, 10:220; the most complete discussion of these issues is contained in former governor-general Galissonnière's "Memoir on the French Colonies in North America" (1750), in ibid., 220–32; ibid., 239–40; see also Eccles, "Fur Trade and Eighteenth Century Imperialism."

22   NYCD, 10:240–41; de Longueuil to Rouillé, April 21, 1752, ibid., 245–51; Earl of Albemarle to Earl of Holderness (Paris), March 1, 1752, ibid., 241–42; Peters to Penn, October 15, 1750, Penn MSS, Official Correspondence, 5:73, HSP; William Johnson to Clinton, September 25, 1750, NYCD, 6:600; Donald H. Kent, *The French Invasion of Western Pennsylvania*, 10–11.

23   De Longueuil to Rouillé, April 21, 1752, NYCD, 10:246; Bigot to Rouille, October 26, 1752, Stevens and Kent, *Wilderness Chronicles*, 39–40; the best summaries of Marin's expedition are found in Eccles, "Fur Trade and Eighteenth Century Imperialism," 356–62, and Kent, *French Invasion*, passim; see also Duquesne to Rouille, October 31, 1753, Stevens and Kent, *Wilderness Chronicles*, 55–58 (complaints about Canadian foot-dragging).

24 *Pa. Council Minutes*, 5:614–15; Walter Butler to William Johnson, June 12, 1753, *SWJP*, 9:106.

25 Hamilton to Dinwiddie, May 6, 1753, *Pa. Archives*, 4th ser., 2:182–83; Goodwin, *Trent Journal*, 21.

26 *Pa. Council Minutes*, 5:614–15; Tanaghrisson and Scarouady to Pennsylvania, June 22, 1753, ibid., 635.

27 Duquesne to Rouillé, August 20, 1753, *NYCD*, 10:256; Goodwin, *Trent Journal*, 18–21 (emphasis added).

28 Goodwin, *Trent Journal*, 23; Kent, *French Invasion*, 36–40, 53–55; Deposition of Stephen Coffin (January 10, 1754), Stevens and Kent, *Wilderness Chronicles*, 46–47.

29 Goodwin, *Trent Journal*, 19; *Pa. Council Minutes*, 5:155–56; Shawnees to Pennsylvania, February 8, 1752, ibid., 569; Kent, *French Invasion*, 52; Sylvester K. Stevens and Donald H. Kent, eds., *Journal of Chaussegros de Lery*, 28.

30 Kent, *French Invasion*, 51; Donald Jackson and Dorothy Twohig, eds., *The Diaries of George Washington, 1748–1770*, 1:11.

31 Goodwin, *Trent Journal*, 23–25; Hunter, *Forts on the Pennsylvania Frontier*, 25; periodic attacks continued into 1754, see Stevens and Kent, *Journal of de Lery*, 28, for Ojibwa-Delaware conflict.

32 Jackson and Twohig, *Diaries of Washington*, 1:15; *Pa. Council Minutes*, 5:666–68; Goodwin, *Trent Journal*, 17–18; Hunter, *Forts on the Pennsylvania Frontier*, 67.

33 John Frazer to [?], August 27, 1753, *Pa. Council Minutes*, 5:660; ibid., 666–69; Deposition of Stephen Coffin, Stevens and Kent, *Wilderness Chronicles*, 46–47; Kent, *French Invasion*, 47, 50–52; Peters to Thomas Penn, November 6, 1753, Penn MSS, Official Correspondence, 6:113, HSP.

34 *Pa. Council Minutes*, 5:685; on the Carlisle council see Boyd, *Indian Treaties*, esp. 129–31; Pennsylvanians seemed put out at the Indians' arrival, and the council was hastily organized with the barest of protocol—the colony wished to keep expenses to a minimum: see Boyd, *Indian Treaties*, 129, 134.

35 *Pa. Council Minutes*, 5:685; Boyd *Indian Treaties*, 130; CO 5/1328 ff., 896–924, on Winchester council.

36 Council between the Onondagas and La Jonquière, July 11, 1751, *NYCD*, 10:232–36; Peters to Thomas Penn, May 3, 1753, Penn MSS, Official Correspondence, 6:47, HSP; Hamilton to Assy, [July] 1753, *Pa. Council Minutes*, 5:635; Six Nations to Pennsylvania, [July] 1753, ibid., 637; ibid., 614–15; see also Johnson to Clinton, March 12, 1754, *SWJP*, 9:132.

37 Duquesne to Rouille, August 20, 1753, *NYCD*, 10:255–57; Duquesne to Rouille, October 7, 1753, Stevens and Kent, *Wilderness Chronicles*, 63.

38 *Pa. Council Minutes*, 5:645.

39 *SWJP*, 9:117 (emphasis added).

40 *Pa. Council Minutes*, 5:645; *NYCD*, 6:785–88, esp. 788 on Albany conference; Daniel Claus to Hamilton, January 10, 1754, *Pa. Archives*, 1st ser., 2:116; Hamilton to Assembly, May 22, 1753, ibid., 4th ser., 2:178–79; Jackson and Twohig, *Diaries of Washington*, 1:205 (Covenant Chain quotation); Jennings, *Empire of Fortune*, 80–84.

41 *Pa. Council Minutes*, 5:734, on request for forts; Hamilton to Dinwiddie, November 16, 1753, *Pa. Archives*, 4th ser., 2:211; Jackson and Twohig, *Diaries of Washington*, 1:141.

42 Jackson and Twohig, *Diaries of Washington*, 1:140–42, 147, 150–52.

43 Goodwin, *Trent Journal*, 38; *Pa. Council Minutes*, 5:732–33; Jackson and Twohig, *Diaries of Washington*, 1:144–46, 152.

44 Croghan to Hamilton, February 3, 1754, *Pa. Archives*, 1st ser., 2:119.

45 Donald H. Kent, ed., *Contrecoeur's Copy of George Washington's Journal for 1754*, 12; Jackson and Twohig, *Diaries of Washington*, 1:181–82; see also Trent to Washington, February 19, 1754, W. W. Abbot, and Dorothy Twohig, eds., *The Papers of George Washington, Colonial Series*, 1:68.

46 Washington to the Earl of Loudoun, January 10, 1757, Abbot and Twohig, *Papers of Washington*, 1:64; Washington to Dinwiddie, March 7, 1754, ibid., 72; ibid., 76 (n. 3); Washington to Dinwiddie, March 9, 1754, Brock, *Official Records of Dinwiddie*, 1:92.

47 Kent, *Contrecoeur's Copy of Washington's Journal*, 17, 24; Washington's version of the Jumonville affair is in Washington to Dinwiddie, May 29, 1754, Abbot and Twohig, *Papers of Washington*, 1:110–12, 114 nn. 12, 14; see also Dinwiddie to Sir Thomas Robinson, June 18, 1754, Brock, *Official Records of Dinwiddie*, 1:202–3; Scarouady's account is in Indian Affairs, fols. 250–51, APS (council at Philadelphia, December 20, 1754).

48 Kent, *Contrecoeur's Copy of Washington's Journal*, 27, 29–30; Washington to Dinwiddie, May 29, 1754, Abbot and Twohig, *Papers of Washington*, 1:112; Washington to Dinwiddie, June 3, 1754, ibid., 123; one Ohio Indian message to the British included the marks of Shingas, Delaware George, and Netawatwees in support of Tanaghrisson and Scarouady; see Indian Affairs, [1754], fols. 144–45, APS.

49 Kent, *Contrecoeur's Copy of Washington's Journal*, 36; Washington to Dinwiddie, June 3, 1754, Abbot and Twohig, *Papers of Washington*, 1:123; on the Aughwick remove, Andrew Montour to Hamilton, July 21, 1754, Indian Affairs, APS; on Fort Necessity, see Kent, *Contrecoeur's Copy of Washington's Journal*, 35; Jackson and Twohig, *Papers of Washington*, 1:155–56, 162 [n. 3]; Tanaghrisson quoted in *Pa. Council Minutes*, 6:151–52.

50 Croghan to Hamilton, August 16, 1754, *Pa. Council Minutes*, 6:141; ibid., 247, 150–59 (Tamaqua quoted on 156).

Chapter Six

1 Proceedings of the December 4 council are found in *BP*, 2:621–26; *Pa. Archives*, 1st ser., 3:571–74.

2 On the Delawares as "women," see Heckwelder, *History, Manners, and Customs*, 58–59; Jennings, *Ambiguous Empire*, 301–2; Jay Miller, "The Delaware as Women: A Symbolic Solution."

3 *Pa. Council Minutes*, 6:152–53.

4 Ibid., 150–51.

5 Ibid., 141, 156–57; Philadelphia council, December 20, 1754 (Scarouady) fols. 258, 260, Indian Affairs of Pennsylvania, APS; Croghan to Hamilton, December 2, 1754, *Pa. Archives*, 1st ser., 2:209.

6 For the opening phases of the Seven Years' War, see Lawrence Henry Gipson, *The British Empire before the American Revolution*, vol. 6, *The Great War for the Empire: The Years of Defeat, 1754–1757*, chaps. 4, 6; and Guy Fregault, *Canada: The War of the Conquest*, chaps. 1–3; for military affairs in the west, see Eccles, *Canadian Frontier*, chap. 8.

7 *Pa. Council Minutes*, 6:370–71; the Braddock-Shingas exchange was reported by a returned captive, Charles Stuart, to whom Shingas had meticulously explained his

motives for waging war: Beverly W. Bond, Jr., ed., "The Captivity of Charles Stuart, 1755–1757," 63–65; plans of the large fort Braddock intended to build at the Forks reflect British intent quite clearly and were doubtless shown to curious Indians when taken by the French at Braddock's defeat; see Charles M. Stotz, "Defense in the Wilderness," in Stotz and James, *Drums in the Forest*, 156–57; see also Wainwright, *George Croghan*, 88–94; Braddock's army took few Indians with it to the Ohio, and most of those were Iroquois led by Andrew Montour: D. Claus to Peters, Canajoharie, July 10, 1755, *SWJP*, 9:196, 199; on Ohio Indian hostilities in the wake of Braddock's defeat: *Pa. Council Minutes*, 6:703–5; *NYCD*, 10:408, 423; for a summary of these early raids, see Hunter, *Forts on the Pennsylvania Frontier*, 122–25; Jennings, *Empire of Fortune*, 164–66.

8   Bond, "Captivity of Charles Stuart," 63–65; *Pa. Council Minutes*, 6:766–68; ibid., 8:198.

9   *Pa. Council Minutes*, 6:682–87; Croghan to Johnson, May 15, 1755, *SWJP*, 1:496; also on Shawnees: Hamilton to Glen, October 30, 1753, *Pa. Archives*, 4th ser., 2:204; Hamilton to Dinwiddie, October 30, 1753, ibid., 207, 213; Hamilton to Tanaghrisson and Scarouady, n.d., ibid., 214–17; *Pa. Council Minutes*, 5:733; *Pa. Archives*, 1st ser., 2:414.

10   Washington to Dinwiddie, Great Meadows, June 3, 1754, Abbot and Twohig, *Papers of George Washington*, 1:123; Peters to Thomas Penn, September 11, 1753, Penn MSS, Official Correspondence, 6:105, HSP; Johnson to Board of Trade, May 28, 1756, *DHSNY*, 2:717–26; Thomas Pownall to Johnson, December 21, 1755, *SWJP*, 12:76–77; *Pa. Council Minutes*, 7:532. In 1758 the Shawnee headman Kakowatchiky (Ackowanothio), indignant about British inquiries as to why the Ohio Indians were at war, sent a letter to the Pennsylvanians with a bill of particulars. High on his list of causes was colonial "land hunger"; see *Pa. Archives*, 1st ser., 3:548–49; see also Daniel Claus to Johnson, April 5, 1756, *SWJP*, 2:438–40.

11   *Pa. Council Minutes*, 6:781–82; *Pa. Archives*, 1st ser., 3:548–49; Bond, "Captivity of Charles Stuart," 63–65; Hulbert and Schwarze, *Zeisberger's History*, 98, 100.

12   Hunter, *Forts*, 173, and chaps. 5 and 6 on border warfare in Pennsylvania; Bond, "Captivity of Charles Stuart," 60–61; Anthony F. C. Wallace, *King of the Delawares: Teedyuscung, 1700–1763*, chap. 6.

13   Lawrence Henry Gipson, *The British Empire before the American Revolution*, vol. 7, *The Great War for the Empire: The Victorious Years*, 36, 45, 46, 47, 52, 53; Hunter, *Forts*, 211, 307, 363, 380; Nicholas B. Wainwright, ed., "George Croghan's Journal, April 3, 1759 to April [30], 1763," passim, (on references to returned captives), 1759–61; Edmund de Schweinitz, ed., "The Narrative of Marie Le Roy and Barbara Leininger, for Three Years Captives among the Indians," 417–20; *Pa. Council Minutes*, 6:781–82 (number of captives); on private forts: William A. Hunter, ed., "Thomas Barton and the Forbes Expedition," 441; Elisha Saltar to Morris, Carlisle, April 5, 1756, *Pa. Archives*, 1st ser., 2:613; French reports include much detail on the activities of raiding parties based in the Ohio Country, though claims are doubtless inflated and based on partial and confused reports from the field: Vaudreuil to Minister of Marine, August 8, 1757, *NYCD*, 10:435–38; same to same, February 13, 1758, Stevens and Kent, *Wilderness Chronicles*, 108–10; same to same, June 10, 1758, ibid., 111; on the war along the Virginia border see Dinwiddie to Col. John Buchanan, August 11, 1755, Brock, *Official Records of Dinwiddie*, 2:154; Dinwiddie to Henry Fox, May 24, 1756, ibid., 413; Dinwiddie to Colonel Read, August 3, 1757, ibid.

14   Morris to Johnson, April 24, 1756, *SWJP*, 2:443; Heckewelder, quoted in Paul A. W.

Wallace, ed., *The Travels of John Heckewelder in Frontier America*, 38; Hunter, *Forts*, 380, Dinwiddie to Colonel Patton, August 1, 1755, Brock, *Official Records of Dinwiddie*, 2:132; Jerome H. Wood, Jr., *Conestoga Crossroads: Lancaster, Pennsylvania, 1730–1790*, 74–75; John Duffy, *Epidemics in Colonial America*, 87–88; Gipson, *British Empire before the American Revolution*, 7:34–53.

15   Paul A. W. Wallace, *Conrad Weiser, 1696–1760: Friend of Colonist and Mohawk*, 413–15.

16   *Pa. Council Minutes*, 7:74–76, 88–89; Johnson to Board of Trade, May 28, 1756, *DHSNY*, 2:721–22; on the bounties themselves, see Charles Hamilton, ed., *Braddock's Defeat*, 113; *Pa. Council Minutes*, 7:78; Dinwiddie to Washington, April 8, 1756, Brock, *Official Records of Dinwiddie*, 2:381–82; Daniel Claus to Johnson, April 5, 1756, *SWJP*, 2:438–40; on the Maryland volunteers: Forbes to General James Abercrombie, September 4, 1758, Alfred Proctor James, ed., *The Writings of John Forbes relating to His Service in North America*, 200.

17   Fauquier to Board of Trade, January 5, 1758, George Reese, ed., *The Official Papers of Francis Fauquier, Lieutenant Governor of Virginia, 1758–1768*, 1:146; Fauquier to W. H. Lyttleton, October 13, 1758, ibid., 89; Fauquier to Board of Trade, November 30, 1761, ibid., 2:597. On the history of scalp bounties and their moral implications, see Axtell, *European and the Indian*, 207–41; see also "A Narrative of Facts Furnished by Robert Robison," in Washburn, *Narrative of Indian Captivities*, 57:126: Armstrong's troops took at least fourteen scalps at Kittanning.

18   Smith, "Account of the Remarkable Occurrences in the Life and Travels of Colonel James Smith," 219; Myndert Wemp to Johnson, April 29, 1756, *NYCD*, 7:100–101; Johnson to Amherst, May 26, 1760, *SWJP*, 3:253; Howard H. Peckham, ed., "Thomas Gist's Indian Captivity, 1759," 301; [John M'Cullough], "A Narrative of the Captivity of John M'Cullough, Esq.," in Washburn, *Narratives of North American Indian Captivities*, 57:94; women seem to have borne a heavier share of domestic work during the war; see Schweinitz, "Narrative of Marie Le Roy and Barbara Leininger," 409.

19   Edward P. Hamilton, ed., *Adventures in the Wilderness: The American Journals of Louis Antoine de Bougainville, 1756–1760*, 204; *NYCD*, 10:840; Eccles, *Canadian Frontier*, 176; see also the geographic distribution of this and other epidemics in Tanner, *Atlas of Great Lakes Indian History*, 169–74, and map 32: "Epidemics among the Indians, c. 1630–1880"; Forbes's army, which entered the region in late summer 1758, was a mobile germ factory of major proportions, containing hundreds of men stricken with smallpox, "Fluxes, Diarhoas, Agues, [and] Fevers"; see Hunter, "Thomas Barton and the Forbes Expedition," 452.

20   Stevens and Kent, *Wilderness Chronicles*, 117; the Armstrong raid is examined in detail by William Hunter in "Victory at Kittanning"; see also *Pa. Council Minutes*, 7:341–43.

21   Croghan to Denny, April 2, 1757, ibid., 7:466; Forbes to Bouquet, June 27, 1758, James, *Writings of Forbes*, 124; Vaudreuil to Minister of Marine, August 8, 1756, Stevens and Kent, *Wilderness Chronicles*, 95; *NYCD*, 10:436; *Pa. Council Minutes*, 6:781–82.

22   On Teedyuscung see Wallace, *King of the Delawares*, esp. 108–9, 131–48; Jennings, *Empire of Fortune*, chap. 12.

23   Denny to Proprietors, April 9, 1757, *Pa. Archives*, 1st ser., 3:108–9; ibid., 147–48; *Pa. Council Minutes*, 7:514–17.

24   William A. Hunter, "Provincial Negotiations with the Western Indians, 1754–58," 217; Teedyuscung to Denny, August 30, 1757, *Pa. Council Minutes*, 7:725–26; ibid., 531; Denny to Johnson, November 20, 1757, *SWJP*, 2:752–53.

25 Teedyuscung to Denny, March 15, 1758, *Pa. Council Minutes*, 8:32–35; Hunter, "Provincial Negotiations," 218; Boyd, *Indian Treaties*, 223 (Easton Treaty Minutes, 1758).

26 Hamilton, *Adventures in the Wilderness*, 180; Fregault, *War of the Conquest*, 160–61, 213; Eccles, *Canadian Frontier*, 176–77, 179; *Pa. Council Minutes*, 7:341–43; *Pa. Archives*, 1st ser., 3:305–8.

27 Hamilton, *Adventures in the Wilderness*, 114, 204; *SWJP*, 2:774–75; ibid., 13:100; Thwaites, *Wisconsin Historical Collections*, 18:202; *Pa. Archives*, 1st ser., 3:147–48; James, *Writings of Forbes*, 116, 194.

28 *SWJP*, 13:100; Hamilton, *Adventures in the Wilderness*, 180; Thwaites, *Wisconsin Historical Collections*, 18:202, 209; *SWJP*, 2:774–75; *Pa. Council Minutes*, 7:531; *Pa. Archives*, 1st ser., 3:83.

29 Bond, "Captivity of Charles Stuart," 77; Johnson to Abercrombie, April 28, 1758, *SWJP*, 2:829–30.

30 Francis Jennings, "A Vanishing Indian: Francis Parkman versus His Sources," 307–8; *Pa. Council Minutes*, 8:142–45, 456–59; Forbes to Bouquet, June 16, 1758, James, *Writings of Forbes*, 115–16; Forbes to Bouquet, July 20, 1758, ibid.; see also Jennings, *Empire of Fortune*, chap. 17, on army-Quaker cooperation.

31 Thwaites, "Two Journals of Western Tours by Charles Frederick Post," in idem, *Early Western Travels*, 1:195, 200, 212. For another interpretation of Post's activities, see Walter T. Champion, Jr., "Christian Frederick Post and the Winning of the West.".

32 Thwaites, "Two Journals," 199, 212, 215, 221–22; *Pa. Archives*, 1st ser., 3:548–49; Timothy Alden, ed., "An Account of the Captivity of Hugh Gibson among the Delaware Indians of the Big Beaver and Muskingum from the Latter Part of July 1756 to the Beginning of April, 1759," 148.

33 Thwaites, "Two Journals," 213–14.

34 Boyd, *Indian Treaties*, 224; on Pisquetomen, see Jennings, *Empire of Fortune*, 392–93.

35 Boyd, *Indian Treaties*, 223; Charles M. Stotz, "Defense in the Wilderness," in James and Stotz, *Drums in the Forest*, 160; Thwaites, "Two Journals," 219.

36 Boyd, *Indian Treaties*, 213–44 (Easton Treaty, 1758); Jennings, "Vanishing Indian," 317.

37 Boyd, *Indian Treaties*, 215–43; "Benjamin Chew's Journal during the Easton Treaty of 1758," ibid., 307; Jennings, *Empire of Fortune*, 396–403.

38 Boyd, *Indian Treaties*, 237; *Pa. Council Minutes*, 8:206–8.

39 Forbes to Peters, October 16, 1758, James, *Writings of Forbes*, 234–35; Forbes to Fauquier, November 5, 1758, Reese, *Official Papers of Fauquier*, 1:102; Washington to Forbes, November 28, 1758, ibid., 115; see also Jennings, "Vanishing Indian," 317–18.

40 Thwaites, "Two Journals," 240.

41 Ibid., 256, 258, 273–74; *Pa. Council Minutes*, 8:206–8; James, *Writings of Forbes*, 251–53.

42 Thwaites, "Two Journals," 246–48.

43 Ibid., 254, 258.

44 Ibid., 254, 270–73.

45 Ibid., 271–72, 274–76, 278.

46 Ibid., 273.

47 Jennings, "Iroquois Alliances in American History," 52–53; John R. Alden, "The Albany Congress and the Creation of the Indian Superintendencies"; Jones, *License for Empire*, 38–39.

48 *SWJP*, 2:125–26; ibid., 9:234–38.

49 Ibid., 2:414, 9:368.

50 Jack Stagg, *Anglo-Indian Relations in North America to 1763, and an Analysis of the Royal Proclamation of 7 October 1763,* 210–17; Francis Jennings, "'Pennsylvania Indians' and the Iroquois," in Richter and Merrell, *Beyond the Covenant Chain,* 90–91; Jennings, "Iroquois Alliances," 54–55; Boyd, *Indian Treaties,* 215–43; "Benjamin Chew's Journal," ibid., 317.

51 Johnson to Gage, January 12, 1764, *SWJP,* 4:296; Johnson to Gage, January 27, 1764, ibid., 308; Johnson to Gage, March 16, 1764, ibid., 368; Clarence Walworth Alvord and Clarence Edwin Carter, eds., *Collections of the Illinois State Historical Library,* vol. 10, *The Critical Period, 1763–1765,* 273–80; Jones, *License for Empire,* 58–59; Peter Marshall, "Colonial Protest and Imperial Retrenchment: Indian Policy, 1764–1768," esp. 1–7.

52 Thwaites, "Two Journals."

53 *SWJP,* 3:444, 446–47.

54 Wainwright, *George Croghan,* 153; Bouquet to William Allen, November 25, 1758, *BP,* 2:611; Thwaites, "Two Journals," 274.

55 *BP,* 2:622–23

56 On the relocation of Ohio Indians see Tanner, *Atlas,* 46–47 and map 9: "The French Era, 1720–c. 1761."

57 On the impact of the war see Peckham, "Gist's Captivity," 301 (Wyandot town with no men at home); Schweinitz, "Narrative of Marie Le Roy and Barbara Leininger," 409.

58 Thwaites, "Two Journals," 288; *BP,* 2:623–24.

Chapter Seven

1 Wainwright, "Croghan's Journal," 316–17; *Pa. Council Minutes,* 8:382–93, esp. 386, 390.

2 *BP,* 3:507–11.

3 *Pa. Council Minutes,* 8:389; *BP,* 3:510–11; Wainwright, "Croghan's Journal," 344–436 passim.

4 Ibid., 330–31, 332; Croghan to General John Stanwix, July 23, 1759, *BP,* 3:450–51; Mercer to Stanwix, August 6, 1759, ibid., 503–4; Croghan to Stanwix, August 6, 1759, ibid., 502; *Pa. Council Minutes,* 8:396.

5 *BP,* 3:470; Wainwright, "Croghan's Journal," 317–18; Croghan to Horatio Gates, May 25, 1759, *BP,* 2:319–20; Bouquet to Captain Sinclair, August 8, 1759, ibid., 516; Stanwix to Denny, August 16, 1759, *Pa. Council Minutes,* 8:379; Bouquet to Gen. Robert Monckton, July 19, 1760, *BP,* 4:649–50.

6 Wainwright, "Croghan's Journal," 366; Croghan to Stanwix, July 21, 1759, *BP,* 3:434–35; *Pa. Council Minutes,* 8:311–12; John W. Jordan, ed., "James Kenny's 'Journal to ye Westward,' 1758–59," 433.

7 *Pa. Council Minutes,* 8:388–89; Wainwright, "Croghan's Journal," 350; Johnson to Gage, February 19, 1764, *SWJP,* 4:331.

8 *Pa. Council Minutes,* 8:387, 388–89, 430, 752.

9 Jack M. Sosin, *Whitehall and the Wilderness: The Middle West in British Policy, 1760–1775,* chap. 2, esp. 46.

10 Johnson to Board of Trade, May 17, 1759, *NYCD,* 7:375–78; Johnson to Earl of Egremont, May 1762, *SWJP,* 10:460–65; Egremont to Amherst, December 12, 1761, ibid., 3:588; Sosin, *Whitehall and the Wilderness,* 4; Louise Phelps Kellogg, *The British Regime in Wisconsin and the Northwest,* chap. 1 (on "interregnum").

11 Bouquet to Fauquier, February 8, 1762, Reese, *Official Papers of Fauquier,* 2:677–78; on

the army's role in the west see John Shy, *Toward Lexington: The Role of the British Army in the Coming of the American Revolution*, esp. chap. 2; Stanley McCrory Pargellis, *Lord Loudoun in America*, passim (on the administration of the army); on the concept of garrison government and its place in British imperial history see Stephen Saunders Webb, "Army and Empire: English Garrison Government in Britain and America, 1569–1763."

12   Shy, *Toward Lexington*, 98–99, 100–101, 116, 118; J. Clarence Webster, ed., *Journal of Jeffrey Amherst, Recording the Military Career of General Amherst in America from 1758 to 1763, 328–30, 332*; on dwindling troops strengths: Amherst to Bouquet, *March 20, 1761, BP*, 5:357–58; Bouquet to Major William Walters, April 25, 1761, ibid., 444–45; Pargellis, *Lord Loudoun*, 110–12.

13   On the occupation of the upper Ohio Valley: *BP*, 4:640–43, 669–70; Sylvester K. Stevens and Donald H. Kent, eds., *Wilderness Chronicles of Northwestern Pennsylvania*, 183–206; Bouquet quoted in Bouquet to Mrs. Gually [?], October 18, 1761, *BP*, 5:825–28.

14   On army logistics, Harry Kelsey, "The Amherst Plan: A Factor in the Pontiac Uprising," *Ontario History* 65 (1973): 149–58; on the condition of western garrisons, Stewart to Bouquet, December 20, 1760, Stevens and Kent, eds., *Wilderness Chronicles*, 199; Walters to Bouquet, September 15, 1760, *BP*, 5:188–90; Bouquet to Amherst, March 28, 1763, BP/BM Add. MSS. 21634, 147–48; on officers, Campbell to Bouquet, March 10, 1761, *BP*, 5: 340–41; Mather to Bouquet, March 11, 1761, ibid., 343; Cochrane to Bouquet, May 14, 1761, ibid., 480; discipline: de Couagne to Johnson, May 26, 1763, *SWJP*, 10:684; Bouquet to Monckton, July 21, 1761, *BP*, 5:654; Ensign Hay to Bouquet, October 10, 1760, ibid., 66; Bouquet to Amherst, April 7, 1763, BP/BM Add. MSS. 21634, 152; health, Meyer to Bouquet, October 22, 1761, *BP*, 5:833–37; Meyer to Bouquet, November 15, 1761, BP/BM Add. Mss. 21634, 195–96; Meyer to Bouquet, November 29, 1761, ibid., 213–14; quotations from Cochrane to Bouquet, June 30, 1761, *BP*, 5:600–602; Bouquet to Amherst, May 24, 1762, BP/BM Add. MSS. 133–34.

15   Campbell to Bouquet, May 21, 1761, *BP*, 5:491.

16   Croghan to Johnson, January 30, 1759, *SWJP*, 10:91–92; Meyer to Bouquet, December 9, 1761, BP/BM Add. MSS. 21647, 232; Kellogg, *British Regime*, 10–12, on Michilimackinac; Bouquet to Monckton, January 26, 1761, *BP*, 5:265. The scramble evidently quickly saturated the market: latecomers like Frederick Hambach found few opportunities at Detroit by late spring 1761; see Hambach to Bouquet, May 24, 1761, *BP*, 503.

17   On native participation in the Ohio trade see Wainwright, "Croghan's Journal," 399–437 passim; Campbell to Bouquet, June 8, 1761, *BP*, 5:533; on the dispersal of traders: Wainwright, "Croghan's Journal," 399, 421; John W. Jordan, ed., "Journal of James Kenny, 1761–1763," 26; Wallace, *Travels of John Heckewelder*, 41; [James Gorrell], "Lieutenant James Gorrell's Journal," 37; liquor abuse: Campbell to Bouquet, May 21, 1761, *BP*, 5:492; Campbell to Bouquet, June 1, 1761, ibid., 517; Jordan, "Journal of Kenny," 38; Wainwright, "Croghan's Journal," 422; Johnson to John Tabor Kempe, December 18, 1762, *SWJP*, 3:976–77; Bouquet to Monckton, March 18, 1761, *BP*, 5:349; Amherst to Johnson, February 22, 1761, *SWJP*, 3:343–45.

18   Theodore Thayer, *Pennsylvania Politics and the Growth of Democracy, 1740–1776*, 80; for examples of friction between traders: Jordan, "James Kenny's Journal," 437–38; Jordan, "Journal of Kenny," 13–14, 18, 34; Fort Pitt traders to Bouquet, February 27, 1761, *BP*, 5:315; Bouquet to John Langdale, February 28, 1761, ibid., 317; Langdale to Bouquet, March 5, 1761, ibid., 328–31, 332–33; Langdale to Bouquet, October 1, 1761, ibid., 791–92; Adam Stephen to Fauquier, October 29, 1759, Reese, *Official Papers of*

Fauquier, 1:258; on the Friendly Association: Jennings, *Empire of Fortune*, 28; Mulkearn, *Mercer Papers*, 153–64, for Pennsylvania's attempt to regulate trade in 1759; on Quaker confrontations with the army and Indian Department, Peters to Monckton, August 29, 1760, "The Aspinwall Papers," 9:305; Bouquet to Croghan, June 14, 1763, BP/BM Add. MSS. 21648, 178–79; Indian perceptions of Quaker influence vs. royal government, Johnson to Amherst, May 26, 1762, *SWJP*, 3:744.

19 Johnson to Thomas Pownall, September 7, 1757, *SWJP*, 2:737; Washington to Fauquier, December 2, 1758, Reese, *Official Papers of Fauquier*, 1:117–18; John Mercer to Fauquier, November 1759, ibid., 259–61; Fauquier to Board of Trade, December 1, 1759, ibid., 275–76; see also James, *Ohio Company*, chap. 8; Mulkearn, *Mercer Papers*, 49–152.

20 Forbes to Amherst, January 26, 1759, James, *Writings of John Forbes*, 283; Forbes to Amherst, January 28, 1759, ibid., 286; Johnson to Board of Trade, May 17, 1759, *DHSNY*, 2:781–85; Francis Jennings, "The Imperial Revolution: The American Revolution as a Tripartite Struggle for Sovereignty," in Jennings, *American Indian and the American Revolution*, 42–59; idem, "The Indians' Revolution," in Young, *American Revolution*.

21 The most complete study of the British Indian Department is Robert S. Allen, *The British Indian Department and the Frontier in North America, 1755–1830*, esp. 7–22, on the formative years of the deparment; Johnson to Board of Trade, October 8, 1764, Alvord and Carter, *Collections*, 10:327–42.

22 Johnson to de Lancey, August 8, 1755, *SWJP*, 1:841; see also ibid., 212–13, 217–20.

23 A recent summary of Amherst's American career can be found in *DCB*, s.v. "Amherst, Jeffery, lst Baron Amherst"; Amherst to Johnson, July 8, 1761, *SWJP*, 3:505; Amherst to Johnson, August 9, 1761, ibid., 514–15; Edward P. Hamilton, *Sir William Johnson, Colonial American*, 275–77 (on the Montreal campaign); for examples of Amherst on Indians, see, WO 34/23 Amherst to Colonel Farquar, September 11, 1759; Amherst to Monckton, November 3, 1760, "Aspinwall Papers," 347; Amherst to Johnson, June 24, 1761, *SWJP*, 3:421; Amherst to Johnson, August 18, 1761, ibid., 519; on Amherst's difficulties with the home government, Shy, *Toward Lexington*, 89–106; on Johnson's ties to colonies and home government, David S. McKeith, "The Inadequacy of Men and Measures in English Imperial History: Sir William Johnson and the New York Politicians, a Case Study" (Ph.D. diss.); Johnson to Board of Trade, May 17, 1759, *DHSNY*, 2:784; Johnson to the Earl of Egremont, May 1762, *SWJP*, 10:460–65; Johnson to Daniel Claus, March 10, 1761, ibid., 3:354. There is as yet no study on Amherst's American career that directs attention to his views of, and relations with, Indians, but see two older biographies: John Cuthbert Long, *Lord Jeffrey Amherst*, and Lawrence Shaw Mayo, *Jeffrey Amherst: A Biography*.

24 On the Cherokee wars, Stagg, *Anglo-Indian Relations in North America*, 254; W. Stitt Robinson, *The Southern Colonial Frontier 1607–1763*, 217–23; Croghan to Horatio Gates, May 20, 1760, "Aspinwall Papers," 247.

25 Quotation from Wainwright, "Croghan's Journal," 355; *BP*, 5:625; *Pa. Council Minutes*, 8:391; Mercer to Bouquet, August 20, 1759, *BP*, 3:591–92; Campbell to Monckton, June 1, 1761, "Aspinwall Papers," 416; Wainwright, "Croghan's Journal," 416, 419–20, 422, 423–24, 431–32; Lieutenant Meyer to Bouquet, September 30, 1761, *BP*, 5:786–88; Ensign Pauli to Bouquet, February 19, 1762, BP/BM Add. MSS. 21648, 33; Jordan, "Journal of Kenny," 153.

26 *Pa. Archives*, 1st ser., 3:746; *BP*, 5:152.

27 Meyer to Bouquet, October 22, 1761, *BP*, 5:833; same to same, November 8, 1761,

BP/BM Add. MSS. 21647, 188–89; Lt. Stair Campbell Carre to Bouquet, February 2, 1762, ibid., 21648, 17; Campbell to Bouquet, December 11, 1760, *BP*, 5:170; Carre to Bouquet, August 30, 1761 (corn), ibid., 721–22; Monckton Papers, 40: Fort Pitt, Accounts and Receipts, 1760–61.

28 Mathers to Bouquet, January 29, 1761, *BP*, 5:273; Stewart to Monckton, August 22, 1760 (prices), Monckton Papers, 38; Bouquet to Lieutenant Guy, May 18, 1762, BP/BM Add. MSS. 21653, 129–30; Holmes to Bouquet, May 17, 1762, ibid., 21648, 52–53; Johnson to Amherst, January 7, 1762, *SWJP*, 3:601; Meyer to Bouquet, October 12, 1761, *BP*, 5:819–20; Carre to Bouquet, November 26, 1761, BP/BM Add. MSS. 21647, 208.

29 Kent, *Iroquois Indians*, 2:216; Archer Butler Hulbert and William Nathaniel Schwarze, eds., "The Diaries of David Zeisberger relating to the First Missions in the Ohio Basin," 103; Sergeant McDonald to Bouquet, April 10, 1762, BP/BM Add. MSS. 21648, 61; same to same, April 15, 1761, ibid., 69–70; Bouquet to Amherst, March 24, 1761, ibid., 75–76; Jordan, "Journal of Kenny," 158; Wainwright, "Croghan's Journal," 423.

30 Stewart to Monckton, August 18, 1760, Northcliffe Collection, Monckton Papers, 38; Jordan, "Journal of Kenny," 10; Monckton Papers, 41, on Indian expenses at Fort Pitt.

31 On desertion and motives, Bouquet to Monckton, July 27, 1761, *BP*, 5:660; William Harris to Bouquet, November 23, 1762, BP/BM Add. MSS. 21648, 160–61; Bouquet to Amherst, October 5, 1762, ibid., 21634, 99–100; Bouquet to Amherst, December 1, 1763, ibid., 294; on Niagara deserters: WO 34/22, Court-Martial at Fort Niagara, December 4, 1762; ibid., Amherst to Major Wilkins, December 5, 1762; *SWJP*, 3:700; on Sandusky and Detroit, Campbell to Bouquet, July 7, 1761, *BP*, 5:618–20; Bouquet to Amherst, February 3, 1762, BP/BM Add. MSS. 21634, 63–64.

32 Wainwright, "Croghan's Journal," 369; WO 34/21, Major Walters to Amherst, September 15, 1760; Johnson to Major Wilkins, December 22, 1762, *SWJP*, 13:280–81.

33 On Owen, BP/BM Add. MSS. 21655, 264, where he is listed as "John Owens"; Bouquet to Johnson, November 15, 1764, *SWJP*, 4:586; Johnson to Bouquet, December 17, 1764, ibid., 620; ibid., 10:451; Johnson to Bouquet, February 20, 1765; ibid., 585; David Jones, *A Journal of Two Visits Made to Some Nations of Indians on the West Side of the River Ohio in the Years 1772 and 1773*, 18.

Chapter Eight

1 Croghan to Horatio Gates, May 21, 1760, "Aspinwall Papers," 252; Wainwright, "Croghan's Journal," 365; on Swain, Captain Richard Mather to Bouquet, February 13, 1761, *BP*, 5:295; Cochrane to Bouquet, June 30, 1761, ibid., 600; Lieutenant Gordon to Bouquet, August 18, 1762, BP/BM Add. MSS. 21648, 63–64.

2 *SWJP*, 13:227–28; Bouquet to Lt. Stair Campbell Carre, October 15, 1761, *BP*, 5:822; on theft, *SWJP*, 3:453; 13:227–28; on theft of Indian horses, ibid., 10:329; soldiers' attacks on Indians, Lieutenant Carre to Bouquet, November 5, 1761, BP/BM Add. MSS. 21647, 184; Lieutenant Carre to Bouquet, July 3, 1761, ibid., 5:613.

3 Little work has yet been done on the use of horses among northeastern Indians, but see Clifton, *Prairie People*, 128–29, for suggestive material on the Potawatomis; Jordan, "James Kenny's Journal," 437; Mercer to Bouquet, August 15, 1759, *BP*, 3:566; see also Merrell, *Indians' New World*, 184, 189, for horses and horse theft among the Catawbas.

4 Wainwright, "Croghan's Journal," 324, 352; *Pa. Council Minutes*, 8:385; *SWJP*, 3:531–32; Croghan to Gen. John Stanwix, August 6, 1759, *BP*, 3:502.

5   Callender to Bouquet, May 23, 1761, *BP*, 5:501; Bouquet to Monckton, July 24, 1761, ibid., 654.

6   Amherst to Johnson, January 12, 1762, *SWJP*, 3:792; Amherst to Major Walters, September 12, 1760, WO 34/23; Johnson to Amherst, February 12, 1761, *SWJP*, 3:331; ibid., 214; Amherst to Johnson, August 14, 1763, ibid., 4:189; on liquor and its effects, Johnson to Amherst, April 1, 1762, ibid., 3:664–65; Wainwright, "Croghan's Journal," 358; Johnson to Board of Trade, June 18, 1757, *DHSNY*, 2:745–48; Croghan to Horatio Gates, May 23, 1760, "Aspinwall Papers," 252; restrictions on weapons, Capt. Donald Campbell to Johnson, June 9, 1762, *SWJP*, 3:758; Amherst to Johnson, May 7, 1761, ibid., 387–88.

7   Pennsylvania trade regulations are found in Mulkearn, *Mercer Papers*, 153–65; Johnson's proposed regulations are found in *SWJP*, 3:531–32 (for Fort Pitt), 533 (Sandusky), 534–35 (Fort Miami); traders' passes are preserved in WO 34/22; on evasion of regulations, Jordan, "Journal of James Kenny," 26, 31; Wainwright, "Croghan's Journal," 421; Lieutenant Carre to Bouquet, February 2, 1762, BP/BM Add. MSS. 21648, 17; Lt. Archibald Blane to Bouquet, March 12, 1762, ibid., 46; Johnson to Amherst, September 24, 1762, *SWJP*, 3:883; BP/BM Add. MSS. 21655, 221–22; ibid., 21654, 122–23; Johnson quoted in Johnson to John Tabor Kempe, December 18, 1762, *SWJP*, 3:976–77.

8   Amherst to Maj. William Walters, January 17, 1761, WO 34/23; Amherst to Johnson, April 3, 1763, *SWJP*, 10:649; Amherst to Monckton, August 2, 1760, "Aspinwall Papers," 291; Bouquet to Capt. Simeon Ecuyer, February 18, 1763, BP/BM Add. MSS.. 21653, 171–72; on gifts as bribes, Amherst to Bouquet, July 25, 1762, ibid., 21634, 95–96; Amherst to Johnson, August 9, 1761, *SWJP*, 3:515; Amherst to Johnson, December 20, 1761, ibid., 594; see also Croghan to [?], March 23, 1762, Cadwallader Collection, George Croghan Papers, sec. 23, HSP, on Amherst and Indian Department expenses.

9   The foregoing is based on Mauss, *Gift*, esp. chap. 1; Sahlins, *Stone Age Economics*, 150, 153, 155, 169, 174, 183; Wilbur R. Jacobs, *Wilderness Politics and Indian Gifts: The Northern Colonial Frontier, 1748–1763*, 13–18 and passim; Francis Jennings, *The Invasion of America: Indians, Colonialism, and the Cant of Conquest*, 122–23.

10 Croghan to Horatio Gates, May 1, 1760, "Aspinwall Papers," 246–47; Croghan to Bouquet, December 10, 1762, *SWJP*, 10:597; Johnson to Amherst, June 21, 1761, ibid., 291; Johnson to Amherst, January 21, 1763, ibid., 612; "custom" quotation in Campbell to Bouquet, May 21, 1761, *BP*, 5:491; Wainwright, "Croghan's Journal," 403; for local commanders taking latitude, Major Walters to Amherst, August 14, 1760, WO 34/21; [Gorrell], "Lieutenant James Gorrell's Journal," 32; Campbell to Johnson, June 9, 1762, *SWJP*, 3:758; Campbell to Bouquet, June 3, 1762, BP/BM Add. MSS. 21648, 1–2; Campbell to Bouquet, August 28, 1762, ibid., 74–75; Campbell to Bouquet, October 27, 1762, ibid., 132–33; for rigorous enforcement of Amherst's policy in the Ohio Country, Bouquet to Ecuyer, February 18, 1763, ibid., 21653, 171–72; Croghan to Johnson, May 10, 1762, *SWJP*, 3:733; Croghan to Johnson, October 8, 1762, ibid., 10:549.

11 Wainwright, "Croghan's Journal," 423–24; Croghan to Johnson, March 31, 1762, *SWJP*, 3:663; Croghan to Johnson, October 8, 1762, ibid., 10:548–49; Croghan to Bouquet, November 25, 1762, BP/BM Add. MSS. 21648, 167–68.

12 *Pa. Council Minutes*, 8:388; BP/BM Add. MSS. 21655, 98; Wainwright, "Croghan's Journal," 324; Jordan, "Journal of Kenny," 185; Croghan to Monckton, July 26, 1761, Cadwallader Collection, George Croghan Papers, sec. 23, HSP.

13   Jordan, "Journal of Kenny," 194, 196; Edward St. Leger to Bouquet, June 22, 1762, BP/BM Add. MSS. 21648, 161; Capt. Henry Balfour to Miamis, September 25, 1761, *SWJP*, 10:322; ibid., 3:693; John Baird to Bouquet, June 8, 1762, BP/BM Add. MSS. 21648, 137; Croghan to Monckton, April 19, 1761, Cadwallader Collection, George Croghan Papers, sec. 23, HSP.

14   Wainwright, "Croghan's Journal," 432; Croghan to Johnson, December 22, 1759, *SWJP*, 10:131–32; Johnson to Amherst, March 18, 1763, ibid., 624; Peters to Monckton, September 18, 1760, "Aspinwall Papers," 324–27.

15   Johnson to Croghan, July 26, 1761, *SWJP*, 10:319; Ensign Pauli to Bouquet, February 19, 1762, BP/BM Add. MSS. 21648, 33.

16   Croghan to Johnson, July 25, 1761, *SWJP*, 10:316; on the Mississauga exchange, ibid., 3:455–56.

17   Sgt. Angus McDonald to Bouquet, October 25, 1761, *BP*, 5:840; Bouquet to James Livingston, October 31, 1761, ibid., 847; Bouquet to Fauquier, February 8, 1762, Reese, *Official Papers of Fauquier*, 2:677; Croghan to Johnson, May 10, 1762, *SWJP*, 10:452.

18   Bouquet to Fauquier, February 8, 1762, Reese, *Official Papers of Fauquier*, 2:667–68; *BP*, 5:844; Bouquet to Amherst, April 1, 1762, BP/BM Add. MSS. 21634, 81–85; Thayer, *Pennsylvania Politics*, 80.

19   Fauquier to Bouquet, January 17, 1762, Reese, *Official Papers of Fauquier*, 2:663–64; Bouquet to Fauquier, February 8, 1762, ibid., 677–78; Amherst to Fauquier, February 28, 1762, ibid., 693; Bouquet to Cresap, September 12, 1760, *BP*, 5:32; Thomas Hay to Bouquet, April 9, 1761, ibid., 401.

20   Thayer, *Pennsylvania Politics*, 77.

21   "Aspinwall Papers," 240–42; compare this version of Amherst's message with later efforts to make his plans more acceptable to the natives: see *BP*, 4:531–36; *SWJP*, 3:34, 214; Amherst to Hamilton, March 30, 1760, ibid., 205–6; Amherst to Johnson, June 11, 1761, ibid., 506; BP/BM Add. MSS. 21653, 46–47.

22   The material above is based on "A List of Houses and Inhabitants at Fort Pitt, 24 April 1761," *BP*, 5:407–21, and an analysis of these data found in James Patrick McClure, "The Ends of the American Earth: Pittsburgh and the Upper Ohio Valley to 1795" (Ph.D. diss.), 61–68; Bouquet to Cochrane, July 12, 1761, *BP*, 5:629–30; Bouquet to Monckton, March 20, 1761, ibid., 355.

23   Amherst to William Sharpe, October 20, 1762, WO 34/74; Amherst to Johnson, August 9, 1761, *SWJP*, 3:515; Rutherford to Johnson, May 12, 1761, ibid., 10:265–66; Amherst to Pitt, May 4, 1761, Gertrude Selwyn Kimball, ed., *Correspondence of William Pitt, When Secretary of State, with Colonial Governors and Military and Naval Commissioners in America*, 2:426–27; on the size of the grant: Johnson to Colonel Vaughan, August 15, 1765, *SWJP*, 11:895; Rutherford's petition is in Rutherford to Amherst, April 28, 1761, WO 34/21.

24   Rutherford to Amherst, April 28, 1761, WO 34/21; Amherst to Major Walters, July 25, 1761, WO 34/23; Johnson to Walters, April 29, 1761, *SWJP*, 3:728; Johnson to Amherst, July 29, 1761, ibid., 10:320–21.

25   Johnson to Amherst, July 29, 1761, *SWJP*, 10:320–21; Johnson to Daniel Claus, May 20, 1761, ibid., 270.

26   Walters to Amherst, July 30, 1761, WO 34/21.

27   Amherst to Johnson, August 7, 1761, *SWJP*, 3:515; Amherst to Walters, August 9, 1761, WO 34/23; Amherst to Major Wilkins, October 17, 1762, ibid.; Johnson to Walters,

April 29, 1762, *SWJP*, 3:728; Henry van Schaak to Johnson, November 7, 1762, ibid., 928; Amherst to William Sharpe, October 20, 1762, WO 34/74.

28 On the origin of the belts, see Croghan to Monckton, October 3, 1761, Cadwallader Collection, George Croghan Papers, sec. 23, HSP; Wainwright, "Croghan's Journal," 409–10; *SWJP*, 3:459–60.

29 Campbell to Amherst, June 17, 1761, *SWJP*, 3:348–49; ibid., 456, 460; Wainwright, "Croghan's Journal," 410–11.

30 Major Walters to Amherst, June 29, 1761, WO 34/21; Wainwright, "Croghan's Journal," 411; *SWJP*, 3:456, 460; Campbell to Croghan, May 10, 1761, Cadwallader Collection, George Croghan Papers, sec. 12, HSP.

31 *SWJP*, 3:439, 440, 462, 465; Campbell to Amherst, June 17, 1761, ibid., 348–49. For a different interpretation of Seneca involvement, see Gregory Evans Dowd, "The French King Wakes up in Detroit: 'Pontiac's War' in Rumor and History," 258–59. Dowd's work represents a significant advance in our understanding of Great Lakes Indians' motives for war in 1763.

32 *SWJP*, 3:697–98; see also Wallace, *Death and Rebirth of the Seneca*, 47–48; DCB, s.v. "Kayahsota."

33 Campbell to Bouquet, June 16, 1761, *BP*, 5:555–56; Wainwright, "Croghan's Journal," 410–11.

34 Campbell to Bouquet, July 7, 1761, *BP*, 5:618–20; Campbell to Johnson, July 8, 1761, *SWJP*, 3:449, 452, 453.

35 Campbell to Major William Walters, June 17, 1761, *BP*, 5:560–61.

36 Bouquet to Campbell, June 30, 1761, *BP*, 5:596–97; Wainwright, "Croghan's Journal," 408; Alexander Henry, *Travels and Adventures in Canada and the Indian Territories between the Years 1760 and 1776*, 44–45.

37 On the importance of 1763 in Indian-English relations see Wilbur R. Jacobs, *Dispossessing the American Indian: Indians and Whites on the Colonial Frontier*, chap. 9.

38 Jordan, "Journal of Kenny," 43, 156–57, 163; Campbell to Bouquet, February 10, 1762, BP/BM Add. MSS. 21648, 22–23; Croghan to Johnson, March 31, 1762, *SWJP*, 3:663.

39 Jordan, "Journal of Kenny," 152; Croghan to Bouquet, November 25, 1762, BP/BM Add. MSS. 21648, 167–68; Heckewelder and Pipe, quoted in Wallace, *Travels of John Heckewelder*, 41–42; on Pipe see Wallace, *Indians in Pennsylvania*, 180.

40 Ensign Pauli to Bouquet, August 8, 1762, BP/BM Add. MSS. 21648, 48; Campbell to Bouquet, August 4, 1762, ibid., 42–43; Ensign Christie to Bouquet, August 15, 1762, ibid., 57; Jordan, "Journal of Kenny," 165–66; Amherst to Major Wilkins, November 21, 1762, WO 34/23.

41 *SWJP*, 3:543; Campbell to Bouquet, October 12, 1761, *BP*, 5:815; Amherst to Johnson, December 20, 1761, *SWJP*, 3:594; Lieutenant Carre to Bouquet, December 24, 1761, BP/BM Add. MSS. 21647, 241; Heckewelder, *History, Manner, and Customs*, 159; the same severe weather that plagued Ohio Indian hunters also wrought havoc with the army: floods from spring melt-offs and an early thaw inundated Fort Pitt and destroyed precious supplies and a good part of the ramparts. See Charles M. Stotz, "Defense in the Wilderness," in James and Stotz, *Drums in the Forest*, 169–72.

42 BP/BM Add. MSS. 21655, 171–73; Duffy, *Epidemics in Colonial America*, 198–99; for Hutchins's instructions, BP/BM Add. MSS. 21655, 185–86; Hutchins's journal is in ibid., 167–74, and *SWJP*, 10:521–29; see also Jordan, "Journal of Kenny," 169.

43   BP/BM Add. MSS. 21655, 169, 171, 172, 173–74.

44   BP/BM Add. MSS. 21655, 167–74; Wainwright, "Croghan's Journal," 423–24; Croghan to Bouquet, November 25, 1762, BP/BM Add. MSS. 21648, 167–68; Croghan to Johnson, October 5, 1762, SWJP, 3:890.

45   On Neolin's revitalization movement, see Charles E. Hunter, "The Delaware Nativist Revivial of the Mid-Eighteenth Century"; Anthony F. C. Wallace, "New Religious Beliefs among the Delaware Indians, 1600–1900," 9; idem, "Revitalization Movements: Some Theoretical Considerations for Their Comparative Study"; Dowd, "French King Wakes up in Detroit," 259–61; for details of Neolin's teaching as understood by one colonial observer, see Jordan, "Journal of Kenny," 171–75, 188.

46   Hunter, "Delaware Nativist Revival," 40; Jordan, "Journal of Kenny," 12; Croghan to Johnson, July 25, 1761, SWJP, 10:316; Wainwright, "Croghan's Journal," 410.

47   Wallace, Travels of Heckewelder, 67; on the background to the Lancaster Treaty, see Wainwright, George Croghan, chap. 9; text appears in Boyd, Indian Treaties, 263–98; Jordan, "Journal of Kenny," 161–62; Wainwright, "Croghan's Journal," 426; on Delaware responses, Jordan, "Journal of Kenny," 175; Wainwright, "Croghan's Journal," 426–27, 429.

48   Jordan, "Journal of Kenny," 157, 168, 170; Wainwright, "Croghan's Journal," 426; Heckewelder, History, Manners, and Customs, 253, on the subsequent influential role of Netawatwees.

49   Jordan, "Journal of Kenny," 169–70; Captain Ecuyer to Bouquet, November 25, 1762, BP/BM Add. MSS. 21653, 160–61; Bouquet to Amherst, December 12, 1762, BP/BM Add. MSS. 21634, 116–17; Ensign Holmes to Gladwin, March 30, 1763, WO 34/49; Croghan to Amherst, December 10, 1762, SWJP, 3:965; Croghan to Bouquet, December 10, 1762, ibid., 10:597.

50   Bouquet to Amherst, December 12, 1762, BP/BM Add. MSS. 21634, 116–17; on the treaty news see Tanner, Atlas of Great Lakes Indian History, 48; Wainwright, "Croghan's Journal," 436–38; Jordan, "Journal of Kenny," 187; Croghan to Amherst, April 30, 1763, BP/BM Add. MSS. 21634, 158–59; Gladwin to Amherst, February 21, 1763, WO 34/49; Wainwright, "Croghan's Journal," 438.

51   On Canadian influence among the Indians, SWJP, 10:534; Johnson to Amherst, March 18, 1763, ibid., 624; on La Baye, see [Gorrell], "Lieutenant James Gorrell's Journal," 24–27 and passim; Howard H. Peckham, Pontiac and the Indian Uprising, 165; on the Ohio Country, Captain Barnsley to Bouquet, June 13, 1762, BP/BM Add. MSS. 21648, 151–52; Wainwright, "Croghan's Journal," 399, 403; BP/BM Add. MSS. 21653, 54; on the 1763 conflict as a "defensive war" see R. Cole Harris and Geoffrey Matthews, eds., Historical Atlas of Canada, vol. 1, From the Beginning to 1800, map 44: "Indians' Defensive War of 1763"; Dowd, "French King Wakes up in Detroit," passim, for the Great Lakes Indians' quest for a restoration of the French regime. Capt. Gavin Cochrane, who served in the Ohio Country and at Fort Niagara before and during the war, offered a detailed explanation of the conflict that would have met with approval from Ohio Indian leaders, see Cochrane, "Treatise on the Indians of North America Written in the Year 1764," Ayer MSS. NA 176, chap. 7, Newberry Library.

52   A. T. Volwiler, ed., "William Trent's Journal at Fort Pitt, 1763," 393–94.

53   BP/BM Add. MSS. 21655, 212; Volwiler, "William Trent's Journal," 399.

54   Croghan to Johnson, July 2, 1763, SWJP, 10:728; on Delaware George see Jordan, "Journal of Kenny," 154; Wainwright, "Croghan's Journal," 429; on Shingas see Hecke-

welder, *History, Manners, and Customs*, 268–76; Hulbert and Schwarze, *Zeisberger's History*, 88–90; Weslager, *Delaware Indians*, 99–100.

55 BP/BM Add. MSS. 21655, 221–22, 249–50; *SWJP*, 10:685–88.

56 Volwiler, "William Trent's Journal," 405–8.

57 Johnson to Amherst, June 6, 1763, *NYCD*, 7:522–23; ibid., 553–54; *SWJP*, 10:769, 902–3; Johnson to Gage, November 8, 1764, ibid., 11:400; ibid., 619; Walter Pilkington, ed., *The Journals of Samuel Kirkland, Eighteenth-Century Missionary to the Iroquois, Government Agent, Father of Hamilton College*, 21–28; Johnson to Amherst, October 6, 1763, *SWJP*, 10:866–68; ibid., 770.

58 *SWJP*, 10:767–78; ibid., 11:228–29; Bouquet to Johnson, November 30, 1764, ibid., 4:607; ibid., 627–28; on Great Lakes Indians' anticipation of French restoration see Dowd, "French King Wakes up in Detroit," 261–71; on Kelerac, *SWJP*, 10:819–23; ibid., 13:317–21; Peckham, *Pontiac*, 192–93.

59 Volwiler, "Trent's Journal," 399; Johnson to Amherst, October 6, 1763, *SWJP*, 10:866–67; Croghan to Johnson, July 2, 1763, ibid., 727–28.

60 BP/BM Add. MSS. 21655, 202; on regional cooperation, *SWJP*, 11:228–29; ibid., 4:553–55, 504; *NYCD*, 7:583; Alvord and Carter, *Collections*, 10: 306; on Shawnees, Croghan to Johnson, May 13, 1765, *SWJP*, 11:737.

61 Peckham, *Pontiac*, 167, 224–25; Tanner, *Atlas*, 48–50; Johnson to Amherst, June 16, 1763, BP/BM Add. MSS. 21634, 212–13; Bouquet to Amherst, September 7, 1763, ibid., 263; Amherst to Bouquet, October 3, 1763, ibid., 281–82.

62 Croghan to Johnson, July 2, 1763, *SWJP*, 10:727–28; BP/BM Add. MSS. 21655, 208–9; Ecuyer to Bouquet, June 26, 1763, BP/BM Add. MSS. 21648, 175–76.

63 Lt.-Col. William Browning to Johnson, October 22, 1763, *SWJP*, 10:906; Jean-Baptiste de Couagne to Johnson, November 11, 1763, ibid., 921.

64 Bouquet to Amherst, June 14, 1763, BP/BM Add. MSS. 21634, 191; Bouquet to Amherst, June 29, 1763, ibid., 205; Fauquier to Amherst, August 2, 1763, Reese, *Official Papers of Fauquier*, 2:1001; Gage to Halifax, July 13, 1764, Alvord and Carter, *Collections*, 10:284; Harris, *Historical Atlas of Canada*, vol. 1, map 44: "Indians' Defensive War, 1763," for the extent of native attacks in 1763–64.

65 Alden T. Vaughan, "Frontier Banditti and the Indians: The Paxton Boys' Legacy, 1763–1775," 1–3; James Axtell, *The European and the Indian: Essays in the Ethnohistory of Colonial North America*, 207–41, for additional context see also Henry J. Young, "A Note on Scalp Bounties in Pennsylvania."

66 "A Declaration and Remonstrance," in John R. Dunbar, ed., *The Paxton Papers*, 101–4, 108; "An Historical Account of the Late Disturbances," ibid., 129; "The Squabble a Pastoral Ecologue," ibid., 145; see also [Benjamin Franklin], "A Narrative of the Late Massacres," ibid., 57–75; Vaughan, "Frontier Banditti," 3–4; see also Brooke Hindle, "The March of the Paxton Boys."

67 For Pennsylvania's scalp bounty see *Pa. Council Minutes*, 9:190–92; "open season" taken from Vaughan, "Frontier Banditti," 2.

68 Amherst to Johnson, May 29, 1763, *SWJP*, 10:688–89; Amherst to Bouquet, June 6, 1763, BP/BM Add. MSS. 21634, 181–82; Amherst to Bouquet, June 23, 1763, ibid., 197–98; Amherst's initial optimism was shared by Bouquet, who was destined to lead the regular forces in the west; see Bouquet to Amherst, June 25, 1763, ibid., 203.

69 On the 1763 operations see Peckham, *Pontiac*, 175, 206–7; Shy, *Toward Lexington*, 120–22; Amherst to Bouquet, July 16, 1763, BP/BM Add. MSS. 21634, 218–19; Amherst to

Bouquet, June 29, 1763, ibid., 204; Bouquet to Amherst, July 13, 1763, ibid., 214–15; Amherst to Bouquet, July 16, 1763, ibid., 216–17; Bouquet to Amherst, August 27, 1763, ibid., 250–51; on the use of dogs in warfare against Indians, see Mark A. Mastromarino, "Teaching Old Dogs New Tricks: The English Mastiff and the Anglo-American Experience."

70 Bouquet to Amherst, June 16, 1763, BP/BM Add. MSS. 21634, 189–90; Bouquet to Amherst, July 26, 1763, ibid., 222–24; Bouquet to Fauquier, April 11, 1764, Reese, *Official Papers of Fauquier*, 3:1094; BP/BM Add. MSS. 21650, 128–29.

71 Niles Anderson, "Bushy Run: Decisive Battle in the West"; this essay encapsulates the traditional view of the battle and its place in frontier history; Bouquet to Amherst, August 11, 1763, BP/BM Add. MSS. 21634, 243–44; Bouquet to Amherst, August 27, 1763, ibid., 250–51; Bouquet to Amherst, August 26, 1763, WO 34/40; Bouquet to Campbell, September 7, 1763; BP/BM Add. MSS. 21653, 219–20.

72 SWJP, 11:618; Bouquet to Amherst, August 11, 1763, BP/BM Add. MSS. 21634, 243–44; Bouquet to Campbell, September 7, 1763, BP/BM Add. MSS. 21653, 219–20.

73 BP/BM Add. MSS. 21634, 161; ibid., 214–15; see Bernard Knollenberg, "General Amherst and Germ Warfare," for a defense of Amherst and the rejoinder by Donald H. Kent, "Communications," 762–63.

74 Volwiler, "Trent's Journal," 400; BP/BM Add. MSS. 21654, 218–19, for receipts for the smallpox-infested clothing tendered to the trading firm that claimed the loss; on the European officers' code of conduct see Christopher Duffy, *The Military Experience in the Age of Reason*, 74–80.

75 Captain William Grant to Bouquet, April 15, 1764, BP/BM Add. MSS. 21650, pt. 1, 102; Colonel Andrew Lewis to Bouquet, September 10, 1764, ibid., pt. 2, 127; Brose, "Valley Sweets Site," 15–16; [M'Cullough], "Narrative of the Captivity of John M'Cullough," 102.

76 SWJP, 11:618; Edward Ward to Johnson, May 2, 1764, ibid., 169–70.

77 Bouquet to Amherst, July 3, 1763, BP/BM Add. MSS. 21634, 207–8; Amherst to Bouquet, October 16, 1763, ibid., 286; Gage to Johnson, April 22, 1764, SWJP, 4:404; ibid., 488; ibid., 11:284.

78 Johnson to Cadwallader Colden, October 24, 1763, SWJP, 4:274–75; ibid., 11:25–27; Johnson to Gage, July 30, 1764, ibid., 365–66; Gage to Johnson, February 20, 1764, ibid., 4:334; Bouquet to Johnson, October 21, 1764, ibid., 570–71.

79 Gage to Fauquier, February 28, 1764, Reese, *Official Papers of Fauquier*, 3:1089–90; Gage to Johnson, June 24, 1764, SWJP, 4:408–9; ibid., 11:244; Johnson to Board of Trade, January 20, 1764, NYCD, 7:600; Shy, *Toward Lexington*, 135–39; Tanner, *Atlas*, 50–51 and map 11: "Pontiac's War, 1763–1764: Principal Theatre; Harris, *Historical Atlas of Canada*, vol. 1, map 44: "Indians' Defensive War, 1763–64."

80 Gage to Johnson, June 24, 1764, SWJP, 11:244; on the issue of ammunition, see Capt. James Grant to Gage, April 2, 1764, Gage Papers, American Series, vol. 16, Clements Library; Shy, *Toward Lexington*, 135–36; on Bradstreet's army, see John Bradstreet Orderly Book (June 27 to November 29, 1764), Orderly Book Collection, American Antiquarian Society (microfilm); on Bouquet see Edward .G. Williams, ed. "The Orderly Book of Colonel Henry Bouquet's Expedition against the Ohio Indians, 1764"; idem, ed., *Bouquet's March to the Ohio: The Forbes Road*, passim.

81 SWJP, 11:25–27; Johnson to Colden, April 6, 1764, ibid., 4:386–87; ibid., 11:139–57; NYCD, 7:621–23.

82 Johnson to Colden, August 23, 1764, SWJP, 4:511–12; Johnson to Gage, August 5,

1764, ibid., 11:324–27; Johnson to Gage, September 30, 1764, ibid., 365–66; Johnson to the Earl of Halifax, August 30, 1764, *NYCD*, 7:647.

83   *SWJP*, 11:25–27; *NYCD*, 7:652–53; on Gaustarax, see *SWJP*, 11:619; Wallace, *Indians in Pennsylvania*, 175; Johnson to the Earl of Hillsborough, April 4, 1772, *NYCD*, 7:282–83, 291, and below.

84   The Niagara Treaty minutes are in *SWJP*, 11:262–324; ibid., 153–57; ibid., 4:500–501 (on captives); ibid., 291 (on Senecas against Ohio Indians); ibid., 11:310.

85   Ibid., 11:328–33; on Bradstreet's offer of peace, see *Pa. Council Minutes*, 9:194–97.

86   Gage's instructions to Bradstreet are found in Gage to Bradstreet, April 2, 1764, Gage Papers, American Series, vol. 16, Clements Library. The progress of Bradstreet's expedition can be followed in G. D. Scull, ed., "The Montresor Journals." Bradstreet's negotiations are in *Collections of the New York Historical Society*, 1881, 526–30; Bradstreet's negotiations are also found in "Papers relating to the Expeditions of Colonel Bradstreet and Colonel Bouquet, in Ohio, A.D. 1764," 4; John Penn to Fauquier, September 6, 1764, Reese, *Official Papers of Fauquier*, 3:1157; Gage to Johnson, September 2, 1764, *SWJP*, 11:342–44; Gage to Johnson, September 4, 1764, ibid., 4:524; Johnson to Gage, September 11, 1764, ibid., 534–35; Gage to Johnson, September 16, 1764, ibid., 538–39; a different version of Bradstreet's actions has recently appeared in Jennings, *Empire of Fortune*, 450–51; the experience of Captain Thomas Morris, Bradstreet's emissary to Pontiac, confirms the Ohio Indians' continued hostility through the summer and early autumn of 1764. See Thomas Morris, *Journal of Captain Thomas Morris from Miscellanies in Prose and Verse*, 18–19, 27–28.

87   *SWJP*, 11:374; Gage to Johnson, October 26, 1764, ibid., 391–92.

88   On renewed Ohio Indian raids see Capt. James Grant to Gage, April 2, 1764, Gage Papers, American Series, vol. 16, Clements Library; Gage to Colden, June 12, 1764, ibid., vol. 20; Bouquet to Gage, June 12, 1764, ibid.; Gage to Johnson, February 20, 1764, *SWJP*, 4:334; Bouquet left Fort Pitt on October 2, and by the twelfth Bradstreet was set to depart from Sandusky for the voyage back to Niagara; see Williams, *Bouquet's March*, 135, 137; Tanner, *Atlas*, map 11: "Pontiac's War, 1763–1764: Principal Theatre"; on Bradstreet's treaty at Detroit see *SWJP*, 4:526–33.

89   On the availability of arms and munitions, see BP/BM Add. MSS. 21650, 101, Deposition of Gershom Hicks, April 14, 1764; Samuel Wharton to Franklin, December 19, 1764, Leonard W. Labaree and William B. Willcox, eds., *The Papers of Benjamin Franklin*, 11:528; [M'Cullough], "Narrative of the Captivity of John M'Cullough," 103; on Shawnee losses, see Bouquet to Johnson, January 25, 1765, *SWJP*, 4:641.

90   On the magnitude of Indian successes on the battlefield see Peckham, *Pontiac*, 156–214.

91   BP/BM Add. MSS. 21655, 228; Alexander McKee to Johnson, October 21, 1764, *SWJP*, 11:385–86; Gage to the Earl of Halifax, November 9, 1764, Clarence Edwin Carter, ed., *The Correspondence of General Thomas Gage with the Secretaries of State*, 1:43.

92   Clarence W. Alvord and Clarence E. Carter, eds., *Collections of the Illinois State Historical Library*, vol. 11, *The New Regime, 1763–1765*; ibid., 8; see also Bouquet to Johnson, October 21, 1764, *SWJP*, 4:570–71.

93   *SWJP*, 11:435–46, 452–56.

94   Ibid., 450–67.

95   Bouquet to Captain McNeill, November 15, 1764, BP/BM Add. MSS. 21651, 48–49; Bouquet to Johnson, November 15, 1764, *SWJP*, 4:585; ibid., 11:515, 617.

96 *SWJP*, 11:461–67; Bouquet to Johnson, November 15, 1764, ibid., 4:585–86; Bouquet to Fauquier, November 15, 1764, Reese, *Official Papers of Fauquier*, 3:1161–62.
97 Bouquet to Johnson, December 3, 1764, *SWJP*, 4:606–7.
98 Bouquet to Custaloga, Tamaqua, Samuel (Netawatwees's replacement), December 3, 1764, ibid., 11:483–84; Gage to Halifax, January 23, 1765, Carter, *Correspondence of Gage*, 1:48.
99 *SWJP*, 11:723–38; Alvord and Carter, *Collections*, 11:40; Johnson to Robert Leake, August 16, 1765, ibid., 75.
100 Johnson to Gage, February 22, 1765, *SWJP*, 11:592; Johnson to Colden, February 22, 1765, ibid., 4:655; *NYCD*, 7:730; divisions and conflicts among Ohio Indians at the Fort Pitt congress are summarized in Capt. William Murray to Gage, May 12, 1765, Gage Papers, American Series, vol. 36, Clements Library.
101 On the April and May proceedings, see *NYCD*, 7:718–41, esp. 725–26, 728; quotation ibid., 740; the July proceedings are in ibid., 751–58.
102 Gage to Johnson, April 25, 1764, *Johnson Papers*, 4:408–9; Gage to Johnson, June 24, 1764, ibid., 11:244; Johnson to Gage, December 6, 1764, ibid., 495; Croghan to Johnson (Carlisle), February 18, 1765, ibid., 577; on Pontiac after the siege of Detroit, see Peckham, *Pontiac*, chaps. 17–19.
103 Gage to Fauquier, February 28, 1764, Reese, *Official Papers of Fauquier*, 3:1089–90.
104 On Amherst, Shy, *Toward Lexington*, 124, 125, 260.

Chapter Nine

1 Wallace, *Death and Rebirth of the Seneca*, 117.
2 Tanner, *Atlas of Great Lakes Indian History*; compare map 9: "The French Era, 1720 to c. 1761" and map 13: "Indian Villages and Tribal Distribution, 1768."
3 Kent, *Iroquois Indians*, 2:214, 217; Schweinitz, "Narrative of Marie Le Roy and Barbara Leininger," 412; Wainwright, "George Croghan's Journal," 358; Hunter, "Documented Subdivisions of the Delaware Indians," 34–35; Thomas Hutchins, "Plan of . . . Indian Country [1764]," reproduced in Thomas H. Smith, *The Mapping of Ohio*, 62–63.
4 Reuben Gold Thwaites, ed., "Two Journals of Western Tours by Charles Frederick Post," in idem, ed., *Early Western Travels*, 1:281.
5 Wainwright, "George Croghan's Journal," 356; Jordan, "Journal of Kenny," 177; Tanner, *Atlas*, map 13: "Indian Villages and Tribal Distribution, 1768"; Edmunds, *Shawnee Prophet*, 7–8.
6 Helen Hornbeck Tanner, "The Location of Indian Tribes in Southeast Michigan and Northern Ohio," in Wheeler-Voegelin and Tanner, *Indians of Northern Ohio and Southeast Michigan*, 217–18, 220–21; Wainwright, "Croghan's Journal," 351, 354, 405–6; *SWJP*, 13:129–30.
7 Tanner, *Atlas*, map 13: "Indian Villages and Tribal Distribution, 1768"; *BP*, 4:405.
8 Kent, *Iroquois Indians*, 2:215; Thwaites, "Journals of Post," 294; *BP*, 4:405–8; *Pa. Council Minutes*, 7:531; *Pa. Archives*, 1st ser., 3:560–63.
9 Guy Soulliard Klett, ed., *Journals of Charles Beatty*, 1762–1769, 46; Jones, *Journal of Two Visits*, 52, 76; Peter Wood, "The Changing Population of the Colonial South: An Overview by Race and Region, 1685–1790," in Wood, Waselkov, and Hatley, *Powhatan's Mantle*, 84–87, 90, for population trends in the lands immediately south of the Ohio River during this period; Wainwright, "Croghan's Journal," passim, on captives returned

between 1759 and 1762 at Fort Pitt; William S. Ewing, "Indian Captives Released by Colonel Bouquet"; *SWJP*, 11:484–91, on captives returned to Bouquet in 1764; see also Axtell, *European and the Indian*, 173–78.

10   Archaeological sites in the upper Ohio Valley are limited in number. However, sites from same period elsewhere in the northeast, notably eastern Pennsylvania and western New York, can offer clues to what Ohio Indian artifact inventories would have looked like. See Marco M. Hervatin, "Refuge[e] Wyandot Town of 1748," John A. ZaKucia, "Chambers Site, 36 La11" (1957) (unpublished artifact inventory and field notes on file with the Pennsylvania Historical and Museum Commission; my thanks to Barry C. Kent for providing a copy of this material); see also Kent, *Susquehanna's Indians*, 386–89, on Conestoga about 1763; Mark F. Seeman and Janet Bush, "The Enderle Site: An Historic Burial Locality in Erie County, Ohio"; the discussion above also is based on an inspection of artifacts from Seneca sites occupied between 1745 to 1778; my thanks to Richard Rose of the Rochester Museum and Science Center for allowing me access to these collections.

11   Hulbert and Schwarze, *Zeisberger's History*, 86–87; Jones, *Journal*, 84; Franklin B. Dexter, ed., *Diary of David McClure Doctor of Divinity, 1748–1820*, 42; [M'Cullough], "Narrative of the Captivity of John M'Cullough," 90; Bailey, *Ohio Company Papers*, passim for traders' inventories.

12   On housewares, Hulbert and Schwarze, *Zeisberger's History*, 16–17; on housing, Dexter, *Diary of McClure*, 61; Klett, *Journals of Beatty*, 61; Jones, *Journal*, 88; "Zeisberger's and Senseman's Journey," Moravian Archives, box 135, folder 7, item 1 (typed transcript on microfilm), 82; BP/BM Add. MSS. 21655, 261; on the "piquet" houses, Peter Moogk, *Building a House in New France*, 31; for similar transformations in other parts of the native east, see M. Thomas Hatley, "The Three Lives of Keowee: Loss and Recovery in Eighteenth-Century Cherokee Villages," in Wood, Waselkov, and Hatley, *Powhatan's Mantle*.

13   Hulbert and Schwarze, *Zeisberger's History*, 13; "Journal of a Mission to the Indians in Ohio, by Friends from Pennsylvania, July–September, 1773," 105–6; Dexter, *Diary of McClure*, 75; Heckewelder, *History, Manners, and Customs*, 197; Marshall J. Becker, "Lenape Bands prior to 1746: The Identification of Boundaries and Processes of Change Leading to the Formation of the 'Delawares,'" in Kraft, *Lenape Indians*, 27.

14   Hulbert and Schwarze, *Zeisberger's History*, 14; Wallace, *Travels of John Heckewelder*, 41, 44; Johnson to Gage, April 16, 1764, *SWJP*, 11:132; Jones, *Journal*, 57; Jordan, "Journal of Kenny," 22.

15   Smith, "Remarkable Occurrences in the Life," 210, 214; Hulbert and Schwarze, *Zeisberger's History*, 61 (traps), 29 (firearms), 144 (currency); Major William Walters to Johnson, April 5, 1762, *SWJP*, 10:427; [M'Cullough], "Narrative of the Captivity of John M'Cullough," 96.

16   On captives, see Axtell, *European and the Indian*, 168–206; Alden T. Vaughan and Daniel K. Richter, "Crossing the Cultural Divide: Indians and New Englanders, 1605–1763," from which last I have borrowed the term "transculturation"; Dexter, *Diary of McClure*, 61.

17   Pilkington, *Journals of Samuel Kirkland*, passim; and Klett, *Journals of Beatty*, passim; James Axtell, *The Invasion Within: The Contest of Cultures in Colonial North America*, chaps. 7–10, on New England missionaries.

18   Weslager, *Delaware Indians*, 285–91; Emma Gray and Leslie Robb Gray, *Wilderness*

Christians: The Moravian Mission to the Delaware Indians, 48–50; Jones, *Journal*, 92, 95; Dexter, *Diary of McClure*, 50.

19 August C. Mahr, trans. and ed., "Diary of a Moravian Indian Mission Migration across Pennsylvania in 1772," 250, 259, 263, 265, 267; Hulbert and Schwarze, *Zeisberger's History*, 24–25.

20 John Heckewelder, *A Narrative of the Mission of the United Brethren among the Delaware and Mohegan Indians, from Its Commencement in the Year 1740 to the Close of the Year 1808*, 157; Dexter, *Diary of McClure*, 68.

21 Hulbert and Schwarze, *Zeisberger's History*, 27, 131.

22 Ibid., 21 (metalworking), 63 (traps), 85 (rifles); Wainwright, "Croghan's Journal," 352; smithy and armorers' skills could have been learned easily enough from resident artisans like John Fraser, who kept a shop at Venango until he was driven out by Marin's army in 1753; see Hunter, *Forts on the Pennsylvania Frontier*, 24. See p. 36 above for references to kettles and guns.

23 Hulbert and Schwarze, *Zeisberger's History*, 16; Capt. William Murray to Gage, May 12, 1765, Gage Papers, American Series, vol. 36, Clements Library.

24 Jones, *Journal*, 77; Hulbert and Schwarze, *Zeisberger's History*, 118; see Howard, *Shawnee!* 133–34, 298–301; William W. Newcomb, Jr., *The Culture and Acculturation of the Delaware Indians*, 31–39; on animal sacrifice, see "Diary of David Zeisberger's and Gottlob Senseman's Journey to Goschgoschink on the Ohio and Their Arrival There in 1768," Moravian Archives, box 135, folder 7, item 1 (typed transcript on microfilm), 66.

25 John A. Zakucia, "The Chambers Site, an Historic Burial Ground of 1750–75," passim; Seeman and Bush, "Enderle Site," 2–4; see also Robert C. Mainfort, Jr., *Indian Social Dynamics in the Period of European Contact: The Fletcher Site Cemetery, Bay County*, on burial customs and the use of coffins in the Great Lakes region; on Shingas's wife's funeral: Heckewelder, *History*, 269–72; [M'Cullough], "Narrative of the Captivity of John M'Cullough," 93; Dexter, *Diary of McClure*, 90; Hulbert and Schwarze, *Zeisberger's History*, 89. For a general discussion of change and persistence in native burial rituals see Axtell, *European and the Indian*, 110–28.

26 Wallace, "Revitalization Movements," 267; this summary is based on Hunter, "Delaware Nativist Revival"; see also Jordan, "Journal of Kenny," 171, 175; the reference to Neolin in 1766 is in Klett, *Journals of Beatty*, 65.

27 Jordan, "Journal of Kenny," 188; [M'Cullough], "Narrative of the Captivity of John M'Cullough," 98–99.

28 On the history of revitalization movements among the Delawares, see Wallace, "New Religious Beliefs among the Delaware Indians"; see also William N. Fenton, "The Iroquois in History," in Leacock and Lurie, *North American Indians in Historical Perspective*, 131.

29 Jordan, "Journal of Kenny," 188; Klett, *Journals of Beatty*, 65, 70; Dexter, *Diary of McClure*, 68; Hunter, "Delaware Nativist Revivial," 47.

30 Heckewelder, *History*, 291, 293–95; Hulbert and Schwarze, "Diaries of Zeisberger," 24; Hulbert and Schwarze, *Zeisberger's History*, 134; "Zeisberger's and Senseman's Journey," 58.

31 On "Winginum" at Fort Pitt, see BP/BM Add. MSS. 21655, 213; Hulbert and Schwarze, "Diaries of Zeisberger," 23, 28; George H. Loskiel, *History of the Mission of the United Brethren among the Indians of North America*, pt. 3, 35.

32 Hulbert and Schwarze, "Diaries of Zeisberger," 23, 28; Loskiel, *History*, pt. 3, 31; "Zeisberger's and Senseman's Journey," 58, 97.

33 Pilkington, *Journal of Kirkland*, 18–29.

34 Marshall Becker, "Native Settlements in the Forks of Delaware, Pennsylvania, in the Eighteenth Century: Archaeological Implications," 54. Becker identifies Killbuck as a "Jersey" Indian; he later succeeded Netawatwees as headman of this Delaware group in the west. The Schuylkill-Brandywine Delawares were led throughout the period by kin of Allumapees—notably Tamaqua—and their successors. See also Marshall Becker, "A Summary of Lenape Socio-political Organization and Settlement Pattern at the Time of European Contact: The Evidence for Collecting Bands," 87; idem, "The Boundary between the Lenape and Munsee: The Forks of Delaware as a Buffer Zone"; idem, "Lenape Bands prior to 1740," 19–32; idem, *The Forks of Delaware, Pennsylvania during the First Half of the Eighteenth Century: The Migration of Some "Jerseys" into a Former Shared Resource Area North of Lenape Territory and Its Implications for Cultural Boundaries and Identities*, 55; my thanks to Dr. Becker for providing a copy of this last publication. See also Ives Goddard, "Delaware," in Trigger, *Northeast*, 223, and Thurman, "Delaware Social Organization," 128.

35 Evidence of earlier cooperation between Tamaqua's and Netawatwees's people can be found in *Pa. Archives*, 1st ser., 3:537: messages sent to Pennsylvania in 1758 were signed by Tamaqua and Shingas, but also by Killbuck, later Netawatwees's successor.

36 Klett, *Journals of Beatty*, 67–68; on Netawatwees, see Wainwright, "Croghan's Journal," 364.

37 Hulbert and Schwarze, *Zeisberger's History*, 111; Jones, *Journal*, 104–5; on mission Indian migrations, Hulbert and Schwarze, "Diaries of Zeisberger," 30; "Zeisberger's and Senseman's Journey," 69, 76, 79, 86–87; Loskiel, *History*, pt. 3, 55, 56, 72–75; the departure of the Moravian converts from Goschgosching was hastened by Wingenund, who—doubtless eager to see the troublemakers off—acted as their intermediary with the Delaware council at Newcomer's Town; Loskiel, *History*, 62–63.

38 On Delaware and Munsee cultural differences, see Wallace, *Travels of Heckewelder*, 104; Thurman, "Delaware Social Organization," 128; Hunter, "Documented Subdivisions," 34; Wallace, *Indians in Pennsylvania*, 174.

39 Loskiel, *History*, pt. 3, 35, 55, 56; Hulbert and Schwarze, "Diaries of Zeisberger," 14, 30, 47; "Zeisberger's and Senseman's Journey," 53, 69, 76, 79, 86–87, 93; *DCB*, s.v. "Glikhikan."

40 Loskiel, *History*, pt. 3, 56–58, 69, 71, 72–74; Dexter, *Diary of McClure*, 42; Heckewelder, *Narrative*, 112–15.

41 Loskiel, *History*, Pt. 3, 32; Wallace, *Travels of Heckewelder*, 111; Jones, *Journal*, 103; "Zeisberger's and Senseman's Journey," 94; Klett, *Journals of Beatty*, 67.

42 Heckewelder, *Narrative*, 112–15.

43 Wallace, *Travels of Heckewelder*, 102.

44 Tanner, *Atlas*, 57–67 and map 13: "Indian Villages and Tribal Distribution, 1768."

45 Hulbert and Schwarze, *Zeisberger's History*, 18–19, 122.

46 Klett, *Journals of Beatty*, 62, 67; Jones, *Journal*, 100; Dexter, *Diary of McClure*, 79–83; David Brainerd to Eleazer Wheelock, June 23, 1767, *SWJP*, 5:570–71.

47 Dexter, *Diary of McClure*, 79–83 (emphasis added), 109–10 (on Jones and the Shawnees); Jones, *Journal*, 64, 99–100.

48 Dexter, *Diary of McClure*, 66, 75; Wallace, *Travels of Heckewelder*, 41–43; Axtell, *Invasion Within*, 265.

49 Jordan, "Journal of Kenny," 160; Wallace, *Travels of Heckewelder*, 68.

50   Jones, *Journal*, 98–100; William Franklin to Johnson, May 25, 1774, *SWJP*, 8:1159; "Zeisberger's and Senseman's Journey," 67 (Senecas), 73.

51   "Journal of a Mission to the Indians in Ohio," 105 (Quakers rejected); "Zeisberger's and Senseman's Journey," 94 (Tamaqua quotation).

52   Wallace, *Travels of Heckewelder*, 104, 111; Dexter, *Diary of McClure*, 51; Jones, *Journal*, 98.

Chapter Ten

1   The discussion of policy that follows is drawn from Sosin, *Whitehall and the Wilderness*, chaps. 2–3, and Marshall, "Colonial Protest and Imperial Retrenchment."

2   On the 1763 Proclamation, see Stagg, *Anglo-Indian Relations in North America*, 350–92; see also D. W. Meinig, *The Shaping of America: A Geographical Perspective on Five Hundred Years of History*, vol. 1, *Atlantic America, 1492–1800*, 284–87.

3   Gage to Johnson, October 14, 1764, *SWJP*, 11:377; Johnson to Gage, December 18, 1764, ibid., 4:622–23; Lords of Trade to Johnson, August 5, 1763, *NYCD*, 7:535–36; Johnson to Board of Trade, November 13, 1763, ibid., 572–81; Johnson's plan is reproduced in ibid., 637–41.

4   Sosin, *Whitehall and the Wilderness*, chaps. 2–3, esp. 76–78; Johnson to Gage, August 5, 1764, *SWJP*, 11:326; William Eyre to Johnson, January 7, 1764, ibid., 6; Gage to Johnson, December 25, 1765, ibid., 987; Johnson to Gage, September 1, 1764, ibid., 4:519.

5   Gage to Johnson, May 16, 1764, ibid., 4:425; Johnson to Board of Trade, January 20, 1764, *NYCD*, 7:600.

6   Johnson to Earl of Dartmouth, November 4, 1772, K. G. Davies, ed., *Documents of the American Revolution, 1770–1783*, 5:213; Johnson to Alexander McKee, January 20, 1774, *SWJP*, 8:1012; for Kiashuta's role as messenger and mediator, see Lt. George Phyn to Johnson [Fort Pitt], September 19, 1767, ibid., 5:681; *Pa. Council Minutes*, 9:515; and below.

7   Johnson to Amherst, August 20, 1765, *NYCD*, 7:541–42, on Kanestio; Instructions for Henry Montour, February 9, 1764, *SWJP*, 4:321–22; Johnson to John Penn, February 9, 1764, ibid., 322–24; Henry Montour, William Hare, and John Johnson to Johnson, April 7, 1764, ibid., 392–94; Johnson to Gage, November 8, 1765, ibid., 11:399–400.

8   Sosin, *Whitehall and the Wilderness*, chap. 4; *NYCD*, 7:740.

9   Gage to Johnson, December 25, 1765, *SWJP*, 11:987.

10   On army reductions in the west see Shy, *Toward Lexington*, 258–65; Sosin, *Whitehall and the Wilderness*, 110–17; Shelburne to Johnson, December 11, 1766, Alvord and Carter, *Collections*, 11:449; Gage to Shelburne, February 22, 1767, Carter, *Correspondence of Gage*, 1:123.

11   Marshall, "Colonial Protest and Imperial Retrenchment," 1–17, esp. 17; Sosin, *Whitehall and the Wilderness*, chaps. 6–9; Shy, *Toward Lexington*, 280–81.

12   Johnson to Cadwallader Colden, December 18, 1764, *SWJP*, 4:622; Josiah Davenport to Commissioners, May 8, 1765, Gratz Collection, Indian Commissioners' Papers, box 9: Correspondence, HSP.

13   Croghan to Johnson, May 12, 1765, *SWJP*, 11:736–37; Croghan to Johnson, May 13, 1765, ibid., 737 ; *NYCD*, 7:735; Croghan to Gage, May 26, 1765, Cadwallader Collection: George Croghan Papers, sec. 26, HSP.

14   John Penn to Johnson, March 21, 1765, *SWJP*, 11:643–44; Fauquier to Board of Trade,

February 13, 1764, Reese, *Official Papers of Fauquier*, 3:1076–78; the army's contradictory role is revealed in letters from Gage in 1764 urging that a new road be opened from Augusta County to the Scioto River via the Kanawha River to serve as the "great Road to the Illinois, *when we get possession of it.*" See Gage to Fauquier, December 10, 1764, ibid., 3:1192–93; Gage to Johnson, December 31, 1764, *SWJP*, 11:516 (emphasis added); this was the same general who soon lamented the illegal settlement of the Ohio Country, settlement promoted by new trails blazed through the borderlands.

15 *SWJP*, 11:791, 793; Alvord and Carter, *Collections*, 11:5.

16 Ibid.; Gage to Johnson, January 18, 1765, *SWJP*, 11:540; Gage to Earl of Halifax, January 23, 1765, Carter, *Correspondence of Gage*, 1:48; Vaughan, "Frontier Banditti and the Indians," 3–8.

17 Johnson to William Franklin, June 20, 1766, Alvord and Carter, *Collections*, 11:319; John Penn to Johnson, March 11, 1766, *SWJP*, 12:41; Proclamation of Augusta Boys, ca. June 4, 1765, Reese, *Official Papers of Fauquier*, 3:1255–56; Capt. Ralph Phillips to Gage, June 14, 1766, ibid., 1370; Gage to Johnson, April 5, 1766, *SWJP*, 12:295; for other incidents before 1768 see Col. John Reid to Gage, June 18, 1765, *SWJP*, 4:769; Johnson to Gage, May 27, 1766, ibid., 5:224–25; ibid., 260; Johnson to Gage, June 27, 1766, ibid., 12:115–16; Fauquier to Johnson, April 4, 1767, ibid., 294; Fauquier to Johnson, April 4, 1767, Reese, *Official Papers of Fauquier*, 3:1435; Fauquier to Capt. William Murray, April 2, 1767, ibid., 1437–38; *Pa. Archives*, 1st ser., 4:217–18; *SWJP*, 11:790–91; Gage to Johnson, June 28, 1767, ibid., 5:574.

18 *SWJP*, 11:790–91; Reese, *Official Papers of Fauquier*, 3:1369–70.

19 Fauquier to Johnson, April 4, 1767, *SWJP*, 12:294; Gage to Johnson, April 5, 1767, ibid., 295; Gage to Johnson, December 14, 1767, *DHSNY*, 2:890; Croghan to Johnson, January 15, 1767, Cadwallader Collection, George Croghan Papers, sec. 29, HSP.

20 Croghan to Gage, June 3, 1767, Howard H. Peckham, ed., *George Croghan's Journal of His Trip to Detroit in 1767, with His Correspondence relating Thereto*, 15–16; Delawares to Fauquier, September 10, 1767, *SWJP*, 5:665–66; Gage to Johnson, March 17, 1766, ibid., 12:44.

21 Capt. William Murray to Gage, May 16, 1767, Gage Papers, vol. 65, Clements Library; Croghan to Gage, October 18, 1767, ibid., vol. 67; *SWJP*, 13:139; Jehu Hay to Johnson, August 1767, ibid., 5:648–49; Croghan to Gage, September 27, 1767, Peckham, *Croghan's Journal*, 20–21; ibid., 31–35; Croghan to Benjamin Franklin, October 20, 1767, Cadwallader Collection, George Croghan Papers, sec. 29, HSP.

22 Peckham, *Croghan's Journal*, 33–34.

23 Ibid., 32, 36, 41, 46; Alexander McKee to Croghan, September 20, 1767, *SWJP*, 5:686–87.

24 Croghan to Johnson, September 25, 1767, ibid., 701; Gage to Fauquier, December 7, 1767, Reese, *Official Papers of Fauquier*, 3:1519–20.

25 Nathaniel McCulloch to Croghan, March 12, 1765, *SWJP*, 11:635–36; Gage to Halifax, April 27, 1765, ibid., 4:731–32; Gage to Halifax, June 8, 1765, Carter, *Correspondence of Gage*, 1:62; Vaughan, "Frontier Banditti," 6–7; Stephen H. Cutcliffe, "The Sideling Hill Affair: The Cumberland County Riots of 1765."

26 Cutcliffe, "Sideling Hill Affair," 45–46; Croghan to Gage, July 6, 1766, *SWJP*, 5:307; Delawares (Netawatwees) to commanding officer, Fort Pitt, September 24, 1766, ibid., 481–82; Joseph Spear et al. to Johnson, October 4, 1766, ibid., 384–85; Johnson to Gage, April 1, 1767, *DHSNY*, 2:843; Croghan to Gage, October 18, 1767, Peckham, *Croghan's Journal*, 26; Croghan to Johnson, October 18, 1767, *SWJP*, 12:375.

27   Gage to Johnson, June 10, 1765, *SWJP*, 11:785; Johnson to Gage, June 19, 1767, ibid., 798; Gage to Johnson, May 19, 1766, ibid., 12:91–92; Gage to Johnson, June 22, 1766, ibid., 111–12; Johnson to Shelburne, April 1, 1767, Alvord and Carter, *Collections*, 10:543; Gage to Shelburne, April 7, 1767, Carter, *Correspondence of Gage*, 1:133; Gage to Shelburne, June 13, 1767, ibid., 142; Sosin, *Whitehall and the Wilderness*, 107.

28   Marshall, "Colonial Protest and Imperial Retrenchment," passim; compare with Sosin, *Whitehall and the Wilderness*, chaps. 5–7; policy issues and disputes are revealed in Alvord and Carter, *Collections*, 10:234–45, 422–30; Shelburne to Townshend, March 30, 1767, ibid., 536–41; Gage to Shelburne, April 3, 1767, ibid., 544–52.

29   Johnson to Shelburne, February 28, 1766, *SWJP*, 12:31–32; Johnson to John Penn, January 15, 1767, ibid., 256–57; Croghan to Johnson, October 18, 1767, ibid., 374; Croghan to Thomas Penn, October 1767, Cadwallader Collection, George Croghan Papers, sec. 29, HSP; Croghan to Benjamin Franklin, February 12, 1768, ibid., sec. 30; on the Stump affair, see Vaughan, "Frontier Banditti," 8–10; Alexander McKee to Croghan, February 13, 1768, *SWJP*, 6:101–2; Croghan to Gage, February 17, 1768, ibid., 110–11; Croghan to Johnson, March 1, 1768, Clarence W. Alvord and Clarence Edwin Carter, eds., *Collections of the Illinois State Historical Library*, vol. 16, *Trade and Politics, 1767–1769*, 179; Croghan to Gage, April 14, 1768, Cadwallader Collection, George Croghan Papers, sec. 30, HSP.

30   *Pa. Council Minutes*, 9:521–23; Vaughan, "Frontier Banditti," 11–12.

31   Croghan to Johnson, October 18, 1767, Alvord and Carter, *Collections*, 16:89; *Pa. Council Minutes*, 9:527–28, 537.

32   *Pa. Council Minutes*, 9:528–35; a different version of this face-off, from a Six Nations perspective, is found in Jones, *License for Empire*, 90–91.

33   Johnson to Gage, April 18, 1767, *DHSNY*, 2:849.

34   Croghan to Benjamin Franklin, October 2, 1767, Labaree and Willcox, *Papers of Franklin*, 14:69–71; Croghan to Benjamin Franklin, December 12, 1765, Alvord and Carter, *Collections*, 11:62; a year earlier (1764) Ohio Indians had also agreed to cede land to Colonel Bradstreet; see *SWJP*, 11:328–35; Gage to Johnson, October 4, 1767, ibid., 12:367; emphasis added.

35   *Pa. Council Minutes*, 9:522–23, 532; Johnson to Bouquet, December 17, 1764, BP/BM Add. MSS. 21651, 80–81; Johnson to Board of Trade [1767], Alvord and Carter, *Collections*, 16:33.

36   Johnson to Shelburne, October 26, 1767, *SWJP*, 5:762–63; Guy Johnson to Gage, May 4, 1768, ibid., 12:488–89; for Stuart's negotiations with the Cherokees and other southern Indians see Jones, *License for Empire*, 99, 110, 114; Peter Marshall, "Sir William Johnson and the Treaty of Fort Stanwix, 1768," 165–66.

37   Johnson to Gage, April 23, 1768, *SWJP*, 12:476 (italics in original); Johnson to John Penn, August 24, 1768, ibid., 6:334–35.

38   Sosin, *Whitehall and the Wilderness*, 46; Marshall, "Johnson and the Treaty of Fort Stanwix," 173–74 (on missionaries); *NYCD*, 8:111–37, for the treaty minutes and a list of Crown and colonial participants.

39   Johnson to Baynton, Wharton, Morgan, January 30, 1766, *SWJP*, 5:16; Johnson to John Blair, September 25, 1768, ibid., 6:406–7; Johnson to Governor Moore, September 28, 1768, ibid., 411; on Johnson's instructions see Hillsborough to Johnson, March 12, 1768, *NYCD*, 8:35–36; Gage to Johnson, May 8, 1768, *SWJP*, 12:494; Board of Trade to Shelburne, December 23, 1767, *NYCD*, 7:1004–5 (boundary line limits); Shelburne to

Johnson, January 5, 1768, ibid., 8:2 (Johnson to negotiate on basis of Board of Trade recommendations).

40 *SWJP*, 6:569 (expenses); ibid., 12:628–29 (number of Indians).

41 Treaty minutes found in *NYCD*, 8:111–37, esp. 113, 120–26; Samuel Wharton to Franklin, December 2, 1768, Labaree and Willcox, *Papers of Franklin*, 15:275–79; Johnson to Hillsborough, October 23, 1768, *DHSNY*, 2:912–14.

42 Gage to Johnson, April 3, 1769, *SWJP*, 12:709–10.

43 Ibid.

44 Hillsborough to Gage, March 24, 1769, Alvord and Carter, *Collections*, 16:513; Hillsborough to Johnson, May 13, 1769, *DHSNY*, 2:938–39; Gage to Johnson, July 23, 1769, *SWJP*, 7:65–66; see Lester J. Cappon et al., eds. *Atlas of Early American History*, vol. 2, *The Revolutionary Era, 1760–1790*, on southern cession and boundary lines, 1768–74, 92–93; Johnson to Gage, April 14, 1769, *SWJP*, 12:715.

45 Johnson to Hillsborough, June 26, 1769, *NYCD*, 8:172–73; Johnson to Gage, August 9, 1769, *SWJP*, 12:746–47; Johnson to Dartmouth, November 4, 1772, Davies, *Documents of the American Revolution*, 5:213.

Chapter Eleven

1 Gage to Johnson, October 4, 1767, *SWJP*, 12:366–67; ibid., 406–8 (emphasis added); Croghan to Benjamin Franklin, October 2, 1767, Alvord and Carter, *Collections*, 16:75–86; Hulbert and Schwarze, "Diaries of Zeisberger," 72.

2 On the arrival of the news, Hulbert and Schwarze, "Diaries of Zeisberger," 101; *SWJP*, 7:184–85; Croghan to Johnson, May 10, 1770, ibid., 651–52; Gage to Johnson, September 10, 1769, ibid., 160; Croghan to Gage, January 1, 1770, Davies, *Documents of the American Revolution*, 2:21–22.

3 Gage to Johnson, May 20, 1770, *SWJP*, 12:822; Netawatwees to Richard Penn, November 1771, *Pa. Council Minutes*, 10:13; Davies (C.O. 5) Johnson to Dartmouth, December 26, 1772, Davies, *Documents of the American Revolution*, 5:248.

4 Johnson to Hillsborough, April 4, 1770, *DHSNY*, 2:990; Newcomer to John Penn, April 1, 1771, *Pa. Council Minutes*, 9:736; Gage to Johnson, June 10, 1771, *SWJP*, 8:142; Johnson to Gage, June 27, 1771, ibid., 160; Johnson to Gage, September 19, 1771, ibid., 259–62; Johnson to Gage, November 16, 1771, ibid., 315–17; Johnson to Gage, December 23, 1771, ibid., 349; Johnson to Gage, September 2, 1772, ibid., 586–87; Gage to Hillsborough, October 6, 1772, Carter, *Correspondence of Gage*, 1:335. King never returned home; he died at Charleston while en route to New York; see Johnson to Hillsborough, April 4, 1772, *NYCD*, 8:290–91.

5 Gage to Johnson, August 27, 1769, *SWJP*, 12:140; on speculators and colonizing plans see Wainwright, *George Croghan*, chap. 10, which traces the complex efforts of one such speculator; Thomas Perkins Abernethy, *Western Lands and the American Revolution*, chaps. 1–6, on post-1773 speculative ventures throughout the west.

6 Johnson to Hillsborough, August 14, 1770, *DHSNY*, 2:975; Robert Callender to John Penn, April 21, 1771, *Pa. Archives*, 1st ser., 4:412; Wade and Keiuser to Johnson, June 15, 1772, *SWJP*, 8:519; Gage to Hillsborough, July 1, 1771, Carter, *Correspondence of Gage*, 1:328–29. On Black Boys: Johnson to Governor Moore, September 1, 1769, *SWJP*, 7:154; Normand MacLeod to Johnson, March 12, 1770, ibid., 483; last quotation: Johnson to Hillsborough, August 26, 1769, *DHSNY*, 2:953.

7   Jackson and Twohig, *Diaries of Washington*, 2:297; Alexander McKee to Johnson, July 3, 1773, *SWJP*, 8:842–43; ibid., 12:1079; Gage to Johnson, May 20, 1770, ibid., 822; Gage to Hillsborough , February 5, 1772, Davies, *Documents of the American Revolution*, 5:32.

8   Dexter, *Diary of McClure*, 93; Capt. Gordon Forbes to Gage, July 28, 1768, *SWJP*, 6:294; Gage to Hillsborough (Cherokees), April 25, 1770, Carter, *Correspondence of Gage*, 1:258; Johnson to Gage, September 19, 1771, *SWJP*, 8:262; Johnson to Gage, December 23, 1771, ibid., 348; Johnson to Dartmouth, November 4, 1772, Davies, *Documents of the American Revolution*, 5:213. On Kentucky as a borderland, see Wood, "Changing Population of the Colonial South," 84–85.

9   Dexter, *Diary of McClure*, 101; "Journal of a Mission to the Indians," 105; *SWJP*, 12:1080; Robert Callender to John Penn, April 21, 1771, *Pa. Archives*, 1st ser., 4:412.

10   Klett, *Journals of Beatty*, 51; Baynton, Wharton, and Morgan to Lauchlin Macleane, October 9, 1767, Alvord and Carter, *Collections*, 16:85; Capt. Harry Gordon to Gage, June 4, 1766, Gage Papers, American Series, vol. 52, Clements Library; Robert L. Hooper, Jr., to Johnson, February 9, 1771, *SWJP*, 7:1132; Robert Callender to John Penn, March 21, 1771, *Pa. Archives*, 1st ser., 4:412; Croghan to Samuel Wharton, November 2, 1771, Cadwallader Collection, George Croghan Papers, sec. 32, HSP; Dexter, *Diary of McClure*, 41; see also Jones, *Journal of Two Visits to Some Nations of Indians*, 14–18; Johnson to Gage, November 18, 1772, *SWJP*, 8:640; on food shortages, Jones, *Journal*, 29; Clark to Jonathan Clark, January 9, 1773, James A. James, *Collections of the Illinois State Historical Library, George Rogers Clark Papers, 1771–1781*, 8:2.

11   Ibid. (*Clark Papers*); Wallace, *Travels of Heckewelder*, 108; August C. Mahr, trans. and ed., "A Canoe Journey from the Big Beaver to the Tuscarawas in 1773: A Travel Diary of John Heckewelder," 289.

12   Ibid. ("Canoe Journey"), 292; Wallace, *Travels of Heckewelder* (Friedensstadt to Schönbrunn Journal—1773), 106–7; Dexter, *Diary of McClure*, 93, 118–19; Captain Charles Edmonstone to Gage, May 17, 1772, Gage Papers, American Series, vol. 111, Clements Library; same to same, December 24, 1772, ibid., vol. 116; Gage to Hillsborough, October 7, 1772, Carter, *Correspondence of Gage*, 1:336; Thomas P. Slaughter, *The Whiskey Rebellion: Frontier Epilogue to the American Revolution*, chap. 4, provides a portrait of Ohio Valley settler society in the late eighteenth century.

13   Jones, *Journal*, 22; Gage to Hillsborough, October 7, 1772, Davies, *Documents of the American Revolution*, 5:203; Croghan to Gage, November 2, 1771, Cadwallader Collection, George Croghan Papers, sec. 32, HSP.

14   Dexter, *Diary of McClure*, 84–85; Hulbert and Schwarze, "Diaries of Zeisberger," 63; Johnson to Shelburne, April 1, 1767, Alvord and Carter, *Collections*, 11:543; Gage to Johnson, October 22, 1769, *SWJP*, 7:225.

15   Jackson and Twohig, *Diaries of Washington*, 2:316 (emphasis added); Gage to Hillsborough, October 7, 1772, Davies, *Documents of the American Revolution*, 5:203; Guy Johnson to General Frederick Haldimand, August 26, 1773, Sir Frederick Haldimand Papers, BP/BM Add. MSS., 21670.

16   Dexter, *Diary of McClure*, 83, 84–85.

17   Delawares, Munsees, and Mahicans to Pennsylvania, Maryland, and Virginia, December 4, 1771, Davies, *Documents of the American Revolution*, 3:254–55; Delawares (Netawatwees) to Virginia, September 10, 1767, Reese, *Papers of Fauquier*, 3:1497–98; "Zeisberger's and Senseman's Journey," Moravian Archives, box 135, folder 7, item 1 (typed transcript on microfilm), 100; see also Johnson to Hillsborough, April 4, 1772, Davies,

Documents of the American Revolution, 5:60, on Shawnee complaints about settlements above the Kanawha in Kentucky: Johnson rejected them as "fallacious pretence," but the Shawnees persisted in challenging the British for control of this vital territory; see below.

18 Quotation: Johnson to Gage, April 18, 1771, *SWJP,* 8:76–77; Johnson to Gage, August 9, 1771, ibid., 219–20; quotation: Johnson to Gage, August 9, 1769; ibid., 7:86; Capt. John Brown to Johnson, October 17, 1770, ibid., 184–85, 942; Johnson to Gage, July 31, 1770, ibid., 817.

19 *DHSNY,* 2:869 (reference to Gaustarax as "Casteehe: chief of the Genesees" [1767]); Six Nations to Johnson, July 1771, *NYCD,* 7:282–83, refers to Guastarax, "who is now under the ground"; on Sayenquaraghta, Normand MacLeod to Johnson, May 10, 1769, *SWJP,* 6:750; *NYCD,* 8:362–67.

20 On Genesee messages to the Ohio Indians, Croghan to Johnson, October 18, 1767, *SWJP,* 12:374; Croghan to Johnson, May 10, 1770, ibid., 7:652; Johnson to Croghan, April 18, 1771, ibid., 8:6–9, 75–76; on the Niagara portage, Johnson to Gage, April 4, 1766, Alvord and Carter, *Collections,* 11:209; Croghan to Gage, May 12, 1765, Gage Papers, American Series, vol. 36, Clements Library; efforts to recall war belts, *NYCD,* 8:362–67; quotation on sachems, Croghan to Johnson, May 19, 1770, *SWJP,* 7:689.

21 Normand MacLeod to Johnson, September 8, 1767, *SWJP,* 5:662; Johnson to Hillsborough, August 29, 1769, *DHSNY,* 2:949; Johnson to Gage, September 19, 1771, *SWJP,* 8:259.

22 Alexander McKee to Croghan, February 20, 1770, *SWJP,* 7:404; Johnson to Croghan, February 1, 1771, ibid., 1121; Gage to John Stuart, October 16, 1770, Davies, *Documents of the American Revolution,* 2:203–4; Edmunds, *Tecumseh,* 11–13.

23 *SWJP,* 13:407–8; see Tanner, *Atlas of Great Lakes Indian History,* map 13: "Indian Villages and Tribal Distribution, 1768," map 15: "Frontier in Transition, 1770–1784: Pennsylvania, New York, Canada," map 16: "Frontier in Transition, 1772–1781: The Ohio Country and Canada"; Helen Hornbeck Tanner, "Land and Water Communication Systems of the Southeastern Indians," in Wood, Waselkov, and Hatley, *Powhatan's Mantle,* 8–10; Edmunds, *Tecumseh and the Quest for Indian Leadership,* 10–12.

24 Captain Charles Edmonstone to Gage, May 13, 1770, Gage Papers, American Series, vol. 92, Clements Library; Robert Callender to John Penn, April 21, 1771, *Pa. Archives,* 1st ser., 4:412; Captain Pipe to Pennsylvania [1771], ibid., 441; Croghan to Captain Charles Edmonstone, February 19, 1771, *SWJP,* 7:1149–50 (on Ohio Indians' plans to remove); ibid., 12:914–15; Wainwright, *George Croghan,* 273; on Cherokees, *SWJP,* 8:339–40.

25 Croghan to Johnson, August 8, 1769, ibid., 7:78–79; on the Miamis' role in the Wabash Confederacy, ibid., 12:1044–45; on the Ohio Indians' cooperation, message from Killbuck to Gov. Richard Penn, November 1771, *Pa. Council Minutes,* 10:10, 12; see also Gage to Dartmouth, January 6, 1773, Carter, *Correspondence of Gage,* 1:343; Gage to Dartmouth, February 8, 1773, ibid., 345.

26 Johnson to Hillsborough, February 10, 1770, Davies, *Documents of the American Revolution,* 2:38; Johnson to Gage, January 5, 1770, *SWJP,* 7:328; *NYCD,* 8:227–44; Theda Perdue, "Cherokee Relations with the Iroquois in the Eighteenth Century," in Richter and Merrell, *Beyond the Covenant Chain,* 146–47.

27 Gage to Hillsborough, January 9, 1770, Davies, *Documents of the American Revolution,* 2:22–25; Johnson to Hillsborough, February 18, 1771, *DHSNY,* 2:980–81.

28 Johnson to Croghan, March 16, 1768, *SWJP,* 12:472; Gage to Johnson, April 4, 1768, ibid., 6:176; Stuart to Gage, February 8, 1771, ibid., 7:1131; Gage to Johnson, April 15,

1771, ibid., 8:70; Gage to Johnson, March 9, 1772, ibid., 418–19; Gage to Johnson, April 1, 1771, ibid., 57–58.

29 Croghan to Gage, August 8, 1770, Gage Papers, American Series, vol. 92, Clements Library; Captain Edmonstone to Gage, February 24, 1771, ibid., vol. 100; Johnson to Hillsborough, August 14, 1770, DHSNY, 2:978; Gage to John Stuart, October 16, 1770, Davies, Documents of the American Revolution, 2:203–4; Gage to Hillsborough, November 12, 1770, Carter, Correspondence of Gage, 1:281; Johnson to Hillsborough, February 18, 1771, NYCD, 8:262; John Stuart to Alexander Cameron, February 23, 1771, Davies, Documents of the American Revolution, 3:43.

30 Robert Callender to John Penn, April 21, 1771, Pa. Archives, 1st ser., 4:411–12; Newcomer to John Penn, April 1, 1771, Pa. Council Minutes, 9:736; SWJP, 12:1047–48; see also Goddard, "Delaware," 223.

31 NYCD, 8:230; Johnson to Gage, September 19, 1771, SWJP, 8:259–60.

32 On King, Johnson to Gage, June 27, 1771, SWJP, 8:160; Gov. William Bull to Johnson, September 6, 1771, ibid., 247; Johnson to Gage, November 16, 1771, ibid., 317–18; Johnson to Gage, February 15, 1772, ibid., 406–8; on the Wabash Indians' rejection of the Six Nations' messages, Johnson to Gage, September 2, 1772, ibid., 586–87; on Kiashuta, ibid., 12:1034–35, 1048.

33 Johnson to Gage, September 19, 1771, SWJP, 8:262; Croghan to Alexander McKee, April 26, 1772, Cadwallader Collection, George Croghan Papers, sec. 23, HSP; "Journal of a Mission to the Indians in Ohio," 104; Johnson to Hillsborough, November 4, 1772, NYCD, 8:316; Gage to Johnson, January 20, 1772, SWJP, 8:373; on the Illinois French, Gage to Johnson, March 9, 1772, ibid., 8:417; Gage to Johnson, December 15, 1772, ibid., 661; Johnson to Haldimand, January 26, 1774, Haldimand Papers, BM Add. MSS. 21670; Hillsborough quoted in Hillsborough to Johnson, July 1, 1772, Davies, Documents of the American Revolution, 5:135.

34 Traders to Croghan, December 18, 1767, SWJP, 6:19; Alvord and Carter, Collections, 16:58; Hillsborough to Fauquier, April 15, 1768, Reese, Official Papers of Fauquier, 3:1544–46; Gage to Capt. John Brown, August 29, 1768, SWJP, 6:346–47; Johnson to Gage, January 7, 1766, ibid., 5:1–5; Gage to Johnson, February 3, 1766, ibid., 30; Capt. Harry Gordon to Johnson, March 4, 1766, ibid., 49; Gage to Johnson, August 7, 1768, ibid., 313; on troop reductions, Gage to John Penn, March 30, 1765, Pa. Archives, 1st ser., 4:214–15; Gage to Johnson, September 7, 1772, SWJP, 8:592–93.

35 Johnson to Thomas Penn, July 4, 1770, ibid., 7:785; ibid., 8:755–56; Captain Edmonstone to Gage, September 28, 1772, Gage Papers, American Series, vol. 114, Clements Library; quotation from Dexter, Diary of McClure, 85.

36 Richard Penn to Assembly, January 29, 1773, Pa. Council Minutes, 10:68–69; McClure, "Ends of the American Earth," chap. 4; on intercolonial border disputes, see Cappon et al., Atlas of Early American History, 91–93 and map 16: "De Facto Government, 1775," map 17: "De Facto Government, 1785."

37 William H. Smith, The St. Clair Papers: The Life and Public Service of Aurthur St. Clair, 1:7–9; McClure, "Ends of the American Earth," 193–95.

38 George Wilson to St. Clair, August 14, 1771, Smith, St. Clair Papers, 1:257–59; St. Clair to Joseph Shippen, Jr., September 24, 1771, ibid., 260; Robert Lettis Hooper to St. Clair, July 10, 1772, ibid., 264; St. Clair to Joseph Shippen, Jr., July 18, 1772, ibid., 265–67.

39 Croghan to St. Clair, June 4, 1772, ibid., 262–64; Dunmore to John Penn, March 3, 1774, Pa. Council Minutes, 10:156–57; Sosin, Whitehall and the Wilderness, chap. 8; Wain-

wright, *George Croghan*, 277–81; McClure, "Ends of the American Earth," 205–19; Slaughter, *Whiskey Rebellion*, chap. 5, on Washington's landholdings and interests in the Ohio Valley.

40 Aeneas MacKay to St. Clair, January 11, 1774, *Pa. Council Minutes*, 10:140–42; Smith, *St. Clair Papers*, 1:10; St. Clair to Penn, February 2, 1774, *Pa. Archives*, 1st ser., 4:476–77; St. Clair to Joseph Shippen, Jr., February 25, 1774 (Connolly jailbreak), Smith, *St. Clair Papers*, 1:284–85; *SWJP*, 12:1083; Croghan to St. Clair, June 4, 1774, *Pa. Archives*, 1st ser., 4:507; see also Wainwright, *George Croghan*, 286–88; McClure, "Ends of the American Earth," 227–39; Dunmore to Dartmouth, March 18, 1774, Davies, *Documents of the American Revolution*, 8:65–66 (on Dunmore's 1773 meeting with Connolly at Pittsburgh).

41 On population, Dunmore to Dartmouth, March 18, 1774, ibid., 65; Johnson to Dartmouth, June 20, 1774, *NYCD*, 8:460–61.

42 McKee to Johnson, October 16, 1773, *SWJP*, 12:1039; ibid., 1082, 1084; on Shawnee warriors, Shawnees to McKee, March 8, 1774, *NYCD*, 8:461–62; "Reminiscences of Judge Henry Jolly," in Thwaites and Kellogg, *Dunmore's War*, 12–13; on Ohio Iroquois, *SWJP*, 12:1032–33.

43 Devereaux Smith to Dr. William Smith, June 10, 1774, *Pa. Archives*, 1st ser., 4:511–13; ibid., 568–70, Richard Butler deposition, August 23, 1774; ibid., 495–96; Thwaites and Kellogg, *Dunmore's War*, 9–14 (Henry Jolly); Edmunds, *Tecumseh*, 11–18.

44 Capt. Daniel Smith to Col. William Preston, March 22, 1774, Thwaites and Kellogg, *Dunmore's War*, 2–3; John Floyd to Col. William Preston, April 26, 1774, ibid.; *SWJP*, 12:1082, 1089.

45 Clark to Samuel Brown, June 17, 1798, James, *Collections*, 8:3–9; Johnson to Haldimand, June 9, 1774, *SWJP*, 8:1164–65; St. Clair, by no means an impartial observer, reported that the Virginians were "enraged" to learn that Pennsylvania continued to trade with Delawares in 1774, even though these natives were not involved in hostilities with Virginia; see St. Clair to Penn, June 26, 1774, Smith, *St. Clair Papers*, 1:334; see also *Pa. Archives*, 1st ser., 4:496.

46 Devereaux Smith to Dr. William Smith, June 10, 1774, *Pa. Archives*, 1st ser., 4:511–13; Smith, *St. Clair Papers*, 1:316 n. 1 (Connolly's proclamation of June 18, 1774); Clark to [?] Brown, June 17, 1798, James, *Collections*, 8:7; on the local militia at Fort Dunmore, William Crawford to Penn, April 8, 1774, Smith, *St. Clair Papers*, 1:291–92; on Virginians' Indian hating, St. Clair to Penn, June 22, 1774, ibid., 329; on scalping, Dunmore to Dartmouth, August 14, 1774, Davies, *Documents of the American Revolution*, 8:160; on the unreliability of local militias, Col. William Christian to Col. William Preston, July 12, 1774, Thwaites and Kellogg, *Dunmore's War*, 80–84.

47 On the scalping of Indians by Virginians, Johnson to Haldimand, June 9, 1774, *SWJP*, 8:1164–65; Devereaux Smith to Dr. William Smith, June 10, 1774, *Pa. Archives*, 1st ser., 4:513; St. Clair to Penn, June 22, 1774, ibid., 496, 525; Col. William Christian to Col. William Preston, November 8, 1774, Thwaites and Kellogg, *Dunmore's War*, 303.

48 *NYCD*, 8:466; Nicholas B. Wainwright, ed., "Turmoil at Pittsburgh: Diary of Augustine Prevost, 1774," 151–52; *Pa. Archives*, 1st ser., 4:498–99 (Zeisberger); St. Clair to Penn, May 29, 1774, ibid., 501.

49 Cornstalk to Alexander McKee, May 20, 1774, *Pa. Archives*, 1st ser., 4:497; St. Clair to Penn, June 8, 1774, ibid., 510; ibid., 508 (last quotation); Shawnees to Connolly, May 21, 1774, *NYCD*, 8:465–66.

50   *Pa. Archives*, 1st ser., 4:521; on the attack on the Shawnees, St. Clair to Penn, June 22, 1774, ibid., 523–24; St. Clair to Penn, June 26, 1774, ibid., 530; on Dunmore's campaign see also Robert L. Kerby, "The Other War in 1774: Dunmore's War"; Downes, *Council Fires on the Upper Ohio*, chap. 7.

51   Wainwright, "Turmoil at Pittsburgh," 131–32; Dartmouth to Dunmore, September 8, 1774, *Pa. Archives*, 1st ser., 4:577–78.

52   Dunmore's justification for his actions is found in Dunmore to Dartmouth, December 24, 1774, Davies, *Documents of the American Revolution*, 8:254; Wainwright, *George Croghan*, 294; McClure, "Ends of the American Earth," 229–230, 243, 246–47; on mixed signals sent to the Indians, Wainwright, "Turmoil at Pittsburgh," 142–43.

53   St. Clair to John Penn, August 25, 1774, *Pa. Archives*, 1st ser., 4:576; on the death of Sir William Johnson, Guy Johnson to Dartmouth, July 12, 1774, *NYCD*, 8:471; Guy Johnson to Dartmouth, July 26, 1774, ibid., 473; Guy Johnson to John Penn, July 22, 1774, *SWJP*, 8:1187; *NYCD*, 8:476; Guy Johnson to Gage, October 21, 1774, *SWJP*, 12:688–89.

54   Guy Johnson to Dartmouth, July 26, 1774, *NYCD*, 7:473; Sir William Johnson to Gage, July 4, 1774, *SWJP*, 12:1114–15; Wainwright, "Turmoil at Pittsburgh," 126; Guy Johnson to Gage, September 29, 1774, *SWJP*, 13:680–81; Guy Johnson to Gage, October 6, 1774, ibid., 686–87.

55   Croghan to Connolly and McKee, May 4, 1774, Cadwallader Collection, George Croghan Papers, sec. 35, HSP; same to same, May 5, 1774, ibid., Wainwright, "Turmoil at Pittsburgh," 134–35, 142 (Delaware comment on Dunmore), 149; Loskiel, *History of the Mission of the United Brethren*, pt. 3, 94; *Pa. Archives*, 1st ser., 4:500; Delawares (White Eyes) to Virginia and Pennsylvania, July 23, 1774, ibid., 552–53.

56   Delawares (White Eyes) to Virginia and Pennsylvania, July 23, 1774, ibid., 552–53; Guy Johnson to Gage, August 19, 1774, *SWJP*, 13:669–70; Lt. Col. Caldwell to the Six Nations, September 29, 1774, *NYCD*, 8:507–8; *Pa. Archives*, 1st ser., 4:508; St. Clair to John Penn, June 16, 1774, ibid., 519; William Thompson to John Penn, June 19, 1774, ibid., 622.

57   Wainwright, "Turmoil at Pittsburgh," 140; Col. William Fleming's Journal, in Thwaites and Kellogg, *Dunmore's War*, 290; St. Clair to Joseph Shippen, Jr., November 2, 1774, *Pa. Archives*, 1st ser., 4:586; on the battle of Point Pleasant, Dunmore to Dartmouth, December 24, 1774, Davies, *Documents of the American Revolution*, 8:261–62; Christian to Col. William Preston, November 8, 1774, Thwaites and Kellogg, *Dunmore's War*, 304; on the continued hostility of Ohio Iroquois, St. Clair to John Penn, December 4, 1774, *Pa. Archives*, 1st ser., 4:586–88; Tanner, *Atlas*, 71–72, 79–80.

Conclusion

1   For a discussion of the aggressiveness Americans displayed on the frontier see John Shy, *A People Numerous and Armed: Reflections on the Military Struggle for American Independence*, 278–80.

2   Colin G. Calloway, *Crown and Calumet: British-Indian Relations, 1783–1815*, chaps. 1, 8, and 9.

3   Edmunds, *Shawnee Prophet*, esp. 11–17, for the post-1774 conflict between Shawnees and the United States; idem, *Tecumseh*, for Tecumseh's role; Wallace, *Death and Rebirth of the Seneca*, chap. 6, on the Senecas' role in events after Dunmore's invasion.

4   On Tenskwatawa, see Edmunds, *Shawnee Prophet*, chaps. 3 and 4; on Handsome Lake and

the Seneca revitalization, see Wallace, *Death and Rebirth of the Seneca*, passim; on the Delawares' westward trek see C. A. Weslager, *The Delaware Indian Westward Migrations, with the Text of Two Manuscripts (1821–22) Responding to General Lewis Cass's Inquiries about Lenape Culture and Language*, 35–77, 209–50; the retreat of Indians from the Ohio Country can be followed in Tanner, *Atlas of Great Lakes Indian History*, 74–104, and maps 15, 16, 17, 18, and 20.

Bibliography

Primary Sources

Manuscript Collections

American Antiquarian Society, Worcester, Massachusetts
  John Bradstreet Papers, 1742–1782: Orderly Book Collection
American Philosophical Society, Philadelphia, Pennsylvania
  Chalmers Collection
  Indian and Military Affairs of Pennsylvania
  Logan Papers
  Miscellaneous Manuscripts
  Shippen Papers
Bethlehem, Pennsylvania
  Moravian Archives (microfilm)
British Library, London
  Additional Manuscripts, series 21661–21892, Sir Frederick Haldimand Papers (micro-film)
William L. Clements Library, University of Michigan, Ann Arbor
  Thomas Gage Papers, American Series, 1755–75
Historical Society of Pennsylvania, Philadelphia
  Cadwallader Collection, George Croghan Papers
  Etting Collections
  Gratz Collection, Indian Commissioners' Papers
  Logan Papers
  Pemberton Papers
  Penn MSS, Proprietary Records: Indian Affairs
  Penn MSS, Official Correspondence
  Peters Papers

National Archives of Canada, Ottawa
    Records relating to Indian Affairs, RG 10, series 2, Commissioners of Indian Affairs, Albany, 1677–1748
    MG 18 M; series 1, Monckton Papers of the Northcliffe Collection
The Newberry Library, Chicago, Illinois
    Ayer Manuscripts
Public Record Office, London
    Colonial Office Records, Class 5, America and the West Indies (Microfilm: University Publications of America, 1972 [Part 1, Westward Expansion])
    War Office Records, Series 34, Sir Jeffery, First Baron Amherst, Official Papers (microfilm)

Published Sources

Abbot, W. W., and Dorothy Twohig, eds. *The Papers of George Washington, Colonial Series.* 7 vols. to date. Charlottesville: University of Virginia Press, 1983—.

Adolph, Henry F. "Wyoming Described in Letter Written by Rev. John Heckewelder." *Pennsylvania Archaeology* 6 (1937): 46–49.

Alden, Timothy, ed. "An Account of the Captivity of Hugh Gibson among the Delaware Indians of the Big Beaver and Muskingum from the Latter Part of July 1756 to the Beginning of April, 1759." *Collections of the Massachusetts Historical Society*, 3d ser., 6 (1837):140–53.

Alvord, Clarence Walworth, and Clarence Edwin Carter, eds. *Collections of the Illinois State Historical Library.* vol. 10. *The Critical Period, 1763–1765.* Springfield: Illinois State Historical Library, 1915.

———. *Collections of the Illinois State Historical Library.* Vol. 11. *The New Regime, 1765–1767.* Springfield: Illinois State Historical Library, 1916.

———. *Collections of the Illinois State Historical Library.* Vol. 16. *Trade and Politics, 1767–1769.* Springfield: Illinois State Historical Library, 1921.

"The Aspinwall Papers." *Collections of the Massachusetts Historical Society*, 4th Ser., vol. 9 (1871).

Bailey, Kenneth P., ed. *The Ohio Company Papers, 1753–1817, Being Primarily Papers of the "Suffering Traders" of Pennsylvania.* Arcata, Calif., 1947.

[Bard, Richard.] "An Account of the Captivity of Richard Bard, Esq." In Washburn, *Narratives of North American Indian Captivities*, 57:115–22.

Bartram, John. *Observations on the Inhabitants, Climate, Soil, Rivers, Productions, Animals, and Other Matters Worthy of Notice Made by Mr. John Bartram in His Travels from Pensilvania to Onondago, Oswego, and the Lake Ontario, in Canada.* London: Whiston and White, 1751.

Beauchamp, William Martin, ed. *Moravian Journals relating to Central New York, 1745–66.* Syracuse, N.Y.: Onondaga Historical Association, 1916.

Bond, Beverly W., Jr., ed. "The Captivity of Charles Stuart, 1755–1775." *Mississippi Valley Historical Review* 13 (1926–27): 58–81.

[Bonnecamps]. "Account of the Voyage on the Beautiful River Made in 1749, under the Direction of Monsieur de Céloron, by Father Bonnecamps." *Ohio Archaeological and Historical Quarterly* 29 (1920): 397–423.

Boyd, Julian P., ed. *Indian Treaties Printed by Benjamin Franklin, 1736–1762.* Philadelphia: Historical Society of Pennsylvania, 1938.

Brock, R. A., ed. *The Official Records of Robert Dinwiddie, Lieutenant-Governor of the Colony of Virginia, 1751–1758*. 2 vols. Collections of the Virginia Historical Society, n.s., 3–4. Richmond: Virginia Historical Society, 1883–1884.

Browne, William Hand, et al., eds. *Archives of Maryland*. 72 vols. to date. Baltimore, 1883–.

Carter, Clarence Edwin, ed. *The Correspondence of General Thomas Gage with the Secretaries of State, 1763–1775*. 2 vols. New York: Archon, 1989.

Cochrane, Captain Gavin. "Treatise on the Indians of North America Written in the Year 1764." Ayer MSS. NA 176, Newberry Library.

Darlington, William M. *Christopher Gist's Journals with Historical, Georgraphical and Ethnological Notes and Biographies of His Contemporaries.*. Pittsburgh: J. R. Weldin, 1893.

Davies, K. G., ed. *Documents of the American Revolution, 1770–1783*. 20 vols. Shannon: Irish University Press, 1972–79.

Dexter, Franklin B., ed. *Diary of David McClure, Doctor of Divinity, 1748–1820.*. New York: Knickerbocker Press, 1899.

Dunbar, John R., ed. *The Paxton Papers*. The Hague, 1975.

Goodwin, Alfred T., ed. *Journal of Captain William Trent from Logstown to Pickawillany, A.D. 1752*. Cincinnati: Clark, 1871.

[Gorrell, James]. "Lieutenant James Gorrell's Journal." *Collections of the State Historical Society of Wisconsin* 1–2 (1854): 24–48.

Hamilton, Charles, ed. *Braddock's Defeat*. Norman: University of Oklahoma Press, 1959.

Hamilton, Edward P., trans. and ed. *Adventures in the Wilderness: The American Journals of Louis Antoine de Bougainville, 1756–1760*. Norman: University of Oklahoma Press, 1964.

Hazard, Samuel, ed. *Minutes of the Provincial Council of Pennsylvania* [spine title, *Colonial Records*]. 16 vols. Harrisburg, 1838–53.

Heckewelder, John. *An Account of the History, Manners, and Customs of the Indian Nations Who Once Inhabited Pennsylvania and the Neighboring States* (1819). Ed. William C. Reichel. *Memoirs of the Historical Society of Pennsylvania* 12 (1826).

———. *A Narrative of the Mission of the United Brethren among the Delaware and Mohegan Indians, from Its Commencement in the Year 1740 to the Close of the Year 1808*. Philadelphia: McCarty and Davis, 1820.

Henry, Alexander. *Travels and Adventures in Canada and the Indian Territories between the Years 1760 and 1776*. Ed. James Bain. Rutland, Vt.: Charles Tuttle 1969.

Hulbert, Archer Butler, and William Nathaniel Schwarze, eds. *David Zeisberger's History of the North American Indians*. Columbus: Ohio State Archeological and Historical Society, 1910.

———. "The Diaries of David Zeisberger relating to the First Missions in the Ohio Basin." *Ohio Archaeological and Historical Quarterly* 21 (1912): 1–25.

Hunter, William A., ed. "Thomas Barton and the Forbes Expedition." *Pennsylvania Magazine of History and Biography* 105 (1971):431–83.

Jackson, Donald, and Dorothy Twohig, eds. *The Diaries of George Washington, 1748–1770*. 2 vols. Charlottesville: University of Virginia Press, 1976.

Jacobs, Wilbur R., ed. *The Appalachian Indian Frontier: The Edmund Atkin Report and the Plan of 1755*. Lincoln: University of Nebraska Press, 1967.

James, Alfred Proctor, ed. *Writings of General John Forbes relating to His Service in North America*. Menasha, Wis.: Collegiate Press, 1938.

James, James A., ed. *Collections of the Illinois State Historical Library*. Vol. 8. *George Rogers Clark Papers, 1771–1781*. Springfield: Illinois State Historical Library, 1912.

Johnson, Joseph E., ed. "A Quaker Imperialist's View of the British Colonies in America, 1732." *Pennsylvania Magazine of History and Biography* 60 (1936): 97–130.

Jones, Rev. David. *A Journal of Two Visits Made to Some Nations of Indians on the West Side of the River Ohio in the Years 1772 and 1773.* Fairfield, Wash.: Galleon Press, 1973.

Jordan, John W., ed. "James Kenny's 'Journal to ye Westward' 1758–59." *Pennsylvania Magazine of History and Biography* 37 (1913): 295–449.

———, "Journal of James Kenny, 1761–1763." *Pennsylvania Magazine of History and Biography* 37 (1913): 1–47, 152–201.

"Journal of a Mission to the Indians in Ohio, by Friends from Pennsylvania, July–September, 1773." *Historical Magazine and Notes and Queries, concerning the Antiquities, History and Biography of America,* 2d ser., 7 (1870): 103–7.

Kalm, Peter. *The America of 1750: Peter Kalm's Travels in North America: The English Version of 1770.* Ed. Adolph B. Benson. 2 vols. New York: Dover 1966.

Kellogg, Louise Phelps, ed. *Narratives of the Old Northwest, 1635–1699.* Original Narrative of Early American History, ed. J. Franklin Jameson. New York: Charles Scribner's Sons, 1917.

Kent, Donald H., ed. *Contrecoeur's Copy of George Washington's Journal of 1754.* Harrisburg: Pennsylvania Historical and Museum Commission, 1952.

———, *Pennsylvania and Delaware Treaties.* Vol. 1. *1629–1737. Early American Indian Documents: Laws and Treaties, 1607–1789.* Ed. Alden T. Vaughan. Washington, D.C.: University Press of America, 1979.

Kimball, Gertrude Selwyn, ed. *Correspondence of William Pitt When Secretary of State, with Colonial Governors and Military and Naval Commissioners in America.* 2 vols. New York: Macmillan, 1906.

Klett, Guy Soulliard, ed. *Journals of Charles Beatty, 1762–1769.* University Park: Pennsylvania State University Press, 1962.

Labaree, Leonard W., and William B. Willcox, eds. *The Papers of Benjamin Franklin.* 26 vols. to date. New Haven: Yale University Press, 1959–.

Lafitau, Joseph François. *Customs of the American Indians Compared with the Customs of Primitive Times.* Ed. and trans. William N. Fenton and Elizabeth L. Moore. 2 vols. Publications of the Champlain Society 48–49. Toronto: Champlain Society, 1974, 1977.

Lambing, A. A., ed. "Céloron's Journal." *Ohio State Archaeological and Historical Quarterly* 29 (1920): 335–95.

Lawson, John. *A New Voyage to Carolina.* Ed. Hugh Talmage Lefler. Chapel Hill: University of North Carolina Press, 1967.

Loskiel, George H. *History of the Mission of the United Brethren Among Indians in North America.* Trans. Christian Ignatius La Trobe. 3 parts. London, 1794.

[M'Cullough, John.] "A Narrative of the Captivity of John M'Cullough, Esq." In Washburn, *Narrative of North American Indian Captivities,* 57:87–113.

McDowell, William L., Jr., ed. *Documents relating to Indian Affairs May 21, 1751–August 7, 1754.* Colonial Records of South Carolina, ser. 2. Columbia, S.C., 1958.

Mahr, August C., trans. and ed. "A Canoe Journey from the Big Beaver to the Tuscarawas in 1771: A Travel Diary of John Heckewelder." *Ohio State Archaeological and Historical Quarterly* 61 (1952): 283–98.

———, "Diary of a Moravian Indian Mission Migration across Pennsylvania in 1772." *Ohio State Archaeological and Historical Quarterly* 62 (1953): 247–70.

Moore, Charles, ed. "The Gladwin Manuscripts." In *Michigan Pioneer and Historical Collections*, 27: 605–80. Lansing: Michigan State Historical Society, 1896.

Morris, Thomas. *Journal of Captain Thomas Morris from Miscellanies in Prose and Verse.* London, 1791. Reprinted Ann Arbor, Mich.: University Microfilms, 1966.

Mulkearn, Lois, ed. *George Mercer Papers relating to the Ohio Company of Virginia.* Pittsburgh: University of Pittsburgh Press, 1954.

O'Callaghan, Edmund B., ed. *The Documentary History of the State of New York.* 4 vols. Albany: Weed, Parsons, 1849–51.

O'Callaghan, Edmund B., and Berthold Fernow, eds. *Documents relative to the Colonial History of the State of New York.* 15 vols. Albany: Weed, Parsons, 1856–87.

"Papers relating to the Expeditions of Colonel Bradstreet and Colonel Bouquet, in Ohio, A.D. 1784." *Western Reserve and Northern Ohio Historical Society Tract*, no. 13 (February 1872): 1–5.

Pease, Theodore C., and Ernestine Jenison, eds. *Collections of the Illinois State Historical Library.* Vol. 29. *Illinois on the Eve of the Seven Years' War, 1747–1755.* Springfield: Illinois State Historical Library, 1940.

Peckham, Howard H., ed. *George Croghan's Journal of His Trip to Detroit in 1767, with His Correspondence relating Thereto.* Ann Arbor: University of Michigan Press, 1939.

———. "Thomas Gist's Indian Captivity, 1758–1759." *Pennsylvania Magazine of History and Biography* 80 (1956): 285–311.

Pennsylvania Archives. 9 ser., 138 vols. Philadelphia, 1852–1949.

Pilkington, Walter, ed. *The Journals of Samuel Kirkland, Eighteenth-Century Missionary to the Iroquois, Government Agent, Father of Hamilton College.* Clinton, N.Y.: Hamilton College, 1980.

[Post, Charles Frederick]. "Two Journals of Western Tours, by Charles Frederick Post: One, to the Neighborhood of Fort Duquesne (July–September, 1758); the Other, to the Ohio (October, 1758–January, 1759)." In *Early Western Travels, 1748–1846*, ed. Reuben Gold Thwaites, 1:175–291. Cleveland: Arthur H. Clark, 1904.

Reece, Frances R., ed. "Colonel Eyre's Journal of His Trip from New York to Pittsburgh, 1762." *Western Pennsylvania Historical Magazine* 27 (1944): 37–50.

Reese, George, ed. *The Official Papers of Francis Fauquier, Lieutenant Governor of Virginia, 1758–1768.* 3 vols. Virginia Historical Society, Virginia Historical Documents, 14, 15, 16. Charlottesville: University of Virginia Press, 1980–83.

[Robison, Robert]. "A Narrative of Facts Furnished by Robert Robison. . . ." In Washburn, *Narratives of North American Indian Captivities*, 57:123–29.

Rogers, Robert. *Journals of Major Robert Rogers.* London, 1765. Reprinted Ann Arbor, Mich.: Readex Microprint Corporation, 1967.

Schweinitz, Edmund de, ed. "The Narrative of Marie Le Roy and Barbara Leininger, for Three Years Captives among the Indians." *Pennsylvania Magazine of History and Biography* 29 (1905): 407–20.

Scull, G. D., ed. "The Montresor Journals." *Collections of the New York Historical Society*, 1881, 252–321.

Smith, James. "An Account of the Remarkable Occurrences in the Life and Travels of Colonel James Smith (Late a Citizen of Bourbon County, Kentucky) during His Captivity with the Indians, in the Years 1755, '56, '57, '58, and '59." In Washburn, *Narratives of North American Indian Captivities*, 55:178–264.

Smith, William H., ed. *The St. Clair Papers: The Life and Public Service of Arthur St. Clair.* 2 vols. Cincinnati: Robert Clarke, 1882.

Stevens, Sylvester K., and Donald H. Kent, eds. *The Expedition of Baron de Longueuil*. Harrisburg: Pennsylvania Historical Commission, 1940.

——, *Journal of Chaussegros de Lery*. Harrisburg: Pennsylvania Historical Commission, 1940.

——, *The Papers of Colonel Henry Bouquet*. 19 vols. Harrisburg: Pennsylvania Historical Commission, 1940–43.

——, *Wilderness Chronicles of Northwestern Pennsylvania*. Harrisburg: Pennsylvania Historical Commission, 1941.

Stevens, Sylvester K., Donald H. Kent, Louis M. Waddell, et al., eds. *The Papers of Henry Bouquet*. 5 vols. to date. Harrisburg: Pennsylvania Historical and Museum Commission, 1951—.

Sullivan, James, et al., eds. *The Papers of Sir William Johnson*. 14 vols. Albany: State University of New York, 1921–63.

Thwaites, Reuben Gold, ed. *Collections of the State Historical Society of Wisconsin*. Vol. 17. *The French Regime in Wisconsin, 1727–1743*. Madison: State Historical Society of Wisconsin, 1906.

——. *Collections of the State Historical Society of Wisconsin*. Vol. 18. *The French Regime in Wisconsin, 1743–1760*. Madison: State Historical Society of Wisconsin, 1908.

——. *Early Western Travels, 1748–1846*. Cleveland: Arthur H. Clark, 1904.

Thwaites, Reuben Gold, and Louise Phelps Kellogg, eds. *Documentary History of Dunmore's War, 1774*. Madison: Wisconsin Historical Society, 1904. Reprinted: Harrisonburg, Va.: Carrier, 1947.

Timberlake, Henry. *Lieutenant Henry Timberlake's Memoirs, 1756–1765*. Ed. Samuel Cole Williams. Johnson City, Tenn., 1927. Reprinted New York: Arno Press, 1971.

"The Treaty of Logg's Town, 1752." *Virginia Magazine of History and Biography* 13 (1905–06): 148–74.

Volwiler, A. T., ed. "William Trent's Journal at Fort Pitt, 1763." *Mississippi Valley Historical Review* 11 (1924): 390–413.

Wainwright, Nicholas B., ed. "George Croghan's Journal, April 3, 1759 to April [30], 1763." *Pennsylvania Magazine of History and Biography* 71 (1947): 313–444.

——, "Turmoil at Pittsburgh: Diary of Augustine Prevost, 1774." *Pennsylvania Magazine of History and Biography* 85 (1961): 111–62.

Wallace, Paul A. W., ed. *The Travels of John Heckewelder in Frontier America*. Pittsburgh: University of Pittsburgh Press, 1985. Originally published as *Thirty Thousand Miles with John Heckewelder*, 1958.

Washburn, Wilcomb E., ed. *Narratives of North American Indian Captivities*. 111 vol. New York: Garland, 1976–.

Webster, J. Clarence, ed. *Journal of Jeffery Amherst, Recording the Military Career of General Amherst in America from 1758 to 1763*. Chicago: University of Chicago Press, 1931.

Williams, Edward G., ed. *Bouquet's March to the Ohio: The Forbes Road*. Pittsburgh: Historical Society of Western Pennsylvania, 1975.

——, "The Orderly Book of Colonel Henry Bouquet's Expedition against the Ohio Indians, 1764." *Western Pennsylvania Historical Magazine* 42 (1959): 9–33, 179–200, 283–352.

Wraxall, Peter. *An Abridgment of the Indian Affairs Contained in Four Folio Volumes, Transacted in the Colony of New York, from the Year 1678 to the Year 1751*. Ed. Charles H. McIlwain. Cambridge: Harvard University Press, 1915.

Secondary Sources

Books

Abernethy, Thomas Perkins. *Western Lands and the American Revolution.* New York: University of Virginia Institute for Research in the Social Sciences, 1937. Reprinted New York: Russell and Russell, 1959.

Allen, Robert S. *The British Indian Department and the Frontier in North America, 1755–1830.* Ottawa, Canada: National Historic Parks and Sites Branch, Department of Indian Affairs and Northern Development, 1975.

Anderson, Gary Clayton. *Kinsmen of Another Kind: Dakota-White Relations in the Upper Missouri Valley, 1650–1862.* Lincoln: University of Nebraska Press, 1984.

Aquila, Richard. *The Iroquois Restoration: Iroquois Diplomacy on the Colonial Frontier, 1701–1754.* Detroit: Wayne State University Press, 1983.

Axtell, James. *After Columbus: Essays in the Ethnohistory of Colonial North America.* New York: Oxford University Press, 1988.

———. *The European and the Indian: Essays in the Ethnohistory of Colonial North America.* New York: Oxford University Press, 1981.

———. *The Invasion Within: The Contest of Cultures in Colonial North America.* New York: Oxford University Press, 1985.

Bailey, Kenneth P. *The Ohio Company of Virginia and the Westward Movement 1748–1792;* Glendale, Calif.: Arthur H. Clark, 1939.

Bailyn, Bernard. *The Peopling of British North America: An Introduction.* New York: Alfred A. Knopf, 1987.

———. *Voyagers to the West: A Passage in the Peopling of America on the Eve of the Revolution.* New York: Alfred A. Knopf, 1986.

Barth, Fredrik, ed. *Ethnic Groups and Boundaries: The Social Organization of Cultural Difference.* Boston: Little, Brown, 1969.

Becker, Marshall Joseph. *The Forks of Delaware, Pennsylvania, during the First Half of the Eighteenth Century: The Migrations of Some "Jerseys" into a Former Shared Resource Area North of Lenape Territory and Its Implications for Cultural Boundaries and Identities.* Abhandlungen der Volkerkundlichen Arbeitsgemeinschaft, 55. Nortorf, West Germany, 1987.

Bonvillain, Nancy, ed. *Studies on Iroquoian Culture.* Occasional Publications in Northeastern Anthropology 6. Rindge, N.J.: Franklin Pierce College, Fund for Anthropology, 1980.

Bradley, James W. *Evolution of the Onondaga Iroquois: Accommodating Change, 1500–1655.* Syracuse: Syracuse University Press, 1987.

Brasser, Ted J. *Riding the Frontier's Crest: Mahican Indian Culture and Culture Change.* National Museum of Man, Ethnology Division, Paper 13, Ottawa: National Museums of Canada, 1974.

Brose, David, ed. *The Late Prehistory of the Lake Erie Drainage: A Symposium Revised.* Cleveland: Cleveland Museum of Natural History, 1976.

Brown, George W., et al., eds. *Dictionary of Canadian Biography.* Toronto: University of Toronto Press, 1966—.

Calloway, Colin G. *Crown and Calumet: British-Indian Relations, 1783–1815.* Norman: University of Oklahoma Press, 1987.

———. *The Western Abenakis of Vermont, 1600–1800: War, Migration, and the Survival of an Indian People.* Norman: University of Oklahoma Press, 1990.

Cappon, Lester J., et al., eds. *Atlas of Early American History*. Vol. 2 *The Revolutionary Era, 1760–1790*. Princeton: Princeton University Press, 1976.

Clifton, James A. *Hurons of the West: Migrations and Adaptations of the Ontario Iroquoians, 1650–1704*. National Museum of Man, Canadian Ethnology Service Research Report. Ottawa: National Museums of Canada, 1977.

———. *The Prairie People: Continuity and Change in Potawatomi Indian Culture, 1665–1965*. Lawrence: Regents Press of Kansas, 1977.

Deetz, James. *In Small Things Forgotten: The Archaeology of Early American Life*. New York: Doubleday Press, 1977.

Donehoo, George P. *A History of the Indian Villages and Place Names in Pennsylvania*. Harrisburg, Pa.: Telegraph Press, 1928. Reprinted Baltimore: Gateway Press, 1977.

Downes, Randolph C. *Council Fires on the Upper Ohio: A Narrative of Indian Affairs in the Upper Ohio Valley until 1795*. Pittsburgh: University of Pittsburgh Press, 1940. Reprinted 1968.

Duffy, Christopher. *The Military Experience in the Age of Reason*. New York: Macmillan, 1987.

Duffy, John. *Epidemics in Colonial America*. Baton Rouge: Louisiana State University Press, 1971.

Dunn, Richard S., and Mary Maples Dunn, eds. *The World of William Penn*. Philadelphia: University of Pennsylvania Press, 1986.

Eccles, W. J. *The Canadian Frontier, 1534–1760*. Rev. ed. Albuquerque: University of New Mexico Press, 1983.

Edmunds, R. David. *The Shawnee Prophet*. Lincoln: University of Nebraska Press, 1983.

———. *Tecumseh and the Quest for Indian Leadership*. Boston: Little, Brown, 1984.

———. ed. *American Indian Leaders: Studies in Diversity*. Lincoln: University of Nebraska Press, 1980.

Elliott, John B., ed. *Contest for Empire, 1500–1775*. Indianapolis: Indiana Historical Society, 1979.

Fenton, William N. *Symposium on Local Diversity in Iroquois Culture*. Bureau of American Ethnology Bulletin 149. Washington, D.C.: Smithsonian Institution, 1951.

Fischer, David Hackett. *Albion's Seed: Four British Folkways in America*. New York: Oxford University Press, 1989.

Foster, Michael K., Jack Campisi, and Marianne Mithun, eds. *Extending the Rafters: Interdisciplinary Approaches to Iroquoian Studies*. Albany: State University of New York Press, 1984.

Fregault, Guy. *Canada: The War of the Conquest*. Trans. Margaret M. Cameron. Toronto: Oxford University Press, 1969.

Gilman, Carolyn. *Where Two Worlds Meet: The Great Lakes Fur Trade*. Publications of the Minnesota Society Museum Exhibit Series 2. St. Paul: Minnesota Historical Society, 1982.

Gipson, Lawrence Henry. *The British Empire before the American Revolution*. Vol. 4. *Zones of International Friction: North America South of the Great Lakes Region, 1748–1754*. New York: Alfred A. Knopf, 1961.

———. *The British Empire before the American Revolution*. Vol. 6. *The Great War for the Empire: The Years of Defeat, 1754–1757*. New York: Alfred A. Knopf, 1946.

———. *The British Empire before the American Revolution*. Vol. 7. *The Great War for the Empire: The Victorious Years, 1758–1760*. New York: Alfred A. Knopf, 1949.

———. *Lewis Evans, to Which Is Added Evans' "A Brief Account of Pennsylvania" Together with Facsimiles of His Geographical, Historical, Political, Philosophical, and Mechanical Essays, Numbers I and II*. Philadelphia: Historical Society of Pennsylvania, 1939.

Gray, Emma E., and Leslie Robb Gray. *Wilderness Christians: The Moravian Mission to the Delaware Indians*. Ithaca, N.Y.: Cornell University Press, 1956.

Graymont, Barbara. *The Iroquois in the American Revolution.* Syracuse: Syracuse University Press, 1972.

Hamilton, Edward P. *Sir William Johnson, Colonial American.* Port Washington, N.Y.: Kennikat Press, 1976.

Hanna, Charles A. *The Wilderness Trail, or The Ventures and Adventures of the Pennsylvania Traders on the Allegheny Path.* 2 vols. New York: B. P. Putnam's Sons, 1911.

Harris, R. Cole, and Geoffrey J. Matthews, eds. *Historical Atlas of Canada.* Vol. 1. *From the Beginning to 1800.* Toronto: University of Toronto Press, 1987.

Hayes, Charles F., ed. *Charles F. Wray Series in Seneca Archaeology.* Vol. 1. *The Adams and Culbertson Sites,* by Charles F. Wray et al. Rochester, N.Y.: Rochester Museum and Science Center, 1987.

Helm, June, ed. *Essays on the Problem of Tribe.* Seattle: University of Washington Press, 1968.

Howard, James H. *Shawnee! The Ceremonialism of a Native American Tribe and Its Cultural Background.* Athens: Ohio University Press, 1981.

Hunter, William A. *Forts on the Pennsylvania Frontier, 1753–1758.* Harrisburg: Pennsylvania Historical and Museum Commission, 1960.

Jacobs, Wilbur R. *Wilderness Politics and Indian Gifts: The Northern Colonial Frontier, 1748–1763.* Lincoln: University of Nebraska Press, 1967.

———. *Dispossessing the American Indian: Indians and Whites on the Colonial Frontier.* New York: Charles Scribner's Sons, 1972.

James, Alfred Proctor. *The Ohio Company: Its Inner History.* Pittsburgh: University of Pittsburgh Press, 1959.

James, Alfred Proctor, and Charles Morse Stotz. *Drums in the Forest.* Pittsburgh: Historical Society of Western Pennsylvania, 1958.

Jennings, Francis. *The Ambiguous Iroquois Empire: The Covenant Chain Confederation of Indian Tribes with English Colonies.* New York: W. W. Norton, 1984.

———. *The American Indian and the American Revolution.* Occasional Papers 6. Chicago: Newberry Library Center for the History of the American Indian, 1983.

———. *Empire of Fortune: Crowns, Colonies, and Tribes in the Seven Years' War in America.* New York: W. W. Norton, 1988.

———. *The Invasion of America: Indians, Colonists, and the Cant of Conquest.* Chapel Hill: University of North Carolina Press, 1975.

Jennings, Francis, William N. Fenton, Mary A. Druke, and David R. Miller, eds. *The History and Culture of Iroquois Diplomacy: An Interdisciplinary Guide to the Treaties of the Six Nations and Their League.* Syracuse: Syracuse University Press, 1985.

Jones, Dorothy V. *License for Empire: Colonialism by Treaty in Early America.* Chicago: University of Chicago Press, 1982.

Kellogg, Louise Phelps. *The British Regime in Wisconsin and the Northwest.* Madison: State Historical Society of Wisconsin, 1933.

———. *The French Regime in Wisconsin and the Northwest.* Madison: State Historical Society of Wisconsin, 1925. Reprinted New York: Cooper Square, 1968.

Kent, Barry C. *Susquehanna's Indians.* Anthropological Series 6. Harrisburg: Pennsylvania Historical and Museum Commission, 1984.

Kent, Donald H. *The French Invasion of Western Pennsylvania.* Harrisburg: Pennsylvania Historical and Museum Commission, 1954.

———. *The Iroquois Indians.* 2 vols. New York: Garland, 1974.

————, ed. *Pennsylvania and Delaware Treaties, 1629–1737.* Washington, D.C.: University Publications of America, 1979.

Kopperman, Paul E. *Braddock on the Monongahela.* Pittsburgh: University of Pittsburgh Press, 1977.

Kraft, Herbert C. *A Delaware Indian Symposium.* Anthropological Series 4. Harrisburg: Pennsylvania Historical and Museum Commission, 1974.

————. *The Lenape: Archaeology, History, and Ethnography.* Collections of the New Jersey Historical Society, vol. 21. Newark: New Jersey Historical Society, 1986.

————. *The Lenape Indians: A Symposium.* Archeological Research Center, Seton Hall University, Publication 7. South Orange, N.J.: Seton Hall University, 1984.

Levine, Robert A., and Donald T. Campbell. *Ethnocentrism: Theories of Conflict, Ethnic Attitudes, and Group Behavior.* New York: John Wiley, 1972.

Long, John Cuthbert. *Lord Jeffrey Amherst: A Soldier of the King.* New York: Crowell-Collier and Macmillan, 1976.

MacAndrews, Craig, and Robert B. Edgerton. *Drunken Comportment: A Social Explanation.* New York: Aldine, 1969.

Mainfort, Robert C., Jr. *Indian Social Dynamics in the Period of European Contact: Fletcher Site Cemetery, Bay County.* Publications of the Museum, Anthropological Series, vol. 1, no. 4. East Lansing: Michigan State University, 1979.

Mauss, Marcel. *The Gift: Forms and Functions of Exchange in Archaic Societies.* Trans. Ian Cunnnison. New York: W. W. Norton, 1967.

Mayer-Oakes, William J. *Prehistory of the Upper Ohio Valley.* Annals of the Carnegie Museum, vol. 34. Pittsburgh: Carnegie Museum of Natural History, 1955.

Mayo, Lawrence Shaw. *Jeffrey Amherst: A Biography.* London: Longmans, Green, 1916.

Meinig, D. W. *The Shaping of America: A Geographical Perspective on Five Hundred Years of History.* Vol. 1: *Atlantic America, 1492–1800.* New Haven: Yale University Press, 1986.

Merrell, James H. *The Indians' New World: Catawbas and Their Neighbors from European Contact through the Era of Removal.* Chapel Hill: University of North Carolina Press, 1989.

Moogk, Peter. *Building a House in New France.* Toronto: McClelland and Steward, 1977.

Newcomb, William W., Jr. *The Culture and Acculturation of the Delaware Indians.* University of Michigan Museum of Anthropology, Anthropology Papers 10. Ann Arbor: University of Michigan, 1956.

Niemczyki, Mary Ann Palmer. *The Origin and Development of the Seneca and Cayuga Tribes of New York State.* Research Records 17. Rochester, N.Y.: Rochester Museum and Science Center, 1984.

Norton, Thomas Elliot. *The Fur Trade in Colonial New York, 1686–1776.* Madison: University of Wisconsin Press, 1974.

Pargellis, Stanley McCrory. *Lord Loudoun in North America.* New Haven: Yale University Press, 1933. Reprinted New York: Archon Books, 1968.

Parkman, Francis. *The Conspiracy of Pontiac and the Indian War after the Conquest of Canada.* 2 vols. Boston: Little, Brown, 1909.

————. *Montcalm and Wolfe.* 2 vols. Boston: Little, Brown, 1909.

Peckham, Howard H. *Pontiac and the Indian Uprising.* New York: Russell and Russell, 1947.

Quimby, George Irving. *Indian Culture and European Trade Goods: Archaeology of the Historic Period in the Western Great Lakes Region.* Madison: University of Wisconsin Press, 1966.

Ray, Arthur J. *Indians in the Fur Trade: Their Role as Hunters, Trappers, and Middlemen in the Lands Southwest of Hudson's Bay, 1660–1870.* Toronto: University of Toronto Press, 1974.

Reid, John Phillip. *A Better Kind of Hatchet: Law, Trade, and Diplomacy in the Cherokee Nation during the Early Years of European Contact*. University Park: Pennsylvania State University Press, 1976.

Richter, Daniel K., and James H. Merrell, eds. *Beyond the Covenant Chain: The Iroquois and Their Neighbors in Indian North America, 1600–1800*. Syracuse: Syracuse University Press, 1987.

Robinson, W. Stitt. *The Southern Colonial Frontier, 1607–1763*. Albuquerque: University of New Mexico Press, 1979.

Sahlins, Marshall. *Stone Age Economics*. Chicago: Aldine, 1972.

Severance, Frank H. *An Old Frontier of France*, 2 vols. New York: Dodd, Mead, 1917; reprinted in one volume, Arno Press, 1971.

Shy, John. *A People Numerous and Armed: Reflections on the Military Struggle for American Independence*. Rev. ed. Ann Arbor: University of Michigan Press, 1990.

———. *Toward Lexington: The Role of the British Army in the Coming of the American Revolution*. Princeton: Princeton University Press, 1965.

Slaughter, Thomas P. *The Whiskey Rebellion: Frontier Epilogue to the American Revolution*. New York: Oxford University Press, 1986.

Smith, Thomas H. *The Mapping of Ohio*. Kent, Ohio: Kent State University Press, 1977.

Sosin, Jack M. *Whitehall and the Wilderness: The Middle West in British Colonial Policy, 1760–1775*. Lincoln: University of Nebraska Press, 1961.

Stagg, Jack. *Anglo-Indian Relations in North America to 1763, and an Analysis of the Royal Proclamation of 7 October 1763*. Ottawa: Research Branch, Indian and Northern Affairs of Canada, 1981.

Tanner, Helen Hornbeck, ed. *Atlas of Great Lakes Indian History*. Norman: University of Oklahoma Press, 1987.

Tanner, Helen Hornbeck, and Erminie Wheeler-Voegelin. *Indians of Ohio and Indiana prior to 1795*. 2 vols. New York: Garland, 1974.

Thayer, Theodore. *Pennsylvania Politics and the Growth of Democracy, 1740–1776*. Harrisburg: Pennsylvania Historical and Museum Commission, 1953.

Tooker, Elizabeth, ed. *Iroquois Culture, History, and Prehistory: Proceedings of the 1965 Conference on Iroquois Research*. Albany: State University of New York Press, 1967.

Trigger, Bruce G. *The Children of Aataentsic: A History of the Huron People to 1660*. 2 vols. Montreal: McGill–Queen's University Press, 1976.

———. *The Huron, Farmers of the North*. 2d ed. Fort Worth, Tex.: Holt, Rinehart and Winston, 1990.

———. *Natives and Newcomers: Canada's "Heroic Age" Reconsidered*. Montreal: McGill–Queen's University Press, 1985.

———, ed. *Northeast*. Vol. 15 of *Handbook of North American Indians*, ed. William C. Sturtevant. Washington, D.C.: Smithsonian Institution, 1978.

Vecsey, Christopher, and Robert W. Venables, eds. *American Indian Environments: Ecological Issues in Native American History*. Syracuse: Syracuse University Press, 1980.

Wainwright, Nicholas B. *George Croghan, Wilderness Diplomat*. Chapel Hill: University of North Carolina Press, 1959.

Wallace, Anthony F. C. *The Death and Rebirth of the Seneca*. New York: Random House, 1969.

———. *King of the Delawares: Teedyuscung, 1700–1763*. Philadelphia: University of Pennsylvania Press, 1949.

Wallace, Paul A. W. *Conrad Weiser, 1696–1760: Friend of Colonist and Mohawk*. Philadelphia: University of Pennsylvania Press, 1945.

————. *Indian Paths of Pennsylvania*. Harrisburg: Pennsylvania Historical and Museum Commission, 1965.

————. *Indians in Pennsylvania*. Rev. ed. Anthropological Series 5. Harrisburg: Pennsylvania Historical and Museum Commission, 1981.

Weslager, C. A. *The Delaware Indian Westward Migration, with the Text of Two Manuscripts (1821–27) Responding to General Lewis Cass's Inquiries about Lenape Culture and Language*. Wallingford, Pa.: Middle Atlantic Press, 1978.

————. *The Delaware Indians: A History*. New Brunswick, N.J.: Rutgers University Press, 1972.

Wheeler-Voegelin, Erminie, and Helen Hornbeck Tanner, *Indians of Northern Ohio and Southeastern Michigan*. New York: Garland, 1974.

Wood, Jerome H., Jr. *Conestoga Crossroads: Lancaster, Pennsylvania, 1730–1790*. Harrisburg: Pennsylvania Historical and Museum Commission, 1979.

Wood, Peter H., Gregory A. Waselkov, and Thomas M. Hatley, eds. *Powhatan's Mantle: Indians in the Colonial Southeast*. Lincoln: University of Nebraska Press, 1989.

Wray, Charles F., et al. *Charles F. Wray Series in Seneca Archaeology. Vol. 1. The Adams and Culbertson Sites*. Research Records no. 19. Rochester, N.Y.: Rochester Museum and Science Center, 1987.

Young, Alfred F., ed. *The American Revolution: Explorations in the History of American Radicalism*. DeKalb: Northern Illinois University Press, 1976.

Articles

Alber, Thomes S., and Eliabeth Tooker. "Seneca." In Trigger, *Northeast*, 505–17.

Albrecht, Carl. W., Jr. "The Peaceable Kingdom: Ohio on the Eve of Settlement." *Timeline* 2 (1985): 18–25.

Alden, John R. "The Albany Congress and the Creation of the Indian Superintendencies." *Mississippi Valley Historical Review* 27 (1940): 193–210.

Anderson, Niles. "Bushy Run, Decisive Battle in the West." *Western Pennsylvania Historical Magazine* 46 (1963): 211–45.

Becker, Marshall J. "The Boundary between the Lenape and Munsee: The Forks of Delaware as a Buffer Zone." *Man in the Northeast* 26 (1983): 1–20.

————. "The Lenape Bands prior to 1746: The Identification of Boundaries and Processes of Change to the Formation of the 'Delawares.'" In Kraft, *Lenape Indians*, 19–32.

————. "Native Settlements in the Forks of Delaware, in the Eighteenth Century: Archaeological Implications." *Pennsylvania Archaeologist* 58 (1988): 42–60.

————. "A Summary of Lenape Socio-political Organization and Settlement Pattern at the Time of European Contact: The Evidence for Collecting Bands." *Journal of Middle Atlantic Archaeology* 4 (1988): 79–83.

Benson, Evelyn A. "The Huguenot Le Torts: First Christian Family on the Conestoga." *Journal of the Lancaster County Historical Society* 65 (1961): 92–103.

Billington, Ray A. "The Fort Stanwix Treaty of 1768." *New York History* 25 (1944): 182–94.

Bonvillain, Nancy. "Iroquoian Women." In Bonvillain, *Studies on Iroquoian Culture*, 47–58.

Brasser, T. J. "Early Indian-European Contacts." in Trigger, *Northeast*, 78–88.

————. "Group Identification along a Moving Frontier." *Verhandlungen des XXXVIII Internationalen Amerikansten Kongress* (Munich), 2 (1971): 261–65.

Breen, Timothy H. "An Empire of Goods: The Anglicization of Colonial America, 1690–1776." *Journal of British Studies* 25 (1980): 467–99.

Brose, David, "The Valley Sweets Site, 20 SA 24, Saginaw County, Michigan." *Michigan Archaeologist* 12 (1966): 1–21.

Brown, Judith K. "Economic Organization and the Position of Women among the Iroquois." *Ethnohistory* 17 (1970): 151–67.

Callender, Charles. "Shawnee." in Trigger, *Northeast*, 622–35.

Campisi, Jack, "The Iroquois and the Euro-American Concept of Tribe." *New York History* 63 (1982): 165–82.

Champion, Walter T., Jr. "Christian Frederick Post and the Winning of the West." *Pennsylvania Magazine of History and Biography* 104 (1980): 308–25.

Clifton, James A. "The Re-emergent Wyandot: A Study of Ethnogenesis on the Detroit River Borderland, 1747." In *The Western District*, ed. K. G. Pryke and L. L. Kulisek, 1–17. Windsor, Ont.: Essex County Historical Society and Western District Council, 1983.

Cutcliffe, Stephen H. "The Sideling Hill Affair: The Cumberland County Riots of 1765." *Western Pennsylvania Historical Magazine* 59 (1978): 39–53.

Dowd, Gregory Evans, "The French King Wakes up in Detroit: 'Pontiac's War' in Rumor and History." *Ethnohistory* 37 (1990): 254–78.

Downes, Randolph C. "Dunmore's War: An Interpretation." *Mississippi Valley Historical Review* 21 (1934): 311–30.

Druke, Mary A. "Linking Arms: The Structure of Iroquois Intertribal Diplomacy." In Richter and Merrell, *Beyond the Covenant Chain*, 29–40.

Eccles, W. J. "The Fur Trade and Eighteenth Century Imperialism." *William and Mary Quarterly*, 3d ser., 40 (1983): 341–62.

————. "A Belated Review of Harold Adams Innes's *The Fur Trade in Canada*." *Canadian Historical Review* 60 (1979): 419–41.

Edmunds, R. David. "Old Briton." In Edmunds, *American Indian Leaders*, 1–20.

Ewing, William S. "Indian Captives Released by Colonel Bouguet." *Western Pennsylvania Historical Magazine* 39 (1956): 187–203.

Fenton, William N. "Cultural Stability and Change in American Indian Society." *Journal of the Royal Anthropological Institute of Great Britain and Ireland* 83 (1953): 169–74.

————. "Factionalism in American Indian Society." In *Actes des IVe Congrès International des Sciences Anthropologiques et Ethnologiques*, 2:330–46, Vienna, 1954–56.

————. "The Iroquois in History." In *North American Indians in Historical Perspective*, ed. Eleanor B. Leacock and Nancy O. Lurie, 129–68. New York: Random House, 1971.

————. "Locality as a Basic Factor in the Development of Iroquois Social Structure." In *Symposium on Local Diversity in Iroquois Culture*, ed. William N. Fenton, 35–54. Washington, D.C.: Bureau of American Ethnology, 1951.

————. "Problems Arising from the Historic Northeastern Position of the Iroquois." *Smithsonian Miscellaneous Collections* 100 (1940): 159–251.

Foster, Michael K. "On Who Spoke First at Iroquois-White Councils: An Exercise in the Method of Upstreaming." In Foster, Campisi, and Mithun, *Extending the Rafters*, 183–258.

Fried, Morton. "On the Concept of 'Tribe' and 'Tribal Society.'" In Helm, *Essays on the Problem of Tribe*, 3–20.

Gearing, Fred. "Structural Poses of Eighteenth Century Cherokee Villages." *American Anthropologist* 60 (1958): 1148–57.

Goddard, Ives. "Delaware." In Trigger, *Northeast*, 213–39.

Griffin, James B. "Late Prehistory of the Ohio Valley." In Trigger, *Northeast*, 547–59.

Haan, Richard L. "Covenant and Consensus: Iroquois and English, 1676–1760." In Richter and Merrell, *Beyond the Covenant Chain*, 41–57.

———. "The Problem of Iroquois Neutrality: Suggestions for Revision." *Ethnohistory* 27 (1980): 317–30.

Hamilton, Kenneth G. ."Cultural Contributions of Moravian Missions among the Indians." *Pennsylvania History* 17 (1951): 1–15.

Hatley, M. Thomas. "The Three Lives of Keowee: Loss and Recovery in Eighteenth-Century Cherokee Villages." In Wood, Waselkov, and Hatley, *Powhatan's Mantle*, 223–48.

Hauptman, Laurence M. "Refugee Havens: The Iroquois Villages of the Eighteenth Century." In Vecsey and Venables, *American Indian Environments*, 128–39.

Hervatin, Marco M. "Refuge[e] Wyandot Town of 1748." *Newsletter* (Beaver Valley Chapter, Society for Pennsylvania Archaeology), 7 January/February 1958): 1–4.

Hindle, Brooke. "The March of the Paxton Boys." *William and Mary Quarterly*, 3d ser., 3 (1946): 461–86.

Hunter, Charles E. "The Delaware Nativist Revival of the Mid-Eighteenth Century." *Ethnohistory* 18 (1971): 39–49.

Hunter, William A. "Documented Subdivisions of the Delaware Indians." *Bulletin of the Archaeological Society of New Jersey* 35 (1978): 20–40.

———. "History of the Ohio Valley." In Trigger, *Northeast*, 588–93.

———. "Provincial Negotiations with the Western Indians, 1754–58." *Pennsylvania History* 18 (1951): 213–29.

———. "Traders on the Ohio: 1730." *Western Pennsylvania Historical Magazine* 35 (1952): 85–92.

———. "Victory at Kittanning." *Pennsylvania History* 23 (1956): 376–407.

Huston, John W. "The British Evacuation of Fort Pitt, 1772." *Western Pennsylvania Historical Magazine* 48 (1985): 317–29.

Jennings, Francis. "Brother Miquon, Good Lord!" In Dunn and Dunn, *World of William Penn*, 195–214.

———. "The Constitutional Evolution of the Covenant Chain." *Proceedings of the American Philosophical Society* 115 (1971): 88–96.

———. "The Delaware Interregnum." *Pennsylvania Magazine of History and Biography* 89 (1965): 174–98.

———. "The Imperial Revolution: The American Revolution as a Tripartite Struggle for Sovereignty." In Jennings, *American Indian and the American Revolution*, 42–50.

———. "Incident at Tulpehocken." *Pennsylvania History* 35 (1968): 335–55.

———. "The Indians' Revolution." In Young, *American Revolution*, 319–48.

———. "The Indian Trade of the Susquehanna Valley." *Proceedings of the American Philosophical Society* 110 (1966): 406–24.

———. "Iroquois Alliances in American History." In Jennings et al., *History and Culture of Iroquois Diplomacy*, 37–66.

———. " 'Pennsylvania Indians' and the Iroquois." In Richter and Merrell, *Beyond the Covenant Chain*, 75–92.

———. "The Scandalous Policy of William Penn's Sons: Deeds and Documents of the Walking Purchase." *Pennsylvania History* 37 (1970): 19–39.

———. "Susquehannock." In Trigger, *Northeast*, 362–67.

———. "A Vanishing Indian: Francis Parkman versus His Sources." *Pennsylvania Magazine of History and Biography* 87 (1965): 306–25.

Kelsey, Harry. "The Amherst Plan: A Factor in the Pontiac Uprising." *Ontario History* 65 (1973): 149–58.

Kent, Donald H. "Communications." *Mississippi Valley Historical Review* 42 (1955): 762–63.

Kerby, Robert L. "The Other War in 1774: Dunmore's War." *West Virginia History* 36 (1974): 1–16.

King, James C. "Indian Credit as a Source of Friction in the Colonial Fur Trade." *Western Pennsylvania Historical Magazine* 49 (1966): 57–65.

Kinsey, W. Fred, III, and Jay F. Custer. "The Lancaster Park Site (36 LA 96): Conestoga Phase." *Pennsylvania Archaeologist* 52 (1982): 17–56.

Knollenberg, Bernard. "General Amherst and Germ Warfare." *Mississippi Valley Historical Review* 41 (1954): 489–94.

McConnell, Michael N. "Peoples 'in Between': The Iroquois and the Ohio Indians, 1720–1768." In Richter and Merrell, *Beyond the Covenant Chain*, 93–112.

Marshall, Peter. "Colonial Protest and Imperial Retrenchment: Indian Policy, 1764–1768." *Journal of American Studies* 5 (1971): 1–17.

———. "Sir William Johnson and the Treaty of Fort Stanwix, 1768." *Journal of American Studies* 1 (1967): 149–79.

Mastromarino, Mark A. "Teaching Old Dogs New Tricks: The English Mastiff and the Anglo-American Experience." *Historian* 49 (1986): 10–25.

Merrell, James H. "The Indians' New World: The Catawba Experience." *William and Mary Quarterly*, 3d ser., 41 (1984): 537–65.

———. "'Our Bond of Peace': Patterns of Intercultural Exchange in the Carolina Piedmont, 1650–1750." In Wood, Waselkov, and Hatley, *Powhatan's Mantle*, 196–222.

———. "Some Thoughts on Colonial Historians and American Indians." *William and Mary Quarterly*, 3d ser., 46 (1989): 94–119.

———. "'Their Very Bones Shall Fight': The Catawba-Iroquois Wars." In Richter and Merrell, *Beyond the Covenant Chain*, 115–33.

Miller, Christopher L., and George R. Hamell. "A New Perspective on Indian-White Contact: Cultural Symbols and Colonial Trade." *Journal of American History* 73 (1986): 311–28.

Miller, Jay. "The Delaware as Women: A Symbolic Solution." *American Ethnologist* 1 (1974): 507–14.

Mulkearn, Lois. "Half-King, Seneca Diplomat of the Ohio Valley." *Western Pennsylvania Historical Magazine* 37 (1954): 65–82.

Nash, Gary B. "The Quest for the Susquehanna Valley: New York, Pennsylvania, and the Seventeenth Century Fur Trade." *New York History* 48 (1967): 3–27.

Niemczyki, Mary Ann Palmer. "The Genesee Connection: The Origins of Iroquois Culture in West-Central New York." *North American Archaeologist* 7 (1986): 15–44.

Perdue, Theda. "Cherokee Relations with the Iroquois in the Eighteenth Century." In Richter and Merrell, *Beyond the Covenant Chain*, 135–49.

Rawlyk, George A. "The 'Rising French Empire' in the Ohio Valley and Old Northwest: The 'Dreaded Juncture' of the French Settlements in Canada with Those of Louisiana." In Elliott, *Contest for Empire*, 41–59.

Richter, Daniel K. "Ordeals of the Longhouse: The Five Nations in Early American History." In Richter and Merrell, *Beyond the Covenant Chain*, 11–28.

———. "War and Culture: The Iroquois Experience." *William and Mary Quarterly*, 3d ser., 40 (1983): 528–59.

Russell, Peter. "Redcoats in the Wilderness: British Officers and Irregular Warfare in Europe and America, 1740 to 1760." *William and Mary Quarterly*, 3d ser., 35 (1978): 629–52.

Seeman, Mark F., and Janet Bush. "The Enderle Site: An Historic Burial Locality in Erie County, Ohio." *Pennsylvania Archaeologist* 49 (1979): 1–12.

Shriver, Philip R. "The Beaver Wars and the Destruction of the Erie Nation." *Timeline* 1 (1985): 29–41.

———. "A Large Seventeenth Century Historic Contact Interment in the Cuyahoga Valley: An Iroquoian Piece in the Puzzle of What Happened to the Whittlesey Focus?" *Ohio Archaeology* 35 (1985): 20–29.

Snyderman, George S. "Concepts of Land Ownership among the Iroquois and Their Neighbors." In Fenton, *Symposium on Local Diversity in Iroquois Culture*, 15–34.

Sosin, Jack M. "Britain and the Ohio Valley, 1760–1775: The Search for Alternatives in a Revolutionary Era." In Elliott, *Contest for Empire*, 60–76.

Stotz, Charles M. "Defense in the Wilderness." In James and Stotz, *Drums in the Forest*, 59–191.

Tanner, Helen Hornbeck. "The land and Water Communication Systems of the Southeastern Indians." In Wood, Waselkov, and Hatley, *Powhatan's Mantle*, 6–20.

———. "The Location of Indian Tribes in Southeast Michigan and Northern Ohio." In Wheeler-Voegelin and Tanner, *Indians of Northern Ohio and Southeast Michigan*, 319–69.

Thurman, Melburn D. "Delaware Social Organization." In Kraft, *Delaware Indian Symposium*, 111–34.

Thwaites, Reuben Gold, ed. "Two Journals of Western Tours by Charles Frederick Post." In Thwaites, *Early Western Travels*, 1:184–291.

Tooker, Elizabeth. "The League of the Iroquois: Its History, Politics, and Ritual." In Trigger, *Northeast*, 418–41.

Trigger, Bruce G. "Iroquoian Matriliny." *Pennsylvania Archaeologist* 48 (1978): 55–65.

Tully, Alan. "Politics and Peace Testimony in Mid-Eighteenth Century Pennsylvania." *Canadian Review of American Studies* 13 (1982): 159–77.

Vaughan, Alden T. "Frontier Banditti and the Indians: The Paxton Boys' Legacy, 1763–1775." *Pennsylvania History* 51 (1984): 1–29.

Vaughan, Alden T., and Daniel K. Richter. "Crossing the Cultural Divide: Indians and New Englanders, 1605–1763." *Proceedings of the American Antiquarian Society* 90 (1981): 23–99.

Wallace, Anthony F. C. "New Religious Beliefs among the Delaware Indians, 1600–1900." *Southwestern Journal of Anthropology* 12 (1956): 1–21.

———. "Political Organization and Land Tenure among the Northeastern Indians, 1600–1830." *Southwestern Journal of Anthropology* 13 (1957): 301–21.

———. "Revitalization Movements: Some Theoretical Considerations for Their Comparative Study." *American Anthropologist* 58 (1956): 264–81.

———. "Women, Land, and Society: Three Aspects of Aboriginal Delaware Life." *Pennsylvania Archaeologist* 17 (1947): 1–35.

Webb, Stephen Saunders. "Army and Empire: English Garrison Government in Britain and America, 1569–1763." *William and Mary Quarterly*, 3d ser., 34 (1977): 1–31.

White, Marian E. "Erie." In Trigger, *Northeast*, 412–17.

Wickwire, Franklin B. "'Go on and Be Brave': The Battle of Point Pleasant." *Timeline* 4 (1987): 2–19.

Witthoft, John, and William A. Hunter. "The Seventeenth-Century Origins of the Shawnee." *Ethnohistory* 2 (1955): 42–57.

Wood, Peter H. "The Changing Population of the Colonial South: An Overview by Race and Region, 1685–1790." in Wood, Waselkov, and Hatley, *Powhatan's Mantle*, 35–103.

Wray, Charles F., and Harry L. Schoff. "A Preliminary Report on the Seneca Sequence in Western New York, 1550–1687." *Pennsylvania Archaeologist* 24 (1954): 53–63.

Young, Henry J. "A Note on Scalp Bounties in Pennsylvania." *Pennsylvania History* 24 (1957): 207–18.

Zakucia, John A. "The Chambers Site, an Historic Burial Ground of 1750–75." *Eastern States Archaeological Federation Bulletin* 19 (1960): 12.

Zoltvany, Yves F. "The Frontier Policy of Philippe Rigaud de Vaudreuil, 1713–1725." *Canadian Historical Review* 48 (1967): 227–50.

———. "New France and the West, 1701–1713." *Canadian Historical Review* 46 (1965): 301–22.

Dissertations

Cutliffe, Stephen. "Indians, Furs, and Empires: The Changing Policies of New York and Pennsylvania, 1674–1768." Ph.D. diss., Lehigh University, 1976.

Druke, Mary A. "Structure and Meaning of Leadership among Mohawk and Oneida during the Mid-Eighteenth Century." Ph.D. diss., University of Chicago, 1981.

Haan, Richard L. "The Covenant Chain: Iroquois Diplomacy on the Niagara Frontier, 1687–1730." Ph.D. diss., University of California, Santa Barbara, 1976.

McClure, James Patrick. "The Ends of the American Earth: Pittsburgh and the Upper Ohio Valley to 1795." Ph.D. diss., University of Michigan, 1963.

McKeith, David S. "The Inadequacy of Men and Measures in English Imperial History: Sir William Johnson and the New York Politicians, a Case Study." Ph.D. diss., Syracuse University, 1971.

Richter, Daniel K. "The Ordeal of the Longhouse: Change and Persistence on the Iroquois Frontier, 1609–1700." Ph.D. diss., Columbia University, 1984.

Zimmerman, Albright G. "The Indian Trade of Colonial Pennsylvania." Ph.D. diss., University of Delaware, 1966.

index